TENNESSEE WILLIAMS

NEW SELECTED ESSAYS: WHERE I LIVE

TENNESSEE WILLIAMS

POETRY
• • • • • • • • • •

COLLECTED POEMS

IN THE WINTER OF CITIES

PROSE
• • • • • • • • •

COLLECTED STORIES

HARD CANDY AND OTHER STORIES

ONE ARM AND OTHER STORIES

MEMOIRS

THE ROMAN SPRING OF MRS. STONE

THE SELECTED LETTERS OF TENNESSEE WILLIAMS, VOLUME I

THE SELECTED LETTERS OF TENNESSEE WILLIAMS, VOLUME II

NEW SELECTED ESSAYS: WHERE I LIVE

PLAYS

··········

TENNESSEE WILLIAMS

NEW SELECTED ESSAYS: WHERE I LIVE

Introduction by

JOHN LAHR

—

Edited, with an Afterword, by

JOHN S. BAK

A NEW DIRECTIONS BOOK

Grateful acknowledgment is given to the editors and publishers of the following publications in which some of the essays in this volume first appeared: *Esquire, Five Young American Poets, '48, Harper's Bazaar, Life, The London Observer, The New York Herald Tribune, The New York Star, The New York Times, Caedmon Records, Michigan Quarterly Review, A Collaborative of Artists and Writers, Conjunctions, Smart Set, Performing Arts, Dramatist Guild Quarterly, Tennessee Williams Review, Harvard Advocate, Shaw Review, Playbill, The Saturday Review of Literature*, and *Vogue*.

New Selected Essays: *Where I Live* is published by special arrangement with The University of the South, Sewanee, Tennessee.

Cover design by Rodrigo Corral
Manufactured in the United States of America
New Directions Books are printed on acid-free paper.
An earlier, shorter collection was first published clothbound and as New Direction Paperbook 468 as *Where I Live: Selected Essays* in 1978, edited by Christine R. Day and Bob Woods. *New Selected Essays: Where I Live*, edited by John S. Bak, first published as New Directions Paperbook 1143 in 2009.
Published simultaneously in Canada by Penguin Canada Books, Ltd.

Library of Congress Cataloging-in-Publication Data:

Williams, Tennessee, 1911-1983.
[Essays. Selections]
New selected essays : where I live / Tennessee Williams ; foreword by John Lahr ; edited, with an introduction by John S. Bak.
p. cm.
Rev. and expanded ed. of: Where I live : selected essays. 1978.
ISBN 978-0-8112-1728-6 (pbk. : alk. paper)
I. Bak, John S. II. Williams, Tennessee, 1911-1983. Where I live. III. Title.
PS3545.I5365A6 2009
814'.54—dc22

2008052179

New Directions Books are published for James Laughlin
by New Directions Publishing Corporation
80 Eighth Avenue, New York 10011

CONTENTS

INTRODUCTION

Tennessee Williams made much of the atmosphere of family violence that shaped his personality; he said less about the family eloquence that shaped his prose. The Dakins, Ottes, and Williamses who made up his family tree were well-educated and well-spoken. They were talkers. Williams grew up in an environment of fluency, in which Biblical imperative, Puritan platitude, classical allusion, patrician punctilio, and Negro homily were tumbled together in a rich linguistic brew. His beloved maternal grandfather, the Reverend Walter Dakin, who was the formative male figure of his early years, had a mellifluous voice and enjoyed reading aloud. ("He could recite poetry by the yard," Williams's mother, Edwina, said. "I'm sure Tom got some of his love of books from Father.") The Reverend Dakin was also something of a ham in the pulpit. Delivering his sermons, which were written out in a hand as limpid and florid as his speech, he spoke with particular dramatic flair. "Pitch now your tents toward Heaven and the Sure Rising," he intoned, in a sermon first given in 1901, a decade before Williams was born, and last delivered in 1920, by which time Williams was in the habit of clinging to his grandfather's every word. Reverend Dakin continued, "As the storm of sin rages more fiercely about you and within you, as the horizon of the world grows darker with new and ever newer forms of evil, learn to shelter yourself more and more closely in the Rock of Ages till the storm shall cease, and the blackened sky be pierced by radiant rays of glory from the Sun of Righteousness who will come to you with healings in His wings."

Williams's growing up was not happy, but it was noisy. At the center of the verbal hubbub—full of complaint, contention, and concern—was the puritanical Edwina, a hysteric who poured her inner life into her children. (" 'Miss Edwina' will still be talking for at least half an hour after she's laid to rest," Williams writes, in "Let Me Hang It All Out," concurring with his brother Dakin's droll assessment.) Once, when he was a child, Williams, mispronouncing the word "young," referred to his mother as a "lung lady." So she was. Edwina wasn't just a talker; she was a narrative event, a torrent of vivid, cadenced speech that could not be denied. Williams referred to his mother's barrage of language as a "spell," which kept his young self both entranced and confounded; by the time he was an adult, however, it left him exhausted. "Yammer, yammer, yammer" was how Clark Mills, Williams's close friend and early literary collaborator, described Edwina's wall of words. "From a distance it had a comical aspect, but, close up, watch out: It was absolutely destructive. . . . To me the word *nightmare* was strictly applicable."

In time, Williams, his mother's understudy, would also become adept at projecting his feelings into others and using language as a means of seduction and control. He also inherited her obsession with the narration of self. (His addiction to writing—he wrote for about eight hours of every day for most of his professional life—is comparable to his mother's logorrhea, though his words made beauty out of emptiness, while hers compounded it.) *The Glass Menagerie* not only delivered Edwina's version of her fractious marriage; it mimicked her verbal performance and the strategy behind it. "I understand the art of conversation," Amanda says, as she tells her son about her long list of former suitors. "Girls in those days knew how to talk, I can tell you. They knew how to entertain their gentleman callers. It wasn't enough for a girl to be possessed of a pretty face and a nimble figure . . . she also needed to have a nimble wit and a tongue to meet all occasions." Although the play reduces the father to a ghostly presence—a photo on the wall and the few phonograph records he left behind—Williams's own father, C.C., had a picturesque vocabulary of his own, which also had its influence on Williams's literary style, a fact that he could acknowledge only after a few years of psychoanalysis and his father's death in 1957. "My father had a great gift for phrase," Williams said of the carousing C.C. "All Southerners have a great gift for idiom. Most of it comes from the blacks, you know, a great many of our idioms come from the blacks." Williams went on, "The title *Cat on a Hot Tin Roof*, for instance, was a favorite phrase of my father's. When he would come home at night, having had a little too much to drink, he'd say, 'Now, Edwina, cut it out. You're making me as nervous as a cat on hot tin roof.' " C.C. disdained his son's passion for writing; Edwina encouraged it. When Williams was twelve, she bought him his first typewriter, and from then on referred to him as "mah writin' son." Writing strengthened Williams's bond with his overbearing mother at the same time that it provided yet another wedge against his feared father.

In "Person–To–Person," Williams describes a group of little girls on a Mississippi sidewalk, "all dolled up in their mothers' and sisters' cast-off finery . . . enacting a meeting of ladies in a parlor with a perfect mimicry of polite Southern gush and simper":

But one child was not satisfied with the attention paid her enraptured performance by the others, they were too involved in their own performances to suit her, so she stretched out her skinny arms and threw back her skinny neck and shrieked to the deaf heavens and her equally oblivious playmates, "Look at me, look at me, look at me!"

And then her mother's high-heeled slippers threw her off balance and she fell to the sidewalk in a great howling tangle of soiled white satin and torn pink net, and still nobody looked at her.

I wonder if she is not, now, a Southern writer . . .

Collapse is the trope of the little girl's plea for attention; Williams also made a spectacle of his inner turmoil, turning his self into theater. His sentences often jump off the page, in shocking exhibitions of loss: "I am not a good writer. Sometimes I am a very bad writer indeed"; "I remember this summer as the one when I got along best with people and they seemed to like me"; "I am widely regarded as a ghost writer, a ghost still visible." Williams's sense of his own absence requires witnesses; his confidential tone—the "you," the "we," to whom many of his best essays are pitched—broadcasts the seductive, projective ambition of his prose. With this strategic pronominal shift, Williams creates an illusion of intimacy with his audience. "I only know that I have felt a release in this work," he writes in the foreword to *Camino Real*, "which I wanted you to feel with me." He uses his own emptiness to hold the other's attention, to make himself felt. "Meanwhile!—I want to go on talking to you as freely and intimately about what we live and die for as if I knew you better than anyone else whom you know," he concludes in "Person–To–Person."

As a child, Williams was a helpless victim of the idiom of family madness; as an adult, as a writer, he recapitulates and controls these otherwise threatening feelings, mastering them. "How can you expect audiences to be impressed by plays and other writings that are created as a release for the tensions of a possible or incipient madman?" Williams asked himself in an interview in the London *Observer* in 1957. His answer: "It releases their own." The liberation is mutual. Williams's prose works to establish a kind of psychic exchange, during which what is inside Williams is cunningly forced into the reader. "We come to each other, gradually, but with love," he writes in "The History of a Play (With Parentheses)," "It is a short reach of my arms that hinders, not the length and multiplicity of theirs. With love and honesty, the embrace is inevitable."

An original prose style is not easily achieved; once perfected, however, it serves the writer as both a mask and a peephole into personality. Williams claimed to have "a very divided nature"; he evolved styles that spoke for each aspect of his self. His high-theatrical style, coaxed out of his unconscious, is the pure sound of his hysteria. "Having always to contend with this adversary fear, which was sometimes terror, gave me a certain tendency toward hysteria and violence in my writing," he writes, in the foreword to *Sweet Bird of Youth*. The result is an almost operatic display of terror, at once full-throated, panic-struck, truth-telling, and seductive, full of startling observation and gorgeous music. "We are two monsters, but with this difference," Alexandra Del Lago tells Chance Wayne, in a typical aria from *Sweet Bird of Youth*. "Out of the passion and torment of my existence I have created a thing that I can unveil, a sculpture, almost heroic, that I can unveil, which is true."

Williams's epistolary style, unless he is pulling his punches with Hollywood producers or critics, is direct, unbuttoned, and loosey-goosey, an improvisational display of his sharpness of mind and tongue. For instance, to Jane Lawrence, in early 1950, he wrote, "Is it the Flapper Age that is coming back, or the age of the Prima Donna? I guess I would be equally at home in either, so I have nothing to worry about. High bosom or saucy butt, it is all the same to me! A turn, a twist, a flick of the wrist, for Mme. Tennessee!"

Williams's public prose style, which this volume of collected journalism represents, is a different kind of discourse with the world. These essays, the well-structured and stately by-products of his reasoning mind, deal mostly with the perception of his plays, his players, and himself. In pieces that were written on demand, to curry pre-opening favor for his plays with the New York public, Williams's rolling rhythms and piquant turns of phrase impose a sense of equipoise on his frantic heart; his eloquence, a mixture of the mundane and the metaphoric, serves as a gorgeous raiment over his "drizzle-puss self," a show of laconic command, which distracts the world and Williams from his emotional disarray. "Fear and evasion are the two little beasts that chase each other's tails in the revolving wire-cage of our nervous world," he writes, for instance, in "The Timeless World of a Play." "They distract us from feeling too much about things. Time rushes towards us with its hospital tray of infinitely varied narcotics." If Williams's writing is not as sinuous or poetic in print as it is onstage, the two styles nonetheless share the "sidewalk histrionics" that he refers to in "Person–To–Person."

Style is metabolism. Williams acknowledged as much. "If the writing is honest it cannot be separated from the man who wrote it," he writes. "It isn't so much his mirror as it is the distillation, the essence, of what is strongest and purest in his nature." The strut of Williams's sonorous sentences is a distinguishing part of his spell, an exhibition of the liberty of expressiveness to which his life was dedicated. The refinement of his tone and the pomp of his rhythm put charm between him and his madness, both diffusing his suffering and expanding its legend:

> When one has passed through an extensive period of that excess of privacy
> which is imposed upon a person almost willfully drifting out of contact

with the world, anticipating that final seclusion of the nonbeing, there comes upon him, when that period wears itself out and he is still alive, an almost insatiable hunger for recognition of the fact that he is, indeed, still alive, both as a man and an artist. ("Too Personal?" [1972])

Williams's confessional courtliness works the hysteric's fillip of seduction and transgression; it puts the conventional to unconventional use in order to shock, to undermine, and to captivate. "I call it God when something good happens, though perhaps there are many times when a Protestant Deity would violently disclaim the authorship of the blessing," Williams jokes, at his most baroque, in "Chicago Arrival." His decorum plays best against un-decorous circumstances: after the first-night cataclysm of his play *Battle of Angels*, for instance, the audience is described fleeing the smoke-filled stage, pushing up "the aisles like heavy, heedless cattle." In the short story, "Two on a Party," Williams describes Billy, a gay hustler, whose bald spot on the crown of his head "was becoming a fact of existence which he couldn't disown." "Of course, the crown of the head doesn't show in the mirror unless you bow to your image in the glass," he writes. "But there is no denying that the top of a queen's head is a conspicuous area on certain occasions which are not unimportant."

All great stylists have to teach their idiom to the public. Williams's essays, with their polite phrasings, make a shrewd case for what was actually a radical revolt against theatrical naturalism and its shallow, melodramatic rendering of human emotion. "I'm trying to catch the true quality of experience in a group of people, that clouding, flickering, evanescent—fiercely charged!—interplay of live human beings in the thundercloud of common crisis," he wrote of *Cat on a Hot Tin Roof* in "Critic Says 'Evasion,' Writer Says 'Mystery,'" though the description applies to all his plays. To Williams, a play was like a poem; it resonated beyond words—and with all the allusive, subliminal power the stage had to offer: light, sound, space, and symbol. Williams saw "plastic theatre" as an extension of sculpture. Instead of imposing points of view on his characters, he let them find both the play and its meaning. "They build the play about them like spiders weaving their webs, sea creatures making their shells," he said. "They take on spirit and body in my mind. Nothing that they say is arbitrary or invented." Although he was in show *business*—was, in fact, the king of legitimate theater in the mid-forties and fifties—Williams insisted on working as an artist, not as a merchant. He actively promoted the notion of art theater and regional repertory as an antidote to Broadway's show shop. He dubbed Broadway "a big slot machine"; dramatic art had fallen, he said, into "the receivership of businessmen and gamblers"—his term for producers—which was like "the conduct of worship becoming the responsibility of a herd of water-buffalos." Williams's essays tilt at the constraints and the follies of commercial theater, on which, according to Arthur Miller, he "planted the flag of beauty." He bemoaned the four-to-five-week out-of-town gestation process, "the scrambling rush to Broadway," as he called it. "Why does it have to hop, skip and jump across the schedule as briskly as something that hinges upon the loss of a G-string or getting someone's garter?" he writes, adding, "Answer: Money." Even in this polemical public debate, Williams boxed clever; defending his vision of dynamic and organic play in *Camino Real*, he wrapped his clenched fist in the velvet glove of eloquence. Of the words "dynamic" and "organic," he writes, "Those terms still define the dramatic values that I value most, and which I value more as they are deprecated by the ones self-appointed to save what they have never known."

Over the decades, Williams's pulse changed from one of exhilaration to one of exhaustion. At the beginning of his great theatrical adventure, in "'Amor Perdido'" (1944), he met life with a palpable thrill; the verve is audible in his writing: "Dark life. Confused, tormented, uncomprehendable and fabulously rich and beautiful." After enough time and success, however, he began to flat-line. By 1973, in "Where My Head is Now and Other Questions" Williams, seized by the delirium of output and sustained by drugs and drink, made it clear that the report from his interior was bad. Here, he can't find the energy for even a six-hundred-word assignment, vamping instead with an old poem that begins, "I run, cried, the fox, in circles . . ." Those circles continued to narrow. Toward the end of his life, comparing himself to a furtive alley cat, he embodied "the negative, unhomed." The lacerating self-portrait that he offers in "The Man In the Overstuffed Chair," a memoir of his father, written in 1960 and published in 1982, shows that the great discovery of his late years was not beauty but barbarity.

> To the world I give suspicion and resentment, mostly. I am not cold. I am never deliberately cruel. But after my morning's work, I have little to give but indifference to people. I try to excuse myself with the pretense that my work justifies this lack of caring much for almost everything else. Sometimes I crack through the emotional block. I touch, I embrace, I hold tight to a necessary companion. But the breakthrough is not long lasting. Morning returns, and only work matters again.

In the end, Williams's talent and his tragedy boiled down to the same hard fact: his big heart had become an atrophied one. He had dedicated himself to the fulfillment of his romantic imagination, only finally to be betrayed by it.

John Lahr
December 2008

ESSAYS

"AMOR PERDIDO"
or
How It Feels to Become a Professional Playwright

It is about a month ago today. I am seated in an open *cantina* facing the square in Acapulco, Gro., Mexico, and in accordance with one of my oldest and most respected traditions, I have just finished spending my last silver coin on a drink. I am seated with two favorite companions. At my left elbow is a juke-box which is playing what I seriously believe to be the most beautiful of all musical compositions, a bolero called *Amor Perdido*. At my right elbow is Mr. Orrin Beebe who is a confessed cousin of Lucius and has just opened a rival *cantina* on the other side of the square.

We are drinking rum-cocos which is a drink made by knocking one end off a coconut and pouring in a couple of jiggers of rum, a dash of lemon and a little cracked ice and sugar.

We are blinking and squinting into the strong yellow sunlight of the square and the dark natives are drifting meaninglessly about us like figures in a dream. Not far from our table is a wretched old dog, slowly dying. I have noticed him before, slinking among the tables with quiet, pleading eyes. Careful not to approach too closely, his large yellow eyes expressing wisdom and sadness and complete acquiescence. I have given him scraps of *tortillas* and *tacos* and he has gulped them down with the frenzied haste of starvation. But now the old dog is dying. The pleading look has gone out of his eyes, he has finally given up his mendicant career. He lies on his side in the sun, breathing in spasms, and his eyes have a look of dark and patient endurance. Nobody seems to notice his condition. The death of dogs in the street is a Mexican commonplace and the natives of Acapulco, a gentle and kindly people, pay no attention to it. I look at the dog and I feel a sympathy for him. I pull his desiccated body into the shade of the *cantina* and pour a little water on the concrete in reach of his tongue. He ignores the water but glances up at me for an instant of recognition. His brief look is apologetic. Then he stares back into space and I return to my table.

A small boy is selling newspapers, *Excelsior* and *El Universal*. In great black type are such words as *Londres* and *Bombas* and *Destrucciónes*.

It seems less immediate, less important than the mongrel's death.

A dusty old *camión*, beach-taxi, is taking on passengers for Los Hornos, which is the afternoon beach. A stout American woman in one of those huge, gaudy sombreros which only Americans wear is bawling out the driver for his delay in starting.

But drinking is a process of insulation against such things and in a few moments my interest has returned to its usual center, inside my own skull.

After a while I turn to Mr. Beebe.

"Well, Beebe, it looks like I am back on the beach."

"How do you mean?"

"I sold a play in New York a few months ago. Ever since then I've been in a fool's Paradise, living on ninety dollars a month with nothing to do but write and lie around here. Now that's all over."

"They dropped your play?"

"Uh-huh. I knew they would sooner or later but hoped it would be a little later than this. The cheque for this month's advance royalties was due about five days ago and it hasn't come yet. So I feel petty goddam sure they've already dropped it."

"What are you going to do?"

"I'm going back to my old profession."

"What's that?"

"Waiting tables."

"You got a job lined up?"

"Yes."

"Where?"

"In your *cantina*."

"Huh!—How much experience have you had?"

"Quite a good deal," I tell him. "I've waited tables in New Orleans, Iowa City, St. Louis, Memphis, Chicago, Los Angeles, San Francisco and Laguna Beach."

"Can you sing?"

"Sing? Like a nightingale!"

"Okay," he says finally. "You'll need a clean white shirt and a black bow tie."

Beebe rises from the table and wanders across the square. But I remain at the table. The jukebox has started again. That amazingly over-dressed woman known as the Princess Olga appears on the square. Three men follow about one step behind her. She talks very loudly, the three men listen and smile. I think she is explaining the mysteries of the universe to them. That's the nice thing about a language you don't understand—it is possible to believe the conversation is so much more elevated than it probably is.

After a while I get up. I think I will go over to Wells-Fargo on the opposite corner and see if any mail has come in for me. I am no longer concerned about it—but go anyway.

My name is printed at the top of the telegraph list. Mr. Tennessee Williams.

I receive the yellow envelope and seat myself in a wicker chair beneath the mildly-agitated punkas.

I tear the envelope open and read this message.

BETTER RETURN AT ONCE. WE ARE CASTING YOUR PLAY
FOR IMMEDIATE PRODUCTION.

Signed: Theresa Helburn, Theatre Guild, New York.

When people are facing imminent destruction their lives are supposed to pass before them in lightning review. What I faced at the moment was something quite different from imminent destruction, and yet that same phenomenon occurred.

As I sat in the wicker chair beneath the languid punkas I thumbed my way back through twenty-six years of living.

Various periods in the past were revived before me. I remembered particularly the *Vieux Carré* of New Orleans where I first learned how a poor artist lives. I remembered the Quarter Rats, as we were called. The prostitute Irene who painted the marvelous pictures and disappeared, Helen who entered my life through a search for a lost black cat, the jobless merchant seaman, Joe, who wrote sea-stories more exciting than Conrad's which were destroyed when the house he lived in burned. I remembered The Quarter Eat Shop, Meals for a Quarter in the Quarter, and passing out pink, yellow, and blue cards on Royal, Bourbon, and Canal. The sunlight rich as egg-yolk in the narrow streets, great, flat banana leaves, and the slow, slow rain. The fog coming up from the river, swallowing Andrew Jackson on his big iron horse. Tamale vendors at midnight, their haunting voices. Mother O'Neill pouring kettles of boiling water through the floor to break up a studio party. The big fight, the riot call, the Black Maria, Night Court and the House of Detention. The big bare room and the filthy, desperate prisoners. Words scrawled on the dirty white walls. Life getting bigger and plainer and uglier and more beautiful all the time.

I remembered thumbing a ride from Santa Monica to San Francisco to see William Saroyan and the Golden Gate Exposition. Saroyan wasn't there but the fair was marvelous. Sunset from Telegraph Hill and a room that I slept in half-way down it and curious scraps of conversation heard through a very thin wall. I remembered days of slightly glorified beach-combing in Southern California. Picking squabs and dropping one feather for each bird in a bottle and collecting afterwards two cents for each feather. Selling shoes across from the M.G.M. lot in Culver City and spending lunch hour watching for Greta Garbo. Never with any success. Taking care of a small ranch up Canyon Road in Laguna Beach. And the sound of dogs barking a long way off at night when the moon started rising. A thirty-year-old schoolteacher from Oklahoma having her last fling before marriage on the California beaches. Waking up at two or three in the morning to find her at the foot of my bunk with a middle-aged man in a crumpled white linen suit, saying, "Tenn, this is Jack, Jack's come here to bring me home, we're getting married tomorrow!" Sitting up all night, drinking, playing the guitar, singing *El Rancho Grande*—celebrating sadly. And Jacobs who used to conk the "queers" in back of Mona's place with an ice-cleaver wrapped in a towel and roll them for their money, and yet was the most good-natured person I've known. And Jim who played juvenile leads in Miami University productions and was going to crash Hollywood—and worked with me as a pin-boy in a Hollywood bowling alley. Trying to get on the W.P.A. Writers' Project once in Chicago. My negro friends there who had so much more charm than white intellectuals have. Joe Jones' free art-class in the old Court-house in St. Louis, the Artists and Writers League there being evicted by the Police because they were Communistic. Screaming and bloody noses and hours in the bull-pen.

School-days in Mississippi. Walking along aimless country roads through a delicate spring rain with the fields, flat, and wide, and dark, ending at the levee and at the cypress brakes, and the buzzards wheeling leisurely a long way up. Dark life. Confused, tormented, uncomprehendable and fabulously rich and beautiful. . . .

When finally I got up from the wicker chair, the brilliant yellow sunlight outside the Wells-Fargo office had faded. Beebe had gone home and had come forth again in a crisp white linen suit. He was seated once more by the juke-box in the rival *cantina*.

I went over where he was sitting and sat down by him.

"Have you got a white shirt?" he asked me.

"No," I told him.

"What size collar do you wear? Fifteen?"

"Fourteen and half," I told him.

"Okay. I'll lend you one of mine that's shrunk a little."

"No, thanks," I told him.

I handed him the yellow piece of paper.

It was getting so dark he had to bend way over to read it.

When he had made it out, he gravely extended his hand.

"Congratulations, Tenn. How do you feel?"

"Old," I told him.

"Huh?"

"Yes. Old. The irresponsible days of my youth are over."

There was a silence.

After a while Beebe smiled. "Has it occurred to you," he said, "that the play might be a failure?"

"No," I answered honestly. "I hadn't thought of that."

"You'd better think of it, Son."

Another brief silence.

"Beebe," I said, "will you keep that job open for me?"

"Sure," said Beebe. "I'll save the shirt for you, too."

After a while we both got up and crossed the plaza and entered Beebe's *cantina*.

Things were festive and bright. It was going to rain. A cool, damp wind was blowing off the Pacific.

I dropped a nickel in the juke-box and wandered out into the patio which was still unlighted. I had a curious sense of isolation. The old life seemed to be over. The new one had not begun yet. This was a time in between. Somehow it made me think of the time when I tore a hole in my one pair of pants and had to spend a motionless half hour behind a screen in a Jewish tailor's shop while the pants were mended. It was an interlude, a period of suspended animation.

Then all at once the Mexican girl started singing *Amor Perdido,* the Japanese lanterns among the dark mango trees bloomed into pastel color. I caught my breath, for it seemed as though I were standing with empty pockets and greedy hands in Aladdin's orchard of jewels.

ca. 1940

TE MORITURI SALUTAMUS
or
An Author's Address to a First Night Audience

As some of you may remember an earlier version of this play was presented last season in Boston. Because of certain unfortunate occurences on that occasion it seems to be wise to preface tonight's opening with the friendly reminder that you members of the first night audience have presumably come to the theatre for a somewhat difference purpose than that for which later audiences will primarily come. They will come primarily for entertainment or escape from actuality into fiction. I would have no right to speak to them like this. You all have come, as I said, for a somewhat different purpose. You have come for diversion, too, but primarily you have come here tonight to exercise the function of judges—to weigh and evaluate a new and serious piece of theatrical work.

We know that you want to weigh and evaluate it fairly. Therefore it seems appropriate to start you out tonight with certain warnings.

This is, to begin with, a play about human passions. I know from experience, and fairly recent experience, and very sad experience, that there are some members of every audience who don't believe that a serious consideration of fundamental human longings, such as the longing for sexual fulfillment, has any place at all upon the stage. Unless, of course, it is treated as something ridiculous, something legitimately mirth-provoking—like *Charley's Aunt* for instance—which I felt was a marvelous play but I am not competing with it!—Those of you who have that belief, that allergy to serious sex drama, the kindest thing that you all can do is to leave the theatre now before the play commences. Your money will be refunded at the cashier's box. I offer you this invitation because I know what mischief you are capable of doing if you remain at large in the auditorium tonight. Maybe this sounds funny but it isn't. In Boston some strange things happened. The play was then and still is a tragic drama of struggle and defeat, but that opening night in Boston it was nearly as much a tragedy for those who created the characters as it was for the characters which they created. Why? Certainly to some extent because the script was not ready to be seen; but mainly I believe because certain members of the audience were not ready to see it.

I want to tell you about a letter which was received shortly after the abortive opening in Boston from a lady of the Back Bay section who was more than usually articulate about her tastes in the theatre. She wished the Theatre Guild to know what she regarded as an acceptable type of drama and presumably expected them to see to it that the theatre was immediately revolutionized to meet these requirements. When I go to the theatre, she said, I wish to see characters on the stage who dress as I dress, who talk as I talk and who act as I act.—In other words what this lady desired was "RUTHLESS REALISM"!—according to Back Bay.

Perhaps if I had visited Back Bay while I was in Boston I might have run across this lady and made detailed observations upon her dress, her conversation and her behavior so that I could faithfully reproduce them when I sat down at my desk in Key West Florida to revise the play. Unfortunately I did not get out to Back Bay. Nor was I, incidentally, confined to the local asylum for the insane, though that would have been nearly as bad. This being the case, and having only the vaguest suspicions of how the Back Bay lady might dress or act or talk, I found myself unable to revise the play to her complete satisfaction—And therefore it was decided not to open again in Boston. —Too bad.

(Seriously, now, did you ever hear of anything quite so pernicious!—That is, in a democratic state.)

And so I want to ask you tonight to remember that serious workers have worked very hard and with all their hearts to put this play before you in a second effort for success. All that they have done in months of labor, or even possibly years of cumulative thought and feeling, may be thoughtlessly and unfeelingly torn to pieces by the laughter of a man who thinks it is silly to try to find poetic truth on the stage or a woman who is embarrassed into spasms of hysterical giggling by the honest representation of passions which she must have felt inside her own heart at one time or another if she is not lucky enough to exist without that frangible type of organ.—Or—still worse—by the use of honest language such as people would be likely to use in given situations.

It seems that some of you are going to stay.

I'm glad of that.

The actors and the producers and I are gladly submitting ourselves and our parts to your judgment. You may say the play is successful, or you may call it a failure, or anything else in between; that's your just prerogative as a first night audience; we may bore you, we may shock you or confuse you, we may offend you or say things that you disagree with altogether; we may seem to you fantastic or ludicrous or even utterly insane. —But we do humbly beseech you in any case not to allow those negative reactions to impose themselves upon the reactions of other people, sitting next to you or near you, who have paid the same price of admission and who may perhaps, if they are not distracted, discover something in the play tonight that purges their own confused emotions through its very seriously-intended vivisection of the human heart.

Thank you and—good night.

ca. 1941-1942

PREFACE TO MY POEMS

Frivolous Version

I began writing verse at about the time of puberty, and one of my earliest lyrics is still the one recited most frequently at parties. It was an apostrophe to death, and I think it deserves to be quoted here because of its distinctive character and evidence of influences. The sextet follows:

> Rudely you seized and broke proud Sappho's lyre,
> Barret and Wylie went your songless way.
> You do not care what hecatomb of fire
> is split when shattering the urn of clay.
> Yet, Death, I'll pardon all you took away
> while still you spare me—glorious Millay!

Having disposed of women poets in this cavalier manner, I took the field with great audacity from the very beginning. I was quite successful, my poetry was much admired in high school and I won not only plaudits but many little prizes from women's clubs and poetry groups in Mississippi and Missouri. I remember when an officer in my mother's chapter of the DAR passed away, I composed an elegy to her which was read aloud at the services and resulted in a very moving catharsis. Poetry was my undoing, however, for when I left school and had employment in the warehouse of a wholesale shoe corporation, I formed the habit of retiring to a closet of the lavatory and spending unconscionably long periods of time working out rhyme schemes. When such unbusinesslike practices were exposed to the boss, I was slated for early dismissal and have never regained any standing in the commercial world for more than a few weeks' time.

Coeval with these early efforts, I became a friend of Clark Mills who lived in the town of Clayton, Mo., to which we had moved. Clark's admiration for my verse was tempered by a more technical approach than my other admirers'. He was usually given to owlish nods and bronchial noises when

I showed him my verse. However, he did admire my plays and stories, and we subsequently formed what we called a "literary factory" in the basement of his suburban home. Ideas from Clark's verse went into my plays, and ideas from my plays went into Clark's verse, and it was a very creative and delightful arrangement, especially since Clark's mother visited us more regularly than the muse with trays of lemonade and sandwiches, and Clark usually had a bottle of wine stashed behind the shelves of poetry. It was Clark who warned me of the existence of people like Hart Crane and Rimbaud and Rilke, and my deep and sustained admiration for Clark's writing gently but firmly removed my attention from the more obvious to the purer voices in poetry. About this time I acquired my copy of Hart Crane's collected poems which I began to read with gradual comprehension.

The poems included in this volume are a sort of spiritual witness of these years: at least they are the product of an unattached and nomadic existence of six or eight years' duration.

For me there was the dramatic intercession of Broadway, which I regard as fortuitous and beside the point since a poet who happens to stumble into the theater is not a case in point. I found good angels such as Audrey Wood, Margo Jones and the Rockefeller Foundation and some relatively altruistic producers such as the Group Theatre and the Theatre Guild to throw me a lifeline when I had reached the very last moment of endurance.

And today I received a telegram which will take me to Hollywood.

For others, I know, the Army has offered a haven. And they are actually more fortunate, I believe, than the so many more who were too battered and knocked about already to pass the physical and psychological examinations that candidates for extinction in the war are subjected to.

And so I propose the question: *How do we live?*

I can't think of anything more important to say.

Serious Version

If there is ever a world congress of poets, I mean outside the one obliquely described in the section called *Walpurgisnacht* in Joyce's *Ulysses,* I think the problem mainly to be considered is not competitive philosophies of art nor even political ideas. Despite the fuss which many of us make over the latter and its indisputable importance, I think it always remains a little outside our introverted orbit. As for the first, it is altogether a matter of personal feeling and most of the arguments have worn themselves out. I think the problem that we should apply ourselves to is simply one of survival. I mean actual physical survival!

Whenever I meet a young poet, barring such eclectic examples as Charles

Henri Ford and Jesse Stuart, for opposite reasons, I always involuntarily ask them: *How do you live? How do you get along?* just as a callously inquisitive visitor at a sideshow would ask the armless man how he unzipped his trousers.

I think it is almost impossible for a young poet to live in contemporary America, let alone contemporary Europe and Asia, and the fact that some of them do is far more surprising than the fact that so many *don't*.

The most destructible element in our society, the immature and rootless artists or poets, is the one that is subjected to the worst lambasting.

I know this, because I have survived it myself, and how I have survived is a question I ask myself with the same incredulous wonder that I have asked others such as—there are too many to name!

I haven't known them merely in New York, where poets know each other, but in New Orleans and in Los Angeles and in St. Louis and Chicago, all the big cities where groups of them huddle together for some dim, communal comfort—I have been a part of their groups because of the desperate necessity for the companionship of one's own kind, and I remember distinctly such people as Irene who painted the most powerful primitive canvases I've ever seen and whispered through shutters to men who passed on the street because she had a body that had to live. I remember Joe Turner who wrote sea stories, often as vivid and beautiful as Conrad's. He was a merchant sailor because there was nothing else for him to do when the W.P.A. Writers' Project ceased to exist, and now not only Joe but his mss. have disappeared altogether. And even those who were known and recognized, whose talents were given the slow and grudging appraisal of those who have the power to help young artists—I have known even those sparingly elected to find the struggle too complex and exhausting to go on with.

Hart Crane wasn't the only one.

I have lived in the middle of it since I was released from the comparative cocoon of schools and colleges and took to the road because the alternative was something too dull to endure.

About this time I also left Clayton, Mo., and took to moving about the country. During this nomadic period I began to write the poems which are included in this volume and a great many more, none of which left my hands before the present time, because I had no reliable mailing address. Oh, I did make one submission to a magazine of verse in Chicago. It was returned to me with a sharply worded complaint about the omission of return postage and it was signed "G.D.," which I assume were the initials of the editor and not anything more profane!

All at once some plays I had left in New York received the spectacular and simultaneous attention of the Rockefeller Foundation, the Group
Theatre, the Theatre Guild, and Audrey Wood. I was awarded a fellowship
and drafted into the startling world of Broadway from which I have never
altogether emerged, although I continue to knock about the country.

Symbolically I found a lot of books inconvenient to carry with me and
gradually they dropped along the way—till finally there was only one volume with me, the book of Hart Crane.

I have it with me today, my only library and all of it. This does not
mean a snobbish or hysterical exclusion of interest in other poets. On the
contrary, I think my taste is unusually catholic, for I still enjoy all of the lady
poets so briskly disposed of in the first sonnet. Wherever there is a truthful
intensity of feeling, I like it—whether it's in Keats or Auden or even in the
presently outlawed Mr. Pound, whom I heard over the short-wave from an
Axis capital lately.

But I am inclined to value Crane a little above Eliot or anyone else
because of his organic purity and sheer breathtaking power. I feel that he
stands with Keats and Shakespeare and Whitman. Why argue about it? It's
too personal a feeling.

If there is ever indeed a world congress of poets, I think the thing to fuss
over is simply this: a method of survival! I mean actual, physical survival!

I think that we are going to have a hard time of it!

                                                                    1944

THE HISTORY OF A PLAY
(With Parentheses)

Battle of Angels was not my first play. I had previously written four others, long tragedies, innocent of structure. These earlier works were little more than preliminary exercises. Inept as the *Battle* is in certain respects, it was a huge advance over its predecessors, written before I knew what a proscenium arch is. Probably no man has ever written for the theatre with less foreknowledge of it. I had never been back-stage. I had not seen more than two or three professional productions: touring companies that passed through the South and Middle West. My conversion to the theatre arrived as mysteriously as those impulses that enter the flesh at puberty. Suddenly I found that I had a stage inside me: actors appeared out of nowhere; shaggy, undisciplined mummers trooped out of the shadowy wings and took the stage over. This cry of players had a gift for improvisation: they carried with them a greasy bundle of old scripts, crumpled and wadded into the bottom of the brass-bound trunk, beneath the tarnished helmets and rhinestone tiaras, the twisted candelabra and moth-eaten velvet capes and scarlet dominoes of traditional mummery. Now and then they would toss me a sheaf of papers like an old bone: only the title and theme were still apparent: the script illegible. "Write this over!" I was commanded. The work was mainly the actors' improvisations. But how I loved it!—this abuse of Cothurnus—is that her name? And the actors loved it, too. They could not wait for the lines to be set down. What thrilling disorder!

I took to the theater with the impetus of compulsion. Writing since I was a child, I had begun to feel a frustrating lack of vitality in words alone. I wanted a plastic medium. I conceived things visually, in sound and color and movement. The writing of prose was just their description, not their essential being: or so I felt it to be. I was impatient of sentences. Tricks of style, polish, urbanity, all of those things that belong to the successful practitioner of letters seemed all the world removed from what I wanted and what I was writing for. The turbulent business of my nerves demanded something more animate than written language could be. It seemed to me that even the giants of literature, such as Chekhov, when writing narratives were only describing dramas. And they were altogether dependent upon the sensitivity of their readers. Nothing lived of what they had created unless the reader had the stage inside him, or the screen, on which their images could be visibly projected. However with a play, a play on a stage—let any fool come to it! It is there, it is really and truly there—whether the audience understands it or not! This may be a childish distinction: however, I felt it that way.

It seemed to me that all good writing is not just writing but is something organic. I say that as though it was a startling discovery of my own. Excuse me. But that is how it came to me, as a personal revelation. It should have come earlier, for I had been writing since twelve and was already wrapped up in literary style like the bandages of a mummy—and I am still struggling to break out of it. Lately the word "professional" has become odious to me because it seems removed from the flesh and blood business of my vocation. The best avenue away from professionalism in writing is really the stage, because the stage is ideally the most plastic, the most objective exercise for the writer. For me there was no other medium that was even relatively satisfactory. I am speaking for myself, not anyone else. If this sounds like a rejection of poetry—kick my face in! I don't mean any such thing. But poetry is also potentially a plastic medium. Nothing goes more naturally onto the ideal stage.

Later on I became sick and furious, unreasonably so, when I learned that people who feel as I do about the theater cannot possess it. It doesn't belong to us. It belongs to Money. Then, after that, I felt more reasonably about it, for I saw that works for the ideal theatre can live on paper until the emancipated theatre is ready for them: just as a race of slaves can survive their period of bondage and eventually come into the sun as free individuals to realize their destiny. All that we really need is to believe, to work, and to survive with honesty. Virgo intacta.

That is Parenthesis One!

Battle of Angels was the first of these plays to release and purify the emotional storms of my earlier youth. The stage or setting of this drama was the country of my childhood. Onto it I projected the violent symbols of my adolescence. It was a synthesis of the two parts of my life already passed through. And so the history of the play begins anterior to the impulse to write it. It begins as far back as I remember, in the mysterious landscape of the Delta country, the smoky quality of light in the late afternoons when I, as a child, accompanied my grandfather, an Episcopal clergyman, on seemingly endless rounds of rural parishioners about such villages as Columbus, Canton, Clarksdale, and Lyons in Mississippi. Wherever my grandfather went, I tagged along. I remember a sympathetic old lady saying, "Tom looks tired," and my grandfather answering, "Tom is strong as an ox." It seems to me those afternoons were always spent in tremendously tall interiors to which memory gives a Gothic architecture, and that the light was always rather dustily golden. I remember a lady named Laura Young. She was dressed in checkered silk. She had a high, clear voice: a cataract of water. Something about her made me think of cherries and she was very beautiful. She was something cool and green in a sulphurous landscape. But there was a shadow upon her. There was something the matter with her. For that reason we called upon her more frequently than anyone else. She loved me. I adored her. She lived in a white house near an orchard and in an arch between two rooms were hung some pendants of glass that were a thousand colors. "That is a prism," she said. She lifted me and told me to shake them. When I did they made a delicate music.

This prism became a play.

When we stopped going there, I learned that the lady was dead. It was the death of a lady and the beginning of a personal myth. For this bright, misty lady was the beginning of Myra Torrance—even that long ago!

But these childish recollections provided me only with the country and with characters of phantom dimensions. I had to animate them with the turbulent stuff of later experience. The opportunity for this came after I had knocked about the states for five years, much as the character Val, with some such shadowy design as his mysterious "Book" as a fleeting objective. I retreated to the family home, which was then in Clayton, Missouri, and because I was stopped and temporarily worn out, it seemed like a final retreat. I hated Saint Louis, of which this town was the suburb—hated it quite unreasonably, associating it with certain personal disasters which had taken place there—so I immured myself in the attic of our home and wrote the tortured first draft of *Battle of Angels,* never at any time regarding it as more than a katharsis for myself. By this time, however, I had acquired from the distance a few contacts with the professional theatre. They were the Group Theatre and Audrey Wood, the agent. All of a sudden they worked a marvelous change in my situation. They had submitted earlier works of mine to the Rockefeller Foundation, which was at that time distributing fellowships of a thousand dollars each to promising playwrights. I received one of these about a week after completing *Battle of Angels* and so I came with the manuscript to New York and began to explore for the first time the world of the professional theatre.

The absurd though tragic dilemma of that little microcosmos is something that I am not at all prepared to write about. That the most exalted of
the arts should have fallen into the receivership of business men and gamblers is a situation parallel in absurdity to the conduct of worship becoming
the responsibility of a herd of water-buffalos. It is one of those things that a
man of reason had rather not think about until the means of redemption is
more apparent. That in spite of this situation small islands of idealism still
remain in the American theatre is all the more miraculous and to be praised.
Men and women of unquestionable integrity still operate in the American
theatre, many in eminent positions. They only wait for the release of the
money octopus to create out of their own high designs a theatre where truth
can resume its exploration of our spiritual night. But as for the theatre as
it now exists, I will only say that I feel a person desiring to write fine plays
could make a much worse mistake than never visiting a Broadway playhouse.

By the end of this first season in New York my fellowship money had
dangerously dwindled. I had already received enough disturbing impressions of the theatre capital to feel an impulse to travel. Summarily and with
little enough warning to anybody concerned, I packed my property, mostly
paper, and departed for Mexico. I had left behind me the first draft of *Battle
of Angels*. The Theatre Guild, one of those small islands alluded to, had
taken an option on it. No one, least of all myself, thought they would do
more than finger it a little before passing it back to the tangent stream that
poetic properties follow. When the monthly advances no longer reached me
in Acapulco, where I was spending the summer, I assumed without any surprise that this release had already occurred. The fact that I had traveled too
rapidly for mail to catch up with me was the true explanation, and the one I
didn't think of. My life was an approximate paradise at this tropical port. I
called it "La Vie Horizontale." I wrote in a hammock all morning, swam all
afternoon in the warm waters of a land-locked bay, spent the evenings talking lazily to another American writer, Andrew Gun, and drinking rum-cocos
on the verandah of hammocks. I would have been content to pursue this life
for the rest of my days, but, toward the end of summer, too much Mexican
grease or unwashed greens resulted in gastric disturbances in both myself
and Mr. Gun. Mr. Gun was a war refugee from Tahiti and he had spent
nearly all our evenings telling me about that island and a little French girl
who was waiting for him there. Fearing to be immured there for the duration of the war due to the cancellation of passenger shipping, he had fled on
the last boat out—now he regretted the action. He had learned of a means of
returning and had convinced me that I also was a spiritual native of Tahiti.

We were all set to go there, when shortly after we had again entered the States, I got hold of a copy of *The New York Times* and was startled to read in the dramatic columns that the Theatre Guild was doing *Battle of Angels* as their initial play of the season and that Miss Miriam Hopkins had already flown from Hollywood to take the starring role.

Well, I returned post-haste to New York and dived unwittingly into the little maelstrom my play had provoked. I was delighted with the selection of Miss Hopkins for the role of Myra, but I was alarmed that things had gone ahead so rapidly, that casting was already in progress when the script was really only a first draft. I knew that the ending of the play, as it then stood, was a melodramatic *tour-de-force*. Conceptually it was fine—the store was set afire and everything went up in the fiery purgation. Yes, very exciting. "A Wagnerian experience," as someone put it in the Guild office! "But how in hell are you going to stage it?" asked Margaret Webster, who had been engaged as director. This question and others were held in abeyance while the production went rocketing ahead. I realized that I had fooled these people. Because certain qualities in my writing had startled them, they took it for granted that I was an accomplished playwright and that some afternoon when I was not busy with interviews, casting, rehearsals, I would quietly withdraw for an hour or two and work out the dramaturgic problems as deftly as such things were done by men like Barry and Kaufman and Behrman. They had no idea how dazed and stymied I was by the rush of events into which my dreamy self was precipitated. Meantime Peggy Webster and I caught a plane to the Mississippi Delta. We spent two days down there, introducing Peggy to the South—visiting country stores and talking to Delta people. Peggy absorbed the South in twenty-four hours. It was a bit too much for her. She began to look a little punch-drunk, seeing just enough of this extraordinary country and its people to make them more mysterious than they were before. On a plane returning to New York, I recall a talk that we had. We had been reciting verse to each other, mostly lyrics of Shakespeare. I repeated the one containing the lines "Nothing of him that doth fade but doth suffer a sea-change into something rich and strange." "That," said Peggy, "is what they should say about *Battle of Angels*."—"Perhaps," I answered, "but there are so many other things they may say about it."— Peggy assented gravely. Neither of us, however, had at this moment any intimation of the line of attack that really would be taken.

During all this time and the weeks that followed it had somehow occurred to none of us working on the production that we were dealing with a play that might be attacked on grounds of morality. If it was in the minds of others, certainly this suspicion was never communicated to me. Was I

totally amoral? Was I too innocent or too evil—that I remained unprepared
for what the audiences, censors and magistracy of Boston were going to find
in my play? I knew, of course, that I had written a play that touched upon
human longings, about the sometimes conflicting desires of the flesh and
the spirit. This struggle was thematic; implicit in the title of the play. Why
had I never dreamed that such struggles could strike many people as filthy
and seem to them unfit for articulation? Oh, if I had written a play full of
licentious wiggling in filmy costumes, replete with allusions to the latrine, a
play that was built about some titillating and vulgarly ribald predicament in
a bedroom—why, then I would feel apprehensive about its moral valuation.
However, it seemed to me that if *Battle of Angels* was nothing else, it was
certainly clean, it was certainly idealistic. The very experience of writing
it was like taking a bath in snow. Its purity seemed beyond question. But
then—the dogma of the moral censor!—there again is something I cannot
cope with and will have to pass over.

As rehearsals progressed it became more and more apparent that if
nothing else needed fixing, the ending of the play certainly did. The store
did not burn down convincingly nor were we, in the crucial parts of Cassandra and Val, able to find actors who seemed anything better than arbitrarily
thrust into the parts. Three different leading men were unsuccessfully tried
out in the five weeks of rehearsal before Wesley Addy was removed from
Twelfth Night to play opposite Miss Hopkins. Though he did not have the
physical quality the part demanded, Mr. Addy understood the play and certainly had talent enough to do a creative job. Miss Doris Dudley in the role
of Cassandra was cruelly miscast. One of the most beautiful women in the
theatre and also one of the sweetest, the terrifying demands of this part only
increased her embarrassment. It was she who had to stand on the stairs of
the burning store and lift the tragedy into a state of purgation with a set of
lines—nowhere now present in the text—which she and all of us felt were
quite impossible to integrate with the rest of the play as they seemed to come
out of an altogether different script.

Toward the end of rehearsals, a series of frenzied conferences were
held. Miss Hopkins, who played her part with heartbreaking beauty and
something that only a woman of poetic understanding and deep experience could give—whenever the confusion lifted sufficiently to give her a
chance to do so—was now becoming definitely frightened. She looked to
me for salvation. After all, I—poor captive thing—was the author. How it
wrung my heart that I could do nothing for her! She had staked so much
on this play. It was to mark her triumphal return to the stage, where her
talent as a dramatic actress could operate without the bonds that bad

screen vehicles had recently put on her. One could easily see why she regarded the production almost as a matter of life and death. Oh, if only my
head would clear up a little—if I could only find some lucid interval in this
dervish frenzy that was sweeping us all unprepared into Boston and disaster! But all the conferences only added to my feeling of impotence. Miss
Hopkins' pleas and protestations—"For heaven's sake, do something,
something!"—only made it more impossible for me to do anything at all.
At last I went to Peggy and told her exactly how unable I was to cope with
the emergency. "It is too late," I said, "I can't do anything more! If I could
get away from all of you for a month—I could return with a new script.
But that is not possible, so you will just have to take what there is and do
what you can with it!"

"Very well," said Peggy, "the store will burn down! Now you stop worrying about it."

To insert another parenthesis: it seems to me that directly behind capital investment as a menace to good theatre is the fact that everything is
done with such a machine-like haste. Five weeks is not long enough to
prepare a complex play. Ideally it should have three months. Why wasn't
that done with the Federal Theater Project? Why didn't they put on one
great play a season, instead of imitating the scrambling rush of Broadway?
No wonder nearly all players have a tendency to chatter rather than speak
on the stage! A play has become something like a feat of legerdemain. I will
allow that rapid execution is the best policy with most Broadway plays,
but when now and then something comes along that deserves a more leisurely gestation—why does it have to hop, skip and jump across the schedule as briskly as something that hinges upon the loss of a G-string or getting
somebody's garter?

Answer: Money.

So after five weeks, only about three of which were conducted with a
final cast, the company entrained for its opening engagement in the city of
Boston. Only Miss Helburn and Mr. Langner appeared unshaken by any
rumors of premonition. This I set down to their seniority, the fact that they
had out-ridden so many previous storms. It was encouraging to observe
their Olympian calm, but it made one all the more conscious of his own
callow emotionalism.

In Boston we had but one night of rehearsal before we opened, in the
Christmas season of 1940.

That night was about as black as any I'd experienced. Everything that
had gone well, or passably well, at previous rehearsals went about as badly
as possible. All the meaning seemed to have gone from the lines: nothing fit-

ted together: the effect was kaleidoscopic. When it came time for the store to burn down—the little trickles of smoke under the wings, the flickering red lights, the bawling voices—against these had to be played the all-important scene that lifted the play to katharsis. Never had it seemed so impossible to combine the two actions. Either you heard only the mob's demonstration or you heard only the interior scene. Also it was suddenly discovered at this rehearsal that the musical score composed for the play could not be used. In my frank opinion, it was terrible. Miss Hopkins felt the same way about it. Almost tearfully she cried out, "How can I dance to that music?" No doubt it was a fine composition technically; but for the play, it was terrible. All of it went out, and at the last moment recorded selections were substituted: banal and make-shift they were but we were devoutly thankful—at least Miriam Hopkins and I—when the high-brow composition released its depressing grip. Suitable music could have done a great deal for the production, but this was really a solo composition—the sort of thing you would expect to hear at a modern dance recital where it could be accorded the proper deference.

I remember that Peggy jumped off the stage at one point and caught her ankle in a folding seat. She uttered a slight cry of pain—Miriam Hopkins screamed as if the sky had fallen—such was the state of our nerves.

I went home too exhausted to think or to sleep. Toward morning I wrote a new final scene. Dreadful it probably was! Nobody paid any attention to it, but I remember saying dramatically that I would crawl on my belly through brimstone if they would only put off the opening and give me a few more days to contrive something else. Mr. Langner smiled at me fondly. A very kind man, he gave me what comfort and reassurance he could. Miss Helburn sent me a telegram—"Saint Michael and all Good Angels be with you!"—signed "Connecticut Updyke" (her married name, with the territorial appellation she had adapted in imitation of mine).

Opening night. Things started rolling peacefully enough. The elegant first night audience entered the theatre with an air of nobility and refinement which boded little of what was to come in our next three hours of communion with them. They looked on the first scenes with bland satisfaction. Gowned by Bergdorf-Goodman, Miss Hopkins was as radiantly beautiful as any of their debutante daughters. The character women upset the dowagers a little from time to time, but the general attitude toward the earthy humor they brought to the script was still indulgent. It was not till the action concerning Vee's visionary portrait of Val—not until that revelation—that the peculiar attitude which this audience brought to the theatre began to make itself seen, heard, and felt. Up and down the aisles the ladies and gentlemen began to converse with each other in sibilant whispers. Subdued hissings and clucking were punctuated now and then by the banging up of a seat and the regal swish of silken garments drawn hurriedly over projecting knees as here and there it became impossible for some spectator to countenance further infractions of standards.

The nature of this phenomenon, the fashionable first night audience, became shockingly plain to me all at once. What interests them is themselves, their dignity, their prestige and pretenses. What they want is a flattering mirror, a picture that does the opposite of Dorian Gray's, one that takes off all their blemishes in its reflection. After the play had closed a Brookline dowager wrote the Theatre Guild—I saw this letter—to say that when she went to the theater she wanted to see cultivated people, people who talked, acted and dressed as she and her friends. Pictures of other *milieux* were not acceptable to her. I am afraid that she expressed a fairly widespread attitude among what is known as the "carriage trade" on which our theater is still financially dependent. Hence the failure of the theatre really to explore the many levels of society except in the superficial and sensational way of *Tobacco Road* and its prototypes, which pleases the carriage trade inversely to polite drawing-room comedy by representing their social inferiors as laughable grotesques.

Returning to the performance. It was not until the point of the conflagration that the Boston audience was in a strategic position to vent its full displeasure. At the final dress-rehearsal there had not been enough smoke to make the fire convincing. Obviously this deficiency had been thoroughly impressed upon the gentlemen operating the smoke-pots, for on opening night when it came time for the store to burn down it was like the burning of Rome. Great sulphurous billows rolled chokingly onto the stage and coiled over the foot-lights. To an already antagonistic audience this was sufficient to excite something in the way of pandemonium. Outraged squawks, gabbling, spluttering spread through all the front rows of the theatre. Nothing that happened on the stage from then on was of any importance. Indeed the scene was nearly eclipsed by the fumes. Voices were lost in the banging up of seats as the front rows were evacuated.

When the curtain at last came down, as curtains eventually must, I had come to that point where one must laugh or go crazy. I laughed. There was little joy in it, but knowing I had to laugh, I found that I could. Miriam Hopkins accepted the same necessity. I see her coming out to face her audience. The stage is still full of smoke. Before her smiling face she is waving a small white hand, to clear the fumes away. She is coughing a little, apologetically touching her throat and chest. Their backs are turned to her, these elegant first-nighters, as they push up the aisles like heavy, heedless cattle. But she is still gallantly smiling and waving away the smoke with her delicate hand. The curtain bobs foolishly up and down to a patter of hands in the balcony that goes on after the lower floor is emptied.

The failure of a play!

The Boston reviewers tried to judge what they had seen as fairly and calmly as possible. In the reviewers there was none of the downright cruelty that the first-night audience had exhibited. Under the circumstances, the reviewers were as good as could be hoped for. Obviously that is not saying that they were good. References were made, however, to the reality of the atmosphere in the earlier scenes of the play and one lady reviewer went so far as to say that there were occasional lines of beauty in the script. Another reviewer made guarded allusions to good character touches in the lesser figures. There was an atmosphere of wariness and bated breath in all these printed reactions.

The magistracy of Boston did not step in till after the play had run for about a week. Then it was that the censors sat out front and demanded excision from the script of practically all that made it intelligible, let alone moving. Fortunately I had already left Boston at that time and did not take part in this really posthumous disturbance.

The play as you now read it was written many months later.

Some day it will be done again. For that occasion I will probably prepare still another version, omitting the present prologue and epilogue. They were a defensive gesture which I wouldn't have made if it were not for the appalling memory of Boston. But I have never written a play that I thought was completed and I don't think I ever will. There is too much to say and not enough time to say it. Nor is there power enough. I am not a good writer. Sometimes I am a very bad writer indeed. There is hardly a successful writer in the field who cannot write circles around me and I am the first to admit it. But I think of writing as something more organic than words, something closer to being and action. I want to work more and more with a more plastic theatre than the one that I have so far. I have never for one moment doubted that there are people—millions!—to say things to. We come to each other, gradually, but with love. It is the short reach of my arms that hinders, not the length and multiplicity of theirs. With love and with honesty, the embrace is inevitable.

1944

NOTES TO THE READER

A stage can be defined as a section of space in which anything can be made to appear to happen. That is a fairly innocuous-looking statement, on the surface, but when you consider it more closely it may begin to excite you. The world is a section of space and life a section of time in which things happen over which the individual, whether he is an artist or not, has very little influence and virtually no control. That is what makes the stage such an infinitely desirable section of space: it is the section of space in which the individual can play the lord and master and somehow, somewhat make up for his helpless bewilderment in the affairs of the cosmos. If the playwright creates a tragedy he takes hold of the abundant raw material of earthly sorrow, which in reality has no form and seldom any poetry and no more dignity than may be inherent in the embattled spirits of those called on to endure it—he takes hold of this stuff and separates it into various pieces. Then he arranges these pieces in a new order that is congruous to that mysterious sense of design which we have in our hearts like a recollection of a heavenly system we lived in before our birth. The result is a transfiguration. The tragic event may be materially the same as it was in reality, but now, in art, on the stage, it is invested with those properties which give it poetry and meaning.

A great painting shocks and delights us with the mysterious balance and congruity of its arrangements in space. It may be what is called a non-objective painting but if it is excellently done the spectator feels that here is a design and order of things that possesses a curious harmony or rectitude: it is like the correct spelling of a word that is illegibly jumbled on the tablet of nature. If you look at one of the great religious paintings of the Quattrocento perhaps you will see more clearly what the artist can do with the unesthetic facts of the case. In that period of the religious inquisitions, of heretics burned at the stake and tortured upon the rack, of the Borgia Pope who was entertained by spectacles of carnal horror—a painter like Botticelli could create a Madonna and child that is all reverence and tenderness, that is like violin music made visible. Such may be the difference between the world and the stage: For I am thinking of the stage as a section of space that is more like that of the painter's canvas than ordinarily it is allowed to be. When the art of the playwright approaches that of the painter he thinks in corresponding terms of balance, rhythm, harmony. His work then begins to depart from the strictly literary province. It begins to enter that of the plastic arts: painting, sculpture, architecture. A plastic theatre emerges which in the hands of sufficiently gifted artists can offer the same mysterious shock and delight that is given by great paintings, a correction of chance by the longing and vision of poets.

The reader may feel that these statements are posturing a discovery of something that has always existed in the theater. When has the good playwright, or novelist for that matter, not felt the necessity for balance, rhythm, congruity in his arrangements of happenings for the book or the stage? You are right, it has nearly always been there, this is not a recent discovery at all and the plastic theatre has existed as a green sprout in an old potato for a very long time indeed.

But to release the essential spirit of something there needs to be a stripping down, a reduction to abstracts. This was the need that prompted the turn to the non-representative in painting. As the painter becomes more aware of what is fundamental in painting—design and balance and so forth—in order to release those things more strikingly he must clear the deck for their action. So he turns the object into the value. Too often non-objective painting exceeds the requirements of this simplification. A painting of Piet Mondrian, for instance, is a bit too skeletal for mine and the usual taste. The design and rhythm is totally revealed, is played upon a trumpet, but an allowable degree of emotion has fallen by the way and what you have there seems (to me) to be more of a blue-print than a building.

A similar turn to something more abstract may very well be the direction of the plastic theatre. That way has already been taken by the pioneer, Lorca. Perhaps no play has been written in more plastic terms than that one of Lorca's called *If Five Years Pass*. Reading it you are struck by a mysterious congruity of its wild and unlikely events.

1945

THE AUTHOR TELLS WHY IT IS CALLED
THE GLASS MENAGERIE

When my family first moved to St. Louis from the South, we were forced to live in a congested apartment neighborhood. It was a shocking change, for my sister and myself were accustomed to spacious yards, porches, and big shade trees. The apartment we lived in was about as cheerful as an Arctic winter. There were outside windows only in the front room and kitchen. The rooms between had windows that opened upon a narrow areaway that was virtually sunless and which we grimly named "Death Valley" for a reason which is amusing only in retrospect.

There were a great many alleycats in the neighborhood which were constantly fighting the dogs. Every now and then some unwary young cat would allow itself to be pursued into this areaway which had only one opening. The end of the cul-de-sac was directly beneath my sister's bedroom window and it was here that the cats would have to turn around to face their pursuers in mortal combat. My sister would be awakened in the night by the struggle and in the morning the hideously mangled victim would be lying under her window. Sight of the areaway had become so odious to her, for this reason, that she kept the shade constantly drawn so that the interior of her bedroom had a perpetual twilight atmosphere. Something had to be done to relieve this gloom. So my sister and I painted all her furniture white; she put white curtains at the window and on the shelves around the room she collected a large assortment of little glass articles, of which she was particularly fond. Eventually, the room took on a light and delicate appearance, in spite of the lack of outside illumination, and it became the only room in the house that I found pleasant to enter.

When I left home a number of years later, it was this room that I recalled most vividly and poignantly when looking back on our home life in St. Louis. Particularly the little glass ornaments on the shelves. They were mostly little glass animals. By poetic association they came to represent, in my memory, all the softest emotions that belong to recollection of things past. They stood for all the small and tender things that relieve the austere pattern of life and make it endurable to the sensitive. The areaway where the cats were torn to pieces was one thing—my sister's white curtains and tiny menagerie of glass were another. Somewhere between them was the world that we lived in.

1945

A PLAYWRIGHT'S STATEMENT ON DALLAS'S THEATER '45 PLANS

Guadalajara, Mexico. July 21—I have just received a telegram from Margo Jones which reads as follows: "Desperately need short article on playwright's attitude toward Dallas theater to show Dallas and the country what we are trying to do. Wire when I can expect it. Love, Margo."

This is a typical communication from Miss Jones, except that she says "Dallas and the country" instead of "Texas and the world." This unexpected caution might suggest that her horizons are shrinking. Knowing Miss Jones fairly well, I doubt the safety of such conclusion.

As a matter of fact, if Margo had said "inform the world," I don't think it would have been at all impertinent of her, for actually the Dallas Theater idea is something worth shouting to the world about. Especially at this time, immediately after the San Francisco charter has been signed, when now as never before it is important to speak across frontiers, to think and dream globally, the world-language of theater is of no small, local importance. For great theater is an international thing. Like great music and painting it is a world property, but more particularly than any other medium of art it has a way of speaking directly from the heart of one people to the hearts of others and so breeding a sense of the one real community, which is the community of common human impulses, needs and longings. But unfortunately America has not produced her share of playwrights—men such as Chekhov, Shaw, Ibsen, Lorca, Shakespeare—who have voices that carry beyond the national frontiers. I think this may be due considerably to the fact that there has been no great and lasting theater here that could offer the sort of climate in which such dramatists could develop.

At the present time Broadway is a big slot machine or race track where millions are won or lost, where more money is earned by a hit show in a single week than Shakespeare's little company could have dreamed of earning in a lifetime. What comes of it in the way of enduring art? Not enough to fill a baby's silver teaspoon!

No, the gamblers are not the proper groomsmen for the dramatic muse, and she will not have much to say in America as long as she is in their custody.

At the present moment there is no art theater in America. The closest approach we had to one was probably the Group Theater, but the Group Theater was a phenomenon of the thirties and did not seem destined to survive the social climate of that brief period. As for the Theatre Guild, it was formerly what might have been loosely termed an art theater, and still has some such pretensions, but it has lately become just another successful commercial management, putting on shows that are usually quite tasteful though not so usually distinguished and specializing the last few seasons in big musicals like *Carousel* and *Oklahoma!* Nothing wrong with that but it doesn't answer the real theatrical needs of this country.

The importance of these facts is that there is about to become what I hope and believe will be a true art theater in America.

Now don't be alarmed by that alarming word art. It is only alarming because of its mistaken association with things that are special, snobbish and eclectic. Art is actually a very straight-forward thing, as plain and honest as daylight and about as necessary.

Is art a commercial failure?

No!

I put that answer in a paragraph all by itself because it cannot be too distinctly spoken.

The gamblers of Broadway are continually being shocked, baffled and appalled by the fact, altogether unaccountable in their scheme of things, that shows which they dub as "art properties" are emerging as the real successes of the show world. Pitifully few of these shows are getting across the opening barrier because of the same superstitious abhorrence among the people who have the money to back them. But like all superstitions it is based on ignorance, which is insulting to the audience of America.

This article cannot be long enough to go into all that I believe and which I know that Margo believes about the possible power and glory of a new plastic theater in this country.

Margo and I are Southerners, most of the people that will be working in the Dallas theater have sprung from the South, and it does not seem surprising or unnatural to any of us that the location of such a theater should be in the heart of the South. We believe in the emotional richness and the vitality of this part of the country, which is ours by birth and breeding. Some kinds of local pride are ugly and pernicious, but the pride of desiring one's native region to assume the leadership in creating something that will be of value to all people is a good kind of pride and one worth cultivating.

I would like to say one thing more, now, at the end of this article. Millions of American youth have already started returning from war to this country. All have been through experiences of terrific intensity and they are going to resume the more or less commonplace ways of life from which they were drawn by the war. These men will need something more than that. Their nerves are keyed to an excitement which they will find lacking in an ordinary peacetime society at home. Something has to be done to dramatize and enrich that society. A good many things ought to be done. But I can think of nothing richer or more exciting at the moment than the springing up of a vital new theater to serve as expression and release of all the new ideas and emotions this vast cargo of heart-hungry youth is bringing back with it. You've got to give them a richer life than they went away from. Here is one chance to do it. It's a big chance to do a big thing. You can have it, you can make it—it's yours!

(And America's and the world's!)

If there is anything more to say—you say it!

1945

THE CATASTROPHE OF SUCCESS

This winter marked the third anniversary of the Chicago opening of *The Glass Menagerie,* an event which terminated one part of my life and began another about as different in all external circumstances as could well be imagined. I was snatched out of virtual oblivion and thrust into sudden prominence, and from the precarious tenancy of furnished rooms about the country I was removed to a suite in a first-class Manhattan hotel. My experience was not unique. Success has often come that abruptly into the lives of Americans. The Cinderella story is our favorite national myth, the cornerstone of the film industry if not of the Democracy itself. I have seen it enacted on the screen so often that I am now inclined to yawn at it, not with disbelief but with an attitude of Who Cares! Anyone with such beautiful teeth and hair as the screen protagonist of such a story was bound to have a good time one way or another, and you could bet your bottom dollar and all the tea in China that that one would not be caught dead or alive at any meeting involving a social conscience.

No, my experience was not exceptional, but neither was it quite ordinary, and if you are willing to accept the somewhat eclectic proposition that I had not been writing with such an experience in mind—and many people are not willing to believe that a playwright is interested in anything but popular success—there may be some point in comparing the two estates.

The sort of life which I had had previous to this popular success was one that required endurance, a life of clawing and scratching along a sheer surface and holding on tight with raw fingers to every inch of rock higher than the one caught hold of before, but it was a good life because it was the sort of life for which the human organism is created.

I was not aware of how much vital energy had gone into this struggle until the struggle was removed. I was out on a level plateau with my arm still thrashing and my lungs still grabbing at air that no longer resisted. This was security at last.

I sat down and looked about me and was suddenly very depressed. I thought to myself, this is just a period of adjustment. Tomorrow morning I will wake up in this first-class hotel suite above the discreet hum of an East Side boulevard and I will appreciate its elegance and luxuriate in its comforts and know that I have arrived at our American plan of Olympus. Tomorrow morning when I look at the green satin sofa I will fall in love with it. It is only temporarily that the green satin looks like slime on stagnant water.

But in the morning the inoffensive little sofa looked more revolting than the night before, and I was already getting too fat for the $125 suit which a fashionable acquaintance had selected for me. In the suite things began to break accidentally. An arm came off the sofa. Cigarette burns appeared on the polished surface of the furniture. Windows were left open and a rainstorm flooded the suite. But the maid always put it straight and the patience of the management was inexhaustible. Late parties could not offend them seriously. Nothing short of a demolition bomb seemed to bother my neighbors.

I lived on room service. But in this, too, there was a disenchantment. Some time between the moment when I ordered dinner over the phone and when it was rolled into my living room like a corpse on a rubber-wheeled table, I lost all interest in it. Once I ordered a sirloin steak and a chocolate sundae, but everything was so cunningly disguised on the table that I mistook the chocolate sauce for gravy and poured it over the sirloin steak.

Of course all this was the more trivial aspect of a spiritual dislocation that began to manifest itself in far more disturbing ways. I soon found myself becoming indifferent to people. A well of cynicism rose in me. Conversations all sounded as if they had been recorded years ago and were being played back on a turntable. Sincerity and kindliness seemed to have gone out of my friends' voices. I suspected them of hypocrisy. I stopped calling them, stopped seeing them. I was impatient of what I took to be inane flattery.

I got so sick of hearing people say, "I loved your play!" that I could not say thank you any more. I choked on the words and turned rudely away from the usually sincere person. I no longer felt any pride in the play itself but began to dislike it, probably because I felt too lifeless inside ever to create another. I was walking around dead in my shoes and I knew it but there were no friends I knew or trusted sufficiently, at that time, to take them aside and tell them what was the matter.

This curious condition persisted about three months, till late spring, when I decided to have another eye operation mainly because of the excuse it gave me to withdraw from the world behind a gauze mask. It was my fourth eye operation, and perhaps I should explain that I had been afflicted for about five years with a cataract on my left eye which required a series of needling operations and finally an operation on the muscle of the eye. (The eye is still in my head. So much for that.)

Well, the gauze mask served a purpose. While I was resting in the hospital the friends whom I had neglected or affronted in one way or another began to call on me, and now that I was in pain and darkness, their voices seemed to have changed, or rather that unpleasant mutation which I had suspected earlier in the season had now disappeared and they sounded now as they had used to sound in the lamented days of my obscurity. Once more they were sincere and kindly voices with the ring of truth in them and that quality of understanding for which I had originally sought them out.

As far as my physical vision was concerned, this last operation was only relatively successful (although it left me with an apparently clear black pupil in the right position, or nearly so) but in another, figurative way, it had served a much deeper purpose.

When the gauze mask was removed I found myself in a readjusted world. I checked out of the handsome suite at the first-class hotel, packed my papers and a few incidental belongings, and left for Mexico, an elemental country where you can quickly forget the false dignities and conceits imposed by success, a country where vagrants innocent as children curl up to sleep on the pavements and human voices, especially when their language is not familiar to the ear, are soft as birds'. My public self, that artifice of mirrors, did not exist here and so my natural being was resumed.

Then, as a final act of restoration, I settled for a while at Chapala to work on a play called *The Poker Night,* which later became *A Streetcar Named Desire.* It is only in his work that an artist can find reality and satisfaction, for the actual world is less intense than the world of his invention, and consequently his life, without recourse to violent disorder, does not seem very substantial. The right condition for him is that in which his work is not only convenient but unavoidable.

For me a convenient place to work is a remote place among strangers where there is good swimming. But life should require a certain minimal effort. You should not have too many people waiting on you; you should have to do most things for yourself. Hotel service is embarrassing. Maids, waiters, bellhops, porters, and so forth are the most embarrassing people in the world for they continually remind you of inequities which we accept as the proper thing. The sight of an ancient woman, gasping and wheezing as she drags a heavy pail of water down a hotel corridor to mop up the mess of some drunken overprivileged guest, is one that sickens and weighs upon the heart and withers it with shame for this world in which it is not only tolerated but regarded as proof positive that the wheels of Democracy are functioning as they should without interference from above or below. Nobody should have to clean up anybody else's mess in this world. It is terribly bad for both parties, but probably worse for the one receiving the service.

I have been corrupted as much as anyone else by the vast number of menial services which our society has grown to expect and depend on. We should do for ourselves or let the machines do for us—the glorious technology that is supposed to be the new light of the world. We are like a man who has bought a great amount of equipment for a camping trip, who has the canoe and the tent and the fishing lines and the axe and the guns, the mackinaw and the blankets, but who now, when all the preparations and the provisions are piled expertly together, is suddenly too timid to set out on the journey but remains where he was yesterday and the day before and day before that, looking suspiciously through white lace curtains at the clear sky he distrusts. Our great technology is a God-given chance for adventure and for progress which we are afraid to attempt. Our ideas and our ideals remain exactly what they were and where they were three centuries ago. No. I beg your pardon. It is no longer safe for a man to even declare them!

This is a long excursion from a small theme into a large one which I did not intend to make, so let me go back to what I was saying before.

This is an oversimplification. One does not escape that easily from the seduction of an effete way of life. You cannot arbitrarily say to yourself, I will now continue my life as it was before this thing, Success, happened to me. But once you fully apprehend the vacuity of a life without struggle you are equipped with the basic means of salvation. Once you know this is true, that the heart of man, his body and his brain, are forged in a white-hot furnace for the purpose of conflict (the struggle of creation) and that with the conflict removed, the man is a sword cutting daisies, that not privation but luxury is the wolf at the door and that the fangs of this wolf are all the little vanities and conceits and laxities that Success is heir to—why, then with this knowledge you are at least in a position of knowing where danger lies.

You know, then, that the public Somebody you are when you "have a name" is a fiction created with mirrors and that the only somebody worth being is the solitary and unseen you that existed from your first breath and which is the sum of your actions and so is constantly in a state of becoming under your own volition—and knowing these things, you can even survive the catastrophe of Success!

It is never altogether too late, unless you embrace the Bitch Goddess, as William James called her, with both arms and find in her smothering caresses exactly what the homesick little boy in you always wanted, absolute protection and utter effortlessness. Security is a kind of death, I think, and it can come to you in a storm of royalty checks beside a kidney-shaped pool in Beverly Hills or anywhere at all that is removed from the conditions that made you an artist, if that's what you are or were or intended to be. Ask anyone who has experienced the kind of success I am talking about—What good is it? Perhaps to get an honest answer you will have to give him a shot of truth serum but the word he will finally groan is unprintable in genteel publications.

Then what is good? The obsessive interest in human affairs, plus a certain amount of compassion and moral conviction, that first made the experience of living something that must be translated into pigment or music or bodily movement or poetry or prose or anything that's dynamic and expressive—that's what's good for you if you're at all serious in your aims. William Saroyan wrote a great play on this theme, that purity of heart is the one success worth having. "In the time of your life—live!" That time is short and it doesn't return again. It is slipping away while I write this and while you read it, and the monosyllable of the clock is Loss, loss, loss, unless you devote your heart to its opposition.

                                                                            1947

CHICAGO ARRIVAL

Several weeks ago in London while I was staying there for the rehearsal period of the Helen Hayes *The Glass Menagerie*, a lady journalist, becoming a bit desperate over my involuntary failure to produce anything of sensational interest in the way of quotable conversation, asked me how I felt when *Menagerie* was about to open on Broadway.

"Oh, but it didn't open on Broadway," I told her, "it opened in Chicago." She gave me one of those blank looks which the English face can produce with peculiar ease. "Not Broadway?" "No, Chicago," I assured her. She thought for a moment and then said, "Why Chicago?" I shrugged a little, for one does not remain six weeks in London without picking up one or two little English gestures. "I don't know why, exactly, but I think that it must have been an act of God!"

The lady pulled another blank face; then sighed and opened her notebook and wrote that down. She had to write down something and that was it.

The Glass Menagerie opened in Chicago by an act of God!

I call it God when something good happens, though perhaps there are many times when a Protestant Deity would violently disclaim the authorship of the blessing. However, I think He ought to be willing to take the responsibility for the Chicago opening of the Eddie Dowling-Laurette Taylor *Menagerie*. Of course, if He is equitable as a Deity should be, He would happily admit that He had several collaborators in this particular bestowal of a blessing. He was aided particularly by certain members of the Chicago press, which here will be nameless, and He was aided by that special something which makes the Loop of Chicago, and its immediate environs, somehow to my mind, the most violently and wonderfully vital small area of America.

It was not easy to explain this in England where Chicago is still thought of in terms of the sawed-off shotgun. The English are always saying, with sometimes no less a spokesman than J. B. Priestley, that "We have got to TRY to understand and get along with our American cousins." The under-

standing begins and ends with this perennial assertion that it is desirable.
Okay. We are agreed about that. But as a beginning, John Bull, you must
make an effort to believe that everything west of Manhattan is still not an
overgrown game of cowboys and Indians without the war-paint and feath-
ers which once made it picturesque. In Chicago the bars do not shut down
with thunderous unanimity at the stroke of 10:30 P.M. In Chicago you can
get a steak an inch thick and even a glass of milk without having a baby.
But the advantages of the United States are not solely material advantages
even in Chicago.

That's what I tried to explain, and perhaps was successful: at least
I managed to fill several pages of the lady's notebook. I did not tell her
everything about the Chicago opening of *The Glass Menagerie*. I could
have told enough about that to fill a poet-sized volume. Perhaps some day
I shall, for no more exciting nor consequential a thing has occurred in my
life. I would begin this story in a railroad station on a cold winter morning
in December, 1944. A train has just pulled into the station, which by some
optical or nervous illusion seems twice the size of the New York station it
left in the early morning. One car of this train is occupied by a theatrical
troupe, none of whose faces is familiar enough to excite the interest of other
passengers. The train is stopped, the company disembarks, there is great
confusion. The small group is scattered like chickens in a thunderstorm.
The management vanishes busily in one direction, exchanging wild shouts
over something of a non-metaphysical nature, the actors trail individually
off to claim their luggage. The playwright, who has forgotten something,
his portable typewriter or possibly even the portfolio containing the still-
being-worked on script, dives back into the coach to retrieve it. When he
emerges again, he finds himself left behind in a suddenly descending cloud
of anxiety and desolation. His fatigued head, one thing he never forgets but
would sometime like to, is incapable of putting a wish into thought; but
what he most wants at this moment is the sight of any familiar figure in this
cold vastness where he first meets the city which is to make or destroy the
play he brings with him.

Then all at once he sees one! Close at hand, too. It is a short and nearly
square figure in a peculiar costume, like something rooted from the bottom
of an old wardrobe trunk. The coat is grey muskrat, but the many small
pelts of which it is composed are not enjoying the most pacific relation.
Discord threatening disunion is at work amongst them. Almost down the
upturned collar of this coat is a very broad brimmed hat of the type that
is worn by cinema buccaneers. Between these two defensive perimeters is a
pair of eyes that are much too bright to be described as brown and a cloudy

profusion of hair that is lighter than auburn. This is the figure of a star. Her name has been famous. It is still a legend, but the face in the station passes without recognition. The figure passes without assurance among the jostling swarm. The brightness of the eyes has bravery but not certainty. The motion of the figure is hesitant; for a moment it even appears to be lost. One hand which does not wear a glove is clutching a very large purse as if it contained a more secure world than that of a teeming station . . .

"Laurette!"

I called her name and she turned and cried out mine.

Then and there we joined forces. The station diminished to a comfortable size; the bitter cold thawed a little; we moved off together with a feeling of a union deeper than physical, more than accidental, to find a taxi.

Catch one we did! It was Laurette who hailed it with an imperious wave of her ungloved hand, hesitation all gone as she sprang like a tiger out of her cloud of softness; such a light spring, but such an amazingly far one!

But sometimes it seems that I am still in some car that was stopped at my corner by the imperious wave of an ungloved hand; and when I am lucky it always seems like Chicago!

1948

QUESTIONS WITHOUT ANSWERS

Writing an article about your play prior to its New York opening is not going to improve the quality of the play and, moreover, it may have the disadvantage of suggesting to the suspicious that an effort is being made to load the dice.

It is possible, though I prefer to think unlikely, that no ethical consideration would deter me from making this effort if I thought it likely to pay off, and God knows pretension has been known to pay off in some branches of the arts. Inflated reputations and eclectic styles have cast an aura of gravity over much that is essentially vacuous in painting; obscurity has disguised sterility in a good deal of verse.

But the theater, which is called the charlatan of the arts, is paradoxically the one in which the charlatan is most easily detected. He must say intelligibly what he has to say and unless it is well worth saying he does not have a Chinaman's chance of surviving. Even cheap entertainment is honest. It is all honest that does what it professes to do, and there is too much hot light and too many penetrating eyes cast upon the stage for the willful obscurantist to pull his tricks.

But writing an article about your play puts you in a fairly untenable position. Three courses seem to be open. You can praise it or you can denigrate it or you can explain it. The first is surely fatal, although it has been attempted. The second is foolish. If you sincerely thought it was a bad play you would not have put it into production, because the failure of a play is one of the world's more agonizing adventures. To explain is okay if there is something that needs explaining.

Obviously, I have already chosen the third one of these three alternatives. The problem now is to find something in my work which needs explaining.

I have been asked a lot of questions about my plays. Recently, only last week, the cast of *Summer and Smoke* was entertained at a supper given by Lester and Cleo Gruber at a suburb in Detroit. Everything was wonderful: it

was the first good time we had all had together on the road and it was wonderfully relaxing after the tension of two openings and some highly charged
atmosphere in suites at the Statler and the Book-Cadillac.

Earlier in the evening the party was conducted in the rathskeller of this
suburban residence. With our backs to the rathskeller bar, behind which
stood a white-jacketed youth passing out drinks as fast as an elbow can
bend, the director, Margo Jones, and myself withstood a barrage of questions like a pair of antlered beasts, and withstood them successfully. But
it was now later in the evening, the rathskeller bar had shut down and the
party had progressed, if progression you call it, from cocktails and high-
balls to cole slaw and beef tongue.

That comfortable stupefaction which belongs to the late hours of Sunday had fallen over me and I had retreated with a plate of food to an alcove
in the parlor. This alcove was something of a cul-de-sac. It had a fine view
but no exit, and if you've seen or read Sartre you know how discomfiting
no exit can be, especially when there get to be women in it. That was what
happened.

A fresh contingent of visitors arrived at the Gruber residence and
headed straight for this alcove. All at once I found myself hemmed in by
three women in basic black who had been to the Saturday matinee and had
apparently thought of nothing since except the problems of Alma Winemiller, the heroine of *Summer and Smoke*. When you are eating, a great deal
can be accomplished by having a mouth full of food and by making guttural
noises instead of speech when confronted with questions such as, What is
the theme of your play? What happens to the characters after the play is
over? Why do you write? What is your next play about and how do you
happen to know so much about women? On that last one you can spit the
food out if it really begins to choke you!

For a writer who is not intentionally obscure, and never, in his opinion,
obscure at all, I do get asked a hell of a lot of questions which I can't answer.
I have never been able to say what was the theme of my play and I don't
think I have ever been conscious of writing with a theme in mind. I am always surprised when, after a play has opened, I read in the papers what the
play is about, that it was about a decayed Southern belle trying to get a man
for her crippled daughter, or that it was about a boozy floozy on the skids,
or a backwoods sheik in a losing battle with three village vamps.

Don't misunderstand me. I am thankful for these highly condensed and
stimulating analyses, but it would never have occurred to me that that was
the story I was trying to tell. Usually when asked about a theme, I look
vague and say, "It is a play about life." What could be simpler, and yet

more pretentious? You can easily extend that a little and say it is a tragedy of incomprehension. That also means life. Or you can say it is a tragedy of Puritanism. That is life in America. Or you can say it is a play that considers the "problem of evil." But why not just say "life"?

To return to the women in the alcove. On this particular occasion the question that floored me was "Why do you always write about frustrated women?"

To say that floored me is to put it mildly, because I would say that frustrated is almost exactly what the women I write about are not. What was frustrated about Amanda Wingfield? Circumstances, yes! But spirit? See Helen Hayes in London's *The Glass Menagerie* if you still think Amanda was a frustrated spirit! No, there is nothing interesting about frustration *per se*. I could not write a line about it for the simple reason that I can't write a line about anything that bores me.

Was Blanche of *A Streetcar Named Desire* frustrated? About as frustrated as a beast of the jungle! And Alma Winemiller? What is frustrated about loving with such white-hot intensity that it alters the whole direction of your life, and removes you from the parlor of an Episcopal rectory to a secret room above Moon Lake Casino?

I did not have to answer the lady who asked me this question. Into the fiery breach jumped—Margo Jones!

"Tennessee does not write about frustrated women!" she shouted. "Tennessee does not write about abnormal characters!"

She had arrived at the alcove and was making an entrance.

"Oh?" said one of the ladies. "Then what does he write about?"

"People!" said Margo. "Life."

"Now, honey," she continued, in a less militant tone, "I don't know a thing about you women, but just looking at you, I can see you have problems!"

By this time I had executed a flanking movement under the cover of Margo's diversionary tactics. The alcove, the women, the questions and finally even the residence were behind me and I stood on the suburban sidewalk, still with a plate of food and no work but ten fingers, and I suddenly felt very happy, not that I had escaped from the questions but that there were people who cared enough to ask them.

The mysterious thing about writing plays about life is that so many people find them so strange and baffling. That makes you know, with moments of deep satisfaction, that you have really succeeded in writing about it!

1948

"SOMETHING WILD . . ."

While I was on the road with *Summer and Smoke* I was entertained one evening by the company of a successful community theater, one of the pioneer outfits of this kind and one of the few that operate on a profitable self-supporting basis. It had been ten years since I had had a connection with a community theater. I was professionally spawned by one ten years ago in St. Louis, but like most offspring, once I departed from the maternal shelter, I gave it scarcely a backward glance. Backward glances are a bit impractical, anyhow, in a theatrical career.

Now I felt considerable curiosity about the contact I was about to renew: but the moment I walked in the door I felt something wrong. Not so much something wrong as something missing. It seemed all so respectable. The men in their conservative business suits with their neat haircuts and highly polished shoes could have passed for corporation lawyers and the women, mostly their wives, were impeccably ladylike. There was no scratchy phonograph music, there were no dimly lit alcoves where dancing couples stood practically still, no sofas with ruptured upholstery, no garlands of colored crepe paper festooning the ceiling and collapsing onto the floor.

In my opinion art is a kind of anarchy, and the theater is a province of art. What was missing here, was something anarchistic in the air. I must modify that statement about art and anarchy. Art is only anarchy in juxtaposition with organized society. It runs counter to the sort of orderliness on which organized society apparently must be based. It is a benevolent anarchy: it must be that and if it is true art, it is. It is benevolent in the sense of constructing something which is missing, and what it constructs may be merely criticism of things as they exist. I felt in this group no criticism but rather an adaptation which was almost obsequious. And my mind shot back to the St. Louis group I have mentioned, a group called The Mummers.

The Mummers were sort of a long-haired outfit. Now there is no virtue, *per se*, in not going to the barber. And I don't suppose there is any particular virtue in girls having runs in their stockings. Yet one feels a kind of nostalgia for that sort of disorderliness now and then.

Somehow you associate it with things that have no logical connection with it. You associate it with really good times and with intense feelings and with convictions. Most of all with convictions! In the party I have mentioned there was a notable lack of convictions. Nobody was shouting for—or against—anything, there was just a lot of polite chitchat going on among people who seemed to have known each other long enough to have exhausted all interest in each other's ideas.

While I stood there among them, the sense that something was missing clarified itself into a tremendous wave of longing for something that I had not been conscious of wanting until that moment. The open sky of my youth!—a peculiarly American youth which somehow seems to have slipped a little bit out of our grasp nowadays. . . .

The Mummers of St. Louis were my professional youth. They were the disorderly theater group of St. Louis, standing socially, if not also artistically, opposite to the usual Little Theater group. That opposite group need not be described. They were eminently respectable, predominantly middle-aged, and devoted mainly to the presentation of Broadway hits a season or two after Broadway. Their stage was narrow and notices usually mentioned how well they had overcome their spatial limitations, but it never seemed to me that they produced anything in a manner that needed to overcome limitations of space. The dynamism which is theater was as foreign to their philosophy as the tongue of Chinese.

Dynamism was what The Mummers had, and for about five years— roughly from about 1935 to 1940—they burned like one of Miss Millay's improvident little candles—and then expired. Yes, there was about them that kind of excessive romanticism which is youth and which is the best and purest part of life.

The first time I worked with them was in 1936, when I was a student at Washington University in St. Louis. They were, then, under the leadership of a man named Willard Holland, their organizer and their director. Holland always wore a blue suit which was not only baggy but shiny. He needed a haircut and he sometimes wore a scarf instead of a shirt. This was not what made him a great director, but a great director he was. Everything that he touched he charged with electricity. Was it my youth that made it seem that way? Possibly, but not probably. In fact not even possibly: you judge theater, really, by its effect on audiences, and Holland's work never failed to deliver, and when I say deliver I mean a sock!

The first thing I worked with them on was *Bury the Dead*, by Irwin

Shaw. That play ran a little bit short of full length and they needed a curtain raiser to fill out the program. Holland called me up. He did not have a prepossessing voice. It was high-pitched and nervous. He said I hear you go to college and I hear you can write. I admitted some justice in both of these charges. Then he asked me: How do you feel about compulsory military training? I then assured him that I had left the University of Missouri because I could not get a passing grade in the ROTC. Swell! said Holland, you are just the guy I am looking for. How would you like to write something against militarism?

So I did.

Shaw's play, one of the greatest lyric plays America has produced, was a solid piece of flame. Actors and script, under Holland's dynamic hand, were one piece of vibrant living-tissue. Now St. Louis is not a town that is easily impressed. They love music, they are ardent devotees of the symphony concerts, but they preserve a fairly rigid decorum when they are confronted with anything offbeat which they are not used to. They certainly were not used to the sort of hot lead which the Mummers pumped into their bellies that night of Shaw's play. They were not used to it, but it paralyzed them. There wasn't a cough or creak in the house, and nobody left the Wednesday Club Auditorium (which the Mummers rented out for their performances) without a disturbing kink in their nerves or guts, and I doubt if any of them have forgotten it to this day.

It was The Mummers that I remembered at this polite supper party which I attended last month.

Now let me give you a picture of the Mummers! Most of them worked at other jobs besides theater. They had to, because The Mummers were not a paying proposition. There were laborers. There were clerks. There were waitresses. There were students. There were whores and tramps and there was even a post-debutante who was a member of the Junior League of St. Louis. Many of them were fine actors. Many of them were not. Some of them could not act at all, but what they lacked in ability, Holland inspired them with in the way of enthusiasm. I guess it was all run by a kind of beautiful witchcraft! It was like a definition of what I think theater is. Something wild, something exciting, something that you are not used to. Offbeat is the word.

They put on bad shows sometimes, but they never put on a show that didn't deliver a punch to the solar plexus, maybe not in the first act, maybe not in the second, but always at last a good hard punch was delivered, and it made a difference in the lives of the spectators that they had come to that place and seen that show.

The plays I gave them were bad. But the first of these plays was a smash hit. It even got rave notices out of all three papers, and there was a real demonstration on the opening night with shouts and cheers and stamping, and the pink-faced author took his first bow among the grey-faced coal miners that he had created out of an imagination never stimulated by the sight of an actual coal mine. The second play that I gave them, *Fugitive Kind,* was a flop. It got one rave notice out of the *Star-Times,* but the *Post-Dispatch* and the *Globe Democrat* gave it hell. Nevertheless it packed a considerable wallop and there are people in St. Louis who still remember it. Bad plays, both of them, amateurish and coarse and juvenile and talky. But Holland and his players put them across the footlights without apology and they put them across with the bang that is theater.

Oh, how long ago that was!

The Mummers lived only five years. Yes, they had something in common with lyric verse of a too romantic nature. From 1935 to 1940 they had their fierce little flame, and then they expired, and now there is not a visible trace of them. Where is Holland? In Hollywood, I think. And where are the players? God knows. . . .

I am here, remembering them wistfully.

Now I shall have to say something to give this recollection a meaning to you.

All right. This is it.

Today we are living in a world which is threatened by totalitarianism. The Fascist and the Communist states have thrown us into a panic of reaction. Reactionary opinion descends like a ton of bricks on the head of any artist who speaks out against the current of prescribed ideas. We are all under wraps of one kind or another, trembling before the spectre of investigating committees and even with Buchenwald in the back of our minds when we consider whether or not we dare to say we were for Henry Wallace. *Yes, it is as bad as that.*

And yet it isn't *really* as bad as that.

America is still America, democracy is still democracy.

In our history books are still the names of Jefferson and Lincoln and Tom Paine. The direction of the democratic impulse, which is entirely and irresistibly away from the police state and away from any and all forms of controlled thought and feeling—which is entirely and irresistibly in the direction of that which is individual and humane and equitable and free—that direction can be confused but it cannot be lost.

I have a way of jumping from the particular to the abstract, for the particular is sometimes as much as we know of the abstract.

Now let me jump back again: where? To the subject of community theaters and their social function.

It seems to me, as it seems to many artists right now, that an effort is being made to put creative work and workers under wraps.

Nothing could be more dangerous to Democracy, for the irritating grain of sand which is creative work in a society must be kept inside the shell or the pearl of idealistic progress cannot be made. For God's sake let us defend ourselves against whatever is hostile to us without imitating the thing which we are afraid of!

Community theaters have a social function and it is to be that kind of an irritant in the shell of their community. Not to conform, not to wear the conservative business suit of their audience, but to let their hair grow long and even greasy, to make wild gestures, break glasses, fight, shout, and fall downstairs! When you see them acting like this—not respectably, not quite decently, even!—then you will know that something is going to happen in that outfit, something disturbing, something irregular, something brave and honest.

The biologist will tell you that progress is the result of mutations. Mutations are another word for freaks. For God's sake let's have a little more freakish behavior—not less.

Maybe ninety percent of the freaks will be just freaks, ludicrous and pathetic and getting nowhere but into trouble.

Eliminate them, however—bully them into conformity—and nobody in America will ever be really young any more and we'll be left standing in the dead center of nowhere.

1948

CARSON MCCULLERS'S
REFLECTIONS IN A GOLDEN EYE

This book, *Reflections in a Golden Eye,* is a second novel, and although its appreciation has steadily risen during the years since its first appearance, it was then regarded as somewhat disappointing in the way that second novels usually are. When the book preceding a second novel has been very highly acclaimed, as was *The Heart Is a Lonely Hunter,* there is an inclination on the part of critics to retrench their favor, so nearly automatic and invariable a tendency that it can almost be set down as a physical law. But the reasons for failure to justly evaluate this second novel go beyond the common, temporal disadvantage that all second novels must suffer, and I feel that an examination of these reasons may be of considerably greater pertinence to our aim of suggesting a fresh evaluation.

To quote directly from book notices is virtually impossible, here in Rome where I am writing these comments, but I believe that I am safe in assuming that it was their identification of the author with a certain school of American writers, mostly of Southern origin, that made her subject to a particular and powerful line of attack.

Even in the preceding book some readers must undoubtedly have detected a warning predisposition toward certain elements which are popularly known as "morbid." Doubtless there were some critics, as well as readers, who did not understand why Carson McCullers had elected to deal with a matter so unwholesome as the spiritual but passionate attachment that existed between a deaf-mute and a half-wit. But the tenderness of the book disarmed them. The depth and nobility of its compassion were so palpable that at least for the time being the charge of decadence had to be held in check. This forbearance was of short duration. In her second novel the veil of subjective tenderness, which is the one quality of her talent which she has occasionally used to some excess, was drawn away. And the young writer suddenly flashed in their faces the cabalistic emblems of fellowship with a certain company of writers that the righteous "Humanists" in the world of letters regarded as most abhorrent and most necessary to expose and attack.

Not being a follower of literary journals, I am not at all sure what title has been conferred upon this group of writers by their disparaging critics, but for my own convenience I will refer to them as the Gothic school. It has a very ancient lineage, this school, but our local inheritance of its tradition was first brought into prominence by the early novels of William Faulkner, who still remains a most notorious and unregenerate member. There is something in the region, something in the blood and culture, of the Southern state that has somehow made them the center of this Gothic school of writers. Certainly something more important than the influence of a single artist, Faulkner, is to be credited with its development, just as in France the Existentialist movement is surely attributable to forces more significant than the personal influence of Jean-Paul Sartre. There is actually a common link between the two schools, French and American, but characteristically the motor impulse of the French school is intellectual and philosophic while that of the American is more of an emotional and romantic nature. What is this common link? In my opinion it is most simply definable as a sense, an intuition, of an underlying dreadfulness in modern experience.

The question one hears most frequently about writers of the Gothic school is this little classic:

"Why do they write about such *dreadful* things?"

This is a question that escapes not only from the astonished lips of summer matrons who have stumbled into the odd world of William Faulkner, through some inadvertence or mischief at the lending library, but almost as frequently and certainly more importantly, from the pens of some of the most eminent book critics. If it were a solely and typically philistine manifestation, there would be no sense or hope in trying to answer it, but the fact that it is used as a major line of attack by elements that the artist has to deal with—critics, publishers, distributors, not to mention the reading public—makes it a question that we should try seriously to answer or at least understand.

The great difficulty of understanding, and communication, lies in the fact that we who are asked this question and those who ask it do not really inhabit the same universe.

You do not need to tell me that this remark smacks of artistic snobbism which is about as unattractive as any other form that snobbism can take. (If artists are snobs, it is much in the same humble way that lunatics are: not because they wish to be different, and hope and believe that they are, but because they are forever painfully struck in the face with the inescapable fact of their difference which makes them hurt and lonely enough to want to undertake the vocation of artists.)

It appears to me, sometimes, that there are only two kinds of people who live outside what E. E. Cummings has defined as "this so-called world of ours"—the artists and the insane. Of course there are those who are not practicing artists and those who have not been committed to asylums, but who have enough of one or both magical elements, lunacy and vision, to permit them also to slip sufficiently apart from "this so-called world of ours" to undertake or accept an exterior view of it. But I feel that Mr. Cummings established a highly defensible point when he stated, at least by implication, that "the everyday humdrum world, which includes me and you and millions upon millions of men and women" is pretty largely something done with mirrors, and the mirrors are the millions of eyes that look at each other and things no more penetratingly than the physical senses allow. If they are conscious of there being anything to explore beyond this *soi-disant* universe, they comfortably suppose it to be represented by the mellow tones of the pipe organ on Sundays.

In expositions of this sort it is sometimes very convenient to invent an opposite party to an argument, as Mr. Cummings did in making the remarks I have quoted. Such an invented adversary might say to me at this point:

"I have read some of these books, like this one here, and I think they're sickening and crazy. I don't know why anybody should want to write about such diseased and perverted and fantastic creatures and try to pass them off as representative members of the human race! That's how I feel about it. But I do have this sense you talk about, as much as you do or anybody else, this sense of fearfulness or dreadfulness or whatever you want to call it. I read the newspapers and I think it's all pretty awful. I think the atom bomb is awful and I think that the confusion of the world is awful. I think that cancer is fearful, and I certainly don't look forward to the idea of dying, which I think is dreadful. I could go on forever, or at least indefinitely, giving you a list of things that I think are dreadful. And isn't that having what you call the Sense of Dreadfulness or something?"

My hesitant answer would be—"Yes, and no. Mostly no."

And then I would explain a little further, with my usual awkwardness at exposition:

"All of these things that you list as dreadful are parts of the visible, sensible phenomena of every man's experience or knowledge, but the true sense of dread is not a reaction to anything sensible or visible or even, strictly, materially *knowable*. But rather it's a kind of spiritual intuition of something almost too incredible and shocking to talk about, which underlies the whole so-called thing. It is the uncommunicable something that we shall have to call *mystery* which is so inspiring of dread among these modern artists that we have been talking about. . . ."

Then I pause, looking into the eyes of my interlocutor, which I hope are beginning to betray some desire to believe me, and I say to him, "Am I making any better sense?"

"Maybe. But I can see it's an effort!"

"My friend, you have me where the hair is short."

"But you know, you still haven't explained why these writers have to write about crazy people doing terrible things!"

"You mean the externals they use?"

" 'Externals?' "

"You are objecting to their choice of symbols."

"Symbols, are they?"

"Of course. Art is made out of symbols the way your body is made out of vital tissue."

"Then why have they got to use—?"

"Symbols of the grotesque and the violent? Because a book is short and a man's life is long."

"That I don't understand."

"Think it over."

"You mean it's got to be more concentrated?"

"Exactly. The awfulness has to be compressed."

"But can't a writer ever get the same effect without using such God damn awful subjects?"

"I believe one writer did. The greatest of modern times, James Joyce. He managed to get the whole sense of awfulness without resorting to externals that departed on the surface from the ordinary and the familiar. But he wrote very long books, when he accomplished this incredibly difficult thing, and also he used a device that is known as the interior monologue which only he and one other great modern writer could employ without being excessively tiresome."

"What other?"

"Marcel Proust. But Proust did not ever quite dare to deliver the message of Absolute Dread. He was too much of a physical coward. The atmosphere of his work is rather womb-like. The flight into protection is very apparent."

"I guess we've talked long enough. Don't you have to get back to your subject now?"

"I have just about finished with my subject, thanks to you."

"Aren't you going to make a sort of statement that adds it up?"

"Neatly? Yes. Maybe I'd better try: here it is: *Reflections in a Golden Eye* is one of the purest and most powerful of those works which are conceived in that Sense of The Awful which is the desperate black root of nearly all significant modern art, from the *Guernica* of Picasso to the cartoons of Charles Addams. Is that all right?"

"I have quit arguing with you. So long."

It is true that this book lacks somewhat the thematic magnitude of the *Chasseur Solitaire,* but there is an equally important respect in which it is superior.

The first novel had a tendency to overflow in places as if the virtuosity of the young writer had not yet fallen under her entire control. But in the second there is an absolute mastery of design. There is a lapidary precision about the structure of this second book. Furthermore I think it succeeds more perfectly in establishing its own reality, in creating a world of its own, and this is something that primarily distinguishes the work of a great artist from that of a professional writer. In this book there is perhaps no single passage that assaults the heart so mercilessly as that scene in the earlier novel where the deaf-mute Singer stands at night outside the squalid flat that he had formerly occupied with the crazed and now dying Antonapoulos. The acute tragic sensibility of scenes like that occurred more frequently in *The Heart Is a Lonely Hunter.* Here the artistic climate is more austere. The tragedy is more distilled: a Grecian purity cools it, the eventually overwhelming impact is to a more reflective order. The key to this deliberate difference is implicit in the very title of the book. Discerning critics should have found it the opposite of a disappointment since it exhibited the one attribute which had yet to be shown in Carson McCullers's stunning array of gifts: the gift of mastery over a youthful lyricism.

I will add, however, that this second novel is still not her greatest; it is surpassed by *The Member of the Wedding,* her third novel, which combined the heartbreaking tenderness of the first with the sculptural quality of the second. But this book is in turn surpassed by a somewhat shorter work. I am speaking of *The Ballad of the Sad Cafe,* which is assuredly among the masterpieces of our language in the form of the novella.

During the two years that I have spent mostly abroad I have been impressed by the disparity that exists between Carson McCullers's reputation at home and in Europe. Translation serves as a winnowing process. The lesser and more derivative talents that have boisterously flooded our literary scene, with reputations inflated by professional politics and by shrewd commercial promotion, have somewhat obscured at home the position of more authentic talents. But in Europe the name of Carson McCullers is where it belongs, among the four or five preeminent figures in contemporary American writing.

Carson McCullers does not work rapidly. She is not coerced by the ridiculous popular idea that a good novelist turns out a book once a year. As long as five years elapsed between her second full-length novel and her third. I understand now that she has begun to work upon another. There could be no better literary news for any of us who have found, as I have found in her work, such intensity and nobility of spirit as we have not had in our prose writing since Herman Melville. In the meantime she should be reassured by the constantly more abundant evidence that the work she has already accomplished, such as this work, is not eclipsed by time, but further illumined.

1950

A WRITER'S QUEST FOR A PARNASSUS

Rome—Among the many misapprehensions held about writers is the idea that they follow a peaceful profession, an idea that derives from the fact that most writers have a sedentary appearance and that most writing is done in a more or less stationary position, usually seated in a chair at a table. But writing is actually a violent activity. It is actually more violent than any other profession that I can think of, including that of the professional wrestler. And writers, when they are not writing, must find some outer violence that is equivalent, or nearly, to the inner one they are used to. They find it difficult to remain long in one place, for writing books and taking voyages are corresponding gestures.

If the writer is truly a writer and not someone who has adopted the vocation as a convenient social pose to excuse his predilection for various kinds of waywardness, his first concern, when he goes traveling, will be to discover that magic place of all places where the work goes better than it has gone before, the way that a gasoline motor picks up when you switch it from regular to high octane. For one of the mysterious things about writing is the extreme susceptibility it shows to the influence of places. Almost every writer has a certain place that he associates, perhaps through mere superstition, with his periods of greatest fertility. But sooner or later this particular place will be exhausted for him and he must find another.

Often this quest will take him out of America. Often it will take him back to America if he has left there. The interval of seeking may be a long one. It may be six months or a year, or the years may be several, but eventually he will find the new place that looks and feels and smells mysteriously like home, and then he will turn around two or three times in his tracks, the way a dog does, sniffing the air in all directions before he sets himself down for the period of outer oblivion and inner violence that his work demands of him.

British and American writers are more inclined to travel than others. I think the British travel to get out of the rain, but the American artist travels for a more particular reason, and for one that I hesitate to mention lest I be summoned before some investigating committee in Congress. Putting that hesitation at least partially aside, let me venture the suggestion that America is no longer a terribly romantic part of the world, and that writers, all except, possibly, Upton Sinclair and Sinclair Lewis, are essentially romantic spirits—or they would not be writing.

Now there are only two cities left in America with a romantic appeal, however vestigial, and they are, of course, New Orleans and San Francisco. Our industrial dynamism has dispelled whatever magic the other great cities may once have possessed. Occasionally an artist may attempt to create a poetic synthesis out of this very dynamism of ours. Hart Crane attempted it, and, in my opinion, he succeeded in it. But one may take warning from the fact that, in spite of his achievement, he jumped off a boat returning to New York from a romantic retreat into Mexico.

Among writers' places there has always been Paris. If you remember the early histories of Hemingway, Fitzgerald, Wescott, Stein and so on, you may well have the impression that Paris offers great stimulation to the expatriate American writers. Well, it no longer does. Paris itself has not changed, it is still the most spacious and elegant capital of the world, and there is now a definite upswing of creative activity among the native French: Jean-Paul Sartre and Albert Camus, for instance. But the effect on young Americans who go there, ostensibly, to write their first books, is one that appears to be vitiating.

You find these new expatriate writers mostly about the Left Bank district known as St. Germain-des-Prés, sitting on the sidewalk in front of the Café de Flore or the Deux Magots or the Reine Blanche, according to their degree of Bohemianism. And they sit there, literally, from dusk until dawn. At daybreak they disappear with each other into shabby little hotels. They go to bed drunk and they wake up hung over and usually in the company of someone they barely remember meeting who looks much worse in the light of noon than in the blur of an alcoholic dawn. It is mid-afternoon before the company has departed and the typewriter hauled from under the bed. The typewriter, of course, needs repairing. The machine is heavy and the repair shop is far, and presently the whole idea is abandoned and they have repaired, themselves, to the sidewalk tables.

The troublesome question, and the one I find it impossible to answer to my own satisfaction, is whether or not these rootless young people would be better off had they remained in America. Obviously they found something lacking at home, and surely they find something in Paris besides the shopworn sophistication of their café circuit. But, whatever it is that they find, it is not a healthy, sustaining center about which their young personalities can form. I did not realize this so keenly when I first knew them in the summer of 1948, but when I came back a year later, and then another year later, and found the same boys and girls sitting on the same sidewalks, circulating among the same changeless cafés, the attritions that they had undergone became starkly evident.

With little effort at cohesion, let's turn sharply south. In Rome there is only one street where people make a social practice of sitting on the sidewalk. That is Via Veneto. It seems, at times, to be given over almost entirely to Americans and streetwalkers and boys picking up discarded cigarette butts. But it's a beautiful street. It winds like an old river among the great hotels and the American Embassy and the fashionable places for Americans to sit in the sun. To some Americans the sun of Rome is stupefying. To others it is merely tranquilizing. To both it is an escape from the feverish, high-pitched atmosphere of a typical urban society.

To me Rome is far more beautiful than Paris. It is not a night city. In Rome there are only two resorts where an American can sit up drinking all night, and I mention that fact because it is entirely relevant. It is what so many Americans seem to want to do in Europe. The two places where they can do it, in Rome, are the Jicky Club and the Caffè Notturno. Most of then go to the Jicky Club, which is on Via Veneto, because it is more like our own American night-spots. The Caffè Notturno is quite another thing. It is where procurers and their ladies get together, about two or three in the morning to exchange their gossip of the Rialto.

Before I came to Rome I was concerned about the change I feared that the Holy Year might have produced in my favorite city of the world. But in Rome you will find no S.R.O. sign. We came down by way of the Italian Alps and on the road we passed only one set of holy pilgrims. It was a cavalcade of motorcyclists from Holland, and it was headed by a young priest in his clerical garments. No doubt it was the strangest crossing of the Alps since Hannibal and his elephants. I had never before seen a priest on a motorcycle, and I must admit that he rode it with dignity and assurance and the look he gave us, as we whizzed past him, was one of grave friendliness.

Rome is actually less crowded than it was last summer. The Vatican has built a lot of new buildings especially for the housing of pilgrims, and that's where they seem to stay. You don't see them in the best restaurants or the interesting worldly places. Since I like to eat well and do not visit churches, I have not seen many of the pilgrims except on the road to Rome.

Rome and Italy cannot be all things to all people, but to me it is the place where I find the sun not only in the sky, where Italy also keeps it, but in the heart of the people. Before I came here for the first time, in the winter of 1948—with the fatigue of years suddenly fallen upon me—I had begun to think that a smile was something that people performed by a muscular contraction at the corners of their mouths. In a short while I found out that a smile can be something that happens between the heart and the eyes, and that the muscular spasm about the mouth may be only the shadow of it.

Rome spells peace, which is what I want above all. But it spells it without isolation, which I don't want. I want to have peace in the middle of many people, and here I find it. And I can work here. That's the thing.

If it is not your city—perhaps you'd like Venice. I could not go to Venice, now, without hearing the haunted cadences of Hemingway's new novel. It is the saddest novel in the world about the saddest city, and when I say I think it is the best and most honest work that Hemingway has done, you may think me crazy. It will probably be a popular book. The critics may treat it pretty roughly. But its hauntingly tired cadences are the direct speech of a man's heart who is speaking that directly for the first time, and that makes it, for me, the finest thing Hemingway has done. But the city is sad, to me, as the memory of the deepest loss I could suffer. It seems to be built, the very gray stones of it and the green-gray water, out of a loss that is almost too bitter to still have poetry in it.

Perhaps you might find the Italian islands to be your place to write. You could go to Capri but it is too much of a picture postcard for my taste and it is the only place I know where the human male manages to outdress the female. Ischia has equally fine bathing at more accessible beaches and the vacationers do not put on such highfalutin airs and outrageous plumage! W. H. Auden lives there, and if you're an American or British writer, you may have to apply to him for your visa.

I have not yet been to Sicily this year. Truman Capote has unfurled his Bronzini scarf above the fashionable resort of Taormina. He is supposedly in D. H. Lawrence's old house. Also there, I am told, is André Gide and the young American writer, Donald Windham, whose new novel, *The Dog Star,* contains the most sensitive new writing since Carson McCullers emerged ten years ago.

Regardless of where you may go in Europe this summer of 1950, you will find that places have a sadness under the surface. Everywhere the people seem to be waiting for the next cataclysm to strike them. They are not panicky, perhaps not even frightened, but they are waiting for it to happen with a feeling of fatality which you cannot help sensing unless you stay drunk the whole time or keep your nose in museums.

Nevertheless, the people want to survive, they want to keep on living through it, whatever it may be. Their history has made them wiser than Americans. It has also made them more tolerant, more patient, and considerably more human as well as a great deal sadder.

If these comments make me seem the opposite of a chauvinist, it is because of my honest feeling, after three years of foreign travel, that human brotherhood that stops at borders is not only delusive and foolish but enormously evil. The Marshall Plan must be translated, now, and amended, into spirit, if the dreaded thing that the Western World is waiting for can still be averted.

1950

THE TIMELESS WORLD OF A PLAY

Carson McCullers concludes one of her lyric poems with the line: "Time, the endless idiot, runs screaming round the world." It is this continual rush of time, so violent that it appears to be screaming, that deprives our actual lives of so much dignity and meaning, and it is, perhaps more than anything else, the *arrest of time* which has taken place in a completed work of art that gives to certain plays their feeling of depth and significance. In the London notices of *Death of a Salesman* a certain notoriously skeptical critic made the remark that Willy Loman was the sort of man that almost any member of the audience would have kicked out of an office had he applied for a job or detained one for conversation about his troubles. The remark itself possibly holds some truth. But the implication that Willy Loman is consequently a character with whom we have no reason to concern ourselves in drama, reveals a strikingly false conception of what plays are. Contemplation is something that exists outside of time, and so is the tragic sense. Even in the actual world of commerce, there exists in some persons a sensibility to the unfortunate situations of others, a capacity for concern and compassion, surviving from a more tender period of life outside the present whirling wire-cage of business activity. Facing Willy Loman across an office desk, meeting his nervous glance and hearing his querulous voice, we would be very likely to glance at our wrist watch and our schedule of other appointments. We would not kick him out of the office, no, but we would certainly *ease* him out with more expedition than Willy had feebly hoped for. But suppose there had been no wrist watch or office clock and suppose there had *not* been the schedule of pressing appointments, and suppose that we were not actually facing Willy across a desk—and facing a person is *not* the best way to *see* him!—suppose, in other words, that the meeting with Willy Loman had somehow occurred in a world *outside* of time. Then I think we would receive him with concern and kindness and even with respect. If the world of a play did not offer us this occasion to view its characters under that special condition of a *world without time*, then, indeed, the characters and occurrences of drama would become equally pointless, equally trivial, as corresponding meetings and happenings in life.

The classic tragedies of Greece had tremendous nobility. The actors wore great masks, movements were formal, dance-like, and the speeches had an epic quality which doubtless was as removed from the normal conversation of their contemporary society as they seem today. Yet they did not seem false to the Greek audiences: the magnitude of the events and the passions aroused by them did not seem ridiculously out of proportion to common experience. And I wonder if this was not because the Greek audiences knew, instinctively or by training, that the created world of a play is removed from that element which makes people *little* and their emotions fairly inconsequential.

Great sculpture often follows the lines of the human body: yet the repose of great sculpture suddenly transmutes those human lines to something that has an absoluteness, a purity, a beauty, which would not be possible in a living mobile form.

A play may be violent, full of motion: yet it has that special kind of repose which allows contemplation and produces the climate in which tragic importance is a possible thing, provided that certain modern conditions are met.

In actual existence the moments of love are succeeded by the moments of satiety and sleep. The sincere remark is followed by a cynical distrust. Truth is fragmentary, at best: we love and betray each other in not quite the same breath but in two breaths that occur in fairly close sequence. But the fact that passion occurred in *passing,* that it then declined into a more familiar sense of indifference, should not be regarded as proof of its inconsequence. And this is the very truth that drama wished to bring us. . . .

Whether or not we admit it to ourselves, we are all haunted by a truly awful sense of impermanence. I have always had a particularly keen sense of this at New York cocktail parties, and perhaps that is why I drink the martinis almost as fast as I can snatch them from the tray. This sense is the febrile thing that hangs in the air. Horror of insincerity, of *not meaning,* overhangs these affairs like the cloud of cigarette smoke and the hectic chatter. This horror is the only thing, almost, that is left unsaid at such functions. All social functions involving a group of people not intimately known to each other are always under this shadow. They are almost always (in an unconscious way) like that last dinner of the condemned: where steak or turkey, whatever the doomed man wants, is served in his cell as a mockingly cruel reminder of what the great-big-little-transitory world had to offer.

In a play, time is arrested in the sense of being confined. By a sort of legerdemain, events are made to remain *events,* rather than being reduced so quickly to mere *occurrences.* The audience can sit back in a comforting dusk to watch a world which is flooded with light and in which emotion and action have a dimension and dignity that they would likewise have in real existence, if only the shattering intrusion of time could be locked out.

About their lives, people ought to remember that when they are finished, everything in them will be contained in a marvelous state of repose which is the same as that which they unconsciously admired in drama. The rush is temporary. The great and only possible dignity of man lies in his power deliberately to choose certain moral values by which to live as steadfastly as if he, too, like a character in a play, were immured against the corrupting rush of time. Snatching the eternal out of the desperately fleeting is the great magic trick of human existence. As far as we know, as far as there exists any kind of empiric evidence, there is no way to beat the game of *being* against *non-being,* in which non-being is the predestined victor on realistic levels.

Yet plays in the tragic tradition offer us a view of certain moral values in violent juxtaposition. Because we do not participate, except as spectators, we can view them clearly, within the limits of our emotional equipment. These people on the stage do not return our looks. We do not have to answer their questions nor make any sign of being in company with them, nor do we have to compete with their virtues nor resist their offenses. All at once, for this reason, we are able to *see* them! Our hearts are wrung by recognition and pity, so that the dusky shell of the auditorium where we are gathered anonymously together is flooded with an almost liquid warmth of unchecked human sympathies, relieved of self-consciousness, allowed to function. . . .

Men pity and love each other more deeply than they permit themselves to know. The moment after the phone has been hung up, the hand reaches for a scratch pad and scrawls a notation: "Funeral Tuesday at five, Church of the Holy Redeemer, don't forget flowers." And the same hand is only a little shakier than usual as it reaches, some minutes later, for a highball glass that will pour a stupefaction over the kindled nerves. Fear and evasion are the two little beasts that chase each other's tails in the revolving wire-cage of our nervous world. They distract us from feeling too much about things. Time rushes toward us with its hospital tray of infinitely varied narcotics, even while it is preparing us for its inevitably fatal operation. . . .

So successfully have we disguised from ourselves the intensity of our own feelings, the sensibility of our own hearts, that plays in the tragic tradition have begun to seem untrue. For a couple of hours we may surrender ourselves to a world of fiercely illuminated values in conflict, but when the stage is covered and the auditorium lighted, almost immediately there is a recoil of disbelief. "Well, well!" we say as we shuffle back up the aisle, while the play dwindles behind us with the sudden perspective of an early Chirico painting. By the time we have arrived at Sardi's, if not as soon as we pass beneath the marquee, we have convinced ourselves once more that life has as little resemblance to the curiously stirring and meaningful occurrences on the stage as a jingle has to an elegy of Rilke.

This modern condition of his theater audience is something that an author must know in advance. The diminishing influence of life's destroyer, time, must be somehow worked into the context of his play. Perhaps it is a certain foolery, a certain distortion toward the grotesque, which will solve the problem for him. Perhaps it is only restraint, putting a mute on the strings that would like to break all bounds. But almost surely, unless he contrives in some way to relate the dimensions of his tragedy to the dimensions of a world in which time is *included*—he will be left among his magnificent debris on a dark stage, muttering to himself: "Those fools. . . ."

And if they could hear him above the clatter of tongues, glasses, chinaware, and silver, they would give him this answer: "But you have shown us a world not ravaged by time. We admire your innocence. But we have seen our photographs, past and present. Yesterday evening we passed our first wife on the street. We smiled as we spoke but we didn't really see her! It's too bad, but we know what is true and not true, and at 3:00 A.M. your disgrace will be in print!"

1951

THE MEANING OF *THE ROSE TATTOO*

The Rose Tattoo is the Dionysian element in human life, its mystery, its beauty, its significance. It is that glittering quicksilver that still somehow manages to slip from under the down-pressed thumbs of the enormous man in the brass-buttoned uniform and his female partner with the *pince-nez* and the chalky smelling black skirts that make you sneeze as she brushes disdainfully past you. It is the dissatisfaction with empiric evidence that makes the poet and mystic, for it is the lyric as well as the Bacchantic impulse, and although the goat is one of its most immemorial symbols, it must not be confused with mere sexuality. The element is higher and more distilled than that. Its purest form is probably manifested by children and birds in their rhapsodic moments of flight and play, especially during the last few minutes of pale blue summer dusk before they light on branches and before their mothers call from the doors, *Come home!* It is not the obedient coming home and going to bed but it is the limitless world of the dream. It is the *rosa mystica,* the light on the bare golden flesh of a god whose back is turned to us or whose face is covered and who flies away from us when we call *Wait!* and rushes past us when we try to stop him. It is the fruit of the vine that takes earth, sun, and air and distills them into juices that deprive men not of reason but of a different thing called prudence. . . .

Finally and incidentally, it is the desire of an artist to work in new forms, however awkwardly at first, to break down barriers of what he has done before and what others have done better before and after and to crash, perhaps fatally, into some area that the bell-harness and rope would like to forbid him.

It may seem curious that I have chosen a woman to be the main protagonist of a play on such a theme. But in the blind and frenzied efforts of the widow, Serafina, to comprehend the mysteries of her dead husband, we sense and learn more about him than would have been possible through direct observation of the living man, the Dionysus himself. Dionysus, being mystery, is never seen clearly. He can not be confined to memory nor an urn, nor the conventions and proprieties of a plump little seamstress who wanted to fortify her happiness with the respect of the community. It was a mistake to fill the house with dummies. It took a long while to learn that eventually the faceless dummies must be knocked over, however elaborate their trappings. It took an almost literal unclothing, a public appearance in a wine-stained rayon slip, a fierce attack on a priest and the neighbor women, to learn that the blood of the wild young daughter was better, as a memorial, than ashes kept in a crematory urn.

In its treatment of this theme the play is no doubt more allusive than direct. Still more undoubtedly its theme overshadows the play. It is the homely light of a kitchen candle burned in praise of a god. I prefer a play to be not a noose but a net with fairly wide meshes. So many of its instants of revelation are wayward flashes, not part of the plan of an author but struck accidentally off, and perhaps these are closest to being a true celebration of the inebriate god.

1951

FACTS ABOUT ME

I was born in the Episcopal rectory of Columbus, Miss., an old town on the Tombigbee River which was so dignified and reserved that there was a saying, only slightly exaggerated, that you had to live there a whole year before a neighbor would smile at you on the street. As my grandfather, with whom we lived, was the Episcopal clergyman, we were accepted without probation. My father, a man with the formidable name of Cornelius Coffin Williams, was a man of ancestry that came on one side, the Williams, from pioneer Tennessee stock and on the other from early settlers of Nantucket Island in New England. My mother was descended from Quakers. Roughly there was a combination of Puritan and Cavalier strains in my blood which may be accountable for the conflicting impulses I often represent in the people I write about.

I was christened Thomas Lanier Williams. It is a nice enough name, perhaps a little too nice. It sounds like it might belong to the son of a writer who turns out sonnet sequences to Spring. As a matter of fact, my first literary award was $25.00 from a Woman's Club for doing exactly that, three sonnets dedicated to Spring. I hasten to add that I was still pretty young. Under that name I published a good deal of lyric poetry which was a bad imitation of Edna Millay. When I grew up I realized this poetry wasn't much good and I felt the name had been compromised so I changed it to Tennessee Williams, the justification being mainly that the Williamses had fought the Indians for Tennessee and I had already discovered that the life of a young writer was going to be something similar to the defense of a stockade against a band of savages.

When I was about twelve, my father, a travelling salesman, was appointed to an office position in St. Louis and so we left the rectory and moved north. It was a tragic move. Neither my sister nor I could adjust ourselves to life in a Midwestern city. The schoolchildren made fun of our Southern speech and manners. I remember gangs of kids following me home yelling "Sissy!" and home was not a very pleasant refuge. It was a perpetually dim little apartment in a wilderness of identical brick and concrete structures with no grass and no trees nearer than the park. In the South we had never been conscious of the fact that we were economically less fortunate than others. We lived as well as anyone else. But in St. Louis we suddenly discovered there were two kinds of people, the rich and the poor, and that we belonged more to the latter. If we walked far enough west we came into a region of fine residences set in beautiful lawns. But where we lived, to which we must always return, were ugly rows of apartment buildings the color of dried blood and mustard. If I had been born to this situation I might not have resented it deeply. But it was forced upon my consciousness at the most sensitive age of childhood. It produced a shock and a rebellion that has grown into an inherent part of my work. It was the beginning of the social consciousness which I think has marked most of my writing. I am glad that I received this bitter education for I don't think any writer has much purpose back of him unless he feels bitterly the inequities of the society he lives in. I have no acquaintance with political and social dialectics. If you ask what my politics are, I am a Humanitarian.

That is the social background of my life!

I entered college during the great American depression and after a couple of years I couldn't afford to continue but had to drop out and take a clerical job in the shoe company that employed my father. The two years I spent in that corporation were indescribable torment to me as an individual but of immense value to me as a writer for they gave me firsthand knowledge of what it means to be a small wage earner in a hopelessly routine job. I had been writing since childhood and I continued writing while I was employed by the shoe company. When I came home from work I would tank up on black coffee so I could remain awake most of the night, writing short stories which I could not sell. Gradually my health broke down. One day, coming home from work, I collapsed and was removed to the hospital. The doctor said I couldn't go back to the shoe company. Soon as that was settled I recovered and went back South to live with my grandparents in Memphis where they had moved since my grandfather's retirement from the ministry. Then I began to have a little success with my writing. I became self-sufficient. I put myself through two more years of college and got a B.A. degree at the University of Iowa in 1938. Before then and for a couple of years afterwards I did a good deal of travelling around and I held a great number of part-time jobs of great diversity. It is hard to put the story in correct chronology for the last ten years of my life are a dizzy kaleidoscope. I don't quite believe all that has happened to me, it seems it must have happened to five or ten other people.

My first real recognition came in 1940 when I received a Rockefeller fellowship and wrote *Battle of Angels* which was produced by the Theatre Guild at the end of that year with Miriam Hopkins in the leading role. It closed in Boston during the tryout run but I have rewritten it a couple of times since then and still have faith in it. My health was so impaired that I landed in 4F after a medical examination of about five minutes' duration. My jobs in this period included running an all-night elevator in a big apartment-hotel, waiting on tables and reciting verse in the Village, working as a teletype operator for the U.S. Engineers in Jacksonville, Florida, waiter and cashier for a small restaurant in New Orleans, ushering at the Strand Theatre on Broadway. All the while I kept on writing, writing, not with any hope of making a living at it but because I found no other means of expressing things that seemed to demand expression. There was never a moment when I did not find life to be immeasurably exciting to experience and to witness, however difficult it was to sustain.

From a $17.00 a week job as a movie usher I was suddenly shipped off to Hollywood where M.G.M. paid me $250.00 a week. I saved enough money out of my six months there to keep me while I wrote *The Glass Menagerie*. I don't think the story from that point on, requires any detailed consideration.

1952

FOREWORD TO *CAMINO REAL*

Since work on *Camino Real* has occupied my thoughts—and lately my dreams—for about two years, not including the couple of months that it took me to do the original sketch for it, it would not only be dishonest but also practically impossible to pretend that I have enough interest in anything else to compose a piece for *The Times* upon some other subject.

It is amazing and frightening how completely one's whole being becomes absorbed in the making of a play. It is almost as if you were frantically constructing another world while the world that you live in dissolves beneath your feet, and that your survival depends on completing this construction at least one second before the old habitation collapses.

More than any other work that I have done, this play has seemed to me like the construction of another world, a separate existence. Of course, it is nothing more nor less than my conception of the time and world that I live in, and its people are mostly archetypes of certain basic attitudes and qualities with those mutations that would occur if they had continued along the road to this hypothetical terminal point in it.

A convention of the play is existence outside of time in a place of no specific locality. If you regard it that way, I suppose it becomes an elaborate allegory, but in New Haven we opened directly across the street from a movie theater that was showing *Peter Pan* in Technicolor and it did not seem altogether inappropriate to me. Fairy tales nearly always have some simple moral lesson of good and evil, but that is not the secret of their fascination any more, I hope, than the philosophical import that might be distilled from the fantasies of *Camino Real* is the principal element of its appeal.

To me the appeal of this world is its unusual degree of freedom. When it began to get under way I felt a new sensation of release, as if I could "ride out" like a tenor sax taking the breaks in a Dixieland combo or a piano in a bop session. You may call it self-indulgence, but I was not doing it merely for myself. I could not have felt a purely private thrill of release unless I had hope of sharing this experience with lots and lots of audiences to come.

My desire was to give these audiences my own sense of something wild and unrestricted that ran like water in the mountains, or clouds changing shape in a gale, or the continually dissolving and transforming images of a dream. This sort of freedom is not chaos or anarchy. On the contrary, it is the result of painstaking design, and in this work I have given more conscious attention to form and construction than I have in any work before. Freedom is not achieved simply by working freely.

Elia Kazan was attracted to this work mainly, I believe, for the same reason—its freedom and mobility of form. I know that we have kept saying the word "flight" to each other as if the play were merely an abstraction of the impulse to fly, and most of the work out of town, his in staging, mine in cutting and revising, has been with this impulse in mind: the achievement of a continual flow. Speech after speech and bit after bit that were nice in themselves have been remorselessly blasted out of the script and its staging wherever they seemed to obstruct or divert this flow, and the process is still going on.

There have been plenty of indications already that this play will exasperate and confuse a certain number of people which we hope is not so large as the number it is likely to please. At each performance a number of people have stamped out of the auditorium, with little regard for those whom they have had to crawl over, almost as if the building had caught on fire, and there have been sibilant noises on the way out and demands for money back if the cashier was foolish enough to remain in his box.

I am at a loss to explain this phenomenon, and if I am being facetious about one thing, I am being quite serious about another when I say that I had never for one minute supposed that the play would seem obscure and confusing to anyone who was willing to meet it even less than halfway. It was a costly production, and for this reason I had to read it aloud, together with a few of the actors on one occasion, before large groups of prospective backers, before the funds to produce it were in the till. It was only then that I came up against the disconcerting surprise that some people would think that the play needed clarification.

My attitude is intransigent. I still don't agree that it needs any explanation. Some poet has said that a poem should not mean but be. Of course, a play is not a poem, not even a poetic play has quite the same license as a poem. But to go to *Camino Real* with the inflexible demands of a logician is unfair to both parties.

Two days ago in Philadelphia a young man from a literary periodical saw the play and then cross-examined me about all its dreamlike images. He had made a list of them while he watched the play, and afterward at my hotel he brought out the list and asked me to explain the meaning of each one. I can't deny that I use a lot of those things called symbols but being a self-defensive creature, I say that symbols are nothing but the natural speech of drama.

We all have in our conscious and unconscious minds a great vocabulary of images, and I think all human communication is based on these images as are our dreams; and a symbol in a play has only one legitimate purpose, which is to say a thing more directly and simply and beautifully than it could be said in words.

I hate writing that is a parade of images for the sake of images; I hate it so much that I close a book in disgust when it keeps on saying one thing is like another; I even get disgusted with poems that make nothing but comparisons between one thing and another. But I repeat that symbols, when used respectfully, are the purest language of plays. Sometimes it would take page after tedious page of exposition to put across an idea that can be said with an object or a gesture on the lighted stage.

To take one case in point: the battered portmanteau of Jacques Casanova is hurled from the balcony of a luxury hotel when his remittance check fails to come through. While the portmanteau is still in the air, he shouts: "Careful, I have—"—and when it has crashed to the street he continues— "fragile—mementoes. . . ." I suppose that is a symbol, at least it is an object used to express as directly and vividly as possible certain things which could be said in pages of dull talk.

As for those patrons who departed before the final scene, I offer myself this tentative bit of solace: that these theatergoers may be a little domesticated in their theatrical tastes. A cage represents security as well as confinement to a bird that has grown used to being in it; and when a theatrical work kicks over the traces with such apparent insouciance, security seems challenged and, instead of participating in its sense of freedom, one out of a certain number of playgoers will rush back out to the more accustomed implausibility of the street he lives on.

To modify this effect of complaisance I would like to admit to you quite frankly that I can't say with any personal conviction that I have written a good play; I only know that I have felt a release in this work which I wanted you to feel with me.

1953

AFTERWORD TO *CAMINO REAL*

Once in a while someone will say to me that he would rather wait for a play to come out as a book than see a live performance of it, where he would be distracted from its true values, if it has any, by so much that is mere spectacle and sensation and consequently must be meretricious and vulgar. There are plays meant for reading. I have read them. I have read the works of "thinking playwrights" as distinguished from us who are permitted only to feel, and probably read them earlier and appreciated them as much as those who invoke their names nowadays like the incantation of Aristophanes's frogs. But the incontinent blaze of a live theater, a theater meant for seeing and for feeling, has never been and never will be extinguished by a bucket brigade of critics, new or old, bearing vessels that range from cut glass punch bowl to Haviland teacup. And in my dissident opinion, a play in a book is only the shadow of a play and not even a clear shadow of it. Those who did not like *Camino Real* on the stage will not be likely to form a higher opinion of it in print, for of all the works I have written, this one was meant most for the vulgarity of performance. The printed script of a play is hardly more than an architect's blueprint of a house not yet built or built and destroyed.

The color, the grace and levitation, the structural pattern in motion, the quick interplay of live beings, suspended like fitful lightning in a cloud, these things are the play, not words on paper, nor thoughts and ideas of an author, those shabby things snatched off basement counters at Gimbel's.

My own creed as a playwright is fairly close to that expressed by the painter in Shaw's play *The Doctor's Dilemma*: "I believe in Michelangelo, Velásquez and Rembrandt; in the might of design, the mystery of color, the redemption of all things by beauty everlasting and the message of art that has made these hands blessed. Amen."

How much art his hands were blessed with or how much mine are, I don't know, but that art is a blessing is certain and that it contains its message is also certain, and I feel, as the painter did, that the message lies in those abstract beauties of form and color and line, to which I would add light and motion.

In these following pages are only the formula by which a play could exist.

Dynamic is a word in disrepute at the moment, and so, I suppose, is the word *organic,* but those terms still define the dramatic values that I value most and which I value more as they are more deprecated by the ones self-appointed to save what they have never known.

1953

PERSON–TO–PERSON

Of course it is a pity that so much of all creative work is so closely related to the personality of the one who does it.

It is sad and embarrassing and unattractive that those emotions that stir him deeply enough to demand expression, and to charge their expression with some measure of light and power, are nearly all rooted, however changed in their surface, in the particular and sometimes peculiar concerns of the artist himself, that special world, the passions and images of it that each of us weaves about him from birth to death, a web of monstrous complexity, spun forth at a speed that is incalculable to a length beyond measure, from the spider-mouth of his own singular perceptions.

It is a lonely idea, a lonely condition, so terrifying to think of that we usually don't. And so we talk to each other, write and wire each other, call each other short and long distance across land and sea, clasp hands with each other at meeting and at parting, fight each other and even destroy each other because of this always somewhat thwarted effort to break through walls to each other. As a character in a play once said, "We're all of us sentenced to solitary confinement inside our own skins."

Personal lyricism is the outcry of prisoner to prisoner from the cell in solitary where each is confined for the duration of his life.

I once saw a group of little girls on a Mississippi sidewalk, all dolled up in their mothers' and sisters' cast-off finery, old raggedy ball gowns and plumed hats and high-heeled slippers, enacting a meeting of ladies in a parlor with a perfect mimicry of polite southern gush and simper. But one child was not satisfied with the attention paid her enraptured performance by the others, they were too involved in their own performances to suit her, so she stretched out her skinny arms and threw back her skinny neck and shrieked to the deaf heavens and her equally oblivious playmates, "Look at me, look at me, look at me!"

And then her mother's high-heeled slippers threw her off balance and she fell to the sidewalk in a great howling tangle of soiled white satin and torn pink net, and still nobody looked at her.

I wonder if she is not, now, a southern writer.

Of course it is not only southern writers, of lyrical bent, who engage in such histrionics and shout, "Look at me!" Perhaps it is a parable of all artists. And not always do we topple over and land in a tangle of trappings that don't fit us. However it is well to be aware of that peril, and not to content yourself with a demand for attention, to know that out of your personal lyricism, your sidewalk histrionics, something has to be created that will not only attract observers but participants in the performance.

I try very hard to do that.

The fact that I want you to observe what I do for your possible pleasure and to give you knowledge of things that I feel I may know better than you, because my world is different from yours, as different as every man's world is from the world of others, is not enough excuse for a personal lyricism that has not yet mastered its necessary trick of rising above the singular to the plural concern, from personal to general import. But for years and years now, which may have passed like a dream because of this obsession, I have been trying to learn how to perform this trick and make it truthful, and sometimes I feel that I am able to do it. Sometimes when the enraptured streetcorner performer in me cries out "Look at me!" I feel that my hazardous footwear and fantastic regalia may not quite throw me off balance. Then, suddenly, you fellow-performers in the sidewalk show may turn to give me your attention and allow me to hold it, at least for the interval between 8:40 and 11-something P.M.

Eleven years ago this month of March, when I was far closer than I knew, only nine months away from that long-delayed, but always expected, something that I lived for, the time when I would first catch and hold an audience's attention, I wrote my first preface to a long play; the final paragraph went like this:

"There is too much to say and not enough time to say it. Nor is there power enough. I am not a good writer. Sometimes I am a very bad writer indeed. There is hardly a successful writer in the field who cannot write circles around me . . . but I think of writing as something more organic than words, something closer to being and action. I want to work more and more with a more plastic theatre than the one I have (worked with) before. I have never for one moment doubted that there are people—millions!—to say things to. We come to each other, gradually, but with love. It is the short reach of my arms that hinders, not the length and multiplicity of theirs. With love and with honesty, the embrace is inevitable."

This characteristically emotional, if not rhetorical, statement of mine at that time seems to suggest that I thought of myself as having a highly personal, even intimate relationship with people who go to see plays. I did and I still do. A morbid shyness once prevented me from having much direct communication with people, and possibly that is why I began to write to them plays and stories. But even now when that tongue-locking, face-flushing, silent and crouching timidity has worn off with the passage of the troublesome youth that it sprang from, I still find it somehow easier to "level with" crowds of strangers in the hushed twilight of orchestra and balcony sections of theatres than with individuals across a table from me. Their being strangers somehow makes them more familiar and more approachable, easier to talk to.

Of course I know that I have sometimes presumed too much upon corresponding sympathies and interests in those to whom I talk boldly, and this has led to rejections that were painful and costly enough to inspire more prudence. But when I weigh one thing against another, an easy liking against a hard respect, the balance always tips the same way, and whatever the risk of being turned a cold shoulder, I still don't want to talk to people only about the surface aspects of their lives, the sort of things that acquaintances laugh and chatter about on ordinary social occasions.

I feel that they get plenty of that, and heaven knows so do I, before and after the little interval of time in which I have their attention and say what I have to say to them. The discretion of social conversation, even among friends, is exceeded only by the discretion of "the deep six," that grave wherein nothing is mentioned at all. Emily Dickinson, that lyrical spinster of Amherst, Mass., who wore a strict and savage heart on a taffeta sleeve, commented wryly on that kind of posthumous discourse among friends in these lines:

> *I died for beauty but was scarce*
> *Adjusted in the tomb,*
> *When one who died for truth was lain*
> *In an adjoining room.*
> *He questioned softly why I failed,*
> *"For beauty," I replied.*
> *"And I for truth, the two are one:*
> *We brethren are," he said.*
> *And so as kinsmen met at night,*
> *We talked between the rooms,*
> *Until the moss had reached our lips*
> *And covered up our names.*

Meanwhile!—I want to go on talking to you as freely and intimately about what we live and die for as if I knew you better than anyone else whom you know.

1955

CRITIC SAYS "EVASION,"
WRITER SAYS "MYSTERY"

In his reviews of *Cat on a Hot Tin Roof,* Mr. Walter Kerr has spoken of an "evasiveness" on my part in dealing with certain questions in the play, mainly questions of character, pertinent mostly to the character of the young male protagonist, Brick Pollitt. This is not the first time that I've been suspected of dodging issues in my treatment of play characters. Critics complained, sometimes, of ambiguities in *Streetcar.* Certainly there were many divergent ideas of Blanche's character and many widely differing interpretations in the playing of her character among the many productions I saw at home and abroad. She was often referred to as a prostitute, often as a dipso or a nympho or liar.

The truth about human character in a play, as in life, varies with the variance of experience and viewpoint of those that view it. No two members of an audience ever leave a theater, after viewing a play that deals with any degree of complexity in character, with identical interpretations of the characters dealt with. This is as it should be. I know full well the defenses and rationalizations of beleaguered writers, a defensive species, but I still feel that I deal unsparingly with what I feel is the truth of character. I would never evade it for the sake of evasion, because I was in any way reluctant to reveal what I know of the truth.

But ambiguity is sometimes deliberate, and for artistically defensible reasons, I can best answer Mr. Kerr's objection by a quote from the manuscript of the play which is not yet available to readers, but will be in a few weeks. It is a long note that occurs in the second act, at the point where Big Daddy alludes to the charge of abnormality in Brick's relation to his dead friend, Skipper:

> Brick's resolute detachment is at last broken through. His heart
> is accelerated; his forehead sweat-beaded; his breath becomes more
> rapid and his voice hoarse. The thing they're discussing, timidly and

painfully on the side of Big Daddy, fiercely, violently on Brick's side, is the inadmissible thing that Skipper and Brick would rather die than live with. The fact that if it existed it had to be disavowed to "keep face" in the world they lived in, a world of popular heroes, may be at the heart of the "mendacity" that Brick drinks to kill his disgust with. It may be the root of his collapse. Or it may be only a single manifestation of it, not even the most important. The bird that I hope to catch in the net of this play is not the solution of one man's psychological problem. I'm trying to catch the true quality of experience in a group of people, that cloudy, flickering, evanescent—fiercely charged!—interplay of live human beings in the thundercloud of a common crisis. Some mystery should be left in the revelation of character in a play, just as a great deal of mystery is always left in the revelation of character in life, even in one's own character to himself. This does not absolve the playwright of his duty to observe and probe as clearly and deeply as he *legitimately* can: but it should steer him away from "pat" conclusions, facile definitions, which make a play just a play, not a snare for the truth of human experience.

This, I believe, states clearly my defense of these so-called ambiguities of character in my plays. The point is, of course, arguable. You may prefer to be told precisely what to believe about every character in a play; you may prefer to know precisely what will be the future course of their lives, happy or disastrous or anywhere in between.

Then I am not your playwright. My characters make my play. I always start with them, they take spirit and body in my mind. Nothing that they say or do is arbitrary or invented. They build the play about them like spiders weaving their webs, sea creatures making their shells. I live with them for a year and a half or two years and I know them far better than I know myself, since I created them and not myself.

But still they must have that quality of life which is shadowy. Was Blanche DuBois a liar? She told many lies in the course of *Streetcar* and yet at heart she was truthful. Was Brick homosexual? He probably—no, I would even say quite certainly—went no further in physical expression than clasping Skipper's hand across the space between their twin beds in hotel rooms—and yet his sexual nature was not innately "normal."

Did Brick love Maggie? He says with unmistakable conviction: "One man has one great good true thing in his life, one great good thing which is true. I had friendship with Skipper, not love with you, Maggie, but friendship with Skipper. . . ."—but can we doubt that he was warmed and charmed by this delightful girl, with her vivacity, her humor, her very admirable courage and pluckiness and tenacity, which are almost the essence of life itself?

Of course, now that he has really resigned from life, retired from competition, her anxious voice, strident with the heat of combat, is unpleasantly, sometimes even odiously, disturbing to him. But Brick's overt sexual adjustment was, and must always remain, a heterosexual one. He will go back to Maggie for sheer animal comfort, even if she did not make him dependent on her for such creature comforts as only a devoted slave can provide. He is her dependent. As Strindberg said: "They call it love-hatred, and it hails from the pit. . . ."

Frankly, I don't want people to leave the Morosco Theatre knowing everything about all the characters they have witnessed that night in violent interplay, I don't want them to be quite certain what will happen to these characters that night or in the morning. Because they themselves, when they step out of the Morosco, cannot be certain that a truck will not run them down while they are hailing a taxi. I give them views, but not certainties.

Every moment of human existence is alive with uncertainty. You may call it ambiguity, you may even call it evasion. I want them to leave the Morosco as they do leave it each night, feeling that they have met with a vividly allusive, as well as disturbingly elusive, fragment of human experience, one that not only points at truth but at the mysteries of it, much as they will leave this world when they leave it, still wondering somewhat about what happened to them, and for what reason or purpose.

1955

THE PAST, THE PRESENT, AND THE PERHAPS

One icy bright winter morning in the last week of 1940, my brave representative, Audrey Wood, and I were crossing the Common in Boston, from an undistinguished hotel on one side to the grandeur of the Ritz-Carlton on the other. We had just read in the morning notices of *Battle of Angels,* which had opened at the Wilbur the evening before. As we crossed the Common there was a series of loud reports like gunfire from the street that we were approaching, and one of us said, "My God, they're shooting at us!"

We were still laughing, a bit hysterically, as we entered the Ritz-Carlton suite in which the big brass of the Theatre Guild and director Margaret Webster were waiting for us with that special air of gentle gravity that hangs over the demise of a play so much like the atmosphere that hangs over a home from which a living soul has been snatched by the Reaper.

Not present was little Miriam Hopkins, who was understandably shattered and cloistered after the events of the evening before, in which a simulated on-stage fire had erupted clouds of smoke so realistically over both stage and auditorium that a lot of Theatre Guild first-nighters had fled choking from the Wilbur before the choking star took her bows, which were about the quickest and most distracted that I have seen in a theater.

It was not that morning that I was informed that the show must close. That morning I was only told that the play must be cut to the bone. I came with a rewrite of the final scene and I remember saying, heroically, "I will crawl on my belly through brimstone if you will substitute this." The response was gently evasive. It was a few mornings later that I received the *coup de grace,* the announcement that the play would close at the completion of its run in Boston. On that occasion I made an equally dramatic statement, on a note of anguish. "You don't seem to see that I put my heart into this play!"

It was Miss Webster who answered with a remark I have never forgotten and yet never heeded. She said, "You must not wear your heart on your sleeve for daws to peck at!" Someone else said, "At least you are not out of pocket." I don't think I had any answer for that one, any more than I had anything in my pocket to be out of.

Well, in the end, when the Boston run was finished, I was given a check for $200 and told to get off somewhere and rewrite the play. I squandered half of this subsidy on the first of four operations performed on a cataracted left eye, and the other half took me to Key West for the rewrite. It was a long rewrite. In fact, it is still going on, though the two hundred bucks are long gone.

Why have I stuck so stubbornly to this play? For seventeen years, in fact? Well, nothing is more precious to anybody than the emotional record of his youth, and you will find the trail of my sleeve-worn heart in this completed play that I now call *Orpheus Descending*. On its surface it was and still is the tale of a wild-spirited boy who wanders into a conventional community of the South and creates the commotion of a fox in a chicken coop.

But beneath that now familiar surface, it is a play about unanswered questions that haunt the hearts of people and the difference between continuing to ask them, a difference represented by the four major protagonists of the play, and the acceptance of prescribed answers that are not answers at all, but expedient adaptations or surrender to a state of quandary.

Battle was actually my fifth long play, but the first to be given a professional production. Two of the others, *Candles to the Sun* and *Fugitive Kind,* were produced by a brilliant, but semiprofessional group called The Mummers of St. Louis. A third one, called *Spring Storm,* was written for the late Prof. E. C. Mabie's seminar in playwriting at the University of Iowa, and I read it aloud, appropriately in the spring.

When I had finished reading, the good professor's eyes had a glassy look as though he had drifted into a state of trance. There was a long and all but unendurable silence. Everyone seemed more or less embarrassed. At last the professor pushed back his chair, thus dismissing the seminar, and remarked casually and kindly, "Well, we all have to paint our nudes!" And this is the only reference that I can remember anyone making to the play. That is, in the playwriting class, but I do remember that the late Lemuel Ayers, who was a graduate student at Iowa that year, read it and gave me sufficient praise for its dialogue and atmosphere to reverse my decision to give up the theater in favor of my other occupation of waiting on tables, or more precisely, handing out trays in the cafeteria of the State Hospital.

Then there was Chicago for a while and a desperate effort to get on the W. P. A. Writers' Project, which didn't succeed, for my work lacked "social content" or "protest" and I couldn't prove that my family was destitute and I still had, in those days, a touch of refinement in my social behavior which made me seem frivolous and decadent to the conscientiously roughhewn pillars of the Chicago Project.

And so I drifted back to St. Louis, again, and wrote my fourth long play which was the best of the lot. It was called *Not About Nightingales* and it concerned prison life, and I have never written anything since then that could compete with it in violence and horror, for it was based on something that actually occurred along about that time, the literal roasting alive of a group of intransigent convicts sent for correction to a hot room called "The Klondike."

I submitted it to The Mummers of St. Louis and they were eager to perform it but they had come to the end of their economic tether and had to disband at this point.

Then there was New Orleans and another effort, while waiting on tables in a restaurant where meals cost only two-bits, to get on a Writers' Project or the Theatre Project, again unsuccessful.

And then there was a wild and wonderful trip to California with a young clarinet player. We ran out of gas in El Paso, also out of cash, and it seemed for days that we would never go farther, but my grandmother was an "easy touch" and I got a letter with a $10 bill stitched neatly to one of the pages, and we continued westward.

In the Los Angeles area, in the summer of 1939, I worked for a while at Clark's Bootery in Culver City, within sight of the M.G.M studio and I lived on a pigeon ranch, and I rode between the two, a distance of ten miles, on a secondhand bicycle that I bought for $5.

Then a most wonderful thing happened. While in New Orleans I had heard about a play contest being conducted by the Group Theatre of New York. I submitted all four of the long plays I have mentioned that preceded *Battle of Angels*, plus a group of one-acts called *American Blues*. One fine day I received, when I returned to the ranch on my bike, a telegram saying that I had won a special award of $100 for the one-acts, and it was signed by Harold Clurman, Molly Day Thatcher, who is the present Mrs. Elia Kazan, and that fine writer, Irwin Shaw, the judges of the contest.

I retired from Clark's Bootery and from picking squabs at the pigeon ranch. And the clarinet player and I hopped on our bicycles and rode all the way down to Tijuana and back as far as Laguna Beach, where we obtained, rent free, a small cabin on a small ranch in return for taking care of the poultry.

We lived all that summer on the $100 from the Group Theatre and I think it was the happiest summer of my life. All the days were pure gold, the nights were starry, and I looked so young, or carefree, that they would sometimes refuse to sell me a drink because I did not appear to have reached twenty-one. But toward the end of the summer, maybe only because it was the end of the summer as well as the end of the $100, the clarinet player became very moody and disappeared without warning into the San Bernardino Mountains to commune with his soul in solitude, and there was nothing left in the cabin in the canyon but a bag of dried peas.

I lived on stolen eggs and avocados and dried peas for a week, and also on a faint hope stirred by a letter from a lady in New York whose name was Audrey Wood, who had taken hold of all those plays that I had submitted to the Group Theatre contest, and told me that it might be possible to get me one of the Rockefeller Fellowships, or grants, of $1,000 which were being passed out to gifted young writers at that time. And I began to write *Battle of Angels,* a lyric play about memories and the loneliness of them. Although my beloved grandmother was living on the pension of a retired minister (I believe it was only $85 a month in those days), and her meager earnings as a piano instructor, she once again stitched some bills to a page of a letter, and I took a bus to St. Louis. *Battle of Angels* was finished late that fall and sent to Miss Wood.

One day the phone rang and, in a terrified tone, my mother told me that it was long distance, for me. The voice was Audrey Wood's. Mother waited, shakily, in the doorway. When I hung up I said, quietly, "Rockefeller has given me a $1,000 grant and they want me to come to New York." For the first time since I had known her, my mother burst into tears. "I am so happy," she said. It was all she could say.

And so you see it is a very old play that *Orpheus Descending* has come out of, but a play is never an old one until you quit working on it and I have never quit working on this one, not even now. It never went into the trunk, it always stayed on the workbench, and I am not presenting it now because I have run out of ideas or material for completely new work. I am offering it this season because I honestly believe that it is finally finished. About seventy-five percent of it is new writing, but, what is much more important, I believe that I have now finally managed to say in it what I wanted to say, and I feel that it now has in it a sort of emotional bridge between those early years described in this article and my present state of existence as a playwright.

So much for the past and present. The future is called "perhaps," which is the only possible thing to call the future. And the important thing is not to allow that to scare you.

1957

THE WORLD I LIVE IN

Tennessee Williams Interviews Himself

Question. Can we talk frankly?

Answer. There's no other way we can talk.

Q. Perhaps you know that when your first successful play, *The Glass Menagerie,* was revived early this season, a majority of the reviewers felt that it was still the best play you have written, although it is now twelve years old?

A. Yes, I read all my play notices and criticisms, even those that say that I write for money and that my primary appeal is to brutal and ugly instincts.

Q. Where there is so much smoke—!

A. A fire smokes the most when you start pouring water on it.

Q. But surely you'll admit that there's been a disturbing note of harshness and coldness and violence and anger in your more recent works?

A. I think, without planning to do so, I have followed the developing tension and anger and violence of the world and time that I live in through my own steadily increasing tension as a writer and person.

Q. Then you admit that this "developing tension," as you call it, is a reflection of a condition in yourself?

A. Yes.

Q. A morbid condition?

A. Yes.

Q. Perhaps verging on the psychotic?

A. I guess my work has always been a kind of psychotherapy for me.

Q. But how can you expect audiences to be impressed by plays and other writings that are created as a release for the tensions of a possible or incipient madman?

A. It releases their own.

Q. Their own what?

A. Increasing tensions, verging on the psychotic.

Q. You think the world's going mad?

A. Going? I'd say nearly gone! As the Gypsy said in *Camino Real,* the world is a funny paper read backwards. And that way it isn't so funny.

Q. How far do you think you can go with this tortured view of the world?

A. As far as the world can go in its tortured condition, maybe that far, but no further.

Q. You don't expect audiences and critics to go along with you, do you?

A. No.

Q. Then why do you push and pull them that way?

A. I go that way. I don't push or pull anyone with me.

Q. Yes, but you hope to continue to have people listen to you, don't you?

A. Naturally I hope to.

Q. Even if you throw them off by the violence and horror of your works?

A. Haven't you noticed that people are dropping all around you, like moths out of season, as the result of the present plague of violence and horror in this world and time that we live in?

Q. But you're an entertainer, with artistic pretensions, and people are not entertained any more by cats on hot tin roofs and Baby Dolls and passengers on crazy streetcars!

A. Then let them go to the musicals and the comedies. I'm not going to change my ways. It's hard enough for me to write what I want to write without me trying to write what you say they want me to write which I don't want to write.

Q. Do you have any positive message, in your opinion?

A. Indeed I do think that I do.

Q. Such as what?

A. The crying, almost screaming, need of a great worldwide human effort to know ourselves and each other a great deal better, well enough to concede that no man has a monopoly on right or virtue any more than any man has a corner on duplicity and evil and so forth. If people, and races and nations, would start with that self-manifest truth, then I think that the world could sidestep the sort of corruption which I have involuntarily chosen as the basic, allegorical theme of my plays as a whole.

Q. You sound as if you felt quite detached and superior to this process of corruption in society.

A. I have never written about any kind of vice which I can't observe in myself.

Q. But you accuse society, as a whole, of succumbing to a deliberate mendacity, and you appear to find yourself separate from it as a writer.

A. As a writer, yes, but not as a person.

Q. Do you think this is a peculiar virtue of yours as a writer?

A. I'm not sentimental about writers. But I'm inclined to think that most writ-
    ers, and most other artists, too, are primarily motivated in their desperate
    vocation by a desire to find and to separate truth from the complex of lies
    and evasions they live in, and I think that this impulse is what makes their
    work not so much a profession as a vocation, a true "calling."

Q. Why don't you write about nice people? Haven't you ever known any
    nice people in your life?

A. My theory about nice people is so simple that I am embarrassed to say it.

Q. Please say it!

A. Well, I've never met one that I couldn't love if I completely knew him
    and understood him, and in my work I have at least tried to arrive at
    knowledge and understanding.

    I don't believe in "original sin." I don't believe in "guilt." I don't be-
    lieve in villains or heroes—only right or wrong ways that individuals have
    taken, not by choice but by necessity or by certain still-uncomprehended
    influences in themselves, their circumstances, and their antecedents.

    This is so simple I'm ashamed to say it, but I'm sure it's true. In
    fact, I would bet my life on it! And that's why I don't understand why
    our propaganda machines are always trying to teach us, to persuade us,
    to hate and fear other people on the same little world that we live in.

    Why don't we meet these people and get to know them as I try to
    meet and know people in my plays? This sounds terribly vain and ego-
    tistical.

    I don't want to end on such a note. Then what shall I say? That I
    know that I am a minor artist who has happened to write one or two
    major works? I can't even say which they are. It doesn't matter. I have
    said my say. I may still say it again, or I may shut up now. It doesn't
    depend on you, it depends entirely on me, and the operation of chance
    or Providence in my life.

                                                                      1957

AUTHOR AND DIRECTOR:
A DELICATE SITUATION

Whether he likes it or not, a writer for the stage must face the fact that the making of a play is, finally, a collaborative venture, and plays have rarely achieved a full-scale success without being in some manner raised above their manuscript level by the brilliant gifts of actors, directors, designers, and frequently even the seasoned theatrical instincts of their producers. I often wonder, for personal instance, if *The Glass Menagerie* might not have been a mere *succès d'estime*, snobbishly remembered by a small coterie, if Laurette Taylor had not poured into it her startling light and power, or if, without the genius of Kazan, *A Streetcar Named Desire* could have been kept on the tracks in those dangerous, fast curves it made here and there, or if the same genius was not requisite to making *Cat on a Hot Tin Roof* acceptable to a theater public which is so squeamish about a naked study of life.

A playwright's attitude toward his fellow workers goes through a cycle of three main phases. When he is just beginning in his profession, he is submissive mostly out of intimidation, for he is "nobody" and almost everybody that he works with is "somebody." He is afraid to assert himself, even when demands are made on him which, complied with, might result in a distortion of his work. He will permit lines, speeches, sometimes even whole scenes to be cut from his script because a director has found them difficult to direct or an actor has found them difficult to act. He will put in or build up a scene for a star at the sacrifice of the play's just proportions and balance. A commercial producer can sometimes even bully him into softening the denouement of his play with the nearly always wrong idea that this will improve its chances at the box office. Or if he is suddenly driven to resistance, he is unable to offer it with a cool head and a tactful tongue. Intimidation having bottled him up until now, he now pops off with unnecessary violence, he flips his lid. That's the first phase of the cycle. The second is entered when the playwright has scored his first notable success. Then the dog has his day. From intimidation he passes into the opposite condition. All of a sudden he is the great, uncompromising Purist, feeling that all ideas but his own are threats to the integrity of his work. Being suddenly a "Name" playwright, explosions of fury are no longer necessary for him to get his way. Now that he has some weight, he throws it around with the assured nonchalance of a major league pitcher warming up by the dugout. When his script is submitted to a producer by his representatives, it is not unlike the bestowal of a crown in heaven, there is a sanctified solemnity and hush about the proceedings. The tacit implication is: Here it is; take it or leave it; it will not be altered, since the slightest alteration would be nearly as sacrilegious as a revision of the Holy Scriptures.

Some playwrights are arrested at this second phase of the cycle, which is really only an aggravated reaction to the first, but sometimes the inevitable eventuality of an important failure after an important success or series of successes, will result in a moderation of the playwright's embattled ego. The temple or citadel of totally unsullied self-expression has not proven as secure a refuge as it seemed to him when he first marched triumphantly into it. It may take only one failure, it may take two or three, to persuade him that his single assessment of his work is fallible, and meanwhile, if he is not hopelessly paranoiac, he has come to learn of the existence of vitally creative minds in other departments of theater than the writing department, and that they have much to offer him, in the interpretation, the clarification, and illumination of what he has to say; and even if, sometimes, they wish him to express, or let him help them express, certain ideas and feelings of their own, he has now recognized that there are elements of the incomplete in his nature and in the work it produces. This is the third phase. There is some danger in it. There is the danger that the playwright may be as abruptly divested of confidence in his own convictions as that confidence was first born in him. He may suddenly become a sort of ventriloquist's dummy for ideas which are not his own at all. But that is a danger to which only the hack writer is exposed, and so it doesn't much matter. A serious playwright can only profit from passage into the third phase, for what he will now do is this: he will listen; he will consider; he will give a receptive attention to any creative mind that he has the good fortune to work with. His own mind, and its tastes, will open like the gates of a city no longer under siege. He will then be willing to supplement his personal conceptions with outside conceptions which he will have learned may be creative extensions of his own.

A mature playwright who has made this third and final step in his relations to fellow workers has come to accept the collaborative nature of the theater: he knows now that each artist in the theater is able to surpass his personal limits by respect for and acceptance of the talent and vision of others. When a gifted young actor rushes up to the playwright during rehearsals and cries out, I can't feel this, this doesn't ring true to me, the writer doesn't put on the austere mask of final authority. He moves over another seat from the aisle of a rehearsal hall, and bows his head in serious reflection while the actor tells him just what about the speech or the scene offends his sense of artistic justice, and usually the writer gets something from it. If he still disagrees with the actor, he says: "Let's get together with (whoever is directing) and talk this over at the bar next door. . . ." Maybe he won't sleep that night, but the chances are that in the morning he will reexamine the challenged segment with a sympathetic concern for an attitude which hasn't originated in his own brain and nerves, where sensibility is seated.

Now all of this that I've been rambling on about is my idea of the healthy course of development for a playwright *except*—I repeat, EXCEPT!—in those rare instances when the playwright's work is so highly individual that no one but the playwright is capable of discovering the right key for it. When this rare instance occurs, the playwright has just two alternatives. Either he must stage his play himself or he must find one particular director who has the very unusual combination of a truly creative imagination plus a true longing, or even just a true willingness, to devote his own gifts to the faithful projection of someone else's vision. This is a thing of rarity. There are very few directors who are imaginative and yet also willing to forego the willful imposition of their own ideas on a play. How can you blame them? It is all but impossibly hard for any artist to devote his gifts to the mere interpretation of the gifts of another. He wants to leave his own special signature on whatever he works on.

Here we encounter the sadly familiar conflict between playwright and director. And just as a playwright must recognize the value of conceptions outside his own, a director of serious plays must learn to accept the fact that nobody knows a play better than the man who wrote it. The director must know that the playwright has already produced his play on the stage of his own imagination, and just as it is important for a playwright to forget certain vanities in the interest of the total creation of the stage, so must the director. I must observe that certain directors are somewhat too dedicated to the principle that all playwrights must be "corrected." I don't think a director should accept a directorial assignment without feeling that, basically, the author of the play, if it's a serious work by a playwright of ability, has earned and deserves the right to speak out, more or less freely, during the rehearsal and tryout period of the production if this can be done in a way that will not disturb the actors. Yet it sometimes happens that the playwright is made to feel a helpless bystander while his work is being prepared for Broadway. It seems to me that the director is privileged to tell the author to "Shut up!" actually or tacitly, only when it is unmistakably evident that he, the director, is in total artistic command of the situation. Sometimes a director will go immediately from one very challenging and exhausting play production into another, being already committed by contract to do so. Then naturally he can't bring the same vitality to the second that he brought to the first. This becomes evident when the play has been blocked out, and after this blocking, little further progress is being made. The play remains at the stage of its initial blocking. The director may say, and quite honestly feel, that what he is doing is giving the public and critics a play precisely as it was written. However, this is evading the need and obligation that I mentioned first in this article, that a play must nearly always be raised above its manuscript level by the creative gifts and energies of its director, and all others involved in its production.

Perhaps it would be a good idea, sometimes, to have a good psychiatrist in attendance at the rehearsals and tryout of a difficult play, one who is used to working with highly charged creative people such as directors and actors and playwrights and producers, so that whenever there is a collision of nervous, frightened, and defensive egos, he can arbitrate among them, analyze their personal problems which have caused their professional problems, and "smooth things over" through the clearing house of a wise and objective observer.

Once in a while the exigencies and pressures of Broadway must step aside for another set of conditions which are too fragile and spiritually important to suffer violence through the silly but sadly human conflict of egos.

The theater *can* be a maker of great friendships!

1957

IF THE WRITING IS HONEST

If the writing is honest it cannot be separated from the man who wrote it. It isn't so much his mirror as it is the distillation, the essence, of what is strongest and purest in his nature, whether that be gentleness or anger, serenity or torment, light or dark. This makes it deeper than the surface likeness of a mirror and that much more truthful.

I think the man William Inge is faithfully portrayed in the work of William Inge the dramatist. The perceptive and tender humanity that shines in *The Dark at the Top of the Stairs* is a dominant trait of Bill Inge as I have known him these past fourteen years. Now the American theater public has begun to know him. When they enter The Music Box theater of Forty-fifth Street, west of Broadway, it is like going next door to call on a well-liked neighbor. There is warmth and courtesy in their reception. There is an atmosphere of serenity in his presence, there is understanding in it, and the kindness of wisdom and the wisdom of kindness. They enter and take comfortable seats by the fireside without anxiety, for there is no air of recent or incipient disorder on the premises. No bloodstained ax has been kicked under the sofa. If the lady of the house is absent, she has really gone to baby-sit for her sister, her corpse is not stuffed hastily back of the coal-bin. If the TV is turned on it will not break into the panicky report of unidentified aircraft of strange design over the rooftops. In other words, they are given to believe that nothing at all disturbing or indecorous is going to happen to them in the course of their visit. But they are in for a surprise, not a violent one but a considerable one, for William Inge the playwright, like William Inge the gentleman from Kansas via St. Louis, uses his good manners for their proper dramatic purpose, which is to clothe a reality which is far from surface. It is done, as they say, with mirrors, but the mirrors may all of a sudden turn into X ray photos, and it is done so quietly and deftly that you hardly know the moment when the mirrors stop being mirrors and the more penetrating exposures begin to appear on the stage before you. All of a sudden, but without any startling explosion, it happens, and you're not sure just when and how. This nice, well-bred next door neighbor, with the accent that belongs to no region except the region of good manners, has begun to uncover a world within a world, and it is not the world that his welcome prepared you to meet, it's a secret world that exists behind the screen of neighborly decorum. And that's when and where you meet the talent of William Inge, the true and wonderful talent which is for offering, first, the genial surface of common American life, and then not ripping but quietly dropping the veil that keeps you from seeing yourself as you are. Somehow he does it in such a way that you are not offended or startled by it. It's just what you are, and why should you be ashamed of it? We are what we are, and why should we be ashamed of it more than enough to want to improve it a little? That's what Bill Inge tells you, in his quiet, gently modulated voice that belongs to no region but the region of sincerity and understanding. No, don't be ashamed of it, but see it and know it and make whatever corrections you feel able to make, and they are bound to be good ones.

X ray photos, coming out of mirrors, may reveal the ravages of tissues turning malignant or of arteries beginning to be obstructed by deposits of calcium or fat. This is God's or the devil's way of removing us to make room for our descendants. Do they work together, God and the devil? I sometimes suspect that there's a sort of understanding between them, which we won't understand until Doomsday.

But Inge reveals the operations of both these powerful mysteries in our lives if you will meet him halfway, and therein lies his very peculiar talent. You hardly know the revelation has happened until you have parted from him and started home, to your house next door to The Music Box on Forty-fifth Street.

This has a great deal to do with the fact that the very handsome and outwardly serene face of William Inge, the gentleman-playwright, looks a bit older than his forty years.

Take fourteen from forty-four years and you are left with thirty, which was Bill's age when I met him in St. Louis in January, 1945. This was just a few weeks after Laurette Taylor had started breaking the ice of a Chicago winter with her performance, there, of my first success, *The Glass Menagerie*. I had returned to my parents' home in St. Louis as a refugee from the shock of sudden fame, but the flight was not far enough to serve its purpose. I had been home hardly a day when my mother interrupted my work in the basement of our rented suburban home—we had recently ascended from the city-apartment level of economy—to tell me the drama critic of the St. Louis *Star-Times* was on the phone. Bill Inge told me that he also did feature stories on theatrical folk passing through St. Louis and he would like to do a sort of "Home Town Boy Makes Good" article on me. He also wondered, sympathetically, if I would not enjoy a little social diversion other than that provided by family friends in St. Louis, since my own small group of past associates in the city had scattered far and wide, by this time, like fugitives from a sanguinary overthrow of state. He gave me his address and a time to come there. He was living in a housing project, way downtown in a raffish part of the city, but when he opened the door I saw over his shoulder a reproduction of my favorite Picasso and knew that the interview would be as painless as it turned out to be.

After I had gone back to Chicago to finish out the break-in run of *Menagerie*, Bill came up one weekend to see the play. I didn't know until then that Bill wanted to be a playwright. After the show, we walked back to my hotel in the Loop of Chicago, and on the way he suddenly confided to me, with characteristic simplicity and directness, that being a successful playwright was what he most wanted in the world for himself. This confession struck me, at the time, as being just a politeness, an effort to dispel the unreasonable gloom that had come over me at a time when I should have been most elated, an ominous letdown of spirit that followed me like my shadow wherever I went. I talked to him a little about this reaction, but I didn't feel that he was listening to me. I think Bill Inge had already made up his mind to invoke this same shadow and to suffuse it with light: and that, of course, is exactly what he has done.

The history of his rise in our theater is deceptively smooth in its surface appearance, for back of it lies the personal Odyssey of Bill Inge, and in the Odyssey, which I know and which has amazed and inspired me, is a drama as fine and admirable as any of the ones he has given, one after another—an unbroken succession of distinguished and successful plays—to the American theater, and someday I hope that he will make a play of it, his personal *Iliad* and *Odyssey*, a truly Homeric drama, but one in which the stairs rise from dark to light through something remarkably fine and gallant in his own nature.

1958

FOREWORD TO *SWEET BIRD OF YOUTH*

When I came to my writing desk on a recent morning, I found lying on my desk top an unmailed letter that I had written. I began reading it and found this sentence: "We are all civilized people, which means that we are all savages at heart but observing a few amenities of civilized behavior." Then I went on to say: "I am afraid that I observe fewer of these amenities than you do. Reason? My back is to the wall and has been to the wall for so long that the pressure of my back on the wall has started to crumble the plaster that covers the bricks and mortar."

Isn't it odd that I said the wall was giving way, not my back? I think so. Pursuing this course of free association, I suddenly remembered a dinner date I once had with a distinguished colleague. During the course of this dinner, rather close to the end of it, he broke a long, mournful silence by lifting to me his sympathetic gaze and saying to me, sweetly, "Tennessee, don't you feel that you are blocked as a writer?"

I didn't stop to think of an answer, it came immediately off my tongue without any pause for planning. I said, "Oh, yes, I've always been blocked as a writer but my desire to write has been so strong that it has always broken down the block and gone past it."

Nothing untrue comes off the tongue that quickly. It is planned speeches that contain lies or dissimulations, not what you blurt out so spontaneously in one instant.

It was literally true. At the age of fourteen I discovered writing as an escape from a world of reality in which I felt acutely uncomfortable. It immediately became my place of retreat, my cave, my refuge. From what? From being called a sissy by the neighborhood kids, and Miss Nancy by my father, because I would rather read books in my grandfather's large and classical library than play marbles and baseball and other normal kid games, a result of a severe childhood illness and of excessive attachment to the female members of my family, who had coaxed me back into life.

I think no more than a week after I started writing I ran into the first block. It's hard to describe it in a way that will be understandable to anyone who is not a neurotic. I will try. All my life I have been haunted by the obsession that to desire a thing or to love a thing intensely is to place yourself in a vulnerable position, to be a possible, if not a probable, loser of what you most want. Let's leave it like that. That block has always been there and always will be, and my chance of getting, or achieving, anything that I long for will always be gravely reduced by the interminable existence of that block.

I described it once in a poem called "The Marvelous Children."

"He, the demon, set up barricades of gold and purple tinfoil, labeled Fear (and other august titles), which they, the children, would leap lightly over, always tossing backwards their wild laughter."

But having, always, to contend with this adversary of fear, which was sometimes terror, gave me a certain tendency toward an atmosphere of hysteria and violence in my writing, an atmosphere that has existed in it since the beginning.

In my first published work, for which I received the big sum of thirty-five dollars, a story published in the July or August issue of *Weird Tales* in the year 1928, I drew upon a paragraph in the ancient histories of Herodotus to create a story of how the Egyptian queen, Nitocris, invited all of her enemies to a lavish banquet in a subterranean hall on the shores of the Nile, and how, at the height of this banquet, she excused herself from the table and opened sluice gates admitting the waters of the Nile into the locked banquet hall, drowning her unloved guests like so many rats.

I was sixteen when I wrote this story, but already a confirmed writer, having entered upon this vocation at the age of fourteen, and, if you're well acquainted with my writings since then, I don't have to tell you that it set the keynote for most of the work that has followed.

My first four plays, two of them performed in St. Louis, were correspondingly violent or more so. My first play professionally produced and aimed at Broadway was *Battle of Angels* and it was about as violent as you can get on the stage.

During the nineteen years since then I have only produced five plays that are *not* violent: *The Glass Menagerie, You Touched Me!, Summer and Smoke, The Rose Tattoo* and, recently in Florida, a serious comedy called *Period of Adjustment,* which is still being worked on.

What surprises me is the degree to which both critics and audience have accepted this barrage of violence. I think I was surprised, most of all, by the acceptance and praise of *Suddenly Last Summer.* When it was done off Broadway, I thought I would be critically tarred and feathered and ridden on a fence rail out of the New York theater, with no future haven except in translation for theaters abroad, who might mistakenly construe my work as a castigation of American morals, not understanding that I write about violence in American life only because I am not so well acquainted with the society of other countries.

Last year I thought it might help me as a writer to undertake psycho-analysis and so I did. The analyst, being acquainted with my work and recognizing the psychic wounds expressed in it, asked me, soon after we started, "Why are you so full of hate, anger, and envy?"

Hate was the word I contested. After much discussion and argument, we decided that "hate" was just a provisional term and that we would only use it till we had discovered the more precise term. But unfortunately I got restless and started hopping back and forth between the analyst's couch and some Caribbean beaches. I think before we called it quits I had persuaded the doctor that hate was not the right word, that there was some other thing, some other word for it, which we had not yet uncovered, and we left it like that.

Anger, oh yes! And envy, yes! But not hate. I think that hate is a thing, a feeling, that can only exist where there is no understanding. Significantly, good physicians never have it. They never hate their patients, no matter how hateful their patients may seem to be, with their relentless, maniacal concentration on their own tortured egos.

Since I am a member of the human race, when I attack its behavior to-ward fellow members I am obviously including myself in the attack, unless I regard myself as not human but superior to humanity. I don't. In fact, I can't expose a human weakness on the stage unless I know it through having it myself. I have exposed a good many human weaknesses and brutalities and consequently I have them.

I don't even think that I am more conscious of mine than any of you are of yours. Guilt is universal. I mean a strong sense of guilt. If there exists any area in which a man can rise above his moral condition, imposed upon him at birth and long before birth, by the nature of his breed, then I think it is only a willingness to know it, to face its existence in him, and I think that, at least below the conscious level, we all face it. Hence guilty feelings, and hence defiant aggressions, and hence the deep dark of despair that haunts our dreams, our creative work, and makes us distrust each other.

Enough of these philosophical abstractions, for now. To get back to writing for the theater, if there is any truth in the Aristotelian idea that vio-lence is purged by its poetic representation on a stage, then it may be that my cycle of violent plays have had a moral justification after all. I know

that I have felt it. I have always felt a release from the sense of meaningless-
ness and death when a work of tragic intention has seemed to me to have
achieved that intention, even if only approximately, nearly.

I would say that there is something much bigger in life and death than
we have become aware of (or adequately recorded) in our living and dying.
And, further, to compound this shameless romanticism, I would say that our
serious theater is a search for that something that is not yet successful but
is still going on.

1959

THE MAN IN THE OVERSTUFFED CHAIR

He always enters the house as though he were entering it with the intention of tearing it down from inside. That is how he always enters it except when it's after midnight and liquor has put out the fire in his nerves. Then he enters the house in a strikingly different manner, almost guiltily, coughing a little, sighing louder than he coughs, and sometimes talking to himself as someone talks to someone after a long, fierce argument has exhausted the anger between them but not settled the problem. He takes off his shoes in the living room before he goes upstairs where he has to go past my mother's closed door, but she never fails to let him know she hears him by clearing her throat very loudly or saying, "Ah, me, ah, me!" Sometimes I hear him say "Ah, me" in response as he goes on down the hall to where he sleeps, an alcove sunroom connected to the bedroom of my young brother, Dakin, who is at this time, the fall and winter of 1943, with the Air Force in Burma.

These months, the time of this story, enclose the end of the life of my mother's mother.

My father's behavior toward my maternal grandmother is scrupulously proper but his attitude toward my grandfather Dakin is so insulting that I don't think the elderly gentleman could have endured it without the insulation of deafness and near-blindness.

Although my grandmother is dying, she is still quite sound of sight and hearing, and when it is approaching the time for my father to return from his office to the house, my grandmother is always downstairs to warn her husband that Cornelius is about to storm in the front door. She hears the Studebaker charging up the drive and cries out to my grandfather, *"Walter, Cornelius is coming!"* She cries out this warning so loudly that Grandfather can't help but hear it. My grandfather staggers up from his chair by the radio and starts for the front stairs, but sometimes he doesn't make them in time and there is an awkward encounter in the downstairs hall. My grandfather says, "Good evening, Cornelius" and is lucky if he receives, in answer, a frigid "Hello, Mr. Dakin" instead of a red-eyed glare and a grunt.

It takes him, now that he's in his eighties with cataracts on both eyes, quite a while to get up the stairs, shepherded by his wife, and sometimes my father will come thundering up the steps behind them as if he intended to knock the old couple down. What is he after? A drink, of course, from a whiskey bottle under his bed in the sunroom, or the bathroom tub.

"Walter, watch out!"

"Excuse me, Mrs. Dakin," my father grunts breathlessly as he charges past them on the stairs.

They go to their bedroom, close the door. I don't hear just what they say to each other, but I know that "Grand" is outdone with Grandfather for lingering too long downstairs to avoid this humiliating encounter. Of course Grandfather finds the encounter distasteful, too, but he dearly loves to crouch by the downstairs radio at this hour when the news broadcasters come on, now that he can't read newsprint.

They are living with us because my grandmother's strength is so rapidly failing. She has been dying for ten years and her weight has dropped to eighty-six pounds. Any other person would be confined to bed, if not the terminal ward of a hospital, but my grandmother is resolved to remain on her feet, and actively helpful about the house. She is. She still does most of the laundry in the basement and insists on washing the dishes. My mother begs her to rest, but "Grand" is determined to show my father that she is not a dependent. And I have come home, this late autumn of 1943, because my mother wrote me, "Your grandmother has had to give up the house in Memphis because she is not strong enough to take care of it and your grandfather, too."

Between the lines of the letter, I read that my mother is expecting the imminent death of her mother and I ought to stop in Saint Louis on my bus trip between the West and East coasts, so I have stopped there.

I arrive there late one night in November and as I go up the front walk I see, through the curtains of the front room windows, my grandmother stalking across the living room like a skeleton in clothes. It shocks me so that I have to set down my luggage on the front walk and wait about five minutes before I can enter the house.

Only my grandmother has stayed up to receive me at this midnight hour, the others thinking that I had probably driven on through to New York, as I had so often before after promising to come home.

She makes light of her illness, and actually she manages to seem almost well for my benefit. She has kept a dinner plate on the stove for me over a double boiler and a low flame, and the living room fire is alive, and no reference is made to my failure in Hollywood, the humiliating termination of my six-months option as a screenwriter at M.G.M. studios.

"Grand" says she's come here to help Edwina, my mother, who is suffering from nervous exhaustion and is very disturbed over Cornelius's behavior. Cornelius has been drinking heavily. Mother found five empty bottles under his bed and several more under the bathtub, and his position as sales manager of a branch of the International Shoe Company is in jeopardy due to a scandalous poker fight in which half of his left ear was bitten off, yes, actually bitten off, so that he had to go to a hospital and have a plastic-surgery operation, taking cartilage from a rib to be grafted onto the ear, and in spite of elaborate precautions to keep it under wraps, the story has come out. Mr. J., the head executive and my father's immediate superior, has at last lost all patience with my father, who may have to retire in order to avoid being dismissed. But otherwise everything is fine, she is telling me about these things because Edwina may be inclined to exaggerate the seriousness of the family situation when we talk in the morning. And now I ought to go up to bed after a long, hard trip. Yes, I ought to, indeed. I will have to sleep in brother Dakin's old room rather than in my usual retreat in the attic, since the bed in the attic has been dismantled so that I won't insist on sleeping up there and getting pneumonia.

I don't like the idea of taking Dakin's room since it adjoins my father's doorless appendage to it.

I enter the bedroom and undress in the dark.

Strange sounds come from my father's sunroom, great sighs and groans and inebriate exclamations of sorrow such as, "Oh, God, oh, God!" He is unaware of my sleepless presence in the room adjoining. From time to time, at half-hour intervals, he lurches and stumbles out of bed to fetch a bottle of whiskey from some place of naive concealment, remarking to himself, "How terrible!"

At last I take a sleeping pill so that my exhaustion can prevail over my tension and my curiously mixed feelings of disgust and pity for my father, Cornelius Coffin Williams, the Mississippi drummer, who was removed from the wild and free road and put behind a desk like a jungle animal put in a cage in a zoo.

At supper the following evening an awful domestic scene takes place.

My father is one of those drinkers who never stagger or stumble but turn savage with liquor, and this next evening after my homecoming he comes home late and drunk for supper. He sits at one end of the table, my mother at the other, and she fixes on him her look of silent suffering like a bird dog drawing a bead on a covey of quail in the bushes.

All at once he explodes into maniacal fury.

His shouting goes something like this: "What the hell, why the hell do you feel so sorry for yourself? I'm keeping your parents here, they're not paying board!"

The shout penetrates my grandfather's deafness and he says, "Rose, let's go to our room." But my grandmother Rose remains at the table as Edwina and Grandfather retire upstairs. I stay as if rooted or frozen to the dining-room chair, the food turning sick in my stomach.

Silence.

My father crouches over his plate, eating like a wild beast eats his kill in the jungle.

Then my grandmother's voice, quiet and gentle: "Cornelius, do you want us to pay board here?"

Silence again.

My father stops eating, though. He doesn't look up as he says in a hoarse, shaky voice: "No, I don't, Mrs. Dakin."

His inflamed blue eyes are suddenly filled with tears. He lurches up from the table and goes to the overstuffed chair in the living room.

This overstuffed chair, I don't remember just when we got it. I suspect it was in the furnished apartment that we took when we first came to Saint Louis. To take the apartment we had to buy the furniture that was in it, and through this circumstance we acquired a number of pieces of furniture that would be intriguing to set designers of films about lower-middle-class life. Some of these pieces have been gradually weeded out through successive changes of address, but my father was never willing to part with the over-stuffed chair. It really doesn't look like it could be removed. It seems too fat to get through a doorway. Its color was originally blue, plain blue, but time has altered the blue to something sadder than blue, as if it had absorbed in its fabric and stuffing all the sorrows and anxieties of our family life and these emotions had become its stuffing and its pigmentation (if chairs can be said to have a pigmentation). It doesn't really seem like a chair, though. It seems more like a fat, silent person, not silent by choice but simply unable to speak because if it spoke it would not get through a sentence without bursting into a self-pitying wail.

Over this chair still stands another veteran piece of furniture, a floor lamp that must have come with it. It rises from its round metal base on the floor to half a foot higher than a tall man sitting. Then it curves over his head one of the most ludicrous things a man has ever sat under, a sort of Chinesey-looking silk lamp shade with a fringe about it, so that it suggests a weeping willow. Which is presumably weeping for the occupant of the chair.

I have never known whether Mother was afraid to deprive my father of his overstuffed chair and weeping-willow floor lamp or if it simply amused her to see him with them. There was a time, in her younger years, when she looked like a fairy-tale princess and had a sense of style that exceeded by far her power to indulge it. But now she's tired, she's about sixty now, and she lets things go. And the house is now filled not only with its original furnishings but with the things inherited from my grandparents' house in Memphis. In fact, the living room is so full of furniture that you have to be quite sober to move through it without a collision . . . and still there is the overstuffed chair.

A few days after the awful scene at the dinner table, my dearly loved grandmother, Rose Otte Dakin, bled to death in the house of my parents.

She had washed the dinner dishes, had played Chopin on the piano, which she'd brought with her from Memphis, and had started upstairs when she was overtaken by a fit of coughing and a lung hemorrhage that wouldn't stop.

She fought death for several hours, with almost no blood left in her body to fight with.

Being a coward, I wouldn't enter the room where this agony was occurring. I stood in the hall upstairs. My grandmother Rose was trying to deliver a message to my mother. She kept flinging out a wasted arm to point at a bureau.

It was not till several days after this death in the house that my mother found out the meaning of that gesture.

My grandmother was trying to tell my mother that all her savings were sewn up in a corset in a drawer of the bureau.

Late that night, when my grandmother had been removed to a mortuary, my father came home.

"Cornelius," said Mother, "I have lost my mother."

I saw him receive this announcement, and a look came over his face that was even more deeply stricken than that of my mother when she closed the eyelids of "Grand" after her last fight for breath.

He went to his overstuffed chair, under the weeping-willow floor lamp, like a man who has suddenly discovered the reality in a nightmare, and he said, over and over again, "How awful, oh, God, oh God, how awful!"

He was talking to himself.

At the time of my grandmother's death I had been for ten years more an irregular and reluctant visitor to the house than a member of the household. Sometimes my visits would last the better part of a year, sometimes, more usually, they would last no more than a week. But for three years after my years at college I was sentenced to confinement in this house and to hard labor in "The World's Largest Shoe Company" in which my father was also serving time, perhaps as unhappily as I was. We were serving time in quite different capacities. My father was the sales manager of that branch that manufactures, most notably, shoes and booties for kiddies, called "Red Goose Shoes," and never before and probably not to this day has "The World's Largest" had so gifted a manager of salesmen. As for me, I was officially a clerk-typist but what I actually did was everything that no one else wanted to do, and since the boss wanted me to quit, he and the straw boss made sure that I had these assignments. I was kept on my feet most of the time, charging back and forth between the office and the connecting warehouse of this world's largest wholesale shoe company, which gave me capable legs and a fast stride. The lowliest of my assigned duties was the one I liked most, dusting off the sample shoes in three brightly mirrored sample rooms each morning; dusting off the mirrors as well as the shoes in these rooms that were intended to dazzle the eyes of retailers from all over the States. I liked this job best because it was so private. It was performed before the retailers came in: I had the rooms and the mirrors to myself, dusting off the sample shoes with a chamois rag was something that I could do quickly and automatically, and the job kept me off the noisy floor of the office. I regretted that it took only about an hour, even when I was being most dreamily meticulous about it. That hour having been stretched to its fullest, I would have to take my desk in the office and type out great sheaves of factory orders. It was nearly all numerals, digits. I made many mistakes, but for an amusing reason I couldn't be fired. The head of the department had gotten his job through the influence of my father, which was still high at that time. I could commit the most appalling goofs and boners and still I couldn't be fired, however much I might long to be fired from this sixty-five-dollar-a-month position. I left my desk more often than anyone else. My branch of "The World's Largest" was on the top floor but I had discovered a flight of stairs to the roof of the twelve-story building and every half hour or so I would go up those stairs to have a cigarette, rather than retiring to the smelly men's room. From this roof I could look across the Mississippi River to the golden wheat fields of Illinois, and the air, especially in autumn, was bracingly above the smog of Saint Louis, so I used to linger up there for longer than a cigarette to reflect upon a poem or short story that I would finish that weekend.

I had several enemies in the office, especially the one called "The Straw Boss," a tall, mincing creature who had acquired the valuable trick of doing nasty things nicely. He was not at all bright, though. He didn't realize that I liked dusting the shoes and running the errands that took me out of "The World's Largest." And he always saw to it that the sample cases that I had to carry about ten blocks from "The World's Largest" to its largest buyer, which was J. C. Penney Company, were almost too heavy for a small man to carry. So did I build up my chest and slightly damage my arterial system, a damage that was soon to release me from my period of bondage. This didn't bother me, though. (I've thought a good deal about death but doubt that I've feared it very much, then or now.)

The thing I most want to tell you about is none of this, however; it is something much stranger. It is the ride downtown that my father and I would take every morning in his Studebaker. This was a long ride, it took about half an hour, and seemed much longer for neither my father nor I had anything to say to each other during the ride. I remember that I would compose one sentence to deliver to my father, to break just once the intolerable silence that existed between us, as intolerable to him, I suspect, as it was to me. I would start composing this one sentence during breakfast and I would usually deliver it halfway downtown. It was a shockingly uninteresting remark. It was delivered in a shockingly strained voice, a voice that sounded choked. It would be a comment on the traffic or the smog that enveloped the streets. The interesting thing about it was his tone of answer. He would answer the remark as if he understood how hard it was for me to make it. His answer would always be sad and gentle. "Yes, it's awful," he'd say. And he didn't say it as if it was a response to my remark. He would say it as if it referred to much larger matters than traffic or smog. And looking back on it, now, I feel that he understood my fear of him and forgave me for it, and wished there was some way to break the wall between us.

It would be false to say that he was ever outwardly kind to his fantastic older son, myself. But I suspect, now, that he knew that I was more of a Williams than a Dakin, and that I would be more and more like him as I grew older, and that he pitied me for it.

I often wonder many things about my father now, and understand things about him, such as his anger at life, so much like my own, now that I'm old as he was.

I wonder for instance, if he didn't hate and despise "The World's Largest Shoe Company" as much as I did. I wonder if he wouldn't have liked, as much as I did, to climb the stairs to the roof.

I understand that he knew that my mother had made me a sissy, but that I had a chance, bred in his blood and bone, to some day rise above it, as I had to and did.

His branch of "The World's Largest" was three floors down from the branch I worked for, and sometimes an errand would take me down to his branch.

He was always dictating letters in a voice you could hear from the elevator before the door of it opened.

It was a booming voice, delivered on his feet as he paced about his stenographer at the desk. Occupants of the elevator, hearing his voice, would smile at each other as they heard it booming out so fiercely.

Usually he would be dictating a letter to one of his salesmen, and not the kind of letter that would flatter or please them.

Somehow he dominated the office with his loud dictation. The letters would not be indulgent.

"Maybe you're eating fried chicken now," he'd boom out, "but I reckon you remember the days when we'd go around the corner for a cigarette for breakfast. Don't forget it. I don't. Those days can come back again . . ."

His boss, Mr. J., approved of C.C.'s letters, but had a soundproof glass enclosure built about his corner in "The World's Largest" . . .

A psychiatrist once said to me, You will begin to forgive the world when you've forgiven your father.

I'm afraid it is true that my father taught me to hate, but I know that he didn't plan to, and, terrible as it is to know how to hate, and to hate, I have forgiven him for it and for a great deal else.

Sometimes I wonder if I have forgiven my mother for teaching me to expect more love from the world, more softness in it, than I could ever offer?

The best of my work, as well as the impulse to work, was a gift from the man in the overstuffed chair, and now I feel a very deep kinship to him. I almost feel as if I am sitting in the overstuffed chair where he sat, exiled from those I should love and those that ought to love me. For love I make characters in plays. To the world I give suspicion and resentment, mostly. I am not cold. I am never deliberately cruel. But after my morning's work, I have little to give but indifference to people. I try to excuse myself with the pretense that my work justifies this lack of caring much for almost everything else. Sometimes I crack through the emotional block. I touch, I embrace, I hold tight to a necessary companion. But the breakthrough is not long lasting. Morning returns, and only work matters again.

Now a bit more about my father whom I have come to know and understand so much better.

My mother couldn't forgive him. A few years after the years that I have annotated a little in this piece of writing, my mother became financially able to cut him out of her life, and cut him out she did. He had been in a hospital for recovery from a drunken spree. When he returned to the house, she refused to see him. My brother had returned from the latest war, and he would go back and forth between them, arranging a legal separation. I suspect it was not at all a thing that my father wanted. But once more he exhibited a gallantry in his nature that I had not then expected. He gave my mother the house and half of his stock in the International Shoe Company, although she was already well set up by my gift to her of half of my earnings from *The Glass Menagerie*. He acquiesced without protest to the terms of the separation, and then he went back to his native town of Knoxville, Tennessee, to live with his spinster sister, our Aunt Ella. Aunt Ella wasn't able to live with him, either, so after a while he moved into a hotel at a resort called Whittle Springs, close to Knoxville, and somehow or other he became involved with a widow from Toledo, Ohio, who became his late autumn love which lasted till the end of his life.

I've never seen this lady but I am grateful to her because she stuck with Dad through those last years.

Now and then, during those years, my brother would be called down to Knoxville to see Dad through an illness brought on by his drinking, and I think it was the Toledo Widow who would summon my brother.

My brother, Dakin, is more of a Puritan than I am, and so I think the fact that he never spoke harshly of the Toledo Widow is a remarkable compliment to her. All I gathered from his guarded references to this attachment between Dad and the Toledo Widow was that she made him a faithful drinking companion. Now and then they would fly down to Biloxi and Gulfport, Mississippi, where Dad and Mother had spent their honeymoon, and it was just after one of these returns to where he had been happy with Mother, and she with him that he had his final illness. I don't know what caused his death, if anything caused it but one last spree. The Toledo Widow was with him at the end, in a Knoxville hospital. The situation was delicate for Aunt Ella. She didn't approve of the widow and would only go to my father's deathbed when assured there would be no encounter between the widow and herself in the hospital room. She did pass by her once in the hospital corridor, but she made no disparaging comment on her when I flew down to Knoxville for the funeral of my father.

The funeral was an exceptionally beautiful service. My brother, Aunt Ella, and I sat in a small room set apart for the nearest of kin and listened and looked on while the service was performed.

Then we went out to "Old Gray," as they called the Knoxville Cemetery, and there we sat in a sort of tent with the front of it open, to witness the interment of the man of the overstuffed chair.

Behind us, on chairs in the open, was a very large congregation of more distant kinfolk and surviving friends of his youth, and somewhere among them was the Toledo Widow, I've heard.

After the interment, the kinfolk all came up to our little tent to offer condolences that were unmistakably meant.

The widow drove off in his car which he had bequeathed to her, her only bequest, and I've heard of her nothing more.

He left his modest remainder of stock in the International Shoe Company in three parts to his sister, and to his daughter, and to my brother, a bequest which brought them each a monthly income of a hundred dollars. He left me nothing because, as he had told Aunt Ella, it didn't seem likely that I would ever have need of inherited money.

I wonder if he knew, and I suspect that he did, that he had left me something far more important, which was his blood in my veins? And of course I wonder, too, if there wasn't more love than hate in his blood, however tortured it was.

Aunt Ella is gone now, too, but while I was in Knoxville for Dad's funeral, she showed me a newspaper photograph of him outside a movie house where a film of mine, *Baby Doll*, was being shown. Along with the photograph of my father was his comment on the picture.

What he said was: "I think it's a very fine picture and I'm proud of my son."

ca. 1960

REFLECTIONS ON A REVIVAL OF A
CONTROVERSIAL FANTASY

If the play, *Camino Real,* were a product being promoted on a TV commercial and I were the spokesman for it, I suppose I would present it in such theatrical terms as these:

"Are you more nervous and anxious than you want people to know?"

"Has your public smile come to resemble the grimace of a lion-tamer in a cage with a suddenly untamed lion, or that of a trapeze performer without a net beneath him and with a sudden attack of disequilibrium coming on him as he's about to perform his most hazardous trick near the top of the big top?"

"And do you have to continue your performance betraying no sign on your face of anxiety in your heart?"

"Then here is the right place for you, the Camino Real, its plaza and dried-up fountain, at the end of it. Here is where you won't be lonely alone, bewildered alone, frightened alone, nor desperately brave alone, either."

Actually, there is a character in the play (she's called the Gypsy and she represents the wonderful, tough-skinned pedestrians of the Camino who were born and bred on it and wouldn't trade it for the Champs Élysées) who delivered a better pitch than mine, above, but hers doesn't precede the play, to introduce it.

I wrote this play in a time of desolation: I thought, as I'd thought often before and have often thought since, that my good work was done, that those "huge cloudy symbols of a high romance" that used to lift me up each morning (with the assistance of coffee so black you couldn't see through it even when you poured it before a fair-weather window), that all those mornings had gone like migratory birds that wouldn't fly back with any change of season. And so it was written to combat or to purify a despair that only another writer is likely to understand fully.

Despair is a thing that you can't live with anymore than you can live with a lover who hates you or a companion who never stops nagging. And even though it was my most spectacular and expensive failure on Broadway, *Camino Real* served for me, and I think for a number of others who saw it during its brief run in 1953, as a spiritual purgation of that abyss of confusion and lost sense of reality that I, and those others, had somehow wandered into.

There are two key speeches in the play, neither of which is more than one sentence. One is the remark of Don Quixote in the Prologue, when he arrives in the midnight plaza of this nowhere, everywhere place and hears all about him the whispering of the word "lonely" from beggar and outcast people asleep on the pavement. He seems oddly comforted by it: he turns to the audience and observes: "In a place where so many are lonely, it would be inexcusably selfish to be lonely alone."

The other key speech is at the end of the play, and is also only one sentence: "The violets in the mountains have broken the rocks." In the final, published version of *Camino Real,* both of these key speeches are given to Don Quixote, not because I regard him as a fool but because I think, and, yet, I do truly believe, that the human coat of arms can and must, finally, bear such romantic mottoes as these, at least in the later stretches of our Camino Reals.

What the play says through this unashamed old romanticist, Don Quixote, is just this, "Life is an unanswered question, but let's still believe in the dignity and importance of the question."

1960

TENNESSEE WILLIAMS PRESENTS HIS POV

The last time I was in Hollywood a famous lady columnist with a way-out taste in millinery but a way-in taste in film fare got me on the phone one morning and lit into me like a mother tigress defending her litter. "I want to know why you are always plunging into sewers!" she demanded.

I happened to like the lady and, as an avid reader of movie fan magazines, I had derived many hours of pleasure from her sometimes withering diatribes against stars whose private behavior had offended her sense of propriety. So, I did not shout back at her but tried to mollify her with a reasonable dissertation on my artistic POV as opposed to hers (and I will pause for one moment to say that POV is a handy contraction of the term "point of view," which is used in the shooting script of movie scenarios). I tried to persuade the lady, in the gentlest possible manner, that from my POV it was not into sewers but into the mainstream of life that I had always descended for my material and characters. I did not succeed in altering her POV, but I did seem to calm her fury.

The POV of Miss Marya Mannes is essentially the same as Miss Hedda Hopper's POV, and even the POV of my mother, who says to me so often, "Son, when there is so much unpleasantness in the world, why is it necessary to put it on the stage?"

Mother's question was more sorrowful in tone than wrathful, but somehow that didn't make it any easier to answer, especially since even a middle-aged son still has a terrible sense of guilt in the presence of Mom. I'm not sure that I even tried to answer it, but one time, to my surprise, I heard her answer it for herself. A visitor was saying, "Mrs. Williams, why does your son waste his talents on such morbid subjects?"

Mother spoke as quickly as if she'd always known the answer. "My son," she said, "writes about life"—and she said it with the conviction of a rebel yell.

I am sorry to be speaking for and about my own work, in response to the POV of Miss Mannes, since I was not the solitary culprit she summoned to justice. My fellow defendants are Lillian Hellman, Albert Camus, Jean Genet, and others, I would assume, such as Bertolt Brecht, Samuel Beckett, Jean Anouilh, Eugene Ionesco, Friedrich Duerrenmatt, and Edward Albee. It's a distinguished list and I am proud to be on it, and hopeful that my plea for the defense will not compromise them too much. I am hoping also that some among them will find an interval in their subversive creative activity to speak for themselves.

Let us begin with statistics. Immediately after reading the piece by Miss Mannes, which would give the impression that virtually all Broadway houses this year had been preempted by works of violence, decadence and stomach-turning morbidity, I consulted the A. B. C. ads of theater attractions then running on Broadway, and I counted fifteen attractions in the musical and revue category.

Of the remaining nine attractions on Broadway, I found that only one or two might conceivably be subversive from the POV of Miss Mannes—that brilliantly witty import, Jean Giraudoux's *Duel of Angels,* and the prize-winning play by Lillian Hellman, *Toys in the Attic.*

The seven other legitimate attractions, although they do recognize with eloquence and dramatic skill that many circumstances in human existence are not as agreeable as all might wish for, could hardly be called "sick" plays, or even decadent, and all of them, from the humanistic POV, are distinctly affirmative. And so, on the basis of statistics, it appears to me that Miss Mannes is sounding a false alarm, or, at least, an alarm which is somewhat exaggerated.

Although she writes with a temperance which is unique among those sharing her POV, she is unmistakably out for blood, and the point I am making is that, quantitatively speaking, there isn't much blood to be out for, at least anywhere near Times Square; not enough to serve as a transfusion for an infant with a moderate thumb cut.

Now let's get down to my POV and that of my codefendants before a very formidable and ever more vocal tribunal. I dare to suggest, from my POV, that the theater has made in our time its greatest artistic advance through the unlocking and lighting up and ventilation of the closets, attics, and basements of human behavior and experience. Miss Hopper calls them "sewers"; so does Dorothy Kilgallen, and so, I'm afraid, at least by implication, does Miss Mannes. I think there has been not a very sick but a very healthy extension of the frontiers of theme and subject matter acceptable to our dramatic art, to the stage, the screen, and even television, despite the POV of "sponsors."

The POV I am speaking for is just this: that no significant area of human experience, and behavior reaction to it, should be held inaccessible, provided it is presented with honest intention and taste, to the screen, play, and TV writers of our desperate time. And I would add that to campaign against this advance in dramatic freedom is to campaign for something that is perilously close to a degree of cultural fascism, out of which came the Nazi book-burning and the "correction" of all the arts in the Russia of Stalin.

And, if you remember the statistics I noted earlier in this piece, you may agree with my POV that such a thing as this sort of cultural rigging is a greater peril than the so-called moral decadence of such works as *Caligula, The Threepenny Opera, The Visit, Toys in the Attic, The Zoo Story, Krapp's Last Tape, Camino Real,* and *The Connection,* most of which are pretty safely off Broadway.

The rallying cry of those who want our creative heads on the chopping block is: let's have plays affirming the essential dignity of mankind. It's a damned good platform. The only trouble with it, from my POV, is that we are not agreed about exactly what that high-sounding slogan really means in the way of truth about dignity and mankind.

People are humble and frightened and guilty at heart, all of us, no matter how desperately we may try to appear otherwise. We have very little conviction of our essential decency, and consequently we are more interested in characters on the stage who share our hidden shames and fears, and we want the plays about us to say "I understand you. You and I are brothers; the deal is rugged but let's face and fight it together."

It is not the essential dignity but the essential ambiguity of man that I think needs to be stated.

Of course I am tempted to talk about my own characters—Blanche DuBois, Serafina Delle Rose, and even the sick Princess Kosmonopolis—at this point, but let me have a bit of dignity and talk instead about Brecht's *Mother Courage,* the greatest of modern plays in my opinion.

Mother Courage was a jackal. She battened on the longest war in history, following the armies, in an ever increasingly beaten-up wagon, with her shoddy merchandise for which she extracted the highest price she could get. At one point she even denied that her son was her son, and let him be executed without an outcry except the awful outcry in her heart. Why? Because of her need to go on with her wagon and her demented daughter and her simple will to endure.

I have specified a work that I think affirms the only kind of essential human dignity and decency, in modern terms, that I can honestly swear by.

Miss Mannes only mentions *My Fair Lady,* and the others sharing her

POV are curiously reluctant to provide us with a list of plays, classic or modern, especially modern, that conform to their moral specifications.

If you were Prince Hamlet and observed the suicidal anguish of Ophelia, would you or would you not rise above all personal concerns, at least for a while, to embrace her kindly? Would you or would you not thrust a dagger through a curtain to kill a man behind it simply because you suspected, but surely weren't certain, that he might be your mother's lover and your father's killer?

From my POV I find Prince Hamlet cruel. How does he strike you from yours?

The magnitude of *Hamlet* does not exist in the matter but in the manner. Dramatic lyricism of the highest, most lasting order, and the passion to reveal the undignified and the often indecent truths about mankind are what make *Hamlet* so great a drama.

This is my POV, exemplified by one classic and one modern play.

The POV of Miss Mannes and company betrays a basic misapprehension of the creative nature and function.

There are two kinds of creative work: organic and non-organic. It is possible to reform, to change the nature of a non-organic (synthetic) work in the arts, meaning that work which is produced through something other than a necessity as built in to the worker as his heartbeat and respiration. But you could flay the skin off a writer whose work is organic and you still would not get out of him a sincere or workable recantation of his faith in what he is doing, however abominable that work may be or strike you as being.

The nervous system of any age or nation is its creative workers, its artists. And if that nervous system is profoundly disturbed by its environment, the work it produces will inescapably reflect the disturbance, sometimes obliquely and sometimes with violent directness, depending upon the nature and control of the artist.

I am giving away no trade secret when I point out how many artists, including writers, have sought refuge in psychiatry, alcohol, narcotics, way-in or way-out religious conversions, and so forth. An extension of the list would be boringly superfluous.

Deny the art of our time its only spring, which is the true expression of its passionately personal problems and their purification through work, and you will be left with a soil of such aridity that not even a cactus plant could flower upon it.

To sum it up for the defense: We have done no worse a deed than the X ray machine or the needle that makes the blood test. And though these are clinical devices, I think we have tried our best to indicate which are the healthy blood cells and which is the normal tissue in the world of our time, through exposing clearly the dark spots and the viruses on the plates and in the blood cultures.

Certainly, there should be a healthy coexistence of My Fair Lady and My Lady of Unwilling Sickness. But if one tries to push out the other, which is the fair one, really?

1960

PRELUDE TO A COMEDY

Perhaps no other occupation is more inclined to infiltrate and finally to absorb the life of the man engaged in it than the writer's calling.

In this context I recall having once written a preface to a poet friend's first volume of verse. The preface began something like this:

"In this time of false intensities, it is exhilarating to know the work of an artist which exists as a natural and joyful accompaniment to his life instead of almost being a substitute for it."

I believe, I went on to say, that I didn't think writing, nor any form of creative work, was ever meant by nature to be a man's way of making a living, that when it becomes one it almost certainly loses a measure of purity.

The first work of creative art was probably a caveman's drawing on the wall of his cave, and it wasn't done for fame or money or even the oh's and ah's of anyone but himself. I think he just picked up a sharp bit of stone and drew on the rock wall of his cave, the pure one-dimensional record in celebration of a bit of personal experience that had deeply moved him.

I suspect that it was the portrait of a dangerous wild beast he had encountered that day in the forest primeval—a beast that he had met in mortal combat and that he obviously had overcome and had, very likely, hauled home for supper. In fact, I suspect that maybe at the back of the cave his wife was broiling some good cuts of meat off the carcass, and it was by the light of her kitchen fire that this aboriginal artist carved with stone onto stone the record, the memorial of the event in the forest that day; an event that moved him to discover, for the first of all times on earth, the impulse of an artist to translate experience into something permanent.

I have seen photographs of these prehistoric rock carvings, which were the beginning of human history in art, and observed the beauty and dignity of them, and sensed the emotional turmoil of the earth's first artist, celebrating the dignity and beauty and valor of his victim even while its carcass was being prepared for supper.

I do wonder, however, if this first artist on earth was hungry enough to gnaw the bones of his conquered adversary with an appetite that wasn't reduced by the shame of devouring the flesh of the valiant victim.

I know he must have had pride in his victory over this slain adversary, but I also know that he must have been paying it homage when he carved its portrait on the cave wall by the light of the fire that prepared its flesh for supper.

What I meant in the opening remark of my preface to the poet's book was that his work had that kind of purity in it, that it had suffered no distortions in its descent from the first creative impulse and action of mankind.

I wrote this preface about twelve years ago, when I was myself a victim of the false intensities that seemed to follow on the transformation of a creative writer to a public figure, especially one who provides material for brilliantly satirical nightclub entertainers.

I felt this danger to the marrow of my bones, and I followed the instinctive reaction of running away. I cut out for Europe, and not one morning during the seven days of the crossing was I able to work with any degree of the joyfulness and naturalness that exhilarated me so much in my friend's first volume of verse.

A psychosomatic illness developed soon after my arrival in Paris and within ten days I was removed to the American hospital there. A coolly sympathetic young doctor told me that I was "threatened with hepatitis and mononucleosis."

These were a pair of disorders I had never heard of before and that had such formidable titles that I wrote in my diary, in my hospital room, "The jig is up: they have some fancy names for it."

Well, the jig wasn't up, I was simply suffering from an exaggerated form of that terrific shock of success that a youngish writer (I was thirty-six) is bound to experience when the privacy and natural joyfulness of his old way of working and living is intercepted like a forward pass in football by his abruptly turning into something less like a serious writer than the latest sensation of the entertainment world, where nothing is staler than the latest sensation a short while later.

Fortunately, I had made in Paris a friend, Mme. Lazareff (the editor of the magazine *Elle*), who didn't take the dreadful names of the two disorders with which I was threatened as seriously as I did. She said to me, "Get dressed quick. I'm checking you out of here."

She not only checked me out of the hospital but also gave me the first dinner that I was able to keep down for a week and put me, that same evening, on a train to the South.

As Blanche said in *A Streetcar Named Desire;* "Sometimes there is God so quickly!"

In Rome there was sunlight and voices, human voices and the daybreak voices of those tiny swallows, which Italians call *ronzini,* thousands of them, swarming up and down at daybreak and dusk like great polka dot veils in a gale, reminding me of not only my lost mornings but my lost evenings, too, the naturalness and the joyfulness of them as they used to be.

I still believe that a writer's safety, especially in his middle years, if he began writing in his adolescence, lies in one of two things, whichever one is more personally suitable to him—living in a remote place, particularly on an island in the tropics, or in a fugitive way of life, running like a fox from place to place. I have tried both and am still trying both, but now I've found one other expedient, which is not to laugh at a problem but to stop taking it as if it affected the whole future course of the world. It surely doesn't: but to write intensely you have to believe intensely in what you're writing, at least for those few hours each day that you work.

One season in Rome I assayed the writing of a novella about the psychological adjustment of a famous actress to retirement from the stage. The actress encounters an old friend of considerable wisdom and candor, who says to her, "You can retire from a business but not from an art; you can't put your talent away like a key to a house where you don't live any more."

She spoke some true words there, and yet when the work of any kind of creative worker becomes tyrannically obsessive to the point of overshadowing his life, almost taking the place of it, he is in a hazardous situation. His situation is hazardous for the simple reason that the source, the fountainhead of his work, can only be his life.

No one ever used the material of his life so well as Marcel Proust, who made out of his life, recollected and continuing, what is possibly the greatest novel of our time, *Remembrance of Things Past,* in which he made the passage of time (from past to present and to the future shadow) a controlled torrent of personal experience and sensibilities to it. It contains all the elements of a man's psychic history—his love, fear, loneliness, disgust, humor, and, most important of all, his forgiving perception of the reasons for the tragicomedy of human confusion.

The midnight dark of the final picture was irradiated and purified by a genius that no other writer of our century has in his command, not even Chekhov or Joyce. But within the limits of each, the writers of our times can use the method of Proust, that of transposing the contents of his life into a creative synthesis of it.

Only in this way can a writer justify his life and work and I think all serious writers know this and their serious audience has a sense of it, too.

1960

FIVE FIERY LADIES

Vivien Leigh is not only the officially appointed first lady of the London theater, but several other things of equal or greater importance: an actress of great talent which has steadily grown through meeting the challenge of many classic roles, Greek, Shakespearean, Restoration, and Shaw, while still appearing so masterfully in such American films as *Gone With The Wind* and my own *Streetcar*. At present she is appearing in a film based on my novel, *The Roman Spring of Mrs. Stone*, a part she accepted with no reluctance despite its being an aging actress, retired from the stage and infatuated with a young adventurer more interested in mirrors than anything except money.

Her beauty, Vivien's, is as delicately flamboyant as an orchid. When she takes the stage, she commands it as if she first arrived there suspended from the bill of a stork.

Vivien, above all else, is incomparably graceful, she moves like a marvelous dancer, on or off stage, and she has an instinct for doing and saying just the one right thing to put you at ease even when you know you are making a fool of yourself. All of these wonderful gifts she has given with no apparent regard for her personal vulnerability: in other words she is not only a stunning actress but a lady with the most important part of that intricate composition, which is kindness of heart.

Right now Geraldine Page is making her first motion picture in seven years, an extraordinarily long lapse of time between films for such a talented and beautiful actress. Her new film is a screen version of *Summer and Smoke* which she revived off Broadway for a year's run a good while after it expired so quickly on Broadway. This revival drew the attention of Hollywood to Gerry. But at that time Hollywood didn't know how to use her. She did not catch on with the picture public because of inept casting. Only in New York did her name continue to mean something, and there it meant something mostly to her own young generation of "method-trained" actors.

Some actresses have the kind of faces you can describe as "neutral." Their beauty must be created by magic, by suitable casting, by technical skill. It exists, but it has to be revealed. This was true of Garbo. She and Gerry have the same kind of beauty, great but unobtrusive until unveiled by some perceptive showman. Garbo had her great impresario, Stiller. Gerry had no one but Gerry. Did this throw her? Hell, no. She has spent the past seven years between her last picture and her new one on the study of her art. She is the most disciplined and dedicated of actresses, possibly the one that fate will select as an American Duse—provided that she continues to love the stage more than the screen. Last night when I called her long distance and inquired about her plans, she said, "I hope to find a new play for Broadway next fall."

MAGNANI! I put the name in caps with exclamation point because that is how she "comes on." She does not do it deliberately, and you can't explain it by the name and the legend. She is simply a rare being who seems to have about her a little lightning-shot cloud all her own that goes in and out with her as inescapably as her shadow. I think this explains her deep suffering from loneliness, her difficulty in human relations, her frequent pronouncement that she likes dogs better. In a crowded room, she can sit perfectly motionless and silent, and still you feel the atmospheric tension of her presence, its quiver and hum in the air like a live wire exposed, and a mood of Anna's is like the presence of royalty. Out of this phenomenon of human electronics has come the greatest acting art of our times. She can play a peasant or an empress, but Anna is haunted by a limitation that exists only in her mind. She feels advancing years may sometimes make her unsuitable for romantic roles. I say that her talent never rested on youth and never will.

Anna and I had both cherished the dream that her appearance in the part I created for her in *The Fugitive Kind* would be her greatest triumph to date, particularly since her co-star would be America's most gifted actor. But Mr. Brando comes at a high price in more ways than one, especially for a foreign co-player, still unsure of the language. Brando's offbeat timing and his slurred pronunciation were right for the part but they were torture for Anna who had to wait and wait for her cue, and when she received it, it would sometimes not be the one in the script. *The Fugitive Kind* is a true and beautiful film, in my opinion, but mutilated by that uncontrollable demon of competitiveness in an actor too great, if he knew it, to resort to such self-protective devices.

Kate is a playwright's dream actress. She makes dialogue sound better than it is by a matchless beauty and clarity of diction, and by a fineness of intelligence and sensibility that illuminates every shade of meaning in every line she speaks. She invests every scene, each "bit," with the intuition of an artist born into her art. Of the women stars that belong to a generation preceding that of "the method," Katharine Hepburn impresses me as having least needed that school of performance-in-depth. Like Laurette Taylor before her, she seems to do by instinct what years of "method" training have taught her juniors to do.

She is limited only by her ladylike voice and manner. Miss Hepburn could never play a tramp or a tenement housewife. No matter. There will always be parts for "ladies," and we need Kate Hepburn to play them.

I don't think Hepburn was happy with the part of the poet's mother in the screen version of *Suddenly Last Summer*. Brilliantly constructed as the screen version was by Gore Vidal, it still made unfortunate concessions to the realism that Hollywood is too often afraid to discard. And so a short morality play, in a lyrical style, was turned into a sensationally successful film that the public thinks was a literal study of such things as cannibalism, madness, and sexual deviation. But I am certain that Kate knew that what the drama truly concerned was all human confusion and its consequence: violence.

Liz Taylor is one of the great phenomena and symptoms of our time in America. Everything she has done with her life has been startling and sometimes implausible. It's hard to guess what Liz wants out of life: the million-dollar contracts and diamond necklaces or the exercise of what is probably the finest raw talent on the Hollywood screen. She has a deeply moving response to fellow artists in trouble, and so I'm inclined to believe that she is more interested in the creative work than the loot.

She thoroughly understands the system she is caught in, and she is not to be bossed or intimidated by it. Hollywood moguls have met their match in our Liz. I've heard her phone conversations with them: mutual understanding and respect. But what will emerge from this is something beyond my conjecture. Naturally I hope that this girl, this cross between a flower and the rock it sprang from, will discover that her greater satisfaction will come from the disciplining of her talent in the stricter conditions of our theater. But this is a personal bias and Liz Taylor, if luck is with her as it must be with us all, will probably wind up with insufficient space on wall or mantel for her big game trophies.

As for Liz's performance in *Suddenly Last Summer*, if it did nothing else, it demonstrated her ability to rise above miscasting. She was marvelously well cast as Maggie in *Cat on a Hot Tin Roof,* and that's when she should have got her Oscar. But it stretched my credulity to believe that such a "hip" doll as our Liz wouldn't know at once in the film that she was "being used for something evil." I think that Liz would have dragged Sebastian home by his ears, and so saved them both from considerable embarrassment that summer.

1961

CARSON MCCULLERS

Ever since a novelist told me that the theater was an art *manqué,* meaning something less than an art, and I got so mad that I nearly drove my car through the lowered gates of an Italian railroad crossing and smack into a *Rapido* from Naples to Rome, I have thought it best to limit my personal encounter with other writers almost as strictly as collisions should be limited between two speeding vehicles in any country. And yet somehow I have managed to make many close and deeply satisfying friendships with other writers, such as Paul and Jane Bowles, Gore Vidal, Truman Capote, Donald Windham, William Inge, Alberto Moravia, and, perhaps most of all, with Carson McCullers, despite the long periods in which we lived in very separate parts of the world. Let's face the fact that the almost constantly irritated sensibilities of writers make it difficult for them to get along together as well as they should. This is especially true between novelists and playwrights. Novelists have the idea that playwrights are the pecuniary favorites of fortune, and they have some justification in this suspicion. Novelists and poets seem to be expected to live on air and subsidies, usually meager, while it is embarrassingly true that playwrights are recipients of comparatively large royalties, have Diners' Club cards, eat at Sardi's, and can travel first class. And so, on the surface, which is always misleading, they appear to be the favorites of fortune, and it is quite understandable and forgivable that their poet and novelist friends are tempted to goad them about the impurities of their medium.

Yet when this invidious attitude is dispelled, it can be agreeable for them to get together. The playwright must put aside his envy of the poet's or novelist's connection with a purer medium, and the novelist or the poet must have the good sense and sensibility to see that the material advantages of the playwright are incidental.

Carson McCullers and I have never had this embarrassment between us, although she is more consistently a writer of fiction than a playwright. From the moment of our first meeting, Carson, with her phenomenal understanding of another vulnerable being, felt nothing for me but that affectionate compassion that I needed so much and that she can give so freely, more freely than anyone else I know in the world of letters.

On the island of Nantucket, the summer of 1946, we worked at opposite ends of a table, she on a dramatization of *The Member of the Wedding* and I on *Summer and Smoke,* and for the first time I found it completely comfortable to work in the same room with another writer. We read each other our day's work over our after-dinner drinks, and she gave me the heart to continue a play that I feared was hopeless.

When I told her that I thought my creative powers were exhausted, she said to me, wisely and truly, an artist always feels that dread, that terror, when he has completed a work to which his heart has been so totally committed that the finishing of it seems to have finished him too, that what he lives for is gone like yesteryear's snow.

At the end of that summer's work I became very ill, and only a few months later so did she, with a mysterious paralysis of her right arm. I have such a fierce resistance to physical illness that I continually push it back; Carson's strength is enormous but primarily exists in her spirit. From 1947 to the present year she has been, as many interested in American writing know, a gallant invalid. She has lived with that paralysis of the right arm and with an excruciating series of operations to correct it, yet all the while she has never surrendered to it. During those fourteen years she has kept on working steadily and with all the creative and personal distinction that makes her an inspiring figure to us relative weaklings. She has completed two plays of the most impressive quality, and at the same time she has given us stories and poems of the purest distinction.

And all this time, these fourteen years, she has also been working on her fifth novel, *Clock Without Hands.*

Before I went abroad last spring, she told me that she felt she couldn't complete it, that she had paid out all her strength. Then I reminded her of what she had told me, those fourteen years ago, that at the end, or near it, of a work to which the artist's heart is totally committed, he always feels that dread, that terror which is greater than the fear of death.

When I returned from abroad, two and a half months later, an advance copy of the completed novel was waiting for me in Key West.

If I hadn't known before that Carson is a worker of miracles, this work would surely have convinced me of it, for without any sign of the dreadful circumstances under which she accomplished it, this work was once again a thing set on paper as indelibly as if it had been carved onto stone. Here was all the stature, nobility of spirit, and profound understanding of the lonely, searching heart that make her, in my opinion, the greatest living writer of our country, if not of the world.

1961

A SUMMER OF DISCOVERY

In those days there was, and for all I know still may be, a share-the-expense travel agency through which people whose funds were as limited as mine, that summer of 1940, go into contact with others who owned cars and were going in roughly the same direction.

A preliminary meeting and interview would be arranged in the office of the agency which was located in the lobby of a rather seedy midtown Manhattan hotel. It was about as embarrassing as applying for a job, perhaps even more so, for a man who is offering you a job can turn you down with some polite little dissimulation such as, "I'm looking for someone with a bit more experience in this type of work." But if you were turned down by a car-owner at this agency, you knew it could only be because you had failed to make an agreeable or trustworthy impression. Inevitably you were nervous and guilty-looking.

On this occasion, the summer that I had decided to go to Mexico for no more definite reason than that it was as far from New York as I could hope to get on the small funds at my disposal, the agency introduced me to a fantastic young honeymoon couple. The bridegroom was a young Mexican who had come up to New York to visit the World's Fair, then in progress, and had encountered and almost immediately married a young blonde lady of ambiguous profession whom he was now preparing to take home to meet his parents in Mexico City.

He had already met with so many unexpected expenses that he needed a paying passenger on his trip home, but it was obvious that my nervous manner aroused suspicion in him. Fortunately they had an interpreter with them, at the meeting, and the bride was more accustomed to and less distrustful of nervous young men. She felt nothing at all alarming about me, and through the interpreter persuaded her bridegroom to accept me as a travelling companion.

They didn't speak the same language in more ways than one and so the young lady, as the journey proceeded, began to use me as her confidant.

About her ambiguous profession she had thoroughly deceived her new mate but she was very uncertain that his well-to-do parents in Mexico City, if we ever got there, would be equally gullible. And so, on the long way South, she would rap at my motel door almost every midnight to tell me about their latest misunderstanding or misadventure, and these clandestine conversations were the best psychological therapy that I could have had in my own state of anxiety and emotional turmoil, which was due to my feeling that my career as a Broadway playwright had stopped almost where it had started and what would follow was unpredictable but surely no good.

The journey was erratic as a blind bird's and took at least twice as long as would be reasonably expected, and the shared expenses were staggering by my standards. However my state of mind and emotion were so depressed that I was fairly indifferent to all practical concerns, even to a bad cold that turned to influenza, to the almost continual dream-state that comes with high fever and chills.

I never again saw this odd young couple after the morning when they delivered me to the YMCA building in Mexico City but, a year or two later, the bride sent me some fairly worthless articles of clothing which I had left in the trunk of the car, along with a note containing sentimental references to the wonderful trip that we had enjoyed together and hoping that sometime, somehow, we'd be able to enjoy another, and I thought to myself as I read it, this poor young woman has gone out of her mind.

Nobody had warned me that Mexico City was, in altitude, one of the highest cities in the world. I felt all the time as if I had taken Benzedrine, couldn't sleep, couldn't stay still. Surmising at last that I was allergic to atmosphere at the 7,500-foot level, I took a bus to Acapulco, some other young American having described it as a primitive place with much better swimming facilities than the "Y."

So I set out for Acapulco, with chills, fever, heart palpitations, and a mental state that was like a somnambulist's, apparently not bothering to inform Audrey Wood, my agent, the Theatre Guild, or the Dramatists Guild that my address would no longer be c/o General Delivery in Mexico City, an oversight which led to much complication some weeks later. Actually I was suffering from incipient tuberculosis, the scars of which are still visible on X ray lung photos.

In Acapulco, I spent the first few days in a fantastic hotel near the central plaza. All the rooms opened onto a large patio-garden containing parrots, monkeys, and the proprietor of the hotel, who was so fat that he could hardly squeeze into a room at the place. Much of his time was devoted to cosmetic treatments which were administered in the patio. Every morning a very lively young barber would arrive to touch up the proprietor's hair with henna and give him a marcel wave and a cold cream facial. Since the dyed, waved hair was quite long and the proprietor spoke in a falsetto voice and was always clad in a bright silk kimono, I wasn't quite sure of his sex till I heard him addressed as Señor something-or-other by one of his employees.

The steaming hot squalor of that place quickly drove me to look for other accommodations, nearer the beaches. And that's how I discovered the background for my new play, *The Night of the Iguana*. I found a frame hotel called the Costa Verde on the hill over the still water beach called Caleta and stayed there from late August to late September.

It was a desperate period in my life, but it's during such times that we are most alive and they are the times that we remember most vividly, and a writer draws out of vivid and desperate intervals in his life the most necessary impulse or, drive toward his work, which is the transmutation of experience into some significant piece of creation, just as an oyster transforms, or covers over, the irritating grain of sand in his shell to a pearl, white or black, of lesser or greater value.

My daily program at the Costa Verde Hotel was the same as it had been everywhere else. I charged my nerves with strong black coffee, then went to my portable typewriter which was set on a card table on a veranda and worked till I was exhausted: then I ran down the hill to the still water beach for my swim.

One morning, taking my swim, I had a particularly bad fit of coughing. I tasted in my mouth something saltier than the waters of the Pacific and noticed beside my head, flowing from my mouth, a thin but bright thread of red blood. It was startling but not frightening to me, in fact I kept on swimming toward the opposite side of the bay, hardly bothering to look back to see if the trajectory of coughed-up blood was still trailing behind me, this being the summer when the prospect of death was hardly important to me.

What was important to me was the dreamworld of a new play. I have a theory that an artist will never die or go mad while he is engaged in a piece of work that is very important to him. All the cells of his body, all of his vital organs, as well as the brain cells in which volition is seated, seem to combine their forces to keep him alive and in control of his faculties. He may act crazily but he isn't crazy; he may show any symptom of mortality but he isn't dying.

As the world of reality in which I was caught began to dim out, as the work on the play continued, so did the death wish and the symptoms of it. And I remember this summer as the one when I got along best with people and when they seemed to like me, and I would attribute this condition to the fact that I expected to be dead before the summer was over and that there was consequently no reason for me to worry about what people thought of me. When you stop worrying what people think of you, you suddenly find yourself thinking of them, not yourself, and then, for the time that this condition remains, you have a sort of crazy charm for chance acquaintances such as the ones that were staying with me that crazy summer of 1940, at the Costa Verde in Acapulco.

By the middle of September the bleeding lungs had stopped bleeding, and the death wish had gone, and has never come back to me since. The only mementos of the summer are the scar on the X ray plate, a story called "The Night of the Iguana," and now this play which has very little relation to the story except the same title and a bit of the same symbolism. But in both the short story and the play, written many years later, there is an incident of the capture of the iguana, which is a type of lizard, and its tying up under the veranda floor of the Costa Verde, which no longer exists in the new Acapulco.

Some critics resent my symbols, but let me ask, what would I do without them? Without my symbols I might still be employed by the International Shoe Co. in St. Louis.

Let me go further and say that unless the events of a life are translated into significant meanings, then life holds no more revelation than death, and possibly even less.

In September, that summer of 1940, the summer when, sick to death of myself, I turned to other people most truly, I discovered a human heart as troubled as my own. It was that of another young writer, a writer of magazine fiction who had just arrived from Tahiti because he feared that the war, which was then at a climax of fury, might cut him off from the magazines that purchased his adventure stories. But in Tahiti he had found that place which all of us spend our lives looking for, the one right home of the heart, and as the summer wore on I discovered that his desolation was greater than my own, since he was so despondent that he could no longer work.

There were hammocks along the sleeping verandas. We would spend the evenings in adjacent hammocks, drinking rum-cocos, and discussing and comparing our respective heartbreaks, more and more peacefully as the night advanced.

It was an equinoctial season, and every night or so there would be a spectacular storm. I have never heard such thunder or seen such lightning except in melodramatic performances of Shakespeare. All of the inarticulate but passionate fury of the physical universe would sometimes be hurled at the hilltop and the veranda, and we were thrilled by it, it would completely eclipse our melancholy.

But the equinox wore itself out by late September, and we both returned to our gloomy introspections.

Day after steaming hot day I would go to Wells-Fargo in town for my option check and it wouldn't be there. It was long overdue and I was living on credit at the hotel, and I noticed, or suspected, a steady increase in the management's distrust of me.

I assumed that the Theatre Guild had dropped their option of *Battle of Angels* and lost all interest in me. The other young writer, still unable to scribble a line that he didn't scratch out with the groan of a dying beast, had no encouragement for me. He felt that it was quite clear that we had both arrived at the end of our ropes and that we'd better face it. We were both approaching the age of thirty, and he declared that we were not meant by implacable nature to go past that milestone, that it was the dead end for us.

Our gloom was not relieved by the presence of a party of German Nazis who were ecstatic over the early successes of the Luftwaffe over the R.A.F. When they were not gamboling euphorically on the beach, they were listening to the radio reports on the battle for Britain and their imminent conquest of it, and the entire democratic world.

My writer friend began to deliver a pitch for suicide as the only decent and dignified way out for either of us. I disagreed with him, but very mildly.

Then one day the manager of the hotel told me that my credit had run out. I would have to leave the next morning, so that night my friend and I had more than our usual quota of rum-cocos, a drink that is prepared in a cocoanut shell by chopping off one end of it with a machete and mixing the juice of the nut with variable quantities of rum, a bit of lemon juice, a bit of sugar, and some cracked ice. You stick straws in the lopped-off end of the cocoanut and it's a long dreamy drink, the most delectable summer night's drink I've ever enjoyed, and that night we lay in our hammocks and had rum-cocos until the stars of the Southern Cross, which was visible in the sky from our veranda, began to flit crazily about like fireflies caught in a bottle.

My friend reverted to the subject of death as a preferable alternative to life and was more than usually eloquent on the subject. It would have been logical for me to accept his argument but something in me resisted. He said I was just being "chicken," that if I had any guts I would go down the hill

with him, right then and now, and take "the long swim to China," as I was
no more endurably situated on earth than he was.

All that I had, he told me, was the uncontrolled emotionalism of a minor lyric talent which was totally unsuited to the stage of life as well as
the theater stage. I was, he said, a cotton-headed romanticist, a hopeless
anachronism in the world now lit by super fire-bombs. He reeled out of his
hammock and to the veranda steps, shouting, "Come on, you chicken, we're
going to swim out to China!"

But I stayed in my hammock, and if he went swimming that night, it
wasn't to China, for when I woke up in the hammock, and it was daylight,
he was dressed and packed and had found an elderly tourist who had a car
and was driving back to Texas, and had invited us to accompany him in his
car free of charge. My friend hauled me out of the hammock and helped me
pack for departure.

This old man, he declared, referring to our driver, is in the same boat
as we are, and the best thing that could happen to all three of us is to miss
a turn through the mountains and plunge off the road down a chasm, to
everlasting oblivion. On this note, we cut out.

We had just reached the most hazardous section of the narrow road
through the mountains when this other young writer asked the tourist if he
couldn't take over the wheel for a while. Oh, no, I exclaimed. But the other
writer insisted, and like a bat out of hell he took those hairpin turns through
the Sierras. Any moment, I thought, we would surely crash into the mountain
or plunge into the chasm on the road's other side, and it was then that I was
all through with my death wish and knew that it was life that I longed for, on
any terms that were offered.

I clenched my hands, bit my tongue, and kept praying. And gradually
the driver's demonic spirit wore itself out, the car slowed, and he turned the
wheel over to the owner and retired to the back seat to sleep off his aborted
flirtation with the dark angel.

The Night of the Iguana is rooted in the atmosphere and experiences
of the summer of 1940, which I remember more vividly, on the emotional
level, than any summer that I have gone through before or after—since it
was then, that summer, that I not only discovered that it was life that I truly
longed for, but that all which is most valuable in life is escaping from the
narrow cubicle of one's self to a sort of veranda between the sky and the
still water beach (allegorically speaking) and to a hammock beside another
beleaguered being, someone else who is in exile from the place and time of
his heart's fulfillment.

A play that is more of a dramatic poem than a play is bound to rest on metaphorical ways of expression. Symbols and their meanings must be arrived at through a period of time which is often a long one, requiring much patience, but if you wait out this period of time, if you permit it to clear as naturally as a sky after a storm, it will reward you, finally, with a puzzle which is still puzzling but which, whether you fathom it or not, still has the beautifully disturbing sense of truth, as much of that ambiguous quality as we are permitted to know in all our seasons and travels and places of short stay on this risky planet.

At one point in the composition of this work it had an alternative title, *Two Acts of Grace,* a title which referred to a pair of desperate people who had the humble nobility of each putting the other's desperation, during the course of a night, above his concern for his own.

Being an unregenerate romanticist, even now, I can still think of nothing that gives more meaning to living.

1961

THE AGENT AS CATALYST

Who is Audrey, what is she, that all our swains commend her?

She is the paradox of the Broadway world. For her clients, she is the mother-image, but the image is a long shot from Whistler's; it's more like Bertolt Brecht's great portrait of *Mother Courage,* an unsentimental portrait which is far more impressive to me; and surely this Lady Mandarin, as I call her, is nothing if not impressive. In fact, she is very likely the most impressive person—as well as influence—in my grown-up professional life.

Audrey is very definitely a lady, and a great one, but she is about as far from my Southern heroines as she is from the irritatingly sweet, passive image of a mother that Mr. Whistler gave us.

She is a startling, almost indecipherable poem of a person, and the poem is intensely modern and representative of the place as well as the time in which she lives and functions.

What is Audrey, really?

To begin with the most obvious thing about her, she is the most successful and powerful agent of the most successful and powerful agency for artists in the world. But that is where anything obvious about her begins and ends.

I always find that people whom I have known a long time, and cared for at least as much as they've cared for me, a good deal more mystifying than those that I simply like or dislike, and I have known Audrey for the past twenty-one years. She is still an enigma to me, and more and more an enigma as time goes by.

When someone is that near and dear to me, I am morbidly uncertain and anxious about their feeling for me, and I can't honestly say, even now, that I know for certain that she cares as much for Tom the person as for Tennessee the playwright, and though this may seem like a left-handed compliment to her, I don't mean it at all that way.

Sometimes I say to myself, "What wonderful friends we could be, Audrey Wood and I, if it weren't for this desperately difficult relationship of agent and client between us!"

The chief difficulty lies in the fact that, like all mother-image people, Audrey Wood, whether she knows it or not, has a will to manage, to control her sometimes recalcitrant son- or daughter-images. She wants to set them straight, to protect them from the dangerous tangents on which they are all too likely to embark, and this is bound to create an ambivalent relationship when the filial image has arrived, as I have, at an age in his life and profession as an artist when he feels humiliated by the acceptance of what he thinks is too much domination, too many decisions for him not made by himself; and if his deepest instinct is that of determination, he would rather make wrong decisions than accept right ones from someone else.

Like most important personalities and persons, Audrey has included in her nature the virtues of both sexes. With the grace and inner delicacy of a most womanly woman she has the combative instincts and vigor of a man and his greater taste for frankness. Her small hands can be firm and strong as iron inside their velvety gloves, and when a situation calls for it she is not reluctant to take the gloves off.

Although she is a woman of her precise moment in history, there is much about her that reminds me of eighteenth-century women of note and distinction. She has their needle-sharp quickness of wit and perception, she would have done very well at the Court of Versailles, she would have gotten along with Du Barry and Mme Pompadour as well as with Marie Antoinette, and the Bourbon Kings would have called her into their councils, readily and wisely. And incidentally, Audrey Wood is one of the best letter writers of her sex since Mme de Sévigné.

But who is Audrey, what is she?

When you stand close to something, the image magnifies, but it also has a tendency to blur.

We are all inclined to think of our friends as less complex than ourselves, since we are naturally more aware of our own ambiguous areas than of theirs.

Ambiguity or complexity of character is what we must first accept in anyone whom we care for in our complex and ambiguous fashion, and it is also, certainly, what is most interesting in them, at least to an artist whose primary concern is avoiding black or white or grey in his character-portraits and seeing his confusing loved ones, in life or in manuscript, as weathers or climates in a continual equinox, with flashes of beautiful color and torrents of darkness.

In human character, simplicity doesn't exist except among simpletons.

Last spring I was invited by *Life* Magazine to write about stars in my professional life, and about one of them I said: "She is a cross between a flower and the rock that it sprang from." Of course the rock was show business and the flower was the heart of a gentle, confused and very vulnerable woman.

For all her strength and her worldly knowledgeability, I believe that Audrey Wood is those three things that I observed in that star of exceptional talent.

The ambiguity, the mysterious contractions in the heart and the life of a human being is a thing that could almost be called my most obsessive concern as a playwright.

Being incapable of absolute convictions, I can't say for sure that Audrey Wood is totally and always on the "side of the angels," meaning altogether devoted to concerns not her own. But let me add: "Who is?"

She is a very, very wise lady, and usually a shrewd one. She has surely risen to her present preeminent position of power in her field through an uncanny sense of not only what is good but what will go. But let me testify that the goodness of a woman has always, to all appearance, been of more concern to her.

For this reason, it is a harrowing thing to submit a script to her. It makes me shiver and shake to deposit in a post-office slot the first draft of a new play addressed to Miss Audrey Wood, and till she gives a report on her reaction, which may be two or three weeks after I mailed it, the shakes and shivers continue and steadily increase.

You may wonder why she waits that long to respond, and sometimes I wonder, too. My guess is that if the wait is a long one, her silence is to let me know that the play is not up to scratch. But when you're so morbidly uncertain about the quality of your work as I am, you are likely to misinterpret expressed opinions of it, as well as the long, silent wait. For instance, in 1945 I mailed Audrey, from New Orleans, the first sketch of *Camino Real*. I waited unusually long, as I recall it, for a word from the lady. Then one evening I was dining at a restaurant in the French Quarter when I was called to the telephone and over it came the voice of Audrey Wood. She said something like this: "Darling, promise me you won't show this to anyone yet."

In retrospect, I would guess that this did not mean what I imagined, which was that the sketch, later published in a book of my one-acts called *American Blues,* was a disgraceful comedown from my previous work. I now think what she meant was merely that she didn't believe it quite ready for public exposure in its shape at that time.

She understands and feels for the acute anxieties of her clients, but she

wisely regards these anxieties as less important than the best possible realization of a work, and this is not an attitude which she imposes only on me.
Sometimes she has asked my opinion of other dear clients' work, delicately
suggesting her own reservations about them as she presents them to me,
usually on a train or a plane as we go to an out-of-town opening of some
play of mine.

When a thing really strikes her as good, even if it is the first draft, she is
likely to give you an immediate reaction of the fullest and warmest enthusiasm, as she did when I gave her a messy mountain of manuscript that turned
into *Cat on a Hot Tin Roof*. That was in Rome, and the very next morning
she had read it and offered the unequivocal opinion that this was my best
play since *A Streetcar Named Desire* and would be a big hit, which it was.

I would say that Audrey can call the shots better than any producer on
or off Broadway. And that, of course, is why it's such a frightening thing to
submit a play to her.

But I still say: Who is Audrey? What is she? Her husband describes her
as "an angel," and as "the little giant of the American theatre." And is livid
with rage at any comparatively reserved estimation of her—and he is far
from being unique in this virtual idolatry of the lady. I have rarely heard
anyone speak disparagingly of her, and even more rarely heard any question
of her integrity in a profession which is necessarily, and almost tragically,
committed to evasions.

And yet I know that if someday our professional relationship should
come to a close, it is she who would close it, not I, and that her reasons
would be the reasons of both a rock and a flower.

1962

T. WILLIAMS'S VIEW OF T. BANKHEAD

I have been invited to contribute to these pages an explication of the meaning and history of my latest version of my "last long play for Broadway," but I am sure you will forgive me for hoping that the play will speak for itself, and to choose the relevant subject of Miss Tallulah Bankhead.

Shall I begin by speaking of her position in her profession, which she says that she hates?

Well, she isn't a Method actress and she is no more a member of the New Wave of theater personalities than I am. We are both veteran performers in our respective departments of the English-speaking theater. And if I should say that I hated writing plays it would be as reliable a statement as Tallulah's statement that she hates the theater.

She loves it with so much of her heart that, in order to protect her heart, she has to say that she hates it. But we know better when we see her onstage. Of course she doesn't know better. The last thing she could ever be, at all consciously, is a liar, despite the fact that she has worked forty years in a world where the Eleventh Commandment often seems to be "Never speak the truth."

Tallulah has never hesitated to speak what she feels to be the truth, no matter about the possible hurt to herself, because when you speak the truth it is you, the speaker, who is most apt to be hurt.

Tallulah is the strongest of all the hurt people I've ever known in my life. And of hurt people I've known a remarkable number, including some whom I have hurt myself, and one of them is Tallulah.

She has forgiven me for it but I am not yet ready to forgive myself.

There is a peculiar sort of consanguinity of spirit between Tallulah and me, despite the fact that she is descended from the plantation Southland and I am descended, on my father's side, from Southern folk who owned no plantations because there are no plantations in the hills of East Tennessee.

We are closely linked in the way of understanding each other to such an extent that we can say anything that we want to say to each other, as long as we say it honestly, without there resulting anything but a bit of temporary glowering between us which leads to more understanding.

Tallulah says to me: "Every good female part you've ever written you've written for *me!*" Tallulah is more than slightly right about that, despite the fact that I have written only four parts for her, Myra Torrance in *Battle of Angels,* Blanche in *A Streetcar Named Desire,* The Princess Kosmonopolis in *Sweet Bird of Youth,* and now, finally, Flora Goforth in *The Milk Train.*

Of these four roles that were written for Tallulah, she has chosen to perform only two, including the one in which you will have a chance to see her on Wednesday.

This intense infatuation of mine began in the summer of 1940. I happened to be in Provincetown, Mass., when Tallulah began an engagement at a playhouse halfway down the Cape. I rode a bicycle down there to see her because she was one of a list to whom the Theatre Guild had submitted my first play bought for Broadway. It so happened that the trip was longer than I had expected and it also so happened that as I was parking the bicycle on the Playhouse lawn, I heard someone calling out, "Five minutes, Miss Bankhead."

There was a response to the call, and this response was delivered in a voice that, having once heard, I would never stop hearing inside my head as I wrote lines for ladies that had somehow resulted from the fantastic crossbreeding of a moth and a tiger. Here was the voice for which I had written the part of Myra Torrance in *Battle of Angels,* and written it for that voice without ever having heard it except in films.

I went backstage after the play that night and she received me in her dressing room with that graciousness that has nothing to do with her Southern origin and genteel breeding but with her instinctive kindness to a person in whom she senses a vulnerability that is kin to her own. I suppose I simply mean that she saw or sensed immediately that I was meeting, for the first time in my life, a great star, and that I was more than just properly awed. I was virtually dumb-struck. I can't quote accurately the conversation between us. I think she asked who I was and then I think she said something like, "Oh, so it's you, the play is impossible, darling, but sit down and have a drink with me."

Which I did.

After a few moments she saw that her rejection of the play had struck me where I lived, and being by nature a person as kind as she is honest, she began to say more about it. Naturally, I can't quote her literally, these twenty-three years later, but I know that she did tell me that she sensed a sort of poetry in the play that was struggling toward theatrical viability but had not arrived there yet. And I know that her sweetness so moved me that the ride back up the Cape was more like floating on a cloud than pedaling a bicycle.

A year or so later this play I'd tried to sell her had failed spectacularly in Boston and I had so declined in favor and fortune that I was passing a month of the winter in the unheated attic of the family home in St. Louis. It was in that city that I next encountered Miss Bankhead. She was storming across the country as the maleficent vixen in *The Little Foxes*. I presented myself once more at her dressing room door and she received me as if she'd last seen me the day before yesterday, not the year before the last. "Well, darling," she roared, "I was luckier than Miriam Hopkins who lost her mind and actually appeared in that abominable Battle of Something that you had the impertinence to write for me!"

Now let's get on the *Streetcar*. It is the winter of 1946–1947 and as always while writing a play very close to my heart, I think I am dying. My worktable is beneath a New Orleans skylight and beside it is the spectral figure of a lady and a star, impatiently keeping watch over my last agony at the typewriter. She is not still for a moment. She is sweeping all about me as I work, crying out, laughing, sobbing, but never losing the arrogance of a lady descended from a queen of Scotland. It is duly submitted to my agent, Audrey Wood, and after a short time that seemed like a century to me, Miss Wood dispatches a wire, mysteriously summoning me to a conference in Charleston, S.C.

In the wire she mentioned that I would there be introduced to a person so important as to be called a personage, and since I have always been hooked on mystery and importance, I pulled my dying body together and caught a plane to the designated place of top-level consultation.

The personage was a lady whose father was a Hollywood monarch and whose husband was another.

"Whom do you have in mind," asked this lady-producer, "for your fantastic Blanche?"

"Well," said I, "while I was writing this play, all of the speeches seemed to be issuing from the mouth of Miss Bankhead."

The lady-producer said that she admired that inimitable voice as much as I did but that she feared that Tallulah would have such power in the part of Blanche that, if she consented to play it, the moth-like side of Blanche would be demolished at once by the tiger-like side of Blanche. And I must shamefully admit that, being a "dying man," I lacked the strength to oppose this strongly stated opinion, being not only a man who thought he was dying but a playwright who had entered that phase of a playwright's remorseless cycle of existence when he may even suspect that unanimous "Yes" notices can add up to a sweetly disguised obituary to his professional being.

The Tiger-Moth called Blanche was superbly played by such stars as Jessica Tandy and Uta Hagen before that part and Tallulah got together, under circumstances that probably only Tallulah Bankhead would have the quixotic valor to confront without fear, or any evidence of it.

I have no wound-up watch and no looked-at calendar and such a dread of time passing, and past, that I can't tell you the year when Tallulah played Blanche; but play it she finally did, and with that Tiger-Moth quality of the lady and star who had haunted the sky-lit workroom in which I had caught Blanche DuBois in the paper facsimile of a jungle trap.

Some people who saw Tallulah's interpretation of Blanche have mistakenly said that she was too strong for the part of this neurasthenic creature, but I personally feel that she gave a magnificent portrayal of the role. I don't suppose anyone reads *Streetcar* anymore, but if they did, they would discover that Blanche is a delicate tigress with her back to the wall. The part must be played opposite an actor of towering presence, a Brando or a Tony Quinn, to create a plausible balance, but circumstances necessitated her playing it opposite an actor who would appear to best advantage as the male lead of a gently poetic play such as, say, something by Chekhov, Synge, or Yeats. And he made Tallulah's incandescent Blanche seem a bit too incandescent.

And now I want to tell you something about Tallulah that I think may convince you that the legend of great Southern ladies is not a myth.

No one could play the part of Flora Goforth in *The Milk Train* with the idea that being selected for the role was exactly a compliment to her, except as an actress of remarkable power.

Well, it's no secret that the play was presented last season on Broadway during the newspaper blackout and ran for only sixty-nine performances and cost its producers, including myself, a pretty tidy sum.

Now here is the lovely story about Tallulah and this play.

One evening before the production my phone rang in Key West.

"Tennessee, darling, I have read your new play and I would like to play it."

My answer? It was an occasion when I might have lied if I had time to think of a lie, believe me, but there was only time to either hang up the phone or speak the truth.

So I said: "Tallulah, I wrote it for you but it wasn't ready for you, so I tried it out in Spoleto with an English actress, Hermione Baddeley, and she was so terrific that I staggered into her dressing room, after the Spoleto opening, and said, 'Hermione, this play will be yours if you want it next season on Broadway.' "

What did Tallulah say? She said: "Well, darling, you did the right thing and that's that. But if it doesn't work because it isn't ready, well, you know me. And I know you wrote it for me and sometime I'm going to play it."

Well, it wasn't ready but now maybe it is, and though I have before me only a Coke laced with a bit of vodka instead of the finest champagne, I raise the glass to drink a toast to Tallulah, lady and star.

1963

GRAND

My grandmother formed quiet but deeply emotional attachments to places and people and would have been happy to stay forever and ever in one rectory, once her bedroom was papered in lemon yellow and the white curtains were hung there, once she had acquired a few pupils in violin and piano, but my grandfather always dreamed of movement and change, a dream from which he has not yet wakened in this ninety-sixth spring of his life.

Although he was married to a living poem, and must have known it, my grandfather's sole complaints against his wife were that she had no appreciation of poetry and not much sense of humor. "When we were quite young," he said, "I used to spend evenings reading poetry to her and she would fall asleep while I read"—which has sometimes made me wonder if her addiction to staying and his to going was the only difference which her infinite understanding had settled between them. My grandfather still is, and doubtless always has been, an unconsciously and childishly selfish man. He is humble and affectionate but incurably set upon satisfying his own impulses whatever they may be, and it was not until the last two or three years of their lives together that my grandmother began to rebel against it, and then it was for a reason that she couldn't tell him, the reason of death being in her, no longer possible to fly in front of but making it necessary, at last, to insist on staying when he wanted to leave.

When she married him she had not expected him to enter the ministry. He was then a schoolteacher and doing well at that vocation. He was a natural teacher, and soon after their marriage he was made head of a private girls' school in East Tennessee and my grandmother taught music there. At one time she had as many as fifty pupils in violin and piano. Their combined incomes made them quite well off for those days.

Then all at once he told her that he had made up his mind to enter the Church, and from that time till the end of her days my grandmother never again knew what it was to live without personal privation. During that interval the reverend and charmingly selfish gentleman would conduct par-

ties of Episcopalian ladies through Europe, deck himself out in the finest
clerical vestments from New York and London, go summers to Chautauqua
and takes courses at Sewanee, while my grandmother would lose teeth to
save dental expenses, choose her eyeglasses from a counter at Woolworth's,
wear at the age of sixty dresses which were made over from relics of her
bridal trousseau, disguise illness to avoid the expense of doctors. She took
eighteen-hour trips sitting up in a day coach whenever summertime or another crisis in her daughter's household called her to St. Louis, did all her
own housework and laundry, sometimes kept two or three roomers, taught
violin, taught piano, made dresses for my mother when my mother was a
young lady, and afterwards for my sister, took an active part in all the wom-
en's guilds and auxiliaries, listened patiently and silently through fifty-five
years of Southern Episcopalian ladies' guff and gossip, smiled beautifully
but not widely in order not to show missing teeth, spoke softly, sometimes
laughed like a shy girl although my grandfather often said that she wouldn't
know a joke if she bumped into one in the middle of the road, skimped all
year long—doing all these things without the aid of a servant, so that once
a year, in the summer, she could take the long day-coach trip to St. Louis to
visit her only child, my mother, and her three grandchildren which included
myself and my sister and our little brother. She always came with a remarkable sum of money sewed up in her corset. I don't know just how much, but
probably several hundred dollars—in spite of the fact that my grandfather's
salary as a minister never exceeded a hundred and fifty dollars a month.

We called her "Grand." Her coming meant nickels for ice cream, quarters for movies, picnics in Forest Park. It meant soft and gay laughter like
the laughter of girls between our mother and her mother, voices that ran up
and down like finger exercises on the piano. It meant a return of grace from
exile in the South and it meant the propitiation of my desperate father's
wrath at life and the world which he, unhappy man, could never help taking
out upon his children—except when the presence, like music, of my grandmother in the furiously close little city apartment cast a curious unworldly
spell of peace over all there confined.

And so it was through the years, almost without any change at all, as we
grew older. "Grand" was all that we knew of God in our lives! Providence
was money sewed in her corset!

My grandmother never really needed a corset and why she wore one I
don't quite know. She was never anything but straight and slender, and she
bore herself with the erect, simple pride of a queen or a peasant. Her family
were German—her maiden name was Rosina Maria Francesca Otte. Her
parents had emigrated to America from Hamburg, I suppose sometime in

the first half of the past century. They were Lutherans but my grandmother was educated in a Catholic convent and at the Cincinnati Conservatory of Music. I never saw my grandmother's father but he looks in pictures like Bismarck. I barely remember her mother, in fact I only remember that she was a spry little old lady who referred to scissors as "shears." About my great grandfather Otto I remember only that it was said of him that he declined to eat salads because he said that grass was only for cows, and that he had come to America in order to avoid military service. He made a large fortune as a merchant and then he lost it all. The last bit of it was exchanged for a farm in East Tennessee, and his farm had an almost legendary character in my grandmother's life.

My grandmother Rose was one of four children who scattered like blown leaves when the family fortune was gone. One of the two brothers disappeared and was never heard of again, and the other, Clemence, still lives in Mobile, Alabama, and must be near ninety. My grandmother had a sister named Estelle who married twice, first to a Tennessee youth named Preston Faller who died young and then to an older man named Ralston, a judge who had the dubious distinction of presiding over the famous Scopes trial in East Tennessee, which was known as the "Monkey trial." Once or twice, in the summer, "Grand" took us to South Pittsburgh, Tennessee, to visit "the Ralstons," about which I remember honey kept in a barrel on the back porch, hot sun on pine needles, and the wildness and beauty of my grandmother's nephew, young Preston Faller Jr., whistling as he dressed for a dance in a room that contains in my memory only a glittering brass bed and roses on the wallpaper and dusk turning violet at the open windows. But I was a child of seven and it is really only the honey in the barrel on the back porch that I remember very clearly, and the watermelons set to cool in the spring water and the well water that tasted of iron, and the mornings being such mornings! I do remember that Preston Faller Jr. would drive his stepfather's car without permission to other towns and stay nights and I remember that once he took me to a minstrel show and that there was an accordion played in this show, and that the keys or buttons of the accordion are remembered as diamonds and emeralds and rubies set in mother-of-pearl. Preston Faller Jr. now lives in Seattle and is doing well there and has sent us pictures of his house and his Cadillac car. And to think that he was such a ne'er-do-well boy! But he was the son of the sister of my grandmother—how time flies!—he's over fifty now . . .

I spoke a while back of my grandmother's inherited farm which her bankrupt parents had retired to in East Tennessee. Actually it was only about two hundred acres of rocky, hilly soil—well, maybe three or four hundred acres—but it was divided by inheritance among the two sisters, my grandmother and Estelle, and their only known living brother, Clemence. Estelle died early of asthma and an overdose of morphine administered by a confused country doctor, and so this legendary farm belonged to my grandmother and her brother and the children of her sister. It was administered by Judge Ralston, the widower of Estelle. I remember only two things about it, or three. One, that my great-aunt Estelle had to live on it prior to her first marriage and that she told my grandmother that she was so lonely that she used to shout hello on the front porch in order to hear an echo from an opposite mountain. Then I remember that some of the timber was sold for several hundred dollars and that the proceeds were passed out among all the inheritors like holy wafers at Communion. And then I remember, finally, that one time, probably after the death of Judge Ralston, my grandmother paid a valedictory visit to this farm, which she had always dreamed might someday prove to contain a valuable deposit of mineral or oil or something, and found that the old homestead had been reduced to a single room which contained an old female squatter. This ancient squatter could not satisfactorily explain how she came to be there on my grandmother's property. "We came by and stayed" was about all she could say. My grandmother inquired what had become of the large porch and the stone chimney and the other rooms and the female squatter said that her husband and sons had had to burn the logs for fire in winter, and that was what had become of the porch and other rooms, that they had disposed financially of the stones in the chimney, too. My grandmother then inquired where they were, these male members of the squatter household, and the finger-thin old lady informed her that the husband had died and that the sons had gone in town a year ago with a big load of lumber and had never returned and she was still sitting there waiting for them to return or some word of them . . .

That was the end of the story of the farm, which had meant to my grandmother an assurance against a future in which she thought maybe all of us might have need of a bit of land to retire to . . .

The one thing that my grandmother dreaded most in the world was the spectre of that dependence which overtakes so many aged people at the end of their days, of having to be supported and cared for by relatives. In my grandmother's case there were no relatives who had ever stopped being at least emotionally dependent on her, but nevertheless this dread hung over her and that was why she continued to keep house in Memphis long after she was physically able to bear it and only gave up and came to St. Louis a few months before her death.

Some years earlier than that, when she and Grandfather were living in

Memphis on his retirement pension of eighty-five dollars a month, I took refuge with them once more, after suffering a nervous collapse at my job in a St. Louis wholesale shoe company. As soon as I was able to travel, I took flight to their tiny cottage in Memphis and slept on the cot in the parlor. That summer I had a closer brush with lunacy than I had had any time since the shattering storms of my earliest adolescence, but gradually once again, as it had in those early crises, my grandmother's mysteriously peace-giving presence drew me back to at least a passable proximation of sanity. And when fall came I set out upon that long upward haul as a professional writer, that desperate, stumbling climb which brought me at last, exhausted but still breathing, out upon the supposedly sunny plateau of "fame and fortune." It began that Memphis summer of 1934. Also that summer, a turning point in my life, something of an opposite nature occurred to "Grand." Through the years, through her miracles of providence, her kitchen drudgery, her privations and music pupils and so forth, she had managed to save out of their tiny income enough to purchase what finally amounted to $7500 in government bonds.

One morning that memorable summer a pair of nameless con men came to call upon my fantastically unworldly grandfather. They talked to him for a while on the porch in excited undertones. He was already getting deaf, although he was then a relatively spry youth of eighty, and I saw him leaning toward them cupping an ear and giving quick nods of mysterious excitement. After a while they disappeared from the porch and he was gone from the house nearly all of that fierce yellow day. He came home in the evening, looking white and shaken, and said to my grandmother, "Rose, come out on the porch, I have something to tell you."

What he had to tell her was that for some unfathomable reason he had sold their bonds and transferred five thousand in cash to this pair of carrion birds who had called upon him that morning and addressed him as "Reverend" in voices of sinisterly purring witchery.

I see my grandmother now, looking off into dimming twilight space from a wicker chair on the porch in Memphis and saying only, "Why, Walter?"

She said, "Why, Walter," again and again, till finally he said, "Rose, don't question me any more because if you do, I will go away by myself and you'll never hear of me again!"

At that point she moved from the wicker chair to the porch swing and for a while I heard nothing, from my discreet position in the parlor, but the rasping voice of metal chain-links rubbed together as my grandmother swung gently back and forth and evening closed about them in their spent silence, which was, I felt without quite understanding, something that all their lives had been approaching, even half knowingly, a slow and terrible facing of something between them.

"*Why,* Walter?"

The following morning my grandfather was very busy and my grandmother was totally silent.

He went into the tiny attic of the bungalow and took out of a metal filing case a great, great, great pile of cardboard folders containing all his old sermons. He went into the back yard of the bungalow with this load, taking several trips, heaping all of the folders into the ashpit, and then he started a fire and fifty-five years of hand-written sermons went up in smoke. The blaze was incontinent. It rose far above the rim of the concrete incinerator, but what I most remember, more than that blaze, was the silent white blaze of my grandmother's face as she stood over the washtub, the stove, the kitchen table, performing the menial duties of the house and not once even glancing out of the window where the old gentleman, past eighty, was performing this auto-da-fé as an act of purification.

"*Why,* Walter?"

Nobody knows!

Nobody but my grandfather who has kept the secret into this his ninety-sixth spring on earth, and those rusty-feathered birds of prey who have gone wherever they came from—which I hope to be hell, and believe so . . .

I think the keenest regret of my life is one that doesn't concern myself, not even the failure of any work of mine nor the decline of creative energy that I am aware of lately. It is the fact that my grandmother died only a single year before the time when I could have given her some return for all she had given me, something material in partial recompense for that immeasurable gift of the spirit that she had so persistently and unsparingly of herself pressed into my hands when I came to her in need.

My grandfather likes to recall that she was born on All Souls' Day and that she died on the Feast of Epiphany, which is the sixth day of January.

The death occurred under merciless circumstances. Her health had been failing for the last five years till finally the thing she had always dreaded came to pass. She had to abandon and sell the home in Memphis and accept the shelter of my father's house in St. Louis because she was literally dying on her feet. Somehow she got through the process of pulling up stakes in Memphis, packing away possessions that had accumulated through sixty years of housekeeping and then that final eighteen-hour day-coach trip to St. Louis. But soon as she arrived there, with a temperature of 104, she collapsed and had to go, for the first time in her life, to a hospital. I was not anywhere near home at this time, the fall of 1943. I was doing a stint for a film studio in California. I got a letter from my mother giving me this news, that my grandmother was fatally ill with a malignant condition of long standing which had now affected her liver and lungs and placed a very brief limit to her remnant of life.

"Your grandmother," she wrote me, "has dropped down to eighty pounds but she won't give up. It's impossible to make her stay in bed. She insists on helping with the housework and this morning she did a week's laundry!"

I came home. It was a week before Christmas and there was a holly wreath on the door and somebody's next-door radio was singing "White Christmas" as I lugged my two suitcases up the front walk. I stopped half-way to the door. Through the frothy white curtains at the parlor windows I saw my grandmother moving alone through the lighted parlor like a stalking crane, so straight and tall for an old lady and so unbelievably thin!

It was a while before I could raise the brass knocker from which the Christmas wreath was suspended. I waited and prayed that some other member of the family, even my father, would become visible through those white gauze curtains, but no other figure but the slowly stalking figure of my grandmother, who seemed to be moving about quite aimlessly to a soundless and terribly slow march tune, a ghostly brass band that was playing a death march, came into view!

The family, I learned later, had gone out to that monthly business banquet of my father's world called the Progress Club.

My grandfather was in bed. "Grand" was waiting up alone to receive me at whatever hour—I had not wired precisely when—I might appear at the family door for this last homecoming of mine that she would take part in.

As my grandmother drew the door open in response to my knock, I remember how she laughed like a shy girl, a girl caught sentimentalizing over something like a sweetheart's photograph, and cried out, in her young voice, "Oh, Tom, oh, Tom!" And as I embraced her, I felt with terror almost nothing but the material of her dress and her own arms burning with fever through that cloth.

She died about two weeks later, after a spurious, totally self-willed period of seeming recuperation.

I left the house right after dinner that evening. She had washed the dishes, refusing my mother's assistance or my grandfather's or mine, and was at the piano playing Chopin when I went out the door.

When I returned only two or three hours later, the whole two-story house which we now occupied was filled with the sound of her last struggle for breath.

On the stairs was a stranger who had heard me knock before I discovered that I did have the key.

He said, with no expression, "Your mother wants you upstairs."

I went upstairs. At the top of the steps, where my grandmother's hemorrhage had begun, was a pool of still fresh blood. There was a trail of dark wet blood into the bathroom and the toilet bowl still unflushed was deep crimson and there were clotted bits of voided lung tissue in the bowl and on the tiles of the bathroom floor. Later I learned that this incontinent giving up of her lifeblood had occurred almost immediately after I had left the house, three hours ago, and still in her bedroom my grandmother was continuing, fiercely, wildly, unyieldingly, her battle with death, which had already won that battle halfway up the stairs . . .

I didn't dare enter the room where the terrible struggle was going on. I stood across the hall in the dark room which had been my brother's before he entered the army. I stood in the dark room, possibly praying, possibly only sobbing, possibly only listening, I don't know which, and across the hall I heard my mother's voice saying over and over again, "Mother, what is it, Mother, what is it, what are you trying to tell me?"

I only dared to look in. My mother was crouched over the figure of my grandmother on the bed, mercifully obscuring her from me. My grandfather was kneeling in prayer beside his armchair. The doctor was hovering helplessly over all three with a hypodermic needle and a bowl of steaming water and this or that bit of useless paraphernalia.

Then all at once the terrible noise was still.

I went into the room.

My mother was gently closing my grandmother's jaws and eyes.

Some hours later neighbors began to arrive. My grandfather went downstairs to let them in, and standing at the top of the stairs, I heard him say to them, "My wife is very weak, she seems to be very weak now."

"Walter will never face the facts about things," was one of my grandmother's sayings about him.

Then a year or so ago my mother happened to tell me that she had finally found out what my grandmother was trying to tell her as she died, but hadn't the strength to. "Your grandmother kept pointing at the bureau, and later I found out that she had her corset in there with several hundred dollars sewed up in it!"

1964

SLAPSTICK TRAGEDY: A PREFACE

During the long, long haul of work on a full-length play there are periods when I am obliged to read what I've been writing to see how it is or isn't shaping up. Almost invariably I am so disappointed or repulsed by what I read that I am unable, for a while, to continue work on it, to start a second, third, or fourth draft of the pachydermous project, and then, since I can't just stop working, I divert myself with some shorter project, a story, a poem, or a less ponderous play. These diversions are undertaken simply as that, as diversions, and they nearly always have a quality in common, which is experimentation in content and in style, particularly in style. The fatigue I felt before this escapade is lifted. I find myself enjoying my work again. The inside weather changes; even the outside weather seems to get lighter and brighter, and I am easier to live with, if anyone's living with me.

The Glass Menagerie was one of these diversions. Over a period of three or four years, whenever I tired of what I supposed were more professional projects, I would pick up and go on with the *Menagerie,* and it would refresh me, although I never believed it would be presented on Broadway. Another one of these diversions was *Camino Real.* A short sketch of that play was published in a paperback called *American Blues* and Elia Kazan happened to come across it and thought it would be fun to do as an Actors Studio exercise. As he and the actors played around with it, Kazan found himself becoming excited by its offbeat style, and when I came through New York, on my way to Rome, he suggested that I drop by the studio to see what Eli Wallach and two or three other highly gifted players had made of the sketch. I was truly amazed. Kazan had found precisely the right key of the little sketch and had invested it with his brilliantly inventive exuberance. Right then and there we decided to put it on Broadway, and I began to expand it into a full-length play.

Slapstick Tragedy is another one of these works that I've done with little thought of anything but self-amusement and relief from the long, long haul of making a full-length play. Last year I showed it to a producer, Charles

Bowden, and to my pleased surprise he felt very strongly that it could and should be produced, the two plays together under the title that fits them both.

I believe that the peculiar style of these two short plays is accurately defined by their mutual title. They are not "Theatre of The Absurd"; they are short, fantastic works whose content is a dislocated and wildly idiomatic sort of tragedy, perhaps a bit like the feature stories in that newspaper, *The National Enquirer*, which I think is the finest journalistic review of the precise time that we live in. The style of the plays is kin to vaudeville, burlesque and slapstick, with a dash of pop art thrown in.

So there you are. Where are you? It was not my idea to write a prefatory explication of these two plays that seem to be hard for most financial backers to understand except as "a play about cancer" and "a play about terrible birds." Categorically speaking, they are not about either, and I think, in production, they may seem to be a pair of fantastic allegories on the tragicomic subject of human existence on this risky planet.

1965

THE WOLF AND I

Some years ago in Rome I entered a restaurant with Anna Magnani and a lupo. A lupo means, literally, a wolf, but in Italy it is the name for a certain breed of dog that isn't a wolf but is next of kin to one, in temperament and appearance. We had hardly entered the restaurant when a waiter rushed up and said, "Oh, I have a young dog the same as yours, Miss Magnani! Would you like to see him?"

The young lupo was fetched out onto the piazza. It was a magnificent creature that acted as if it had just had a shot of adrenalin and Anna Magnani advised me to buy it, despite the fact that the waiter had no papers for it and had named it Satan.

I returned to America with Satan, whom I called the Wolf, taking it down to Key West where it seemed to get along well with my parrot, my English bull-bitch and her litter of eight puppies, not yet distributed as gifts to deserving friends.

The Wolf seemed to be the most devoted dog I'd ever had, so when I started out on a two-month tour of *The Night of the Iguana,* prior to its Broadway opening, I took him along with me, feeling that I might have need of his sympathetic companionship.

But dogs and wolves are uncannily perceptive of human moods. They often think that psychic disturbances are caused by and directed against themselves. They look and look at a tortured human face, trying to figure out what is going on behind it, but they almost always wind up saying to themselves; "I have done something wrong and he is furious with me."

Every evening during the long tour, the Wolf would sit directly in front of me while I hypnotized myself with late movies on TV. Every now and then he would nudge my knees or ankles with his black muzzle and I would took into his oblique yellow eyes, and think, "What a devoted creature, how on earth did I ever live without him?"

We were in the bleak theater town of Detroit, performing in a house that looked as if it had been condemned sixty years ago and the demolition crew had simply overlooked it. It was approaching the pre-Christmas slump, the weather was inexorably awful.

I hadn't had sinus trouble for a good ten years, but during our stay in Detroit I had a sudden recurrence of it, and one evening the discomfort, not to say agony, was so extreme that I phoned the hotel doctor, asking him to drop by at his convenience or sooner. He appeared about midnight. I described my symptoms, and he said, "Oh, you have sinus trouble and probably some fever." He then went into the bathroom to shake down his thermometer, leaving me with the Wolf. The Wolf was taking a suspicious interest in the hotel doctor's bag, which he had left in the bedroom. He was sniffing at the contents. Suddenly he went into a combination of panic and fury, sprang upon my bed and sunk his enormous fangs into both of my ankles. I cried out for help. The doctor and my secretary, Frank Merlo, somehow got the Wolf into the parlor and shut the door on him. Meanwhile I was bleeding copiously. The doctor looked at my ankles and said, "Oh, the Wolf has bitten you to the bone of each ankle," which was an astute and ac-curate observation. He immediately snatched out of his bag a metal appara-tus that looked like a stapling machine, drove metal clamps into my ankles to close the wounds, and then got out of there about as fast as he could.

At this time I was so concerned over the way the play wasn't going that I almost forgot the misadventure of the dog's attack, but late the next evening I was painfully reminded of it when I noticed that my ankles had swollen to nearly the size of an elephant's. I thought it appropriate to call the hotel doctor again, and about midnight of that evening he returned.

"Oh," he said in tone of surprise "you have a staphylococcic infection from the metal clamps in your ankles."

He then removed from his little black bag a huge syringe, the kind used on horses, and pumped me full of a combination of antibiotics.

A minute or two later I began to go into shock. My body started to cover itself with big goose-pimples and I had trouble catching my breath. The doctor seemed to recognize these symptoms of acute allergy and shock, and out of his bag he snatched another hypodermic needle and filled it with an anti-allergy fluid. He shot me with it, but it seemed to do me no good. I got out of bed and went to a window and raised it, hoping that I could breathe better. I was in shorts and it was snowing up a blizzard but I clung tenaciously to the ledge of that open window. I loved the sensation of the snow on my bare chest, it assured me that I was still living. But this relative euphoria was cut short when two men in white jackets entered the room and removed me more or less forcibly from the window to a stretcher. I had never been on a stretcher before nor had I ever before gone downstairs in the freight elevator of a large hotel. The novelty of both experiences did nothing to reassure me, and it was also a new experience to hear from inside an ambulance the wail of an ambulance siren. What I remember thinking in the ambulance is, "Oh, God, I guess I'm dying but I'd better not think about it, just keep on trying to breathe."

It was another new experience to find myself in the emergency ward of a hospital with other patients moaning and gasping around me, separated from view by white canvas curtains. I didn't moan or groan, but I kept on gasping. They gave me oxygen and counter-allergy shots and I was there for roughly three hours, still repeating to myself, "Oh, God, I guess I'm dying but I'd better not think about that." The hotel doctor had considered himself dismissed, but my dear friend and secretary Frank Merlo was still in attendance.

At about 3:00 A.M. I began to pull myself together. Then I insisted that I be taken upstairs to a private hospital room. The emergency doctor and nurse were strongly opposed to my being moved so soon after being in shock, but I had taken a shot or two from a whisky flask that friend Merlo had thought to bring along with him, and Merlo and I assured the medical attendants that I would recuperate more rapidly if I were not lying next to an accident victim who was noisily breathing his last few breaths on this kingdom of earth. At length the attendants conceded. I was wheeled upstairs to a private room, and Merlo, who seemed more exhausted than I by all these novel experiences of mine, told me good night. Then, being alone, I pushed a bell-button for a nurse and asked her for a sedative pill. She brought me one little pink capsule.

"Oh, no," I told her. "I'll need at least two of these."

"I'm sorry," she said, "but we are not permitted to pass out more than one to a patient who's been in shock."

I could only pretend to accept this situation until she had whisked back out of the room. Then I noticed that there was a phone by the bed and immediately called Merlo. I said, "Frank, I hate to get you up again, but they refuse to give me more than one sleeping tablet, so would you please get over here fast as possible with that little cardboard box with sedatives in it."

Frank rushed over with a wrong box and rushed back out before I discovered the mistake. It was then about 5:00 A.M., but I somehow managed to get out of bed and into my clothes, and I started shuffling down the corridor on my elephant ankles, intending to check out of the hospital with the least possible delay. Halfway down the corridor I was intercepted by a nurse who ordered me back to bed. This is a hospital, she told me, and not a hotel. I told her I preferred a hotel to a hospital, and continued on my way downstairs to the front desk, where I phoned for a taxi.

At best, this painful anecdote is only obliquely relevant to my present disinclination to go on tour, with or without a wolf. A pre-Broadway tour is very hard on a wolf and is torture to a playwright. We decided not to go out of town with *Slapstick Tragedy*. Two weeks of previews in New York at reduced prices has a peaceful sound to it.

Where is the wolf? He went to a veterinary in Detroit. I suggested to the veterinary that it might be wise to release the wolf in the forests across the Canadian border, but the veterinary felt there was only one safe solution and that was not it. Goodbye, wolf. . . .

1966

HAPPINESS IS RELEVANT

In a period play on which I sometimes work there is a girl, a high-school student, somewhat dismayed by the onset of romantic longings, who writes themes for her English class that impress her impressionable English teacher.

The English teacher urges the beautiful girl to forsake more frivolous matters and to devote herself to becoming a writer with serious intentions. The girl is sensibly unconvinced of the wisdom of this suggestion, and that evening she discusses it with a romantically handsome youth with whom she is in love.

"Perhaps I write pretty good themes, now and then, but I'm not sure I want to devote myself to being a serious writer. The only one that I know of in this town hanged himself last winter, yes, went about it very carefully, too. He knotted a strong rope about his neck, stood on a chair and kicked it across the room—the day after his dog died, poor man. I mentioned him to my teacher and I asked her if she thought that writers with serious intentions are happy people, and she gave me a very peculiar answer.

"She said: 'Happiness is irrelevant to the life of a serious writer.'

"Well . . . that writer I knew in this town, he made a sorry spectacle. On my way to school last winter I used to see him walking his elderly dog that was as gray as he was. We walked in opposite directions, and whenever he saw me coming toward him, he would cross the street with that elderly, solemn dog. I think he wanted to avoid passing me because he knew that I would look him in the face and wonder about him. One time, only once, we passed each other on the same side of the street, and I think that happened because he was in some deep meditation as gray as he and his dog. And it wasn't pleasant to pass him. He or his dog or both of them had a sour smell to them, as if you'd opened an icebox which hadn't been opened for a long time and had no ice in it, but did have in it some bits of forgotten food in a state of decomposition. No, no, not pleasant, and if my teacher is right and happiness is irrelevant to the life of a writer with serious intentions, why, then, that's something that I would rather avoid. . . ."

The youth whom she loved laughed lightly at her decision, and a moment later both of them started to sing a ragtime song that belonged to the period of the play.

I would say, if anyone asked me, that a writer of serious intentions doesn't choose his calling but has it more or less forced upon him as things are forced on people by something chemical in their bloodstream. A state of relative felicity, or its opposite, is relevant to all things that are organic by nature and still living. Only to the lifeless or mineral world is some kind of sensory well-being irrelevant, Miss English Teacher.

Why should we assume, for instance, as lumbermen have recently found it convenient to assume, that a giant tree, singing with leaves in the red woods of California, is a lesser being than we are simply because the biologists have told us that these ancient and beautiful trees are not afflicted with nervous systems like ours?

Convenient assumptions are too convenient, and to say more about that would be unwisely explicit.

After all, in this piece, I haven't scattered many idioms, to borrow a phrase from Hart Crane. Now I shall try to.

The other day I phoned my mother to see how she was keeping. "Son," she said, "I am coming up to see your play open, if it isn't closed out of New York. I have a lavender lace dress to wear, but I wish you would get me a short white feather boa and white elbow-length gloves, size 6."

What else?

José Quintero's mother may also come up to the New York opening of the play, which we trust will occur, and she will wear a white lace mantilla.

What else?

Not long ago I attended a party in New Orleans. I did not like the guests at my end of the parlor and so I thought I would disperse them. I closed my eyes for a couple of moments and then said gravely, "There is something about me that I think it would be unfair of me not to tell you. I am an octoroon."

I must have been in good form as an actor that evening, since in a minute or two I found myself agreeably alone and went out on the balcony to look over the mistily lovely night of the city and to remember some of the happy times I have had there.

It was in New Orleans that I wrote most of *A Streetcar Named Desire*. At that time I was under the mistaken impression that I was dying. I didn't feel that I could eat much, but in the evenings my only close friend would bring me a bowl of oyster stew and in the afternoons, when I had finished my work, I would go around the corner to a pleasant bar called Victor's and have myself a brandy alexander which I thought would give me strength to get through the rest of the day. It was a somewhat irrational idea, since after the brandy alexander I would always swim about fifteen lengths of the Olympic size pool at the New Orleans Athletic Club, but without that idea of imminent death I doubt that I could have created Blanche DuBois.

What put the moribund idea out of my mind was a visit by my grandfather who was over eighty and was determined to go to the many great restaurants of New Orleans. I discovered in these restaurants that I could eat more than oyster stews. Then I bought a Pontiac convertible and Grandfather and I drove about the parks in the afternoons and abruptly decided to take a trip in the car to Key West. Grandfather had made no concessions to age, so in Key West we swam daily in the Caribbean sea, and by this time I had discovered that I could eat chili, however spicy it was. Miriam Hopkins was there, peppering the scene with her fantastic wit, and there, too, was the divorced wife of Ernest Hemingway. Both of them took a great liking to Grandfather, who was a true cavalier with the ladies.

Every spring I would urge Grandfather to fly to Rome with me, and he would thank me effusively but say, "Oh, Tom, no. I want to be sure to be buried in Dakin's Corner, Ohio, beside your grandmother. She was born on All Souls' Day and she died on the Feast of the Epiphany."

No, he would never go to the loveliest city of the world, however much I assured him that if he should happen to die there, I would make sure that he would be buried in Dakin's Corner.

I once had a huge dog that could and would make you turn right or left according to his caprice. Now I have a little dog, a Boston terrier bitch. She does not have a clock or watch but she knows when it's time for her dinner and after lying perfectly still on the adjoining twin bed, she will get up and stare intently at the telephone, meaning that it's now time for me to call room service and request her bowl of hamburger. In Key West the large and numerous cats of the neighborhood used to make her trot briskly into the house, but now there seems to be a truce between the cats and Gigi. Once I entered the living room and saw Gigi at one end of the sofa and a big cat at the other, both of them staring directly before them. She is theatrical by nature, and in case you're interested, she is professionally represented by Ashley Famous and her modest terms are five grand a week plus twenty percent of the gross.

Happiness is relevant to her life.

1968

"TENNESSEE, NEVER TALK TO AN ACTRESS"

In a state of sobriety, I have always been more or less guarded or diffident in my relations with actresses: that is, with the exceptions of Laurette Taylor, who wouldn't tolerate diffidence in a playwright, and the great and dazzling and sometimes wrathful Tallulah Bankhead, whom I think it is appropriate to mention in the same breath with Laurette.

Let me tell you, at times a little obliquely, about encounters that were somewhat dismaying.

I recall how an actress of great talent and prestige summoned the director and me into her dressing room a short while before the play was to open on Broadway. We naturally obeyed the summons, and there she sat among her bushels of roses.

"At this point in an out-of-town tour," she told us, "I can always tell if a play is going to be well or poorly received in New York."

I assumed, innocently, that there was to be some reassuring pronouncement from the lady, but that was the way in which it didn't work out. After some breathlessly suspended moments of silence, she shook her head at us in negation of any hope for the play.

On other occasions it has been *I* that could be called the spokesman for the party of doom, which is a large and influential party.

Once, when (the incomparable) Mr. Kazan was directing one of my plays, I became panicky over the (irresistible) charm of the leading lady who was supposed to be portraying an unsympathetic part. To my astonishment, a loud and stricken voice rose from me.

"What is she doing? I didn't write this part for an ingenue."

The actress burst into tears and disappeared into the peripheral gloom of the New Amsterdam rehearsal hall. Mr. Kazan followed her and, after fifteen minutes of his silken whisper, the actress returned to the rehearsal stage.

Mr. Kazan said to me: "Tennessee, you must never talk to an actress."

Panic sometimes overtakes me at the first reading of a new play. This happened at the first (reading) rehearsal of *Sweet Bird of Youth*. When the reading had gotten into the second act of the play, I said to Mr. Kazan, "Gadg, I'd like to speak to you a moment."

"O.K."

He came down and sat next to me in the auditorium. I said to him: "Gadg, we've got to stop this thing right here, it mustn't go any further."

I believe he told me to go home and rest. In the evening he and his wife, Molly, came to my apartment and told me, persuasively, that I was just nervous because of my run-down condition, or something like that.

The rehearsals of the play were not discontinued and the play opened successfully on Broadway.

But I am supposed to be writing about my relations with actresses. I'm sorry I got off the track.

Must silence always follow the loss of a star? In my opinion, no.

A revival of *Streetcar* was having its initial opening at the Coconut Grove, Florida, Playhouse, and the brilliant, sometimes tempestuous star was Tallulah Bankhead. The opening night audience at the Coconut Grove Playhouse was out for a good, campy time, and Tallulah sensed the prevailing mood of her audience that night and gave them what they wanted, and what they wanted was not a delicate moth on the stage.

Following the performance there was a party on the bay-shore. I went to this affair and permitted myself a few drinks too many. When Tallulah and I encountered each other, she said to me, "Well, Tennessee, wasn't I the best Blanche you've ever had?"

I said: "No, Tallulah, the worst."

She didn't take that remark as a compliment. "Over that way is the bay," she told me. "Why don't you take a swim in it, straight out?"

This revival of *Streetcar* approached New York with several stops on the way. Despite my savage love for Tallulah, I didn't attend them, but the director, Herbert Machiz, told me that Tallulah worked with the strictest dedication to the inner truth of the part. What pleasure it gave me to say that she gave not an inch to the inescapable camp-followers when the revival opened in New York at the City Center!

(Could it be that Blanche is not as much a moth as she is a tigress?)

Tallulah once said to me: "You wrote all your plays for me except the one you wrote for that Italian." She may have been right about that, in a way.

I saw Diana Barrymore give a stunning performance in the part of

Blanche, too. When I went backstage, afterward, her costume was soaked with perspiration, as if she had been standing in it under a shower, and when I embraced her, I was frightened because her breast was heaving with such a dangerous intensity. I whispered to her manager, "Don't you think we'd better call a doctor?"

Gallantry! Of course, I mean hers, not mine.

I'm sad to admit that I'm still a bit "cagey" with actresses, and I suppose that confession makes you smile. During the rehearsals of my play *Kingdom of Earth,* I was stalking along a backstage corridor in the manner of Napoleon returning from Russia. The star, Estelle Parsons, came up alongside me and linked her arm through mine.

I said: "Oh, Estelle, actresses always hate playwrights."

"Hate?" she said, in a bewildered tone, as if it were a word in a language she didn't know.

Anne Meacham is another actress with whom I've had consistently pleasant relations. Why? Not because she is beautiful, which she is, but because there's nothing she won't say or do on a stage without any sign of embarrassment. She has a totally unconventional kind of elegance.

In spite of my unfailing good humor, you see, I can only write for a tigress.

Now about Maureen Stapleton, she's something else. One evening at dinner I found myself being dull to the point of catatonic, and to remedy that condition I took a goof-ball, washed down with a martini. This gave me a strange sensation and I thought my life was in imminent peril. I had several dinner-guests who were going to Maureen's. I went along with them and told Maureen what I had done. "Well, Tennessee," she said, "you had better have a glass of mustard and water. Go in the bathroom and I'll bring you the glass."

In times since the Roman empire, vomiting is supposed to be done in private, if possible, but I asked Maureen to stay in the bathroom with me while I conducted this experiment with the emetic effect of the mustard and water. I drank it down; no vomiting. "How was it?" Maureen enquired. "Delicious!" I told her, truthfully. "Well, if it was delicious, I'd better mix you another glass of it," she said. The second glass was as delicious as the first, and there was still no emetic effect. "I think you'd better try sticking a finger way down your throat," said Maureen. I took her suggestion and then, finally, the desired action occurred.

All this while a brilliant young actress in the living-room was talking with the subdued tone of an acetylene torch attacking a block of cement. When Maureen and I returned to the front room, I said to this very gifted young actress, a good friend of mine, "Honey, you've got a terrible voice problem."

Tears!—for herself or for me or for the world and all its inhabitants.

I recalled Mr. Kazan saying to me: Tennessee, you must never talk to an actress."

1969

WE ARE DISSENTERS NOW

During the great 1947 blizzard, just following the opening of *Streetcar,* the P.R. man for that vehicle requested of me a write-up on the subject of myself for release to "the media." (How lovely, that word "release," and how seductively pleasant to write yourself up instead of being written up (usually down) by others: but it's much more hazardous, too.)

This P. R. man said that "the media" were especially curious about my name, Tennessee, how I got that name and why and for what honest purpose, if any. It was as if they suspected me of "holding"—or of harboring a Pentagon code-book or a blueprint of its sewers. And the truth was so innocent and so agreeable to record, that my paternal forbearers, the Williamses and Seviers of East Tennessee, had been and still are the fiercely besieged defenders of stockades, savages charging them from all sides still.

("Jump, my bonnie Kate, jump!" And she did and he caught her and the blood went on. But upon another occasion one of Valentine's daughters was less fleet of foot, she was overtaken at the mountain spring and was scalped. And yet she survived the scalping. Bewigged for the rest of her long life, the blood went on and on. And some of it is still running on through my arteries this morning, shouting to you "Right on." "And Jack be nimble, Jack be quick, Jack jump over arithmetic!"—For America the Beautiful is computerized, now, and sold across the blue board which wasn't our dream.)

Halfway through that old ego-trip it occurred to me that it might be appropriate to offer some clue to my political feelings aside from such a phrase as "Huge cloudy symbols of a high romance" which would be stealing from a young dead poet which is worse than stealing from the old and blind. So this is what I said upon that delicate subject, not so delicate, then. I said that if someone should ask me what politics are I would answer that I am a (an) humanitarian. And this was true, I was full of affectionate feelings for the very old and even for some if not all of the young. (I distrusted and disliked most middle-aged folk, but did them no harm.)

However, now, I am no longer certain that it is enough to be humanitarian at heart, even though I know that to be humanitarian at heart makes a man quite subversive to the Pentagon's iced eyes.

I feel, now, that America the Beautiful is sick with killing . . .

About "them." You know who "they" are. I think they have geiger-counters to detect and measure the rebellion in you and if it reaches, if it even approaches a certain level, they whistle their blue boys down on you, they set fools' caps on your heads and stand you in a corner 'til class is dismissed and you're dead.

But right on.

Don't delude yourselves with the comfortable notion that you may not be a Lenny Bruce, too, or his sister, and pay your dues past broke and into the poke.

(How can he love Tom O'Horgan with a dead heart?)

We are repeatedly assured by those who think that reassurances are assurances that a Supreme Court Bench, sagging under the dead-ass weight of "strict constructionists," will never, never dream of denying us our right of heritage to write and speak and cry out freely; but that, boys and girls, is an old ballroom banana and don't buy it. Smell it and trust your olfactory sense and run right by it.

We're all dissenters now: and the heat is on.

This is not the time for the voice of the turtle to be heard in our land, and this is not the time for the voice of the cuckoo to be heard in our land.

I mean this is not the time for such voices, it is the time for the voices of *dissent* to be heard.

These voices must swell in number and not be repressed by terror of "patriotic" reprisal.

But that we must be prepared for, since we will get it.

It is not enough to be simply a humanitarian anymore, for humanitarians may be passive and this is no longer a time for passivity.

I will tell you something.

You don't have to spell America with a "k" to know the condition it's in. You merely have to think beyond and see through.

In the summer of 1940 I shared a verandah at a little hotel over the still-water beach of Acapulco, with a young man who was also a writer and who had just had to give up, because of wartime conditions, residence in what had been an island paradise of the Pacific. This young writer was the son of a top executive in a great American corporation. And yet he had somehow thought beyond that circumstance and seen through.

After a while he started talking to me like a guru on the verandah.

If you saw *Iguana* you know what verandah I am talking about; all along it were hammocks and back of each hammock was a little bedroom with a single white iron bed which occupied most of the interior space. The nights did not cool off till near morning and just off shore there was a tiny island almost completely preempted by an all-night *cantina*. The entertainment there was provided by a marimba band which played the stars out of the sky. And on our verandah the entertainment was drinking "rum-cocos"—and the talk of this young guru who was passionately concerned with social political problems and the intolerable inequities with which the Americas were diseased.

At a distance of thirty-one years, not all of his talk can be accurately reported here. But certain things stand out.

"Humanity is nailed to the two-armed cross of cupidity and stupidity."

He meant the cupidity of the profiteer-imperialists and the stupidity of their victims.

It was, I suppose, a quote from someone and I find a distasteful touch of elitism in it, now, since dialectical ignorance should not be equated with lack of intelligence.

But it was a dramatic image, so it stuck in my mind.

I remember still more his cool, cultivated voice explaining how things had gone wrong with "the American way" as it now existed.

In the beginning we had "frontiers" within our own territory, there was ample room for economic expansion to the West. Now those "frontiers" were exhausted or approaching exhaustion. More and more goods had to be sold at continually higher profit and the goods, the merchandise, had begun to be priced over the buying-capacity of a large part of the people. Consequently, big business, the voracious class of big merchants, had to move beyond our own territorial limits and find new economic frontiers in foreign lands. There was the birth of what is now called "economic imperialism" and it was democracy's death. For in order to protect those markets abroad, it became necessary, said my guru, to virtually invade and occupy foreign states.

And so the modern wars began, always for rhetorically noble purpose, but generally with the basic motive of the rich getting richer and the poor paying for it by something close to bondage. Of course, with young blood.

I know this interpretation has a simplistic sound to it, but truth is often found in the least sophisticated way of interpreting things. And, in the years since then, I have observed not a thing to cause me to doubt at all this simple analysis of what's gone wrong and rotten in our national *modus vivendi*.

I have no brief for any type of socialistic regime that imposes prejudice of race and repression of arts. But *our* kind of socialism when it comes (as it will, perhaps long after my time) will be an altogether new kind. It will have learned so many important lessons from its predecessors and it will not emerge from peasantry and slave-labor, exactly, but more from "the middle class."

An amusing thing happened to me a couple of weeks ago in the London dressing-room of a great English actor. The actor was receiving a visit from a star of the Bulgarian theatre. This visitor said to me, "You know, *Streetcar Named Desire* is being done in Moscow and Sophia now." I told him I'd heard about that and had also heard that Blanche did not go mad over there. "She goes mad in Bulgaria," he told me, "but not in Moscow." And I thought to myself, "Those Moscow cats must have a lot on the ball to keep Blanche in her right mind."

I can't *always* be serious . . .

About that word, that thing called dialectics. I came of age during the "Great Depression" and yet I had only a vague instinct about it, that thing, so formidable in sound, until a fellow-poet introduced me to a young leftist group in St. Louis that was called "The League of Artists and Writers," which met once a week at the Old Court House near the river.

My involvement with it was brief. One night I read them a sequence of love-lyrics and they laughed out loud and I silently and permanently stole away.

These were the years of "message" literature and my lyrics were neither literature nor message.

In the middle thirties I turned to writing plays. Obviously the rather lonely place that I occupied was not even then the ivory tower of an esthete, since my first long play was about the exploitation of Alabama coal miners, and the second about the desperation of derelicts in a flop-house.

At this time I was a student of drama at Washington University in St. Louis. There was an annual one-act play contest. My contribution was a fiercely satirical and, I think, rather eloquently written piece about a great munitions-profiteer: it was titled *Me, Vashya!* and it was far and away the best entry in the contest but it was only given third honorable mention. I was a terribly shy and modest boy at this time, but a mind-blowing fury seized me and I charged into the office of the drama Prof who had put my work down, and I shouted at the man so furiously that he literally blanched and quailed behind his desk.

It was as if Ma Barker had said to me: "Remember, you got to fight the bastards always, boys." And *he* was all of *them* . . .

I have known a certain lady, very closely for a long time, who is no younger than I am.

She has quite a number of eccentricities, some of which are amusing and all of which are poignant with her special sensitivity.

Among these odd ways is her habit, at frequent times, of thrusting her index fingers into her ears and looking attentively into space.

Once I asked her, "Why are you stopping up your ears. Rose?"

She gave me a look of surprise and she answered, with just a touch of reproof in her tone: "I am listening to the doctor in my ears."

While she is tuned in to this interior doctor, her face, still lovely and graced with that nobility that comes from much trouble proudly borne, will have various expressions, she will look desolate sometimes and shake her head. This means that "the doctor in her ears" has given her counsel of a kind that she had hoped not to hear. At other times she will nod happily, for "the doctor" has told her something pleasantly affirmative. Then she will look out the window of the hired car and wave to strangers, usually to children or young people, on the street.

Although we have much in common, I have a slightly different set of eccentricities. However, I also listen to an interior voice.

In the last few years it has kept urging me to forget all the hazards of crying or writing out those faiths that join me to my activist brothers and sisters.

This counselor in my heart has now told me where I am at . . .

Where I am at is where all of us are: the date is July 14, Bastille Day, in our lives, or the day just before that. We are gathered at the gates of such bastions of pig-dom as Attica and San Quentin and practically all other "correctional institutions" in that country, once shining with high purpose, which has been seduced and corrupted by The System to the point where its name is often spelled with a "k" as Kafka spelt it.

That's where we're at and we are facing state-troopers, those creatures from darker space whose faces are masked to give them the look of vicious magnified insects.

More than one side can cry "Charge!" and surely the side with love for and faith in humanity will finally prevail over those whose faith is only in death and whose love is a lust for blood.

1972

TOO PERSONAL?

The greatest danger, professionally, of becoming the subject of so many "write-ups" and personal appearances on TV and lecture platforms is that the materials of your life, which are, in the case of all organic writing, the materials of your work, are sort of telegraphed in to those who see you and to those who read about you. So, when you get to the serious organization of this material into your work, people (meaning audiences and critics—all but the few most tolerant whom you naturally regard as the best) have a sort of *déjà vu or déjà entendu* reaction to these materials which you have submitted to the cathartic process of your "sullen craft and art."

You may justifiably wonder why a man of my years in his profession, recognizing this hazard, has yet been willing to expose himself (with a frequency which seems almost symptomatic of clinical exhibitionism) to all of these interviews and the fewer, but equally personal, exposures on platform and "the tube."

I can offer you at least two reasons for this phenomenon. One is probably something with which you will immediately empathize. When one has passed through an extensive period of that excess of privacy which is imposed upon a person drifting almost willfully out of contact with the world, anticipating that final seclusion of the nonbeing, there comes upon him, when that period wears itself out and he is still alive, an almost insatiable hunger for recognition of the fact that he is, indeed, still alive, both as a man and artist. That's reason number one. The other is rather comical, I'm afraid. You get a devastatingly bad write-up, and you feel that you are washed up for good. Then some magazine editor gets through to you on that phone in the studio of your tropical retreat, the phone that you never pick up till it's rung so persistently that you assume that your secretary and house guests have been immobilized by nerve gas or something of that nature, and this editor speaks to you as sympathetically as the family doctor to a child stricken with a perforated appendix and tells you that he is as shocked as you were by the tasteless exposé-type of interview which appeared about

you in a recent issue of some other mag. And then, of course, you forget
about work, and you rage yourself into a lather over the iniquities and du-
plicities of the "interviewer" referred to. You say, "Why, that creature was
so drunk he didn't know what street I lived on, and the guy that set me up
for him laced my martini with sodium Pentothal, and all I remember about
this occasion is that my head came off my shoulders and hit the ceiling and I
heard myself babbling away like an hysteric and I hadn't the slightest notion
that he had a concealed tape recorder with him, and later he offered to play
bridge with me that night, and he came over again with the tape recorder in
some orifice of his body, I presume, and you know I do not see well and you
know I like to hold forth to apparently amiable listeners, and I just assume
that when they say 'I am interested only in your work,' that that's what they
mean."

Now the editor has you on the hook.

"That's exactly my reaction to the revolting piece and how about letting
us do a piece to correct it?"

You grasp at this offer like a drowning rat climbs on to anything that
will float it. So you get another write-up. Then after this write-up, which
is usually more colorful and better written than the one before, but equally
nonserious, if not downright clownish, you feel that it is a life-or-death matter, professionally, with a new play opening somewhere, to correct the hilar-
ious misquotes and exaggerations which embellished the second write-up,
and so you go on to others and others. Now at last you have poured out,
compulsively and perhaps fatally, all the recent content of your experience
which should have been held in reserve for its proper place, which is in the
work you're doing every morning (which, in my case, is the writing I do an
hour or so before daybreak).

Is it or is it not right or wrong for a playwright to put his persona into
his work?

My answer is: "What else can he do?"—I mean the very root-neces-
sity of all creative work is to express those things most involved in one's
particular experience. Otherwise, is the work, however well executed, not
a manufactured, a synthetic thing? I've said, perhaps repeatedly, that I have
two major classifications for writing: that which is organic and that which
is not. And this opinion still holds.

Now let me attempt to entertain you once more with an anecdote.

Long ago, in the early forties, I attended a very posh party given by the
Theatre Guild. I was comfortably and happily seated at a small table with
my dear friend Miss Jo Healy, who was receptionist at the Guild in those
days, when a lady with eyes that blazed with some nameless frenzy rushed

up to me like a guided missile and seized me by the arm and shrieked to me, "You've got to meet Miss Ferber, she's dying to meet you."

Now in those days I was at least pliable, and so I permitted myself to be hauled over to a large table at which were seated a number of Diamond T trucks disguised as ladies.

"Oh, Miss Ferber," shrieked my unknown pilot, "this is Tennessee Williams."

Miss Ferber gazed slowly up and delivered this annihilating one-liner:

"The best I can manage is a mild 'Yippee.' "

"Madam," I said, "I can't even manage that."

Now everyone knows, who is cognizant of the world of letters, that Miss Edna Ferber was a creature of mammoth productivity and success. She was good at doing her thing; her novel and picture sales are fairly astronomical, I would guess.

I bring her up because she represents to me the classic, the archetypal, example of a writer whose work is impersonal, at least upon any recognizable level. I cannot see her in the oil fields of Texas with Rock Hudson and the late James Dean. Nor can I see her in any of her other impressive epics. I see her only as a lady who chose to put down a writer who was then young and vulnerable with such a gratuitously malicious one-liner. I mean without provocation, since I had literally been dragged to the steps of her throne.

So far I have spoken only in defense of the personal kind of writing. Now I assure you that I know it can be overdone. It is the responsibility of the writer to put his experience as a being into work that refines it and elevates it and that makes of it an essence that a wide audience can somehow manage to feel in themselves: "This is true."

In all human experience, there are parallels which permit common understanding in the telling and hearing, and it is the frightening responsibility of an artist to make what is directly or allusively close to his own being communicable and understandable, however disturbingly, to the hearts and minds of all whom he addresses.

1972

HOMAGE TO KEY WEST

My attachment to the island of Key West dates back to 1941 when I sought solace there from the first important disaster in my profession.

At that time the social life was still affected by Ernest Hemingway's recent presence there. His second wife, née Pauline Pfeiffer, was still in residence that winter: she occupied their charming Spanish colonial house (which has now been converted into a museum where scandalous innuendos are whispered by the custodians about Mr. Hemingway's alleged profligate private life).

It was still a mecca for painters and writers in 1941. I met the poet Elizabeth Bishop and artist Grant Wood there that winter, and Arnold Blanch and his wife.

These things made no difference in Key West; perhaps they don't anywhere now.

There was a genteel boardinghouse called The Trade Winds which had up- and downstairs verandahs encircling the house with a belvedere on the roof, and was constructed of solid mahogany. It was operated by a *grande dame* from Georgia, a lady of great kindliness, humor, and charm, the late Clara Black. She was an Episcopal minister's widow and when I told her that I was the grandson of one, she suddenly remembered that she had a little shack in back of the house which could be converted into living quarters for me. She made it very attractive and even installed a shower; the rent was seven dollars a week.

And since she suspected that I was inadequately fed, she entertained me often at dinner.

Her daughter, Marion Black Vaccaro, became a very close friend of mine. The Vaccaro family of New Orleans, into which she had married, owned the Standard Fruit Company, but the husband was such an alcoholic that in order to get him off booze they had to put him on ether. When he entered my cabin, as he often did when on ether, I would be nearly anesthetized.

Unfortunately this family has passed away now, except for a brother of Marion's, George Black, who lives in Coconut Grove and I think that he will forgive me for these irresistible reminiscences.

Regis Vaccaro had a glass eye, and one night at dinner, for no apparent reason, he snatched it out of its socket and hurled it at Mrs. Black. It landed in her soup plate. Being a true lady, she made no exhibition of dismay at this rather Bohemian gesture. She simply fished the glass eye out of her soup and gave it to Marion in a soup spoon with the casual remark, "I think that Regis lost something."

And then there was the evening when the professional gamblers of Key West, wide open as a frontier town in those days, had threatened to shoot Regis down on sight if he didn't settle some enormous debt which he couldn't settle because his family kept him on a generous but limited allowance; we had to put him on the floor of an old Ford owned by a friend of mine and drive him off the Keys at breakneck speed after dark. The radiator started to leak but this did not phase Miss Clara. She had us fill it with sea water continually till we reached the safe distance of a friend's house in Coconut Grove.

This sort of thing was not then, and would not even be now, a particularly surprising incident in the social life of Key West.

It is still a haven for those who choose to drop out of conventional society.

It is now the final retreat of "the flower children," and Monroe County, to which Key West belongs, was probably carried by Senator McGovern.

Is there a new word for "hippies"? It hardly matters if there is or not, since they appear the same, and the main street of Key West, Duval, is almost preempted by them after midnight.

Very few of them are employed; they are very thin, almost emaciated, but with the inward serenity of young Buddhists.

One night I passed a young man leaning against a wall because he was too weak to stand unsupported.

"What's the matter, son?"

"I need a place to crash. You see, I just got back from South America where I got this amoebic dysentery thing."

"Have you been treated for it?"

"No, man, you know you can't be treated, just diagnosed if you're lucky, but with no bread, who is about to treat you?"

His large, translucent eyes, sunk in deep shadow, betrayed no disturbance over his circumstance.

Key West is like that. It always was and still is.

Sometimes I think most of the kids live on pure air, and the air is the purest I have breathed in the States.

There is still an artists' and writers' colony and there is still a great deal of indigenous, inbred eccentricity among the old "Conch" families of English origin, the first settlers.

Perhaps the preeminent writer is James Leo Herlihy, author of *Midnight Cowboy* and other distinguished novels.

There is a highly original architect, Dan Stirrup, whose style is a combination of Polynesian and contemporary. He did a kitchen for me with a stained glass window, which would have been suitable for a Catholic chapel. At first, I was distressed with a stained glass window in the kitchen, but then I found the morning light coming through it gave me an uplift for work.

There are still outstanding painters such as Edie Kidd and her late husband, Hari Kidd. I speak of him as still being here because his paintings live on in Edie's house beside the charming graveyard.

In winter, there is the explosion of the fantastic painter Henry Faulkner on the scene, never with less than a truck-load of dogs and cats. He seldom passes a police car or a fire station without shouting, "Hello, girls!"—Response? Surprisingly genial.

There is a fabulously successful silkscreen factory called Key West Fabrics. It was founded by a pair of youths who had served as escorts for the late great Tallulah Bankhead. She and Miriam Hopkins, who is also the late as well as the great, were among the important visitors in time past, which has a lovely habit of remaining time present in Key West.

I have entertained the great English director Peter Hall and his dancer wife in my little Key West compound, and at this very moment, my guest house is occupied by a veteran of Vietnam, twenty-five years old, who is the most talented young writer I have met in half a lifetime.

Remember the name: Robert Carroll.

I have mentioned the indigenous eccentricities of the Conches. The town has more than its fair share of recluses. On nights of full moon, ambulance and police sirens are heard almost as continually as the baying of dogs. . . .

Now please don't hurry down here: the island has finally run out of coral-rock extensions into the sea. Almost no one plays bridge and there is almost nothing at all to do but drink or swim or—.

1973

LET ME HANG IT ALL OUT

Much has been made in recent months of the fact that this year marks the silver anniversary of *A Streetcar Named Desire* which most people interested in my writing still regard as my best work for the theater. I am more inclined toward *Cat on a Hot Tin Roof,* that is, toward the play in its original and true form without the anticlimactic reappearance of Big Daddy in Act Three with nothing to do but to tell an off-color story about a male elephant being visibly influenced by the seasonal aura of a female elephant in the adjoining stall.

With that gratuitous bit eliminated from the play, along with the sentimentally ingenuous solution of the marital dilemma between Maggie and Brick, I feel that with this play of 1954–55 I went far as I was likely ever to go in my career as a playwright toward the mastery of that profession: It had a fairly large group of characters most of whom were created "in depth," as they say, and the remainder with sufficiently accurate detail, and the play ran without interruption in time for the exact course in which the curtain was up. And it was based upon what I believe to be the most important theme that I have essayed in my writing for the theater: the mendacity that underlies the thinking and feeling of our affluent society.

You may correctly argue that this same theme was often, if not obsessively, used by Ibsen, but I feel that it is a theme which is virtually inexhaustible and must be tackled again and again and again by playwrights in all centuries and countries until at least one thing is made perfectly clear for all time—man is by instinct not just a "hunter, lover and fighter," as Tom declared to the dismay of his mother Amanda Wingfield in *The Glass Menagerie,* but also the biggest liar among all creatures. In fact, I am not sure that it wasn't man among fish, birds, and mammals that first invented the lie, big or little, as well as laughter, big or little.

I have always been much concerned with the matter of lying and I can honestly say that it is a matter of considerable pride with me and of still more considerable embarrassment to the publishers of my forthcoming memoirs that I simply refuse to dissimulate the facts of my life—or of others, I might add.

Some people who remember *Cat* only for its more sensational aspects think it was a play about homosexuality just as some people, probably more or less the same bunch, persist in claiming that Blanche DuBois in *Streetcar* was really a drag queen. Well, such people pay the same price of admission to a play and are entitled to exercise their triviality of interpretation, if they so choose. It is not to anyone's detriment but their own.

Frankly, and at the risk of alienating some of my friends in Gay Lib, I have never found the subject of homosexuality a satisfactory theme for a full-length play, despite the fact that it appears as frequently as it does in my short fiction. Yet never even in my short fiction does the sexual activity of a person provide the story with its true inner substance. The story "One Arm" was the study of a social victim and of an emotional cripple, as well as a physical cripple, who grew into emotional completeness (an ability to return to love) only a day before his execution in a prison.

(Forgive the digression; it is characteristic of my awkward adventures in the field of non-fictional prose.)

Looking back upon *Cat* once more, it is strange to realize now that it was once considered to be a shocking play. During its Broadway run, one southern matron said to another, at intermission, "What an awful, what a disgusting play!" Her friend made no comment but after the play was over she said to matron number one, "If the play was so awful, why did you stay through it?" And matron one replied, "Oh, I just had to see what disgusting thing would come next."

And to return to the subject of *Streetcar,* I believe that play to be publicly favored chiefly for the vitality of its female protagonist, Blanche DuBois. She had about her an incendiary quality which exploded in her great cries of "Fire, fire!", and I believe it was this quality, this volatility of nature, that has carried the play along for twenty-five years and which I hope will sustain it through the straits and rapids of its forthcoming revivals on the East and West coasts.

I think a great deal will depend upon bringing out the humor in Blanche. She was really a very amusing, as well as pitiable, not-so-young lady, and I have seen her played with great wit as well as pathos last Spring at the University of Minnesota by a young actress named Debra Mooney. She made me howl with laughter at my own work to the indignation of some professors and wives who threatened to have me ejected from the university theater.

Noel Coward says you shouldn't laugh at your own lines. My answer to that one is that if you don't laugh at them, they are simply not very funny. (I am sure that Noel was just being British.)

I hope you'll permit me to pursue the subject of humor in my plays a bit further. It has always been an essential ingredient and the first to make this discovery was the greatest of all my great actresses, Miss Laurette Taylor. Without her discovery of humor in my portrait of Amanda, *The Glass Menagerie* would have been as evanescent as "the fiddle in the wings."

It is simply not in my nature as a dramatist to work without humor, no matter how desperate may be the fates and situations of the protagonists.

I have recently seen a West Coast revival of *Kingdom of Earth* (*The Seven Descents of Myrtle*) in which a good deal of editing had been done, and out of this operation, there emerged a play of such hilarity that once again the more serious-minded members of the audience made angry objections to my decibel of enjoyment.

Do I laugh too much? Do I take too much pleasure in my own use of humor? It would appear to be so, but in a life that has contained so much of a shadowy nature, I have learned that my safest place of refuge is in this very capacity to laugh my head off, in public or in private, and I am afraid that I am incorrigibly blessed or afflicted with this trait—that is, on practically all occasions except when making love or when the curtain comes down upon an opening night and the audience and the critics all appear to me as a single monolithic being whose face is distorted with fury and whose look is concentrated upon me with such a glaring intensity that it would wither an asbestos cabbage.

It is difficult to admit that one is being too garrulous upon the subject of one's self or one's work. In fact, it is almost the same as admitting the approach of senility.

My mother is now eighty-eight and she divides her time between a Spanish stucco house in a pleasant suburb of Saint Louis and a very posh sort of "retirement home" within the city limits. She has acquired, or rather I should say that she has increasingly developed, an inclination to talk and talk and talk, and nearly all of the talk is about matters relating to her "two boys," as she calls my brother and me.

Having bored you quite enough with talk about my plays, let me try to amuse you with an anecdote about Mother at the retirement home.

In the evenings she will descend to the ground floor and enter the dining room. And one recent evening she had not even emerged from the elevator when a lady of her generation cried out to her very loudly, "Not so loud, Mrs. Williams!"

"And, Son, I had not yet so much as opened my mouth," she exclaimed to me. My brother and I both laughed irresistibly at that one, since it is my brother's opinion, shared only with me, that "Miss Edwina" will still be talking for at least half an hour after she's laid to rest.

I can empathize very well with her discontent in a retirement home. Retirement may be a pretty word but not a pleasant condition. I have had to make a number of drastic changes in my own life to avoid a premature state of retirement.

In that pageant of a play, *Camino Real,* the most eloquent romantic of the lot delivers this sad but inescapable observation: "There is a passion for declivity in this world."

And yet he went on across "Terra Incognita" beyond an "Arch of Triumph" on which was perched an interested-looking buzzard.

In life, I would say there are two essential outcries, one of which is "Right On!" and the other "Cursed be he who first cries 'Hold! Enough!'"

1973

WHERE MY HEAD IS NOW AND
OTHER QUESTIONS

There comes a time in the life of an aging writer when he suspects that his work has practically been completed, and this is a time when, if he's a novelist or a poet, he will find himself picking up some early success of his and reading it over with a curious sense of reading the work of some other writer, and he is almost right about that despite the fact that it still bears his name as author. A playwright has the same sensation when he sees the revival of his best-known play at about this distance in time. In the case of *Streetcar,* the time is twenty-five years, a quarter of a century.

Naturally, he has the anxiety that it may seem "dated" since that awful term has been used against some of his more recent work, usually very unfairly in his opinion.

Of course, he has the same anxiety or shock when he looks at himself nowadays in the mirror while shaving.

Perhaps all I need to do is to thank all of you for still being interested in me—if you'll forgive me for the formal humility of that statement.

Having Faye Dunaway, Jon Voight, and Earl Holliman in *A Streetcar Named Desire* under the brilliant, young director, James Bridges, is not an occasion for me to take at all casually, and that is one thing, for sure.

I feel that the American theatre has been very gracious toward me in honoring the twenty-fifth anniversary of *A Streetcar Named Desire* with this production on the West Coast and on the East Coast with Rosemary Harris and James Farentino.

I regret that I can attend only the revival on this Coast. It coincides with my sixty-second birthday, and I simply no longer have the mobility of a jumping flea.

Regardless of a reduced state of mobility I intend (if you're interested in my intentions) to pay the Orient another call and continue on about the world till I reach southern Italy again, and there I plan or, at least, I hope to acquire by the Mediterranean sea a little farm on which to raise goats and geese and to bask in the warm sun and the warm spirit of a people I came to love so much twenty-five years ago.

Frankly, I find it a bit rough in the States and feel that I must absent me from their felicity for a while. My instinct has always been opposed to long stays in places not peaceful.

At the moment I am more interested in writing than in publishing or having further productions, but that is probably only the consequence of having gone through a Broadway production of *Out Cry,* which I honestly didn't think I would survive and am still not quite certain that I did.

Very often a period of rest is one of recuperation, and there is surely some significance in the fact that most of my present luggage on this trip that I'm undertaking consists of manuscripts not yet completed, which I intend to complete.

Intentions are sometimes delusions, but they are as necessary as breath.

So *en avant,* meaning right on.

I understand that you want from me about six hundred words, and, as I look at this piece of paper, I know that I have fallen short of that number.

Will you let me fill up a bit of space, then, shamelessly, with a quote from a poem of mine inscribed to D. H. Lawrence?

> I run, cried the fox, in circles,
> narrower, narrower still,
> across the desperate hollow,
> skirting the frantic hill—

1973

THE BLESSINGS AND MIXED BLESSINGS OF
WORKSHOP PRODUCTIONS

I surely hope that I have expressed my deep gratitude to the off-off-Broadway productions which sometimes seem the principal haven and support of serious American theater in these times, as well as my deep esteem for those artists of the theater who work in them, often for minimal pay, sometimes for none. I have been professionally and morally sustained by a number of these productions, most notably in recent months by a production of *The Two-Character Play* starring Maryellen Flynn and Bob Stattel under the direction of Bill Lentsch.

They read a script of this play which I called "The Bangkok Version" (because I had written it there) in my rooms at a New York hotel. I said to Bill, "If we cut a third out of this work, we'll have a major play." To Bob I said, "Take off ten pounds, young man." To dear Maryellen, words not sufficing, I offered an embrace. A few weeks later, under the work of these artists, that elusive play had a swift, clean-cut story line. Bob had lost the ten pounds and turned in a fine performance; and Miss Flynn—words suffice even less to describe her luminous opening performance at the little Quaigh Theater in the East Sixties.

As for Lentsch's staging—well, I thought, Providence has brought me a magically perceptive director, not only for this play but for any other difficult and neglected play I've written . . .

Then what, you may well ask, do I mean by the phrase "mixed blessings" in the title of this article?

I hope that the Dramatists Guild, a place on whose Council I now occupy with great pride, and my representative Bill Barnes of International Creative Management will add their say to mine about certain abuses, too flagrant to ignore, which are now being practiced to the discredit of that most vital part of our current American theater! To call a spade exactly that and not a teaspoon or a shovel, plays are now being "pirated" by certain managements off off Broadway. I trust that you know what I mean by pirated. They are being put on without the knowledge and permission of the playwright or representative. The playwright is offered no part in their casting, no glimpse of their design, no consultation on any artistic aspect of the surprise presentation. And they are being done without even a token payment of royalties.

Now, I can exist economically without these token payments, which may be one advantage of having been around *and* around so long; but there are many young playwrights who not only deserve some payment, however minimal, for their hard work but also may need it desperately in these stringent times.

To dispense with bushes and with beating around them, I feel justified in citing an experience last season when I was so unfortunate as to see a work of mine called *The Mutilated* subjected to exactly such mutilation. It was a "pirated" production. Neither my representative Mr. Barnes nor I had been informed of its impending production. It appeared to me that they had cast the play almost as mistakenly as they could. If a character was supposed to be ample of bosom, the actress was conspicuously flat-chested. If a gentleman was described onstage as having "red gold" hair, the actor was topped by a crop of raven tresses. Important scenes were visible only in fragments behind an upstage scrim heavily fretted with needless woodwork. Perhaps the performers were gifted, perhaps the director was gifted, but it seemed to me they had deliberately contrived to disguise their gifts. Their candles were hidden as a thief's pocket torch.

Now the saddest thing about this episode is that I had labored a couple of precious months rewriting *The Mutilated*—I think to it's considerable advantage—and if I had known there was to be an off-off-Broadway revival of it, I could have offered them what they could have called a "premiere." And certainly my participation in the casting and my supervision of the design might not have resulted in quite such a dismaying mishap at . . . I shall leave the playhouse unnamed in these pages at present.

A still more serious mishap threatened a more important work of mine off off Broadway. It is more serious because my objection to it might offend some members of the black race, to whom I am devoted (I hate to say that this nation appears to have distinguished itself by something historically infamous: I mean, of course, its generally wanton indifference to the fate of minority ethnic groups). I could not countenance the casting of a black actor in the role of Stanley Kowalski in *A Streetcar Named Desire*.

That play cannot be transposed from its true period of the late 1940s to that of the 1970s. It would ring false all the way through, as every serious "revivalist" of the work has understood—and so has kept it in the period when it was written.

In the 1940s it would have been totally implausible for Stella to have married a black, and unless the script of the play were drastically altered to suit this pointless and cynical purpose, it would be appallingly filled with insults to that heroic and noble people, the blacks, who have suffered the same brutal use in our past and to an extent in our present as have the American Indians.

I will not, I could not consent.

It is with great satisfaction that I have observed the rise of the negro as American artist in all fields with which I'm acquainted; at first, and still most notably, in the field of music; now also very notably in the fields of fiction and of drama, painting and journalism. I doubt that there exist many among these understanding and creative people who fail to agree with my objection to the insolent proposal of the management of the abortively projected *Streetcar '76* to proceed with their project.

The theater does not exist for the purpose of subverting truth. And I am still idealistic enough, where my profession is concerned, to believe that serious theater is spiritually dedicated to the representation of what we know of truth.

I once said that I had accepted the theater as religion. That is no longer quite so true. I mean that theater is no longer my *only* religion. I find myself continually closer to things which are extra-professional; to human relations and to an aroused social conscience and to "parapsychological phenomena."

It is not a thing easily articulated, but . . . now in my middle sixties I think and feel a great deal more of a mystical nature. Time runs out and whatever timelessness is—meaning non-corporeal existence—begins to demand much more consideration.

I realize that there has been a somewhat extravagant note in parts of this article. I don't like putting down honest efforts even when unsuccessful. But piracy is dishonest, especially when it results in such negligent treatment of works that require special delicacy of interpretation. It is like dispatching a box marked "Glass, Handle With Care" in a vehicle with a wheel missing over rough ground in a storm.

Of course it would be a calamity for all theater-lovers if an attack on this practice of pirating productions—a practise which I trust and believe is exceptional, as rare as it is disastrous—should be misconstrued as casting a cold eye at off off Broadway and showcase productions in general or per se. That would surely be throwing the baby out with the bath water: and quite the opposite of my intention in writing this piece for the *Dramatists Guild Quarterly.*

There is no present or imminent sign that Broadway is about to resume its old covenant with seriously creative experiment and innovation in the theater. The chief contemporary protagonist of that old covenant, Mr. Joseph Papp, is providing Broadway with something that makes me think of Custer's Last Stand. Of course he is not quite alone in his heroism. Such folk as Robert Whitehead, Charles Bowden, the Cronyns and Richard Barr show the same spirit in fewer houses.

There will always be two or three plays a season that will require the big-scale production: an *Equus* or a *Seascape* will need to be *first* produced with large expenditures that Broadway alone can provide. I stress first, meaning initially. Later these admirable works will be inherited by off off Broadway, where a public at least equally appreciative of their merits but financially unable (or conscientiously opposed) to meet the wildly inflationary costs of Broadway box office—*wow!*—one thing worse than the incomplete sentence, for which I'm notorious, is the interminable sentence.

I'm sure I have delivered the message, though . . .

Postscript: How fortuitous and heart-warming a thing has occurred! The lady who produced and played the lead in *The Mutilated* phoned me to offer unmistakably sincere apologies for the illicit aspects of the production, which she assured me were somehow accidental. However mystified I may still be by the lapse of communication till now with a living playwright—perhaps she'd sincerely thought me long dead and she'd not be the first to suffer that little misapprehension—her honest-to-God tears of contrition suffice to dismiss my sense of outrage.

I recall an old song with which my mother used to entertain her gentleman callers, she's told me, and with which she enchanted me in my youth:

Oh, dry those tears, Oh, calm those fears,
Life will be sunshine tomorrow!

(Meaning less overcast in the fairly close future.)

1976

I HAVE REWRITTEN A PLAY FOR ARTISTIC PURITY

A literary phenomenon of the Jazz Age was a hugely successful and atrociously bad novel titled *The Green Hat*. It was written by Michael Arlen, perhaps with the late and great Tallullah Bankhead in mind as the heroine of the stage or screen adaptation, since this heroine had many flamboyant mannerisms such as driving a yellow Hispano-Suiza about the late night, nearly dawn, streets of London, a vehicle rendered more notable by a long silver swan on its hood.

This Bankhead-type heroine gave the novel its title by wearing always a green hat when she was about to take on a new lover. She was a lady of high degree who had fallen not out of fashion, exactly, but out of respectable repute because on her wedding night, in Biarritz or Nice, her ideally handsome, youthful and well-born bridegroom, known as Boy Fenwick, I believe, leapt out of the bridal suite to his death on the stones of the courtyard below, which caused a considerable sensation, probably making headlines in two nations, mainly because of the heroine (Iris March) announcing to the press that "Boy died for purity" and declining to go into further details on this intriguing matter.

(Incidentally, I now recall that it was Katharine Cornell, not Tallulah, who appeared as Iris March on the stage: probably the sensational aspects of the novel disqualified it for the purer pretensions of the screen.)

"Boy died for purity." I bring that up, now, to introduce the subject of a semantic variance between the more popular concept of the word "purity" as it applied to Boy Fenwick's reasons for suicide on his wedding night, and the meaning that purity has for those who practice the literary or plastic arts, and I trust you to know it is the latter meaning of the word that concerns me in this piece. I have not died for purity, nor do I plan to, not in this age of penicillin and other antibiotics, but I have all but totally rewritten a play for that latter meaning of the word purity. In that latter meaning, the one affecting a work of art, purity means the disciplined excision from the work of those elements that are inessential or extraneous, and so by one agile leap I bring myself, and possibly you, directly to the stripping away of much inessential, distracting and often incredible material that somehow formed an accretion about the bare and true being of a play, *Summer and Smoke,* thereby turning it into one called *The Eccentricities of a Nightingale,* which is about to lave its premiere as a Broadway production.

This purifying process began back in 1951 during a Roman summer when I was working against time to remove from *Summer and Smoke* the many things which offended me before it went into rehearsal as an H. M. Tennant production in London. It was a radical piece of surgery that I performed. Away went the shooting of the elder Doctor John by Papa Gonzalez and the abrupt revolution of the young Doctor John's character as an act of redemption for his involvement in the aforementioned melodramatic event: in fact, no trace of the Gonzalezes remained, nor did any of what's-her-name—it happily escapes me—after the redeemed hero has conquered the Cuban fever and been received at the town depot with a brass band as the spiritually transmogrified erstwhile wastrel he's now become. Also gone is the cockfight at Moonlake Casino and John's drunken assault on Miss Alma's puritan virtue—which won out . . .

I arrived in London with what I considered, quite correctly I think, was practically a new work excavated from the moldering debris of its predecessor. As usual I was met at the airport by my longest-surviving friend of the female gender, then a young actress under contract to H. M. Tennant, Maria Britneva, now known non-professionally as the Lady St. Just. When I told her that I had arrived with a work purified of all but its humor, poetry and passion, though retaining a pair of protagonists known as Miss Alma and Dr. John, she had to deflate my elation with the news: "But we are already deep into rehearsals with *Summer and Smoke.*"

Observing my crestfallen look, she said, "Oh, never mind. Give me the new play and I'll put it safely away till—"

She didn't specify when, but some ten or fifteen years later, over a preprandial cocktail, she produced *The Eccentricities of a Nightingale,* which I had actually forgotten by that time. "I'm going to put this in your overcoat pocket and I want you to read it tonight if you're sober enough," she informed me. It looked very pretty, all in pale blue type, and I was so happy with it that I read it through non-stop that night.

Space, not time, is of the essence, I believe, and so I now leave it to you who must be its true mentors, at the Morosco on Tuesday.

And now, if any of you still wish to know what Iris March meant in her enigmatic, unqualified assertion, "Boy died for parity"—well, it seems that this young gentleman, famed for impeccable virtue among all friends, was actually afflicted with syphilis and he had taken that dive out the window of the bridal suite to avoid infecting his bride.

One good turn deserving another, she kept his dreadful secret into her early grave. Not so Michael Arlen. He turned it into an atrociously bad novel which became, predictably, a runaway best seller, and he, at least, lived more or less happily, or at least nattily, ever after.

1976

I AM WIDELY REGARDED AS
THE GHOST OF A WRITER

Of course no one is more acutely aware than I that I am widely regarded as the ghost of a writer, a ghost still visible, excessively solid of flesh and perhaps too ambulatory, but a writer remembered mostly for works which were staged between 1944 and 1961.

Of course this is a matter of some chagrin to me and also of some exasperation since I have remained continually a living and practicing writer all this time since. I suspect that what happened is that after *The Night of the Iguana* in 1961, certain radically and dreadfully altered circumstances of my life compelled me to work in correspondingly different styles. There has surely been sufficient exposure in print of my misadventures in the 60's for that subject to be no more than mentioned at this point.

The plays by which I was known in the middle 40's through the first year of two of the 60's were categorized as works of "poetic naturalism." In their written form as well as in their staging, most notably by Elia Kazan, these plays, except for *Camino Real,* were of practically the same genre as say, Arthur Miller's *Death of a Salesman* or William Inge's *Come Back, Little Sheba.*

Once his critics, his audience and the academic communities in which his work is studied have found what they consider a convenient and suitable term for the style of a playwright, it seems to be very difficult for them to concede to him the privilege and necessity of turning to other ways. He truly must make these departures from his past ways, for just as his life has encountered a sudden deviation from its previous course, as if he'd suddenly confronted a wall of fire, his work must follow him in the frantic efforts he makes to go past this flaming barrier.

If his motive impulse in writing is the root-impulse of expressing the present conditions of his life, his world, his work must either be abandoned right there or it must take the dangerous course of reflecting his private panic and cry it out to all who will listen and try to understand.

I went on with my life and I went on with my work and am still going on with them both.

But my dreams are full of alarm and wild suspicion. The world about me seems hostile: I react to unimportant defects and half-imagined slights with an indignation, sometimes exploding into fury not wise in a man with vascular problems. To choose a somewhat amusing incident, Key West's newest and most adventurous dramatic group, the semi-pro Greene Street Theater, quite recently put on a generally admirable production of one of my favorite and most difficult works, *The Eccentricities of a Nightingale*.

I attended the opening and soon became so annoyed by technical deficiencies (no fireworks projected on the scrim, no bells and horns at midnight of New Year's Eve, a rather large white turkey feather instead of a sweeping plume on Miss Alma's rebellious hat) that I stalked out of the theater without a word to actors or director and elbowed my way ungraciously through the genial audience about the doors. An acquaintance asked me, "How'd you like the actors?" and I replied snappishly, "I thought they showed a great deal of endurance and so did I!"

Of course I detest this sort of behavior and tried to make up for it by excessive effusions to the leading lady whom I encountered at a restaurant the next day. I told her not to wait to be cued by other players but "Get off the fly-paper, honey, and just fly, fly, fly!", snapping my fingers so rapidly and loudly that two waiters rushed to the table.

Most of the confidence which I appear to feel, especially when influenced by noon wine, is only a pretense. In my heart an inscrutable bird of dark feather seems to have built a nest which I can never quite dislodge, no matter how loudly I cackle or widely I grin.

Perhaps I've expressed this better in a passage of a poem I worked on last night when I was unable to sleep:

> *The negative. Oh once*
> *I did attempt to speak but what I spoke*
> *seemed to confuse you more. I think I said*
> *'I am a furtive cat, unowned, unknown,*
> *a scavenging sort of blackish alley-cat*
> *distinguished by a curve of white upturned*

at each side of its mouth, which makes it seem to grin
denial of its eyes: the negative, unhomed . . .

I wonder how many of you will feel that I'm indulging in self-pity and how many will feel that I am simply trying to tell you how it is.

1977

THE MISUNDERSTANDINGS AND
FEARS OF AN ARTIST'S REVOLT

Why do they exist, upon what plausible basis, from what do they spring?

No rational, grown-up artist deludes himself with the notion that his inherent, instinctive rejection of the ideologies of failed governments, or power-combines that mask themselves as governments, will in the least divert these monoliths from a fixed course toward the slag-heap remnants of once towering cities.

They are hell-bent upon it, and such is the force of their unconscious deathwish that if all the artists and philosophers should unite to oppose them, by this opposition they could only enact a somewhat comical demonstration, suitable for the final two minutes of a television newscast: desperate farmers driving their pigs and goats up the stately Capitol steps would be scarcely more consequential.

Everywhere tiny bands of terrorists Begin the beguine. In the year 2013 it has been estimated that world population will be doubled. And then?

We do not wish to destroy. We are powerless to prevent.

Young, we may shout: we receive no reply but an echo.

Old, we know, and know better. . . .

In our maturity and our age, what is there for us to do but to seek out places of quiet in which to continue our isolated cave-drawings.

Surely this is known, if anything is known by the monoliths in their (mindless or inscrutable) ongoing.

The question becomes a useless repetition.

Why the misunderstandings and why the fears?

It seems that somehow fear can exist in a monolith with a deathwish: they may not want it spoken by those who still have tongues.

Perhaps we have mentioned some dangerous deceptions, in our time, and so are regarded as criminal offenders. . . .

What implements have we but words, images, colors, scratches upon the caves of our solitude?

In our vocations, we own no plowshares that we can beat into swords, and in our time, swords are used only for gentlemanly fencing in sports clubs or by actors in swashbuckling epics of the screen.

In a California interview I remember once making a statement that has, in retrospect, a somewhat pontifical ring, but the essential meaning of which I'm not inclined to retract. What I said was that civilization, at least as a long-term prospect, had ceased to exist with the first nuclear blasts at Hiroshima and Nagasaki.

I have heard it said that multitudes of "American lives" were saved by these barbaric actions.

And yet I have also heard (I believe it has been officially acknowledged) that the Japanese were attempting to negotiate an all but unconditional surrender before our military command (including the genial Mr. Truman) chose to play games with our new toy, the kind of toy that belonged in, and never should have emerged from, the Devil's workshop, a toy that may eventually extinguish all intelligent life yet known to exist in the expanding (or contracting?) bubble of the cosmos.

Through my studio skylight, no sign of daybreak has appeared, but workhours have grown shorter.

With the providence of luck—redundancy deserved—I'll continue after. . . .

After?—Some hours of sleep and now again, through the skylight of my studio which, half seriously, I call "The Madhouse," another morning's ineffable beginning, pale, very pale, but apparently unclouded. Very soon, I suspect, the rising sun will reveal once again the fathomlessness of blue.

Beginning again, it is the word "Patience" that comes into my head, and what it means to artists in revolt.

By digging in and under, they may pursue their vocation of still giving you words which they hope contain truths.

Hope? I believe they still have it.

I believe they believe more hopefully than their rulers.

Especially when they are old.

They observe while they can, the confused, the fatally wrong moves of men not often evil, themselves, but forced by vested power to give support to evil.

It would seem that our childhood myths of One called God in constant combat with one called Lucifer were an ingenuously incarnated but none the less meaningful concept of the all-pervading dilemma.

It has been said by a sophist that truth is at the bottom of a bottomless well.

Many things have been said that have the ring of a clever epigram: fashionably cynical, yet of what use?

Oh, so many, many things have been said in a tone of graceful defeat. . . . And there is no misunderstanding nor fear of that tone and those sayings.

And so I presume to insist there must be somewhere truth to be pursued each day with words that are misunderstood and feared because they are the words of an Artist, which must always remain a word most compatible with the word Revolutionary, and so be more than a word.

Therefore from youth into age I have continued and will still continue the belief and the seeking, until that time when time can no longer concern me.

1978

MISCELLANY

A Reply to Mr. Nathan (1945)

I have been at this writing game for over ten years now, seven of which have been spent for the most part pretty uncomfortably in the theatre, but for the first time in those years I have come upon a printed comment on work of mine about which I find it impossible to keep a dignified silence. I kept a dignified silence—well, I hope it seemed dignified—about all the charges hurled at an earlier play of mine *Battle of Angels*—I did not answer any of them, including Mr. Nathan's comment in *Esquire* that it was "a cheap sex-shocker"—I am quoting exactly. It may seem strange that I have waited till a play has been praised more lavishly than I ever dreamed any work of mine could be praised—to break this habit of saying nothing in response. The reason is simply that all previous comments have been expressions of opinion but on this occasion, today's article by Mr. Nathan, some statements are made which are not in the realm of opinion but are total misrepresentations and of a sort to seriously compromise my character as a writer if they are accepted as true. Truth is something that I have set up as my single standard, both as a writer and as an individual—this may sound like a very pompous statement and you may think me a very pompous young man for saying it—but I do say it with all earnestness, and will repeat it as often as I am given occasion such as the present.

It will simplify matters for me to quote directly from Mr. Nathan's article the statements which I declare to be untruthful.

They are the following:

"Originally written by Tennessee Williams as a rather freakish experiment and replete with such delicatessen as moving picture titles of silent drama days thrown intermittently on the scenery, it has been metamorphosed under Dowling's guidance into the unaffected and warming simplicity that it should have had in the first place."

This is the first and least offensive of Mr. Nathan's charges.

I would be the last to deny Mr. Dowling's excellence as a director and am second to no one in praising him as a producer of creative plays.

It is true that in the original script I suggested—not insisted—upon the use of magic lantern slides to serve at intervals, carefully chosen, as a sometime satirical and sometimes poetic counterpoint to the dialogue and to sustain the narrator's point-of-view even when he was not present on the stage, for these slides were the narrator's own commentary on what was taking place. I was perfectly willing, made no objection whatsoever, to the removal of this device from the production and I don't regret its removal, for the extraordinary power of Miss Taylor's performance which, I and nobody else had quite anticipated, made this play a play where that performance should be set as a pure jewel in the simplest of all possible settings.

But Mr. Nathan says "replete with such delicatessen" which surely implies that the play contained other such devices. Mr. Nathan, what other devices, or "delicatessen," are you referring to? The script will soon be published as originally written and I will be grateful to anyone, including Mr. Nathan, who can point out the other "delicatessen" that it is "replete with." Scripts can be examined before publication by visiting me or my agent, Audrey Wood, or the stage-manager at the Playhouse and I personally will award a week's royalties—not an inconsiderable sum!—to anyone whosoever succeeds in locating the rest of this "delicatessen" in any script of the play including the one which originally came from my typewriter. More than most scripts, *The Glass Menagerie* has remained in production as it first came to the producer. There has been extraordinary fidelity to the original script, and for that I thank Mr. Dowling and my own determination to keep it so. One scene was added to the show during the Chicago run and that is Mr. Dowling's drunk-scene. This scene was altogether of my own composition, also, though sometimes variations in its performance have taken place—small variations of performance are nothing to quibble about when a play has been projected as faithfully as this one has been.

But Mr. Nathan's next charge is far more disturbing to a character who has really only survived these last five years because he was possessed of an ability to see the humorous along with the sad in existence.

Mr. Nathan says: "Deficient in *any* touches of humor, since Williams forthrightly confesses himself to be a playwright with none, it has been embroidered under that same guidance with suggested flashes of humor."

Let's stop there. To whom, Mr. Nathan, have I ever made this remarkably damaging confession? Certainly never to you!

I have been writing and publishing short comedies for five or six years now, plays which have elicited free and abundant laughter both in reading and performance, and I am happy to cite some of those plays printed since 1940, especially, *The Last of My Solid Gold Watches, The Lady of Larkspur Lotion,* and the one shortly to appear called *Twenty-seven Wagons Full of Cotton*—all in Margaret Mayorga's yearly collections of one-act plays published by Dodd-Mead.

Unless Mr. Nathan means that none of the lines in the play are amusing in themselves, I don't know how to interpret his remark. There are no lines in the play not written by myself, not of my own conception, except the final line of the narrator which I have already cited and which is not altogether the line I would have chosen to end the play with but which I allowed to stand in deference to others' judgment.

Which brings me to the most serious charge of all and the particular one which has elicited this first response to a critic.

"Its narrator character," says Mr. Nathan, "originally the routine wooden compere, has *similarly* been *rewritten* into some living plausibility; and little touches, like, for example, the final illumination of the grinning father's portrait, the final tossing of the play to the audience's imagination, etc., have transformed the script into a medium over which the arts of the theatre can and do play their most hypnotic colors."

The word "rewritten" has only one meaning and that is a fairly strict one. It does not mean "interpreted," it does not mean "acted," it does not mean "produced." It means literally "rewritten." And that I declare to be wholly and completely untrue! There is no line in the script of this play, with the one exception of Mr. Dowling's final line as narrator—"Here's where my memory stops and your imagination begins"—, which is not entirely of my authorship and proof of this statement may be obtained from all who read the play prior to its production and who followed it during that period. I suggest going directly to Laurette Taylor or Mr. Dowling themselves for confirmation of my own word on this subject.

It is not Mr. Nathan's charge that my script was "replete with delicatessen" or his charge that I am a writer without a sense of humor—it is the out and out falsity of the charge that my script has been "rewritten" that has called forth this reply and has aroused in me a feeling of ire the like of which I cannot recall since that remote day in my childhood when the bully on the block seized my red tissue-paper kite and plunged his fist through it just when I was about to give it the first time to the sky!

Mr. Nathan I take this occasion of telling you that you have made me very, very, very, very—*MAD!*

An Appreciation: The Creator of The Glass Menagerie Pays Tribute to Laurette Taylor (1946)

I do not altogether trust the emotionalism that is commonly indulged in over the death of an artist, not because it is necessarily lacking in sincerity but because it may come too easily. In what I say now about Laurette Taylor I restrict myself to those things which I have felt continually about her as apart from any which this unhappy occasion produces.

Of course the first is that I consider her the greatest artist of her profession that I have known. The second is that I loved her as a person. In a way the second is more remarkable. I have seldom encountered any argument about her preeminent stature as an actress. But for me to love her was remarkable because I have always been so awkward and diffident around actors that it has made a barrier between us almost all but insuperable.

In the case of Laurette Taylor, I cannot say that I ever got over the awkwardness and the awe which originally were present, but she would not allow it to stand between us. The great warmth of her heart burned through and we became close friends.

I am afraid it is the only close friendship I have ever had with a player.

Gallantry is the word that best fits those human qualities which made Laurette Taylor so intensely lovable as a person. I do not think it is realized how much she sacrificed of her personal comfort and health during the year and a half that she played in *The Glass Menagerie*. She remained in the part that long because of a heroic perseverance I find as magnificent as her art itself. It is not necessary to mention the mistaken reservation some people had about her ability to remain long with a play.

But Laurette was painfully aware of that reservation and was determined to beat it. She did. She was neither a well nor strong person at any time during the run of the play and often continued her performance when a person of ordinary spirit would not have dared to. Even when throat trouble made it painful for her to speak she continued in her demanding part and I have never seen her physical suffering affect the unfailing wonder of her performance.

It is our immeasurable loss that Laurette Taylor's performances were not preserved on the modern screen. The same is true of Duse and Bernhardt, with whom her name belongs. Their glory survives in the testimony and inspiration of those who saw them. Too many people have been too deeply moved by the gift of Laurette Taylor for that to disappear from us.

In this unfathomable experience of ours there are sometimes hints of something that lies outside the flesh and its mortality. I suppose these intuitions come to many people in their religious vocations, but I have sensed them more clearly in the work of artists and most clearly of all in the art of Laurette Taylor. There was a radiance about her art which I can compare only to the greatest lines of poetry, and which gave me the same shock of revelation as if the air about us had been momentarily broken through by light from some clear space beyond us.

The last word that I received from her was a telegram which reached me early this fall. It was immediately after the road company of our play had opened in Pittsburgh. The notices spoke warmly of Pauline Lord's performance in the part of Amanda. "I have just read the Pittsburgh notices," Laurette wired me. "What did I tell you, my boy? You don't need me."

I feel now—as I have always felt—that a whole career of writing for the theatre is rewarded enough by having created one good part for a great actress. Having created a part for Laurette Taylor is a reward I find sufficient for all the effort that went before and any that may come after.

An Appreciation of Hans Hofmann (1948)

Hans Hofmann is one of the few contemporary painters who have actually taken a step forward in a significant direction. Many others are what is called "advanced" but instead of actually advancing they have made various little private excursions leaving tracks like those of fieldmice in a thin sheet of snow. I do not mean that Hofmann has made a solitary advance but that he walks abreast of the few who have likewise contributed to what progress has been made. His step is in logical sequence to the historical advance of such a painter as Van Gogh who infused the ideas of the Impressionists with a revolutionary vision, and if Vincent were alive today I think he would see in Hans Hofmann a logical inheritor of his passion for seeing more deeply.

The forward step is easily distinguishable from the lateral excursions. It has the authority of pure vision. Van Gogh had that. Picasso has it. And Hans Hofmann also has a place with those giants who move straight into the light without being blinded by it.

It is a relief to turn from the reasonably competent and even gifted painters who paint as if their inspirations were drawn from Esmeralda's Dream-book to this bold and clearheaded man who paints as if he understood Euclid, Galileo and Einstein, and as if his vision included the constellation of Hercules toward which our sun drifts. In his work there is understanding of fundamental concepts of space and matter and of the dynamic forces, identified but not explained by science, from which matter springs. He is a painter of physical laws with a spiritual intuition; his art is a system of co-ordinates in which is suggested the infinite and a causality beyond the operation of chance.

Now at the beginning of an age of demented mechanics, all plastic art is created under a threat of material destruction, for even at the base of the pigment are the explosive elements of the atom. Hans Hofmann paints as if he could look into those infinitesimal particles of violence that could split the earth like an orange. He shows us the vitality of matter, its creation and its destruction, its

angels of dark and of light. Philosophically his work belongs to this age of terrifying imminence, for it contains a thunder of light from the source of matter.
Pure light, pure color, the pure design of pure vision may alone be philosophically indestructible enough to retain our faith, no matter what else falls in ruin,
even our honor and endurance, until the time when truth can come out of exile
and it is no longer dangerous to show compassion and the world is once more
habitable by men of reason.

An Allegory of Man and His Sahara:
The Sheltering Sky by Paul Bowles (1949)

After several literary seasons given over, mostly, to the frisky antics of kids,
precociously knowing and singularly charming, but not to be counted on for
those gifts that arrive by no other way than the experience and contemplation
of a truly adult mind, now is obviously a perfect time for a writer with such a
mind to engage our attention. That is precisely the event to be celebrated in the
appearance of *The Sheltering Sky*, Paul Bowles' first novel.

It has been a good while since first novels in America have come from men
in their middle or late thirties (Paul Bowles is 38). Even in past decades the
first novel has usually been written during the writers' first years out of college.
Moreover, because success and public attention operate as a sort of pressure
cooker or freezer, there has been a discouraging tendency for the talent to bake
or congeal at a premature level of inner development.

In America the career almost invariably becomes an obsession. The "get-
ahead" principle, carried to such extreme, inspires our writers to enormous
efforts. A new book must come out every year. Otherwise they get panicky, and the first thing you know they belong to Alcoholics Anonymous
or have embraced religion or plunged headlong into some political activity
with nothing but an inchoate emotionalism to bring to it or to be derived
from it. I think that this stems from a misconception of what it means to be
a writer or any kind of creative artist. They feel it is something to adopt *in
the place of* actual living, without understanding that art is a by-product of
existence.

Paul Bowles has deliberately rejected that kind of rabid professionalism.
Better known as a composer than a writer, he has not allowed his passion for
either form of expression to interfere with his growth into completeness of personality. Now this book has come at the meridian of the man and artist. And, to
me very thrillingly, it brings the reader into sudden, startling communion with a
talent of true maturity and sophistication of a sort that I had begun to fear was

to be found nowadays only among the insurgent novelists of France, such as Jean Genet and Albert Camus and Jean-Paul Sartre.

With the hesitant exception of one or two war books by returned soldiers, *The Sheltering Sky* alone of the books that I have recently read by American authors appears to bear the spiritual imprint of recent history in the western world. Here the imprint is not visible upon the surface of the novel. It exists far more significantly in a certain philosophical aura that envelopes it.

There is a curiously double level to this novel. The surface is enthralling as narrative. It is impressive as writing. But above that surface is the aura that I spoke of, intangible and powerful, bringing to mind one of those clouds that you have seen in summer, close to the horizon and dark in color and now and then silently pulsing with interior flashes of fire. And that is the surface of the novel that has filled me with such excitement.

The story itself is a chronicle of startling adventure against a background of the Sahara and the Arab-populated regions of the African Continent, a portion of the world seldom dealt with by first-rate writers who actually know it. Paul Bowles does know it, and much better, for instance, than it was known by André Gide. He probably knows it even better than Albert Camus. For Paul Bowles has been going to Africa, off and on, since about 1930. It thrills him, but for some reason it does not upset his nervous equilibrium. He does not remain in the coastal cities. At frequent intervals he takes journeys into the most mysterious recesses of the desert and mountain country of North Africa, involving not only hardship but peril.

The Sheltering Sky is the chronicle of such a journey. Were it not for the fact that the chief male character, Port Moresby, succumbs to an epidemic fever during the course of the story, it would not be hard to identify him with Mr. Bowles himself. Like Mr. Bowles, he is a member of the New York intelligentsia who became weary of being such a member and set out to escape it in remote places. Escape it he certainly does. He escapes practically all the appurtenances of civilized modern life. Balanced between fascination and dread, he goes deeper and deeper into this dreamlike "awayness."

From then on the story is focused upon the continuing and continually more astonishing adventures of his wife, Kit, who wanders on like a body in which the rational mechanism is gradually upset and destroyed. The liberation is too intense, too extreme, for a nature conditioned by and for a state of civilized confinement. Her primitive nature, divested one by one of its artificial reserves and diffidences, eventually overwhelms her, and the end of this novel is as wildly beautiful and terrifying as the whole panorama that its protagonists have crossed.

In this external aspect the novel is, therefore, an account of startling adventure. In its interior aspect, *The Sheltering Sky* is an allegory of the spiritual adventure of the fully conscious person into modern experience. This is not an enticing way to describe it. It is a way that might suggest the very opposite kind of a novel from the one that Paul Bowles has written. Actually this superior motive does not intrude in explicit form upon the story, certainly not in any form that will need to distract you from the great pleasure of being told a first-rate story of adventure by a really first-rate writer.

I suspect that a good many people will read this book and be enthralled by it without once suspecting that it contains a mirror of what is most terrifying and cryptic within the Sahara of moral nihilism, into which the race of man now seems to be wandering blindly.

A Movie by Cocteau . . . :
The Diary of a Film *by Jean Cocteau* (1950)

It is hardly possible to discuss any work of Jean Cocteau without discussing the man himself, for his work is more than usually associated with the public and private character of its creator. The private character of Jean Cocteau, certainly with his consent if not his eager participation, has become an almost totally public one.

In Europe where there exists the Bohemian tradition, accepted and sometimes honored, this exhibitionism has done his reputation no great damage. If his attitudes, artistic or philosophic, have been remarkably flexible, following almost directly along the predominant fashions of more than three decades of avant-gardism, this probably strikes the French, with their realistic and mobile temperament, as a clever and amusing if not a totally admirable quality in the man. As for the rumors of opium-smoking on yachts along the Côte d'Azur and similar irregularities of behavior—well, the French have not forgotten Rimbaud and Verlaine and Baudelaire. The middle-class Frenchman does not approve of such antics, particularly when they occur more or less in public, but he sensibly concludes that poetry itself is a deviation and *chacun à son goût.*

Yet even in Paris one feels the increasing pressure of forces in society that wish to extend their regimentation over the arts. And there is astonishingly little awareness of the fact that this is, basically, a totalitarian point of view. To recognize the ultimate aim of it, one needs only to consider the sterilization of the arts in Fascist nations before the war and the pathetic apology of Shostakovich for not adhering, musically, to what the commissars of culture regard as healthy, wholesome and "positive" in music.

Cocteau's *Beauty and the Beast* is one of the great films to come out of Europe since the war. Its greatness lies mostly in its pictorial values and these, of course, are more attributable to the late Christian Bérard, who did the sets and costumes, than to the author of this "diary." The décor of the film is lavishly baroque. Visually it has an extraordinary luster which I suppose some people would define as "the phosphorescence of decay."

I prefer to think of it as the remembered radiance of that state of innocence in which fairy tales were read and which they wear in our recollection. Like most fairy tales it is basically a parable of good and evil. Compassion and humility are shown in conflict with cruelty, avarice, pride. Beauty, who represents purity of heart, releases the Beast from his evil enchantment: the brutal and arrogant forces are brought to shame: the Beast, resuming his original form of Prince Charming, ascends to some unearthly kingdom with the lovely instrument of his release.

The baroque grandeur of Bérard's visual effects is perfectly mated with the febrile sensibilities of Cocteau, and the result is a film that ranks in poetic and plastic values with Eisenstein's *Alexander Nevsky*.

The diary should be of enormous interest to anyone concerned with the technique of filmmaking, for Jean Cocteau has developed into one of the master craftsmen of the film and this is a fully documented account of how a great film was put together against the enormous odds of the time in which it was made and the personal vicissitudes of the producer-director.

This brings me to what I think is the great and exceptional value of the little volume: its study of the passionate sort of discipline that is involved in creative work, the willpower and the endurance that are demanded. Jean Cocteau is not an "enfant terrible." "Terrible," perhaps, but certainly no longer "enfant." The chronology of his career could only belong to a man who is pushing sixty. Yet when you meet him, you are amazed to find no trace of ennui. He has the youthful exuberance that must have belonged to Rimbaud when he first arrived in Paris, and, mind you, this is after thirty-odd years of leadership in the literary-Bohemian world of Paris which even now he shows no symptom of relinquishing.

During the filming of *Beauty and the Beast* Cocteau was plagued by boils which "nearly drove him mad," a nettle rash which turned out to be eczema, abscessed teeth, swollen eyes, lymphangitis, phlegmon on the neck, impetigo, bronchitis, a strike of the sound technicians and a terrible carbuncle suffered by the leading man, Jean Marais. This is a partial list of difficulties which beset him. Still, the film was made and it is a film of almost flawless quality. Its limpid surface, fluid and effortless as the flow of a dream, bears no reflection of the trials and torments which attended the making of it.

One suspects more than a dash of hypochondria, of psychosomatic ills, in Cocteau's account of what he went through while working on the picture. It is all right to smile now, for the picture is finished. But the smile should be sympathetic, since the accomplishment was just as great as the struggle.

The Human Psyche—Alone:
The Delicate Prey and Other Stories by Paul Bowles (1950)

Paul Bowles is a man and author of exceptional latitude but he has, like nearly all serious artists, a dominant theme. That theme is the fearful isolation of the individual being. He is as preoccupied with this isolation as the collectivist writers of ten years ago were concerned with group membership and purposes. Our contemporary American society seems no longer inclined to hold itself open to very explicit criticism from within. This is what we hope and suppose to be a transitory condition that began with the Second World War. It will probably wear itself out, for it is directly counter to the true American nature and tradition, but at the present time it seems to be entering its extreme phase, the all but complete suppression of any dissident voices. What choice has the artist, now, but withdrawal into the caverns of his own isolated being? Hence the outgrowth of the "new school of decadence," so bitterly assailed by the same forces that turned our writers inward? Young men are writing first novels with a personal lyricism much like that exhibited in the early poems of the late Edna St. Vincent Millay, a comparison which is disparaging to neither party nor to the quality itself. For what is youth without lyricism, and what would lyricism be without a personal accent?

But Paul Bowles cannot be accurately classed with these other young men, not only because he is five or ten years older than most of them but because, primarily, a personal lyricism is not what distinguishes his work. His work is distinguished by its mature philosophical content, which is another thing altogether. As I noted in a review of his first novel, *The Sheltering Sky,* Bowles is apparently the only American writer whose work reflects the extreme spiritual dislocation (and a philosophical adjustment to it) of our immediate times. He has "an organic continuity" with the present in a way that is commensurate with the great French trio of Camus, Genet, and Sartre. This does little to improve his stock with the school of criticism which advocates a literature that is happily insensitive to any shock or abrasion, the sort that would sing "Hail, Hail, the Gang's all Here" while being extricated, still vocally alive, from the debris of a Long Island railroad disaster.

But to revert to the opening observation in this review, Paul Bowles is preoccupied with the spiritual isolation of individual beings. This is not a thing as simple as loneliness. Certainly a terrible kind of loneliness is expressed in most of these stories and in the novel that preceded them to publication, but the isolated beings in these stories have deliberately chosen their isolation in most cases, not merely accepted and endured it. There is a singular lack of human give-and-take, of true emotional reciprocity, in the groups of beings assembled upon his intensely but somberly lighted sets. The drama is that of the single being rather than of beings in relation to each other. Paul Bowles has experienced an unmistakable revulsion from the act of social participation. One may surmise in him the social experience of two decades. Then the withdrawal is logical. The artist is not a man who will advance against a bayonet pressed to his abdomen unless another bayonet is pressed to his back, and even then he is not likely to move forward. He will, if possible, stand still. But Mr. Bowles has discovered that the bayonet is pointed at the man moving forward in our times, and that a retreat is still accessible. He has done the sensible thing under these circumstances. He has gone back into the cavern of himself. These seventeen stories are the exploration of a cavern of individual sensibilities, and fortunately the cavern is a deep one containing a great deal that is worth exploring.

Nowhere in any writing that I can think of has the separateness of the one human psyche been depicted more vividly and shockingly. If one feels that life achieves its highest value and significance in those rare moments—they are scarcely longer than that—when two lives are confluent, when the walls of isolation momentarily collapse between two persons, and if one is willing to acknowledge the possibility of such intervals, however rare and brief and difficult they may be, the intensely isolated spirit evoked by Paul Bowles may have an austerity which is frightening at least. But don't make the mistake of assuming that what is frightening is necessarily inhuman. It is curious to note that the spirit evoked by Bowles in so many of these stories does *not* seem inhuman, nor does it strike me as being antipathetic.

Even in the stories where this isolation is most shockingly, even savagely, stated and underlined the reader may sense an inverted kind of longing and tenderness for the thing whose absence the story concerns. This inverted, subtly implicit kind of tenderness comes out most clearly in one of the less impressive stories of the collection. This story is called "The Scorpion." It concerns an old woman in a primitive society of some obscure kind who has been left to live in a barren cave by her two sons. One of these deserters eventually returns to the cave with the purpose of bringing his mother to the community in which he and his brother have taken up residence. But the old woman is reluctant to leave her cave. The cave, too small for more than one person to occupy, is the only thing in reality that she trusts or feels at home in. It is curtained by rainfall and it is full of scorpions and it is not furnished by any kind of warmth or comfort, yet she would prefer to remain there than to accompany her son, who has finally for some reason not stated in the story decided to take her back with him to the community where he has moved. The journey must be made on foot and it will take three days. They finally set out together, but for the old woman there is no joy in the departure from the barren cave nor in the anticipation of a less isolated existence: there is only submission to a will that she does not interpret.

Here is a story that sentimentality, even a touch of it, could have destroyed. But sentimentality is a thing that you will find nowhere in the work of Paul Bowles. When he fails, which is rarely, it is for another reason. It is because now and then his special hardness of perception, his defiant rejection of all things emollient have led him into an area in which a man can talk only to himself.

The volume contains among several fine stories at least one that is a true masterpiece of short fiction—"A Distant Episode," published first in *Partisan Review*. In this story Paul Bowles states the same theme which he developed more fully in his later novel. The theme is the collapse of the civilized "Super Ego" into a state of almost mindless primitivism, totally dissociated from society except as an object of its unreasoning hostility. It is his extremely powerful handling of this theme again and again in his work which makes Paul Bowles probably the American writer who represents most truly the fierily and blindly explosive world that we live in so precariously, from day and night to each uncertain tomorrow.

Notes on the Filming of The Rose Tattoo (1952)

In a heavy drama the censorship problem is much more serious than in a play that is primarily a comedy such as *Tattoo*. The basic values of *Tattoo* are its warm humanity and its humor and its touching portrayal of a woman's devotion to her husband and daughter. Unless humanity itself has begun to fall under the censor's ban, there should be no serious difficulty in making a film out of this play that will not in any way violate either the story or essential truth of the characters *or* the code.

I have not yet seen the Breen office memoranda on the story but I assume that the major objection will be Serafina's sleeping with Mangiacavallo. This is not essential to the story and can be avoided in the way that I briefly suggested to Mr. Wallis at our recent conference at Paramount Studios.

The long scene between Serafina and Mangiacavallo is played about the same as the stage version up to the point where he, to deceive the neighbors, shouts goodbyes and parks his truck on the other side of the block. This, incidentally, can be an hilariously effective scene on the screen where we could, of course, use an actual banana truck. Mangiacavallo's devious return to the house by back alleys and fences, assaulted by neighborhood dogs, stirring panic among roosters and hens, mistaken for a prowler and even shot at by a patrolman or neighbor, all this can be made into a marvelously funny sequence and prepare for the comic denouement that follows. By the time he has made his way back to the house he has fortified his valor with several big slugs from a bottle of Grappa. He enters the house as before, by the back door, and the lights have been turned out by Serafina who is panting to surrender herself in the parlor. But as he approaches her he embraces a dressmaker's dummy, knocks it over, lunges forward again. As Serafina opens her arms to receive him, he takes a terrific dive, falling flat on his face immediately short of his objective. To revive him she empties over him the water in a vase of roses, shakes him vigorously, applies artificial respiration, all to no avail. He smiles and mumbles "Mama" and passes back into happy oblivion. At last she despairs and hauls him with difficulty to a couch or daybed, or, finding that impossible thrusts a pillow under his head and throws a blanket over him and let's him lie there in some part of the house where he will escape Rosa's attention when she goes to bed. Then, with a profound sigh of regret, Serafina retires alone to her bedroom and in the final shot of the night, after some hesitation, she gets to her knees with her beads.

The scene between Rose and sailor Jack will also be greatly enhanced by the spatial freedom of the film. As neither's chastity is violated, there will be no serious censorship problem in the scene.

As a poetic transitional shot, I think we should see a great wind pushing open the door of the parlor and billowing the window curtains, lifting and whirling the spilt ashes of Rosario and the scattered rose leaves on the floor.

The morning sequence need not be altered at all except in some lines of the dialogue between the mother and daughter.

The scene where Assunta (and I hope the casting and playing of this role will be altogether different from the one on the stage) discovers that the ashes have blown away can be given great poetry and beauty on the screen and it can be built into the important metaphysical or mystic sign that persuades Serafina that Mangiacavallo is indeed the new rose of her heart since he has sprung from the ashes of the old one.

The re-lighting of the vigil light can also be given more emphasis through a close shot on the screen.

As I discussed with Mr. Wallis at our conference, I think the screen story should revert, in the opening sequences, to the original version of the stage play, in which Rosario actually appears and an exciting action sequence can be made out of his shooting and crash on the highway. The original stage version contained, as I mentioned, a highly dramatic scene in which Estelle Hohengarten comes to the Belle Rose house and is locked on the front porch while Rosario plays the electric piano to drown out her voice. Audrey Wood can provide a copy of this first draft of the stage play containing that material.

The censorship problem is not the really important problem in translating this work to the screen. The great problem is an artistic one, and I think the approach to the filming of *Streetcar* has demonstrated the great advantage of being faithful to the artistic concept of the original as opposed to an attempt to "popularize" the material, to appeal on a lower level. This was attempted disastrously in the case of *The Glass Menagerie*. The poetic mood of the play was almost totally lost in the screen version and consequently the picture failed. In *Streetcar* that mood was preserved, and the film play was even better than the play on the stage. In the case of *The Rose Tattoo* the transference to film can and certainly ought to prove a much greater enhancement than it did with *Streetcar*. The stage imposed merciless limitations on what was really the most valuable new aspects of *Tattoo*. This was a play that was built on plastic-poetic elements, and only the barest glimpse of these was provided in the Broadway production. Consequently many people missed altogether what was most original and distinguished in the play on paper. Many of the audience and critics had the mistaken idea that the community life, the Strega, the goat, and crowd scenes and the activities of the children were meant only to fill in and distract the eye. Very few seemed to realize that all of these were an integral part of the artistic conception of the play, that this was a play built of movement and color, almost as much as an abstract painting is made of them. This is arty talk. But what I am talking about is not "artiness" but something very rich and alive and universally appealing. *The Rose Tattoo* should have been a riotous and radiant thing but the spatial limitations of the stage and the limits of time, etc., put it in a straight-jacket and only about two-thirds of its potential appeal came through. In transferring it to the screen, the producer should make sure that the full advantage of his medium is being used. The wild play of the children, the Dionysian antics of the goat's escape and capture, the crazy Strega, the volatile life of the primitive neighborhood, the church, the chanted Mass, the organ music, the simple mysteries of the faith of a simple people, the surrounding earth, and sea, and sky, the great trucks thundering along the highway, the scarlet kite, all of these poetic-plastic elements that were only suggested in fitful, awkward fashion on the stage can be fully exploited to enormous advantage on the screen, and whether or not this is done—and it certainly can be done—is a much more important problem affecting the screen version than the unimportant adjustments that would have to be made to satisfy "the code."

A Tribute from Tennessee Williams to "Heroic Tallulah Bankhead" (1956)

To the considerable and lively controversy about Tallulah Bankhead as Blanche DuBois, in the recent City Center revival of my play, *A Streetcar Named Desire*, I would like, "just for the record," as they say, to add my personal acknowledgment, praise and thanksgiving for what I think is probably the most heroic accomplishment in acting since Laurette Taylor returned, in the Chicago winter of 1944-45, to stand all her admirers and her doubters on their ears in *The Glass Menagerie*.

I have loved all the Blanches I've seen, and I think the question of which was the best is irrelevant to the recent revival. Several weeks ago, on the morning after the opening in Coconut Grove, Miami, Fla., the director and I called on Miss Bankhead in her boudoir where this small, mighty woman was crouched in bed, looking like the ghost of Tallulah and as quiet as a mouse. I sat there gravely and talked to her with the most unsparing honesty that I've ever used in my life, not cruelly, on purpose, but with an utter candor. It seemed the only thing that could save the situation.

If you know and love Tallulah as I do, you will not find it reprehensible that she asked me meekly if she had played Blanche better than anyone else had played her. I hope you will forgive me for having answered, "No, your performance was the worst I have seen." The remarkable thing is that she looked at me and nodded in sad acquiescence to this opinion.

Contrary to rumor, I never stated publicly, to my sober recollection, that she had ruined my play. What I said was phrased in barroom lingo. I was talking to myself, not to all who would listen, though certainly into my cups. But that morning, after the opening, Tallulah and I talked quietly and gently together in a totally truthful vein.

She kept listening and nodding, which may have been an unprecedented behavior in her career. The director and I gave her notes. I went back that night, and every note she was given was taken and brilliantly followed in performance. I left town, then, because I knew that I had hurt her deeply (though for her good) and that she would feel more comfortable without me watching her work.

I doubt that any actress has ever worked harder, for Miss Bankhead is a great "pro," as true as they make them. I think she knew, all at once, that her legend, the audience which her legend had drawn about her, presented an obstacle which her deepest instinct as an artist demanded that she conquer, and for those next three weeks she set about this conquest with a dedication that was one of those things that make faith in the human potential, the human spirit, seem far from sentimental: that give it justification. Think for a moment, of the manifold disadvantages which I won't name that beset her in this awful effort! She had only two weeks rehearsal.

When the play opened at the City Center, this small, mighty woman had met and conquered the challenge. Of course, there were few people there who had my peculiar advantage of knowing what she'd been through, and only a few of her critics appeared to sense it. To me she brought to mind the return of some great matador to the bull ring in Madrid, for the first time after having been almost fatally gored, and facing his most dangerous bull with his finest valor, a bullfighter such as Belmonte or Manolete, conquering himself and his spectators and his bull, all at once and together, with brilliant cape-work and no standing back from the "terrain of the bull." I'm not ashamed to say that I shed tears almost all the way through and that when the play was finished I rushed up to her and fell to my knees at her feet.

The human drama, the play of a woman's great valor and an artist's truth, her own, far superseded, and even eclipsed, to my eye, the performance of my own play. Such an experience in the life of a playwright demands some tribute from him, and this late, awkward confession is my effort to give it.

On Meeting a Young Writer (1956)

Writing is the loneliest of all human occupations, and yet, whenever I meet a new young writer, one whose first book is a sensational best seller, or whose first play has gotten raves and is "the hottest ticket on Broadway," I see behind his shoulder, as I meet him, a phantom crowd of his newly acquired attendants, followers, companions; and I still have enough humanity left in me to almost cry for his plight. For writing is the loneliest of all vocations because it is meant to be so, and when it becomes a terrible public performance, he, the young writer, the beginning talent, is being industriously destroyed at his moment of birth as an artist. I see this phantom crowd over his shoulder. I see the beaming face of the publisher and his whole office staff, faceless but visible; or I see the producer and his whole office staff, particularly those in the publicity department. I see the faces of those who will interview him for the newspapers and television, I see the captains of steamships who will invite him to sit at their table. I see this adulatory host crowded together in the dim, comforting air of the library at the St. Regis or in the Plaza Bar. And I feel as if I were about to place an evergreen wreath on his grave, and that all about me the others are. . . .

The wreath of laurel that is placed on the forehead of a young writer in our time, in our world, can easily turn into a golden band that tightens upon him until it cracks his skull like a dry pea pod.

The work of a writer, his continuing work, depends, for breath of life, on a certain privacy of heart—and how is he to maintain it with that wreath on his head and that crowd at his heels?

Once in a while you meet a young writer who seems able to do it. And this is my gray introduction to the vivid and luminous subject of Françoise Sagan.

When I met Françoise Sagan in Key West (she came down there to meet my house guest, Carson McCullers), I saw behind her this phantom host I've described, for her novel, *Bonjour tristesse,* was already at the head of our American best seller list (as it had been in France); and, seeing back of her the pursuing pack, even hotter than usual on the scent of its quarry, I looked in her eyes for some clue as to the outcome of the race or flight, and I saw something in their gold-freckled brown depths, something cool in its detachment but warm in its sensibility, that made me feel reasonably safe about this young artist's future. I felt that she was the girl in her class most likely to succeed; that fame at nineteen would not be disgrace at twenty, nor ever. There was clarity and humor, not confusion and panic, in her young eyes. It was evening when I met her. I wondered if in the morning she would be at her typewriter banging out a new novel with panicky compulsion. Well, she wasn't. In the morning she was sun-bathing and swimming, and in the afternoon we went deep-sea fishing and in the evening, when it came again, she took the wheel of my sports car and drove it so fast, with such a gay smile, that I had to warn her of the highway patrolmen. I think a passion for speed is a healthy sign in a young artist: it shows that they know already the need to keep distance between them and the pack.

I liked Françoise, and Carson liked her, too. I am not at all surprised, now, that she has scored a second artistic triumph which is, incidentally, another and greater best seller. Of course in this game you are never "out of the woods," but I would bet on this French girl. Perhaps she doesn't have, now, at this moment in her development, the alarming, deeply disturbing, visionary quality of her literary idol, Raymond Radiguet, who died so young after a little great work, nor has she yet written anything comparable to Carson McCullers' *Ballad of the Sad Café,* but I have a feeling that if I had met Mme. Colette at twenty I would have noticed about her the same cool detachment and warm sensibility that I observed in the gold-freckled eyes of Mlle. Sagan. She is young and tender, and she is wise. She will not exchange the cow for a hatful of beans and find herself, the next day, in the ogre's oven!

Concerning Eugene O'Neill (1967)

Eugene O'Neill was not just a playwright but an intensely dedicated artist, and it was singularly painful for him as we see from the fine biographical study written not long ago by Mr. and Mrs. Gelb. It would seem that the whole O'Neill family were destined to suffer more than families should be required to suffer. What was it that required of O'Neill the artist so much torment, above and beyond that degree of torment that comes inevitably with being an artist? I would guess that it was his stature and nobility of spirit. To compromise with the deeply brooding nature of his art was a thing unthinkable for him, and of course he never did it. I don't have the statistics on his failures and successes, but I would venture to guess that he was often misunderstood by his audience and critics. He had the burden of being a truly passionate man and I would suspect he was a man who found it hard to accept and smile at the ways of the world he lived in.

He was a passionate man. I think that quality about him is what is most necessary to understanding O'Neill. Most of us, when we are tormented, turn ourselves into clowns. I mean we laugh at ourselves. But I wonder if O'Neill had that useful trick at his disposal, and from reading his major works, and seeing them in production, I am inclined to think that it must have been unusually hard for him to take, in his profession, a reversal at all lightly.

In 1946, when I was living in New Orleans, I read *The Iceman Cometh*. This was a short while after its production on Broadway and the long-awaited event of a new play by Eugene O'Neill had seemed, to Broadway, a bit of an anti-climax. It was treated with respect but not with the complete elation that might be expected.

I read the play. At first I thought to myself, this play is too long, that's the trouble. But I kept on reading it and soon I became aware that its length was indispensable to its power, its fullness of passion.

I wrote him a letter to this effect, and to my surprise and great pleasure I received a reply. He said that my letter had come to him at the precise time when he needed it, as he always felt, after the opening of a production, a sense of disappointment, of "let-down."

I never met Mr. O'Neill, and these letters were the only communication between us.

Eugene O'Neill was loved, deeply liked, and respected by so many people, which must have given him much comfort and relief that he needed.

But to be an artist is essentially to be lonely.

To be passionate and to be lonely isn't the easiest of things in the world.

I am happy to say that I once met his widow, Carlotta Monterey O'Neill. She was an exceptionally beautiful woman, and I felt in her an almost religious devotion to O'Neill, and this made me much happier for the lonely and passionate man and artist he was, and which he continues to be.

Tennessee Williams Talks about His Play
In the Bar of a Tokyo Hotel (1969)

Please read to the company the following two paragraphs of this letter, as I think it may clarify for them the intention of the play, its "Meaning."

It is about the usually early and peculiarly humiliating doom of the artist. He has made, in the beginning of his vocation, an almost total commitment of himself to his work. As Mark truthfully says, the intensity of the work, the unremitting challenges and demands that it makes to him and of him (in most cases daily) leave so little of him after the working hours that simple, comfortable *being* is impossible for him. In some cases, that may be familiar to us, he is afraid to answer a ringing phone, afraid of a waiter in a restaurant, afraid of his breath and his heart-beat. He is afraid of cutlery on a table. He is afraid of his small dog's attitude toward him.

In the beginning, in his youth, the health of his body enabled him to do his work and cope with his life outside it. He is reticent, but he usually has a strong sexual drive. The same fierce need that he brings to his work, he will bring to finding for himself a wife or a lover. For a few years this wife or lover will accept, or appear to accept, his primary commitment to his work. Then the wife or lover will reasonably resent being so constantly in second place, and will pay him back by promiscuities, sometimes as ravenous as Miriam's. His youth passes. The health of his body fails him. Then the work increases its demand from most of him to practically all of him. At last it seems to him like an impotent attempt at making love. At that point, he is sentenced to death, and as death approaches, he hasn't the comfort of feeling with any conviction that any of his work has had any essential value. The wife or lover is repelled by his shattered condition and is willing to be with him as little a time as possible. Somewhere in her or him there remains, unconsciously, a love for him that can only be expressed in her or his feeling when the artist is dead.

I hope I've said something useful.

Notes for The Two Character Play (1970)

There may be no apparent sexuality in *The Two Character Play* and yet it is actually the *Liebestod* of the two characters from whom the title derives.

This fact should be recognized by the director and players, but then it should appear to be forgotten.

On the surface the story of Felice's *Two Character Play* is dismayingly simple. It seems to revolve upon the question of whether or not Clare and Felice will be able to force themselves out of the house to Grossman's Market and to confront Mr. Conrad Grossman in his office and assure him, falsely, that The Acme Insurance Company is about to pay off their late father's insurance policy which had been forfeited because his death was by suicide.

"Grossman's Market" (and its proprietor) and "The Acme Insurance Company" represent formidable and impersonal forces in the lives of the two characters, as do "Citizen's Relief" and the town's electric plant which has cut off the lights in the house and the telephone company which finally disconnects the phone, and even "the woman next door" to whom they're afraid to call out.

It was my intention to give these outside, impersonal forces a certain "mythic" quality. For instance, the "Acme" responds to a twelve page written and rewritten letter of appeal with only three typewritten sentences and Mr. Conrad Grossman's office in the market is conceived by Clare as being "tucked away in some never discovered corner of a shadowy labyrinth." The son of the next-door neighbors has been given a sling-shot (by his parents, they say) and the recluse brother and sister suspect, now and then, that he uses it to bombard the house with rocks. (The revolver and the box of cartridges are impersonal factors in a way, too.)

The two characters of the play, Clare and Felice, are a pair of vulnerably deviant persons confronted by these implacable forces of the familiar world, and they are defeated in their forlornly gallant attempt to go to the market and tell to Mr. Grossman the lie that would prolong their lives if he believed it and also in their attempt to appeal to "Citizen's Relief" and finally even to call out to the woman next door collecting clothes from her washline.

That is the surface story of *The Two Character Play* and I must hope that it is a parable of enough meaning to compensate for the apparent slightness of its dramatic content.

This play is included in the still more metaphorical (and topical) play of the two performers' imprisonment in "the state theatre of a state unknown," where they have arrived in a manner which is mysterious to them both.

This situation of the "star performers," deserted by their company, corresponds to the play which they perform up to the point where the audience walks out on them. In both the total play and the play within it, two desperately gallant but hopelessly deviant beings, find themselves, in the end, with no escape but self-destruction, which fails them, too.

These notes are not needed, I should think, to cast light upon any intellectual or philosophical obscurity in the play, since I have never traded in obscurity of that kind. But it sometimes seems that in my later plays there is a bit of emotional obscurity, perhaps because the world becomes darker to me as I pass through it, and so it may be of some use to directors and performers of the play for me to have set down this statement of intentions: I must say it has been so to me.

To be effective in the theater now existing, the two performers, who must be very gifted whether they are "stars" or not, must relieve the dark content of the plays, interior and total, with a carefully measured lightness—the jokes of the condemned?—and of course by that virtuosity of performance that very gifted performers always bring to a difficult work.

This is a play that has to seek out its kind with great care, since it is as vulnerable as Clare and Felice, and as deviant.

To William Inge: An Homage (1973)

It was sometime late last winter when Barbara Baxley, a friend and brilliant performer in two of my plays, called me to tell me that William Inge, with whom she had once had a tender "romance," and to whom he was probably closer than almost anyone else outside his family, had fallen into a desperate situation.

Her feeling for him remained as tenderly concerned as ever. "He's going to pieces," she told me in that inimitable voice of hers. "He keeps himself under sedation all day and night, getting up only to drink and then back under sedation."

"Oh, then he is on a suicide course: something has to be done."

"But what? He commits himself voluntarily for two days and then has himself released."

"Isn't his sister with him?"

"Yes, Helen's with him and she's desperate."

"Tell her to commit him herself so he can't get right back out till he has gotten through the present crisis."

"You call her, Ten."

"I don't know her, Barbara."

"Introduce yourself to her on the phone and give her that advice before it's too late. I've tried but she seems immobilized with panic."

Barbara gave me the California telephone number. Before calling, I phoned Maureen Stapleton to confer with her on the advisability of the suggested call to Bill's sister. Maureen was equally disturbed. Being a survivor of nervous crises herself, she could empathize with Bill's and his sister's dilemma.

I then called the number in Hollywood and Bill's sister, Mrs. Helen Connell, answered the phone. I introduced myself to her and she lowered her voice to a whisper, saying she never knew whether Bill was listening to calls. She gave me further details of the predicament. He had, she told me, entered the falling-down stage and a few nights ago had fallen down in the shower and suffered deep scalp cuts and she'd had to assist him back to bed. Under his mattress, she told me, he kept strong sedative pills, seven of them a night, and she confirmed Barbara's report that he only got up now to make a drink and that his pattern was to commit himself to a sanitarium and release himself in two days.

Knowing certain things about Bill from our long association, I was aware of the fact that he was the type of alcoholic who can't tolerate a single drink, that he had put up a very brave and successful struggle to abstain completely, was a member of Alcoholics Anonymous, and that he suffered from extreme claustrophobia, a fact that explained his inability to accept hospital confinement for more than two days.

I suggested to Mrs. Connell that, being his nearest relative, she herself commit him to the best sort of psychiatric hospital, such as Menninger's in his home-state of Kansas, make sure that he had an attractive and spacious room there, and see that he remained till he was back on his feet.

She suddenly cut the phone conversation short, whispering that she heard him stirring about the house and that he was paranoiac about phone calls. Then she assured me that she would follow my advice.

I was in rehearsals with the most difficult play I have written and made no further call and heard no further from Bill's sister.

Two days ago, in Positano, Italy, I opened *The Rome Daily American* and saw a photograph of his anguished face: then the caption declaring that he had committed suicide. And last night my agent, Bill Barnes, called me from New York and inquired if I would care to write something about Bill for *The Times*.

I met Bill Inge in December, 1944, when I returned home briefly to St. Louis. At that time, he was writing for the *Star-Times*, doing dramatic criticism and interviews and, I think, also serving as music critic.

This was during the Chicago break-in of *The Glass Menagerie* and Bill came to our suburban home to interview me. He was embarrassingly "impressed" by my burgeoning career as a playwright. It's always lonely at home now: my friends have all dispersed. I mentioned this to Bill and he cordially invited me to his apartment near the river. We had a gala night among his friends. Later we attended the St. Louis Symphony together. He made my homecoming an exceptional pleasure.

When I returned to *Menagerie* in Chicago, Bill shortly arrived to attend and cover the play, and I believe he was sincerely overwhelmed by the play and the fabulous Laurette Taylor, giving her last and greatest performance.

A year or two later, I was back in St. Louis and we met again. He had now retired as journalist and was teaching English at Washington University, not far from our home, and was living in the sort of neo-Victorian white frame house that must have reminded him of his native Kansas. There, one evening, he shyly produced a play that he had written, *Come Back, Little Sheba*. He read it to me in his beautifully quiet and expressive voice: I was deeply moved by the play and I immediately wired Audrey Wood about it and urged him to submit it to her. She was equally impressed and Bill became her client almost at once.

It was during the rehearsals of that play, starring Shirley Booth and Sidney Blackmer, that Bill had his first nervous crisis. The tension was too much for him, he assuaged it copiously with liquor. Paul Bigelow took him in charge and had him hospitalized away from Broadway's traumas, and I don't think Bill even attended his opening night.

The rest of his career has been well annotated. I should like to make a few personal comments on him as person and as American artist.

Despite all of this "heavy" material about his fate, Bill and his work were suffused with the light of humanity at its best. In each play, there would be one dark scene and it was always the most powerful scene: but he loved his characters, he wrote of them with a perfect ear for their homely speech, he saw them through their difficulties with the tenderness of a parent for suffering children, and they usually came out well.

Bill was a mystery as a person, and he remains one. Ever since he came to New York, probably even before, he found it difficult to open himself up to people, especially at social gatherings. He was inclined to silent moodiness. His face was prematurely etched with hidden sufferings. He would rarely remain at a party longer than half an hour, then he would say quietly, "I think I'd better go now."

Because others were drinking and he couldn't? Or because a shyness, a loneliness beyond reach except by a few such as Barbara Baxley, Elia Kazan and Audrey Wood, was inextricably rooted in his being, despite the many years of analysis and the deserved fame and success?

His shyness was never awkward: he had true dignity and impeccable taste, rarely associated with "middle America." His apartment on the East River contained lovely paintings by "name" painters but reflecting his own taste. Interviews with him contained no touch of vulgarity: Impersonal, perhaps, but impressively thoughtful and modest.

Early last month, after sixteen years of blindness and paralysis in a convent hospital in Malaga, Spain, Jane Bowles succumbed to a cerebral hemorrhage.

Weeks passed before an obituary was printed despite the fact that I am not alone in considering her quite possibly the finest prose writer of the century.

And now Bill . . .

It is pleasant to believe that the work of an artist gives him a certain life after death, usually a thing for which he has paid an enormous price and from which I am afraid he can enjoy no personal satisfaction.

But surely Jane and Bill, she with her deep humanity and he with his, would be happy to know, if they knew, how much of their hearts remain with us cliffhangers.

W. H. Auden: A Few Reminiscences (1975)

I encountered the late Wystan Auden about three or four times, and then but briefly. The first occasion was in a lecture hall somewhere during the penumbrous period of my life in the forties, and I made the mistake of asking him to read some of my verse. I forget his precise response, but it was negative and the encounter was rather chilling. A while later someone took me to his fantastically sordid rooms in the village. It may have been Chester Kallman. I remember a terrible disorder in the premises; it looked like a crash pad of an aging hippie with beer cans and newspapers all about the floors and Mr. Auden himself quite disinclined—or too drunk—to be exactly civil. The later encounters were very agreeable. I suppose he had discovered that I was not a grifter or whatever he took me for, and I discovered that he was a naturally shy and reserved man who could be quite charming when he came to know you. However, I feel that I knew him best through my long friendship with his close friend Christopher Isherwood. These two writers were poles apart in their American life-styles; yet I regard them as being probably the wisest and most civilized men of this age.

I do not feel qualified to discuss Auden as a poet. I liked a lot of his early poems quite a lot, but preferred the love lyrics of his friend Stephen Spender. When his work became more austerely intellectual (and perhaps more important) I was impressed but not moved. Now perhaps I would be. I've always been an impatient reader, never getting through the Cantos of Pound, the epic poems of Byron, preferring to sense vaguely the magnitude of the work than to fasten the seat belt and plough through it.

My final, or rather my latest, recollection of Auden was the shocking announcement of his death which I received (of all places) on TV in The Beverly Hills Hotel. I immediately phoned Isherwood who was naturally far more shocked. It seemed as if we were exchanging reactions to the outbreak of a war between planets.

Foreword to Jane Bowles's **Feminine Wiles** **(1976)**

Persons of note and/or notoriety in the literary and entertainment worlds are often asked to give what are called "quotes" concerning the work of a writer, and often these solicited "quotes" are more in keeping with the market-place than with honesty of statement.

I was never asked to express an opinion of the work of Jane Bowles. I read it, and exclaimed my opinion of it as spontaneously as if I'd stumbled into a wonderland of new, totally fresh sensibility—which, indeed, I had.

I knew Mrs. Bowles personally, but it was not her unique charm as a person that drew from me the opinions which I hold regarding her work. I consider her the most important writer of prose fiction in modern American letters without reference to my close, intuitive friendship with her, and my knowledge of her physical disabilities and spiritual torment during her last years.

Her work doesn't need an appreciation influenced by sympathy with the circumstances of her life. Of course her work was the heart of her life, but it deserves to be appraised as if you had never known her, and it is fully able to stand undiminished by this detached view.

Now having confirmed, unconditionally, my first and lasting opinion of Jane Bowles's work, which doesn't need my opinion, I may speak of her as the totally original and delightful person that she was.

The very first time I met Jane was in Acapulco the summer of 1940; but that was so briefly and so long ago that I have no impression of it except that Janie was totally concerned, it seemed to me, with what you could eat safely in Acapulco at that time, which was practically nothing.

Then, in December 1948, I met her when she came aboard the *Vulcania*, anchored for debarkation in the Strait of Gibraltar, in the presence of Paul Bowles, her husband, and my friend Frank Merlo.

In appearance she was a lovely girl, small, piquant, darting between humor, anxiety, love and distraction. I had met nervous girls before, but her quicksilver animation, her continuous cries, to me and herself, "Shall we do this or shall we do that? What shall we do?", showed such an extreme kind of excited indecision that I was skeptical of its reality—intrigued, certainly, but still somewhat incredulous.

Used to it as Paul must have been, he stood there, simply smiling in a bemused sort of way. It seems to me that Frank Merlo took command of the chaotic situation, much to the relief of us all. (Of course, Paul may already have known how things would go, but was simply waiting for the accustomed flurry to subside.)

Frank saw that the car was put onto the European shore; we settled down for the night at the Rock Hotel in Gib.

"Is she for real?" I asked Frank, when we had retired.

"Are *you* for real?" he countered, a little grimly, perhaps.

I wasn't sure about that, but I soon came to see the reality of Jane. All the indecision was a true and dreadful concern that she might suggest a wrong move in a world that she had correctly surmised to be so inclined to turn wrongly.

There were many subsequent meetings, in Tangier, Paris and New York. What most impressed me about Jane, the person, was her concern for others, for their comfort and their entertainment. The important little things, especially such as providing meals, acquainting you with the right doctors in foreign places, conducting you through markets, introducing you to the interesting people, and somehow, in the midst of confusion, finding the precisely right words to reassure you in your own confusion—these were her particular gifts—ways to get agreeably through day and evening.

Her work, her life: deep truth, observed without pretension, with humor and humanity.

As artist and person, an angel.

Program Note for The Red Devil Battery Sign (1980)

When what you have to say in a work for the theatre is of very great, possibly even dangerous, importance to you, it will make your hands tremble. You will feel inadequate to the assignment. Still you will undertake it.

I confess to you without shame and without apology that this is melodrama, not classically pure tragedy.

The written play reminds me somewhat of a raw, bloody wound. But as I leave it in the hands of these Vancouver Playhouse actors and their gifted director, I am confident that they a will lift the written text above its stature and perhaps they may even offer you a reasonable likeness to the form of that all-but-impossible thing, another work of mine that could stand with *A Streetcar Named Desire.*

Of course I know that in Greek drama there were tragedies and there were comedies and the two were very distinct from each other. But in modern theatre many conditions have changed—the masks have been discarded and also the stilt-like elevations on which the actors walked to give them a super-human aspect.

My kind of serious theatre is to somehow combine humor and terror and sensuality and heart-break. There have been notable occasions on which it seemed to work.

I have a feeling that it can work for you again if you will give it a bit of indulgence: my part of it, I mean. Once a younger playwright whom I much admire said about a new work of his, "Don't try to analyze and understand everything in it. The mysteries it contains are important to its effect: it is a mystery play!" Since I am paraphrasing Edward Albee I should not have put that appeal in quotes. What he meant was if you release yourself to it willingly you will more easily receive its rewards—the elegance, the sense of beauty, and in the end, the catharsis.

I approached the play *Tiny Alice* in that way and I found that he was right: I found in it the poetry, and the mystery and the terror which is life and death.

Finally, don't think of me as someone from a foreign country. I'm not. My work has usually been better done and valued and defended more in England where theatre is deeply loved and cared for.

To have great theatre we must have great audiences too.

Foreword to Dakin Williams's **The Bar Bizarre** (1980)

I am sure that the inimitable and indomitable humor of my brother Dakin will make this book delightful reading, especially since he has the editorial assistance of our friend Lucy Freeman who reproduced so faithfully the southern eloquence of our late mother's *Remember Me To Tom*.

Homage to J. (1981)

It was J. Laughlin who first took a serious interest in my work as a writer. My first notable appearance in print was in a New Directions book called *Five Young American Poets* in 1944. True, I had suffered an abortive play production in 1940, which collapsed in Boston. It appeared to me that this failure was conclusive. J. thought otherwise. Consistently over the years his sense of whatever was valuable in my work was my one invariable criterion.

Among all the multitude of persons I've encountered in the world of letters and theatre (if that distinction is permissible) J. Laughlin remains the one I regard with the deepest respect and affection. My gratitude to him is an inexpressible thing and I trust that he knows it always.

JUVENILIA
and
COLLEGE PAPERS

Can a Good Wife Be a Good Sport? (1927)

Can a woman after marriage maintain the same attitude towards other men as she held before marriage? Can she drink, smoke, and pet with them? Can she do those things which are necessary to good sportsmanship, as the term is generally applied to a girl. Those are questions of really great pertinence to modern married life.

In recounting my own unhappy marital experiences, perhaps I can present convincing answers.

Bernice was an unusually attractive girl, decidedly the flapper type. She had the gift of a quick tongue and a ready wit. I met her and fell in love with her in our mutual place of employment—a wholesale house on Washington Ave. I proposed to her across a glass-topped cafeteria table. However if a girl can accept you under such conditions as prevail in a cheap cafeteria, without the stimulus of moonlight, moonshine, or music, it would seem that her love was strong.

About a month after our marriage I obtained a position as traveling salesman, for the same firm in which I had previously been employed as a clerk.

We had rented a very pleasant little efficiency apartment and it seemed to me at first that my future was to be one of domestic bliss.

Bernice had been a popular girl, so she was naturally dissatisfied to sit at home "darning socks," as she described it. I did not at all object that she should go out reasonably often, or that she should retain her old friends—men as well as women. I reasoned that gradually she would slow down.

However the expected symptoms of slowing down did not appear. In fact, by our second year of marriage, her speed had noticeably increased. Her life seemed, almost, to be one continual stream of dates.

One week, after our third wedding anniversary, I completed my sales tour much sooner than usual. On entering our apartment after giving the customary signal, so that she would not be frightened, I found that she was not there. It was twelve o'clock—midnight. I decided that she must have been lonely and gone to spend the night with a girl friend. I went to bed, but my worry concerning her prevented me from sleeping.

It was almost daylight when I heard her key turn in the lock. I was about to arise to greet her, when I saw through the partially open door between the bedroom and hall that she was accompanied by a young man. She looked cautiously around the parlor. I had placed my suit-case under the bed, and there were no evidences of my return. She then permitted the man to throw his arms around her and kiss her. I was astonished and furious at this. When the man had left, I presented myself. She almost fainted when she saw me.

We were divorced a year later. As I remember "being a good sport" was exactly how she defined her actions. Being a good sport was drinking, smoking, and petting—staying up all night with the boys at cabarets—not sitting at home "darning socks." No, I don't think that a wife can be that kind of "good sport."

High School Travel Articles by Tom Williams (1928–1929)

A Day at the Olympics

The Olympic games, sport in its grandest and most magnificent proportions, were held this year in Amsterdam, the capital of the Dutch nation. We arrived in this city just in time to attend the final event of the games and the awarding of the prizes to winning nations by the Dutch queen.

The grounds on which the games were held presented to us an amazing spectacle. They had the appearance of the grounds of an exposition or fair such as we are acquainted with, grown to an enormous magnitude. When you consider the fact that many of the different sports required each their own amphitheater and that each of these individual amphitheaters had to have a seating capacity adequate for an immense multitude of people, assembled from all parts of the world, who were attending the games, you will be able to conceive the real vastness of the area required for these games and the greatness of their cost.

The event which we witnessed was a competition of skilled horsemanship. The diversity of the nations represented among the spectators of the games on this day was indicated to us by the great variety of languages we heard spoken. Behind us were Germans, in front of us French. The motley of languages was such as to bring one in mind of the tower of Babel. We had programs with us but we were in some confusion as to the point in them at which we had entered. The French to the front of us and the Germans behind us both endeavored to clear our perplexity. Both of them, however, disagreed and fell into violent argument which was settled only when an Englishman, annoyed by their shouting, showed that both of them were wrong and pointed out the right place to us all.

The hurdling proved to be very exciting, since some of the obstacles were very steep and hazardous. There was one wide, wooden platform, sprinkled with sand which made necessary a very careful footing, upon which the horses had to leap, walk across and then jump to the ground again. Some of the most

thrilling moments were provided by the stumblings of the horses upon this platform.

A touch of humor was added to the otherwise intensely serious proceedings
when one of our native horses, titled Miss America, stubbornly refused to stand
before the royal box and present salutations to the queen. She jerked from side
to side, pawed the earth and tossed her head high in the air with every indication of a complete disdain for the Dutch sovereign. Facetiously, one of our party
remarked that Miss America was showing her contempt for royalty.

With the impressive awarding of honors, this year's Olympics came to a
close. None can attend these great games without deepening exceedingly his
respect for Sport.

The Tomb of the Capuchins

To visitors in Rome, one of the city's greatest curiosities is the burial vault of
the venerable old Capuchin monks. These monks were all at one time very decently interred, but for some rather obscure reason they have been dug up and
all heaped together in a single subterranean chamber. This is, perhaps, the largest assemblage of human bones anywhere on exhibition. One feels that if there
were really any truth in the superstitious theory that the spirits of the dead can
rise to avenge themselves for insults or indignities dealt them after death, the
whitened bones of these early Christians would surely be lying much less pas-
sively in the cold and clammy, cob-webbed cellar where by apparently irreverent
hands they have been carelessly thrown.

Upon our entrance to the old Capuchin church, we are placed in the hands
of one of the brown cloaked brethren whose duty it is to conduct the visiting
parties. He leads us down a long, steep flight of stairs, pausing before the low
door at the bottom to look up at us with a sly gleam in his eyes. Slowly he draws
open the heavy door. And instantly there are muffled outcries and hurried stumblings on the stair. The less valiant of the ladies are in precipitate flight. And as
we gaze into the musty interior of the room, we cease to wonder.

Here, before our eyes, is a vast assemblage of those dead beings which in
our early and timorous childhood we have fancied to be lurking in the depths
of our blackest closets. Here, within this room, is a stunning multiplicity of
those creatures of horror that are supposed to lurk behind the sheet and pillow
cases of our Hallowe'en masquerades. Here, in short, are those gruesome things
which heretofore we have never been permitted to see except in our dreams, following a late supper of lobster and sour pickles—here, before our bulging eyes, are
the skeletons of the dead!

No, not even Lon Chaney has ever quite surpassed the grinning skeleton
for sheer ugliness!

There is something about their mocking contemplation of us as we enter that is oddly suggestive of old fraternity members with paddles hidden behind their backs, waiting to perform the rites of initiation upon a group of trembling freshmen; there is very nearly that same cruel and sardonic humor in their faces.

One member of the party voices the question of all of us.

"Don't you ever feel scared when you look at all these skeletons?" she asks the placid guide.

He laughs and shrugs his shoulders with Latin vivacity.

"No, why should I be scared to see bones, nothing but bones?"

We follow him out, all with the profoundest respect for this bright-eyed old brother who sees nothing but bones.

Those who have read Hawthorne's *Marble Faun* will probably remember his description of the celebrated old church, and to them this recollection would no doubt make a visit to the place much more enjoyable.

A Flight Over London

Our bus stopped before a massive brick building. We got out, followed the uniformed person through iron gates and doors; entered a vast field, bright with sun-light, and looked about us breathlessly. We were about to embark upon our first aeronautic excursion. And this was the famous Croydon Field.

It was indeed a very impressive place. Scattered about the field were a great number of yellow hangars and before them were lined the planes flashing in the sun and filling the field with a terrific roar. It was during that exciting period when London was testing her air defenses by a series of mock bombardments and making the disturbing discovery that it was possible for her to be completely annihilated within a few nights. The planes upon the field were those which were to participate in the attack that night and were now undergoing a mechanical inspection.

Our own plane, which naturally for us was the object of principal attention, stood near the edge of the field. As we walked toward it, we saw another equally large plane coming to the ground. It was a trans-channel plane. When we saw the passengers stepping to earth, with such relief upon their faces as might be expected of lost souls who had been wandering in the regions of Erebus, we felt grateful that our flight was a short one and that we were not to be committed simultaneously to the perils of both sea and air.

We stumbled in rather hastily, perhaps in fear that our courage might yet fail us; then took our seats in the wicker chairs, seven on each side of the aisle. In front of us was the pilot's compartment, partitioned by a heavy glass panel. Only the aviator's head and shoulders were visible.

Scarcely had we seated ourselves when the dull throb of the engines quickened with a cyclonic roar. The five propellers, two of them the size of electric fans, flashed dazzlingly in the sun. The vibration became terrific. We felt ourselves palpitating in every joint and fiber of our beings. The plane started to move across the field, slowly at first, but accelerating rapidly to a furious rush. Half-way across the great field it speeds, and then there comes a slight bump, a barely perceptible tilt. You look down and you see the earth skimming lower and lower beneath you. Your breath leaves you for a moment in a gasp of exultation. You are UP! For the first time in your life the earth has released you from its grip.

The trees, the yellow-roofed hangars, the tall, iron fences scud beneath us; then the gleaming concrete road and the open fields. We look down and marvel at the dwindling objects. Roads and fields condense themselves into a checkered pattern. The plane flies toward the city, following the bright line of the road.

Fifteen minutes pass; then we catch the faint glitter of the river. London is beneath us. We have never quite realized its immensity until this moment. It stretches to the horizons.

The plane circles for half an hour over the city. We have the thrill of recognizing the museums which we have visited, the Cathedral, the Abbey, the Houses of Parliament, the parks and even the hotel in which we are stopping. Then the plane turns back. Tea and cakes are served, to the satisfaction of the English passengers. After slightly more than an hour in the air, the plane returns to the field. The cotton has been blown from my ears and as the plane sinks to the ground, I feel a piercing pain in them, due to the rapidity of descent. This, however, is the only unpleasant sensation of the entire trip. When the plane has stopped and we put foot again *in terram*, it is with the conviction that seeing London from the air is one of the great and memorable thrills of a life-time.

A Night in Venice

Venice has been described by all the poets as a city of romance and exquisite beauty. Consequently the cynically-minded tourist arrives in that city fully prepared for the shattering of an illusion. He expects to find orange rinds and banana peels floating upon the "liquid-silver" of the moonlit waterways. He expects the "sea-blown zephyrs" to breathe of stale fish and stagnant, unclean water rather than of blooming gardens and the fresh and fragrant coolness of the starry Adriatic. He expects in short to find that Venice, like most of the things that poets write about, is only a glamorous tradition, a bubble whose color and gloss will fade when subjected to the cold and unimpassioned scrutiny of sensible, practically-minded people.

If the tourist happens to be of that all-too-common species who delight in the fulfillment of their cynical expectations, he is destined to suffer a severe disappointment. He will find that Venice is all that it has ever been called, city of beauty, city of romance, city of enchantment! The most effusive poets, he will find, have never rhapsodized too extravagantly.

There are two modes of transportation in Venice: one by the steamboat, swift, gracelessly built, and noisy craft, the other by gondola. The latter are long, glistening black boats, curving at either end like the toe of a Persian slipper. We selected one that had a little fringed canopy over the middle and a gondolier who had a brilliant sash about his waist. With his huge oar, the length of a vaulting pole, he swept us lightly down the Grand Canal, past palatial white buildings, under dimly lighted bridges. It was a night of glistening clarity, with full, honey-colored moon. Not a single banana peeling floated on the shimmering water and there was no taint of stale fish upon the cool sea breeze. We suffered no broken illusions.

By eloquent sign-language we indicated to the willing, but puzzled, gondolier that we wished him to render a musical accompaniment to the splendor of the night. He graciously complied, singing several Italian songs, one which we recognized as "La Donna E Mobile," or "Woman Is Fickle." His voice was a clear and melodious tenor, and he sang with all the dramatic gestures and flourishes of an opera star.

After having gone a considerable distance, we turned down a crooked side-canal which was even more picturesque. It was narrow as a city alley, and was spanned by numerous little arched bridges. It was lit only by the moonlight, coming in streaks between the houses on either side, and the occasional gleam of a murky lantern, suspended over a door-way.

Shortly we came out into a large and beautiful expanse of water, the Adriatic Bay, around which were located many of the finer hotels. The water scintillated with the reflection of their lights. We drew along-side a miniature show-boat, moored not far from the shore, and listened to the singing and playing of the band of troubadours. At the conclusion of each group of songs, a man stepped from gondola to gondola with an amazing agility, collecting coins in his wide-brimmed hat. Many of the less generous listeners found to their embarrassment, when the hat was passed to them, that the Venetian troubadour has an almost uncanny cleverness at distinguishing between lire and penny-pieces, even in the dark.

When we had had enough of this musical performance, we passed on, winding deviously among the dark shapes of anchored sailing vessels, until we came to a floating dance pavilion, built in the form of a Chinese pagoda and illuminated with brilliant red and yellow lights. The water for yards around sparkled with the colorful reflection of this unique dancing palace.

We floated at a distance for some while, enjoying the gay, animated music and dancing; then, the coolness of the night air having made us sleepy, we directed our gondolier to return us to the hotel.

A Trip To Monte Carlo

Before descending into blazing, Mid-summer Italy, we stopped for a few days at the beautiful city of Nice, on the French Riviera. About twenty or thirty miles from here lies Monte Carlo, the fashionable gambling resort and capital of perhaps the smallest independent state in the world. On the afternoon of our second day in the Riviera we took a motor-trip to this celebrated little city.

Our large bus climbed for an hour through the imposing maritime Alps. On either side of the road were towering, red-rock cliffs, with the pale green of cacti and olive trees growing from crevices and along the rocky slopes. We passed occasional little homesteads, situated picturesquely upon the sides of the mountains. The people, brightly clad as Gypsies, stood in their doorways and waved to us. Many small boys pursued our bus, holding out their hands for coins.

At length, we came out upon a cliff-road, winding directly above the vivid sparkling blue of the Mediterranean. The contract of colors was gorgeous. Brilliant blue of sea, against the dusky green and red of the high cliffs. We passed many handsome villas, surrounded by palm trees. They were built in the Spanish style and very beautifully colored. Some of them were pale pink. Among the most beautiful was one owned by Mary Garden, famous Opera star. We saw the very rock on which she was accustomed to take her sun-baths.

The gleaming roofs of Monte Carlo were visible to us for almost an hour before we entered the city. We had an hour to spend, so we went directly to the main plaza, where the casino is located. It is an impressive building; long, white, ornately decorated with a bright green-tiled roof. It faces a large square, in the center of which is a colorful, beautifully designed bed of flowers, bordered with date palms. On the opposite side of the square is a very "ritzy" looking cafe, with large, vari-colored umbrellas over its outdoor tables. On another side of the square is the magnificent hotel, much handsomer on the interior than the Casino. We brushed some of the dust from our clothes here; then went immediately into the casino. I was admitted to the lobby but when I tried to get a ticket for the gambling room, the man at the desk, in gold-braided uniform, sternly pronounced me "trop jeune." I had forgotten that the age limit at all French gambling resorts is twenty-one. With keen disappointment, for the gambling salon of Monte Carlo is surely one of the world's greatest spectacles, I sank down in a leather chair near the door, so that I could catch glimpses of the interior when the door swung open. After half an hour our party came out again, peering dismally into limp purses. One woman had played very profitably, having won thirteen dollars, but the others had lost, upon the average of five dollars each.

We then crossed over to the cafe to get some cooling drinks. A sumptuous, lavender, Hispano-Suiza limousine had drawn to a stop at the entrance. A very stout woman, dressed with gaudy splendor of a circus queen, stepped out of it. We guessed, by her imperious manner and eccentric mode of dress, that she must be a wealthy Duchess or Russian princess. We sat down at a table near her, thrilled by our proximity to such an important-looking person. A moment later, however, we received a decided shock. She turned to her uniformed attendant and exclaimed fiercely in a language and accent distinctly American, "My Lord, what a headache! Get me my demi-tasse right away."

Before leaving, though, we did have the pleasure of seeing a genuine countess. She was insignificant looking, small and sallow, and she held a crumpled newspaper over her head. Our guide, recognizing her, said that she was immensely wealthy and that she rarely missed a day at the casino.

We returned to Nice by a different route, passing through many long, cool tunnels, obtaining frequent superb views of sea and mountains. We arrived at our hotel in time for a short, refreshing swim in the sea before supper.

The Ruins of Pompeii

One of the most piteous spectacles ever beheld is that of a party of Americans, sight-seeing in Pompeii, during the merry month of August. They stagger about, through the bleached and crumbling ruins, like people lost upon an arid desert. Their eyes are glazed and their tongues are parched. Their foreheads stream with perspiration. They drag themselves wearily up steep inclines, beneath a blazing sun. They lean breathlessly against hot walls, powdering desperately their blistered noses or mopping their brows with handkerchiefs, and caps—even, in extreme cases, with their shorts. Their speech, eager and gay at the beginning of the excursion, has turned to an unintelligible mumbling. They have lost all interest in each other. They are conscious only of their aching legs, their burning skin—and the interminable jabber of the guide.

"Here lad-ees! Here gentlemen! Here is the Pompeian bath house. Notice the marvelous frescoes, the beautiful coloring! These are the benches upon which the leisurely Pompeians reclined, enjoying the delightful steam, and discussing the latest modes and fash-uns."

The party stumbles in; they gaze mutely about them for a minute or two, then stumble out again. They toil listlessly up another narrow, white road, tripping over the deep ruts and crossing stones, until the guide stops again, before a low door in the continuous, white stone wall. "Now we see the typical Pompeian atrium, the courtyard in the center of the house with its picturesque fountain, mosaics and pillared arches. Notice the graceful cupid."

On they go, through the hot, white, dusty maze of Pompeii's ruins. They suffer agonies; but none of them will turn back. To do so would be to make a shameful admission of body triumphant over mind.

Under these conditions described—upon a hot afternoon in August—an extensive tour of Pompeii is a physical torment. It is quite enough to see the theater, the market place, the bath houses, and a few of the more interesting private residences. To tourists the most impressive thing about Pompeii is its compactness. Streets are narrower than city alleys. Houses are built against each other, without even the thinnest strip of intervening lawn. There is no indication of there having ever been any trees—at present, it is entirely barren. It is a well-built city—but it certainly could never have been an attractive city. And how the Pompeians could ever endure the dreadful heat of their August afternoon is a baffling mystery to Americans.

The small museum, situated at the base of the hill upon which Pompeii is built, is generally found most interesting. Contained in this museum is a great number of articles of furniture and pieces of pottery, all perfectly intact, which were taken from the Pompeian household. There is also a gruesome collection of human and animal casts. These were formed by the volcanic dust and ashes which settled upon the victims of the eruption. There is one of a slave, whose facial features are as concisely cut as those of a marble statute.

A tour of Pompeii gives a splendid picture of life among the ancient Romans. It also provides an almost unsurpassed test of physical endurance. As one member of the heroic party expressed it, you feel at the conclusion of the afternoon as though you should be included in Pompeii's ruins.

A Tour of the Battle-fields of France

Upon one of the scant five days of our touring party's stay in Paris, we went on an excursion through the battle-fields and to the quaint, historic old town of Rheims. Most of us had expected to find it a desolate region, grim with blackened ruins. Instead, we found it to be a bright and richly colored country, which, even though we were patriotic Americans, we acknowledged to be the most beautiful we had ever seen.

Our sight-seeing bus bore us swiftly along smooth, well-paved roads, past continuous lines of hills that were patched gaily with fields of variant yellow and green. It seemed scarcely conceivable that this land just ten years before had been ravaged by war; that these fields of golden grain, sprinkled with the night crimson of poppies, were then a barren waste, over which desperate conflicts were waged. Here and there we see a shattered wall, the ruins of a farm house, or a clump of rusted wire. These things, which we would not have noticed had they not been pointed out by the guide, are the only scars of war left upon the land which a decade ago was in a state of almost complete devastation.

We pass through a number of small villages whose tranquility is as perfect as if it had been undisturbed for centuries. We then climb among green hills, on our way to Belleau Woods. It is here that the traces of the war are most distinct. Our guide points out to us the bold summit of a ridge, telling us that before the war it had been thickly wooded. During the battle of Belleau Wood it had been a dividing line between the Allies and the Germans and had been completely stripped by the great artillery fire which swept across it. At frequent intervals along the road we come upon small caves dug into the embankments. These are the dugouts, we are told, where small groups of soldiers had sought refuge from the enemy's bombardment.

When we have reached the highest part of the wooded hills, where the fighting had been most intense, the bus comes to a stop and we walk through the woods, while our guide, an ex-soldier, vividly describes the battle.

The holes which the soldiers dug in the ground remain clearly visible. If one has any imaginativeness in his nature, he is sure to find it a rather thrilling sensation to step down into one of these deep, grass-grown holes, realizing that ten years ago the chill, aching body of a soldier crouched there through some long torturing night, clasping with stiff fingers the handle of his bayonet and waiting tensely for the enemy's attack. It is hard to imagine that these serene, verdant woods, silent except for the chirping of birds, were once filled with the thunder of a terrific battle and that bursting shells scattered fire over the tops of the trees; that this ground over which we walk, now carpeted with soft grass and many colored flowers, was deeply stained with the blood of dead and wounded soldiers. Nature seems to forget even more quickly than men.

When we have finished our walk through the battle-field, we are taken to the American cemetery near-by. It is a large, smooth field, containing a sparkling multitude of white marble crosses, each marking the grave of an American soldier. As we walk among them, each of us lays a few flowers that he has picked upon the hill at the foot of the cross of a soldier from his native state.

A Festival Night in Paris

The day of our arrival in Paris was the fourteenth of July which is a French holiday, commemorating the fall of the Bastille. It corresponds in national importance to our Fourth of July and it is always observed by the French with great festivity. In the evening there are great fire-works exhibitions, torch-light parades, street-dancing and street-fairs.

Wishing to see some of this celebration, we engaged a few cabs after our dinner and directed the driver to take us up the Rue de Rivoli and through the cafe district, where Parisian night-life is gayest. The streets through which we passed presented a thrilling picture. They were filled with a huge and hilariously happy swarm of people. At almost every corner a band was playing. Vividly colored paper lanterns were suspended across the streets and flags were hung from nearly every window. All Paris seemed to be a huge playground.

The crowds were thickest along the Rue de Rivoli for it was down this spacious boulevard that the torch-light parade was going to pass, later in the evening. From the roofs of buildings and elevated platforms on the sidewalks, great flashlights cast beams of red, yellow and purple light making the noisy, crowded street resplendent with color. Rockets drew arcs of flame across the sky and burst into showers of brilliant stars, obscuring momentarily the softer radiance of the real stars above them. Occasionally we glimpsed the immense Eiffel Tower, silhouetted against the purplish dusk of the sky, with its spectacular electric sign, an advertisement of a small French motor car, extending in a golden blaze from the base of the tower to its lofty tip.

We descended from our cabs at the Café de la Paix, the most celebrated of the Parisian cafés, intending to get some refreshments. However, all the tables in this café were occupied, even though they covered the sidewalks in front of the building. We walked on up the street, squeezing breathlessly through the thick crowd, until we came to the café Napolitain, where fortunately two or three tables were vacant. Shoving our way vigorously through the tight mass of tables and chairs and merry Parisians, we finally secured places at these tables, where we had ices, wine and macaroons and from which we had an excellent view of the gayety in the streets. We stayed here for about an hour, listening to the music of the band located near our table, and watching the wild capers and gyrations of the apache-looking couples dancing in the street. Some of the pieces played were of American origin, including the very popular musical comedy hit, *Hallelujah*. It was very interesting to hear the words of these American songs sung in French.

One of the most amusing sights we saw that evening was a negro gentleman, dressed in the most elegant fashion, with spats, silk-hat, gold-headed cane, and a pair of gold-rimmed glasses with a long, black ribbon dangling from one end. He was seated at the table next to ours, with a great siphon bottle and a host of empty glasses in front of him. He was conversing with his wife in the dialect of the typical American negro.

After another brief walk up the Rue de Rivoli, we returned to our hotel, all of us feeling that there was perfect justification for Paris' reputation as the gay and happy city of the world.

The Amalfi Drive and Sorrento

The Amalfi drive, between Naples and Sorrento, is considered by many people the most beautiful and spectacular in the world. It has all the circuitous twists and dips of a scenic railway. It mounts to stupendous heights above the vivid Tyrrhenian sea, tunnels its way through great mountains and loops around huge projections of cliff. With splendid persistence, it defies the most terrific obstacles that nature could thrust in its path. Upon people with weak hearts or easily agitated nerves, it is apt to prove rather a strain; especially when they drive over it in a high-powered car, with one of these marvelous Italian chauffeurs who drive around a horse shoe curve, a thousand feet above the sea, just as casually as you would turn a street corner.

Several other parties accompanied ours upon the drive and we formed a caravan of six or seven cars. While passing along one of the narrowest and most elevated sections of the road, the driver of the car directly behind ours became dissatisfied with the speed that we were making and determined to pass us up. Our chauffeur, however, black-browed and ferocious looking as Mussolini, was equally determined not to let him by. For half an hour they fought over the narrow road, swerving from side to side, honking furiously and howling at each other in terms which probably would have scalded our ears if we had been able to understand the Italian language. To the helpless passengers it seemed like a contest to the death. And when finally it was over—the other car having gained the lead by a daring swoop, close to the edge of the precipice—we all felt as limp and breathless as if we had been through the terrors of a nightmare.

For our lunch we stopped at a small Italian hotel, perched precariously on the lofty brow of a cliff. Our table was set in the court-yard, surrounded by pillared arches and filled with a great variety of flowers. While we ate our lunch, consisting of spaghetti, cheese, fruit and wine, we were serenaded by a band of troubadours, playing stringed instruments and tambourines and singing "Santa Lucia" in lusty baritone and tenor.

Shortly before sunset we arrived in Sorrento. Our hotel, a building of pink stucco enveloped in tall palms, was situated high above the brilliant sea. Directly beneath it lay a narrow, rocky beach. Though we were considerably tired from our long trip, we hurried down, by way of an elevator, for an evening swim.

After supper a group of townspeople, clad in their bright provincial costumes, entertained us with folk dancing. We ended our day by walking through the fragrant garden of the hotel and along the edge of the cliff, towering above the dark sea.

I believe the most poignant memory a traveler can bring with him from Europe is that of standing upon this tall cliff, gazing across the wide expanse of the bay and seeing the huge black cone of Mount Vesuvius with its waving plume of red-tinged smoke, outlined sharply against the deep, starset blue of the night sky.

The First Day Out

You are aroused from sleep by the heavy rap of the steward upon the door, announcing that your bath is ready. You stare stupidly about you for a moment, before the joyous realization comes to you that this strange, white-washed room in which you find yourself is the cabin of a ship—that this is the morning of your first day out at sea! You clamber down from your berth, slip into your bath-robe and hasten after the white-coated steward. You bathe hurriedly in clear salt water which buoys you up as though you were made of cork; you dress still more hurriedly. And in fifteen minutes you are making your way eagerly through the labyrinth of swaying white corridors, bound for the deck to get your first glimpse of the open sea.

As you pass the dining salon you hear the clanging of the breakfast bell, catch a glimpse of polished tables and waiters bearing trays of savory breakfast foods. Though you are ravenously hungry, you walk past without heeding it and mount the short flight of steps that leads onto the deck. In the door-way you pause dizzily. Your last view from the deck the evening before had been of the harbor with the lights of New York shining mistily through the dark night. The huge black piers had stretched on either side, crowded with people holding sleek, wet umbrellas over their heads and shouting and laughing above the loud splash of the falling rain and the sea. Now it is very different. All trace of land has disappeared during the night. Around you on every side is the flashing blue and gold of the sea, stretching in seeming endlessness. It is a magnificent sight. The water is a brilliant royal blue. The waves are crested with snow-white foam.

You spend several minutes gazing raptly over the rail of the deck. And then you remember your breakfast. You hurry down to the dining salon and take a place at the table reserved for your party. After consuming a hearty meal, you return to the deck, find the deck chair assigned to you, extend it to its full length and stretch comfortably out, wrapping yourself in a heavy grey robe. A cool sea breeze sweeps over the deck. The sun shines warmly. Your spirits feel as buoyant as the foamy crests of the waves.

You remain on deck throughout the morning, reading snatches from your book or magazine, playing a few games of bridge or shuffleboard and watching your fellow passengers. They seem to be principally college students, talking and laughing together and having a riotously good time. There are also a considerable number of teachers, clergymen and other professional people. The open sea seems to have a remarkably tonic effect upon the spirits for you see not a single sour face except among those already suffering from the mal-de-mer.

Toward the middle of the morning hot bouillon and crackers are served. The sight of food has already become distressing to those afflicted with seasickness. When the steward passes them with his tray, their faces assume an expression like that of sensitive ladies at a prize-fight. They cast malign glances up on any one who takes out a box of chocolates or happens to make any remark upon the subject of food.

You congratulate yourself that you are such an excellent sailor. However, just at that moment, something very peculiar happens to your head. It seems to come loose and to bob up and down, just like a kite on a windy day. Your legs wobble and the sea and sky whirl dazzlingly around you. You sink into a chair and close your eyes. Only one thought consoles you in your misery. And that is that in five more days you will be once more upon firm land.

Candida (ca. 1936–1937)

Shaw strikes me as being one of the sanest, most balanced individuals that these chaotic times have produced. At the age of eighty, or thereabouts, he is a truly magnificent spectacle, wisecracking his way around the world, as brave and hearty as ever, thumbing his nose at superstitions, conventions, stuffy ideas wherever he goes, winning the affection, even, of people who never get beyond the Sunday magazine section for intellectual or literary exercise. This extraordinary sanity and mental poise of his makes almost everything he has to say witty and more or less enlightening. But as an artist it proved his undoing. No, he is not an artist. In the first place I doubt that artists live to be eighty years old. Old age is the reward of temperance and temperance is not an artistic virtue. Maybe that isn't the complete reason for Shaw's failure as an artist. But the failure itself seems a pretty undeniable fact. Shaw's plays work out like formulas or algebraic problems. His characters move like clockwork figures. It's hard to say why. You can't just put your finger on the source of this unreality. Perhaps seen on the stage, Candida would take on life. Good actors can do amazing things with poor parts. But in manuscript form—well, I can't recall a single speech that impressed me as ringing exactly true, unless it's the long speech of Candida's near the end where she tells the Parson just what she thinks of him. . . .

Marchbanks, the eighteen year old poet-philosopher-lover, is particularly fantastic. It is just impossible to take this character seriously. In the first place such a creature could not exist—not even in the mad-house! Throughout the play (like Shaw himself, who has always professed to be painfully shy) this precocious fellow is ranting about how frightfully timid he is, quite at the mercy of everyone, absolutely unable to lift a finger in his own defense! Then look at the way he acts! Extraordinary! Goes into the Parson's home, tells the Parson he loves the Parson's wife, that the Parson's wife doesn't love the Parson, that the Parson's wife does love him, the young poet, and that he, the young poet, has every intention of taking the Parson's wife because the Parson is just an old windbag and is totally incompetent as the husband of such a celestially refined and exceptional lady as the Parson's wife! How shy of him! Almost obsequious, I would say. . . . And then his poetic gifts—we will have to take the author's word for them! Whenever he becomes lyrical he sounds like the opening chapter of a newspaper serial about tropical castaways or love among artists. . . .

Parson Morell is hardly less fantastic. Any other man in this situation—any other man of a fairly vigorous nature, and Morell is evidently not the pusil-lanimous type of cleric—would have thrown the damned young fool out on his ear. But Parson Morell takes it all very earnestly. Everything must be handled on a high, spiritual plane. Make yourself at home, he says, win my wife if you can—there's nothing I can do about it because I'm a gentleman! And then he practically foams at the mouth with anxiety lest the young poet should actually succeed in his design.

This makes a good, exciting stage situation, perhaps, but it's almost as far from the way real human beings would act as this earth is out of heaven!

Candida herself is fairly possible. A bit cold and fishy, perhaps—and the young poet's absurd, inexplicable adulation of this apparently commonplace woman rather turns us against her—but she does have the saving grace of a sense of humor, which is totally lacking in both Marchbanks and Morell! She does not take either the two men or the situation seriously.

The minor characters are purely stock. Burgess is fairly amusing, in a heavy fashion, Prossy might be—on the stage.

What is the point of the play? Obviously it is supposed to solve some sort of moral or elucidate some kind of problem. I'm not quite sure just what it is. Ob-viously it has something to do with the subtleties of the feminine soul. She is just as likely to love the man for his faults as for his virtues—in fact, more likely, since the maternal instinct requires something to pity or indulge. She does not have to be understood, petted, or set on a pedestal. She doesn't mind cleaning lamps, peeling onions and listening to sermons. But she must feel that she is necessary to the man. . . . Is that it? Maybe so! At any rate, she has the good sense to send romantic halfwits like young Marchbanks "OUT INTO THE NIGHT!" where they certainly belong without worrying herself too much about the mysterious "secret" gnawing at their super-sensitive hearts!

Shaw served an invaluable purpose in transporting the stage from the dilly-dallying society preoccupation that Wilde left it in to the more realistic direction that Ibsen pointed out. But Ibsen was an artist as well as in innovator. Shaw is merely the innovator, the transitionist or pioneer. There is probably going to be something like a dramatic revival now that the worst of the movie influence is passing over [essay breaks off here].

Review of Two Plays by John M. Synge (ca. 1936–1937)

Synge is not only the leading dramatist of the "Irish Renaissance" but it seems to me that he should be ranked as one of the foremost of all dramatists. As an artist I would place him above his fellow countryman, G. B. Shaw. Shaw is eminently practical and down-to-earth and yet this fanciful Irishman, Synge, gives his most fantastic works, according to my notion, an air of reality and an emotional truth which I find lacking in Shaw. Of course Shaw had the artistic handicap of writing problem plays, while Synge's only intention is to portray the Irish character which he loved and understood so well. . . .

With the possible exception of the negros and the Jews, the Irish have the most distinctive racial characteristics to be found among western peoples. The Gaelic nature is full of surprises and contradictions, so it is no wonder that it has been so greatly misinterpreted in literature and misunderstood in life. The early stage conception of the Irishman, and one which still prevails to a considerable extent, is of a drunken, brawling, red-nosed braggart whose every other word is a curse, boast or a lie. But a good-natured likeable fool for all that. Synge explodes this ridiculously false notion, which is just a caricature of the worst Gaelic type. There is a good deal of drunkenness, lying and braggadocio in the Synge Irishman, but there is also an immense fund of poetry, sensitiveness, tenderness, humor, and even spirituality. All of those qualities, hitherto almost completely ignored in literary treatment of the Irish character, are brought out in Synge's characterizations.

The most striking quality of Synge's work is its poetry. And yet there are few obvious efforts at poetic effect. Much of the poetry is derived directly from the folk speech of the characters, the highly colorful idiom which the Irish peasantry employ. Synge, himself a poet, caught this poetic flavor of folk speech and used it in his plays with extreme effectiveness. The language is English (or Anglo-Irish) but so filled with colorful idiom that it seems entirely new and fresh. There is hardly a line without some surprising twist or inversion of phrase or some poetically startling figure of speech. Hence though the action is often slow and the situation without great dramatic tension, the reader's interest is maintained throughout by the sheer poetry of the language.

Riders to the Sea, a one-act tragedy, is a characterization of an old Irish woman, all of whose six sons, husband, and father-in-law were lost in accidents or storms at sea. As the play opens, Michael, eldest of the two remaining, is lost at sea. His fate is not certain. The youngest, Bartley, is about to start on a short voyage. The mother tries uselessly to dissuade him from going. They part in anger. The two daughters urge her to overtake him and give him some bread and a blessing for the trip. She goes out with this intention, and while she is gone a sock and a shirt belonging to Michael are found, washed up on the seashore. This is proof of Michael's death. They are wondering how to break the news to Maurya, the old woman, when she comes in and without a word from them begins a keen for the dead. They ask her if she has given Bartley her blessing. She tells them that she has seen a terrible vision. "The fearfulest thing any person has seen since the day Bride Dara saw the dead man with the child in his arms." She has seen Bartley riding down to the sea on the red mare, and behind him, Michael's ghost astride the grey pony. . . .

Shortly afterwards a crowd of keening women come up to the house and enter the room. Bartley has fallen victim to the sea. But the old woman shows no surprise. She was already prepared for this final tragedy. Now that the last of her six sons is gone she has a strange feeling, almost of relief. . . .

"Michael has a clean burial in the far north, by the grace of Almighty God. Bartley will have a fine coffin out of the white boards, and a deep grave surely. What more can we want than that? No man at all can be living for ever, and we must be satisfied."

The Playboy of the Western World is also a study of Irish peasantry. Christopher Mahon, the playboy or athlete, has had a quarrel with his father and strikes him over the head with a loy (whatever that is) and thinking he has killed him, runs away from home. He takes refuge, finally, after eleven days of flight, in a tavern owned by Michael James and operated by his pretty daughter Pegeen. Pegeen is engaged to a cowardly clown named Shawn Keogh, who has struck a good bargain with her father, but when Christopher tells his story of killing his father, she is completely enamored by the daring young "playboy." The story quickly spreads through the whole locality and Christy, who has been hired as Pot boy at the tavern, becomes a sort of local deity, the most desperate criminal and fearless young playboy the coast of Mayo has ever known. All the young girls bring him presents. The Widow Quin, who has buried her children and destroyed her man, proposes marriage. But Christy is in love with Pegeen. The following day a big athletic tournament is held and Christy wins every contest. While it is going on, Christy's father, old Mahon, arrives at the tavern. He has been following Christy for eleven days. The Widow Quin throws him off the trail for a while, but when he returns he finds Christy in the tavern and exposes the hoax. Pegeen and all the others turn against him. In his rage Christy strikes his father another blow with the loy. Again the old man appears to be dead.

But this does not reinstate the playboy. On the contrary the impulsive peasants decide to hang him for the murder and have him tied up when the old man again recovers, enters the tavern and demands Christy's release. In the end father and son both go off, different ways, and Pegeen is left bitterly lamenting her loss of "the only Playboy of the Western World."

The story sounds merely farcical, and indeed it is, but the characterization is so keen and the language so striking that the play is lifted far above the ordinary level of folk comedy. Phrases and figures of speech which would sound ridiculously theatrical or bombastic in ordinary English seem perfectly natural when expressed in the quaint idiom of the Irish peasants. The love scene between Christy and Pegeen in the third act contains some especially beautiful passages, such as the following:

> Christy: Let you wait to hear me talking till we're astry in Erris when Good Friday's by, drinking a sup from a well and making mighty kisses with our wetted mouths, or gaming in a gap of sunshine, with yourself stretched back unto your necklace, in the flowers of the earth. ****
>
> Pegeen: And myself a girl was tempted often to go sailing the seas till I'd marry a Jew-man with ten kegs of gold, and I not knowing at all there was the like of you drawing nearer, like the stars of God.

These passages and many others, if not the whole play, could easily pass for poetry.

Some Representative Plays of O'Neill And a Discussion of his Art (1936)

As Eugene O'Neill is still a living author critical studies of his work and life have hardly begun to emerge. Unfortunately most critics do not feel free to consider a man's work in its entirety until after his death. The obvious reason is that they are then reasonably safe from being refuted by the most authoritative source. They can give their imaginations a freer rein. Critics have a passion, it seems, for systematizing works of art, for explaining them psychologically, linking them up with some peculiar theory of their own concerning the poet's soul in its struggle between good and evil, the flesh and the devil, or some such thing as that. The only person who is in any position to bear witness to such a relationship between work and poet or such a spiritual struggle is, of course, the poet himself. And the poets are as a rule wisely reticent, feeling correctly that their works are the important things and should stand by themselves.

Mr. Richard Dana Skinner in his study of O'Neill *The Poet's Quest* displayed unusual intrepidity, not waiting till his subject was beyond earshot before he began his spiritual analysis. He got around O'Neill by making an agreement with him that he (O'Neill) was not to see the manuscript before its publication. He admits this in his preface and condones it by the extraordinary excuse that most artists are incapable of understanding what they were trying to say and so it is the critic's mission to inform them.

Mr. Skinner conceives of O'Neill's whole work as representing some sort of mystic quest for truth in the universe. That is all right and quite possible but it seems to me that Mr. Skinner is trying to make the foot to fit the shoe. He searches for spiritual symbols in the most out of the way, often the most ludicrous places. He fails to distinguish between the pure bathos in O'Neill's writing and the comparatively rare passages of real poetry. Apparently he is a man with some knowledge of the theater (judging by the fact that he has reviewed plays for theatrical journals) but he does not even seem to recognize the elements of calculated showmanship, of melodrama, of exciting "Theater" which are so characteristic of even O'Neill's most serious work. It is easy enough to find mysticism in O'Neill and even a conscientious quest for truth but this should not be used as the primary motif for a critical analysis of his whole work. It seems to me that O'Neill was first, last, and always the born showman. Barnum and Bailey are not more replete with tricks for catching and holding public attention. In almost every major production we find him using some new and startling (?) device to give his work a superficial novelty. In *The Great God Brown* it was the use of masks, supposedly drawn from the classic Greek theater. However masks served a totally different purpose in the Greek drama. They were used because the size of the amphitheater and the lack of lighting facilities made facial acting virtually impossible: masks were used so the back-row audience could get a view of the actors. O'Neill used them to express dual personality, a very obvious and unnecessary device which added nothing but a spurious novelty to the value of the play. In *Strange Interlude* he used the soliloquy and the "aside" which was suppose to represent the workings of the subconscious. A subtle dramatist such as Ibsen or Maeterlinck could express the subconscious, the hidden self, without resorting to this obvious device. There was certainly nothing original about it, as soliloquies and asides are as old as drama itself and have been discarded as outworn in the modern theater and inimical to realism.

In the trilogy *Mourning Becomes Electra* the innovation is one of length, primarily, together with a fatalistic theme like that of the Atreus cycle. O'Neill intends to extend the length still further in his new cycle of plays which according to reports will run for a week. It seems to me that this is developing in the wrong direction as modern life tends to speed up everything and the more we can say in a small space the greater will be our probable success. Nevertheless it will have the temporary appeal of something new—new to the modern audience—and will no doubt attract a crowd of novelty seekers.

But of course his innovations represent only one side of his art. Unquestionably O'Neill has made some very serious contributions to American drama.

O'Neill is not a delicate craftsman. He seldom carves with a meticulous or even painstaking file. His usual implements are the rough chisel and hammer. His effects are ponderous, sometimes oppressive, and nearly always have a crude power. His light moments are not frequent and often give the impression of ungainly effort.

O'Neill is sometimes called the poet of the American theater. I'm afraid this is more flattering to O'Neill than it is to the American theater. It is true we have produced very few poet-dramatists. At present there is Maxwell Anderson but his poetry does not seem to be on a very high plane. I think Paul Green comes closest of any within my ken to actually being a poet-dramatist.

O'Neill's poetry comes out of a bucket. It is more often poured on than applied with a brush. It has a tendency to splatter much too copiously and often may be classified as poetry only for the sake of convenience.

O'Neill seems to work with a sullen, muscle-bound fury, whacking off a chunk here, a chunk there, smearing on a generous splash from the bucket, hurriedly patching or glossing over the defects and rushing on to the conclusion. In the end he has something whose approximate effect is one of coarse grandeur. Most of the figures are out of line, the perspective is slightly off, the colors blurred together and laid on too heavy. But surprisingly the final effect is almost invariably impressive.

Unevenness is the most glaring single defect of this technique. O'Neill's characters have a sporadic existence. For stretches they seem to glow and move with a miraculous liveliness. They are fairly transfigured as though infused with the actual breath of life. Then something happens. The machinery suddenly runs down. The characters become rigid as clockwork. They lose countenance. They move heavily. Their speech becomes dull and unreal. Then the animating force resumes its magic. There is another fiercely animated spurt. Then the running down process sets in once more. And so on and on through the play. Of course on the stage this is not so apparent because O'Neill almost always obtains the best of acting and directing talent and those two factors can breathe life into the dullest of dramatic clay. But in manuscript this unevenness of characterization is strikingly evident.

A sincere and sometimes profound search for truth in human personality is perhaps the dominant quality of O'Neill's work. He seems to have discovered a number of fundamental truths about human character which he uses over and over again in his plays. By "discovered" I do not mean that he was the *first* to recognize their existence. Far from that. But he did recognize them and understood them with a perception that is often acute.

Frustration, bewilderment, passion, inarticulate longing, thirst for beauty, for freedom, conflict, duality, selfishness, greed, and tenderness are some of the qualities of character which play most prominently in his work. He is the poet of the inarticulate. He tries to express the inarticulate longings and passions and frustrations of the ordinary human being. He goes about it in a blundering, semi-articulate manner which is not unsuggestive in itself of the people he writes about. Significantly most of his plays are in a dialect or jargon of some sort. The dialect is not recognizable as that of any particular community or locality or time. It is a coarse American language, a sort of composite back-woods-Bronx-bohunk-seaman jargon which O'Neill uses to fit nearly every type of uncultivated character he portrays. It is a powerful and effective language within its limits. But when it tries to scale poetic heights it becomes frequently incongruous. As an example I might cite this passage from *Beyond the Horizon*, O'Neill's first Pulitzer Prize play:

"Suppose I was to tell you it's just Beauty that's calling me, the beauty of the far off and unknown, the mystery and spell of the East which lures me—the joy of wandering on and on—in quest of the secret which is hidden just over there, beyond the horizon?"

I do not see how these lines could be spoken by any farm boy without creating a ludicrously incongruous effect. This is typical of O'Neill's embarrassing directness, his lack of subtlety. It is the ubiquitous tar-brush, the inevitable bucket, which follows O'Neill in all his psycho-artistic meanderings as faithfully as Mary's Little Lamb! [. . .]

The final estimate of O'Neill's work as a dramatist is probably epitomized in the words that the Nobel prize judges used in granting him their dramatic award for the past year:

"To Eugene O'Neill in recognition of his dramatic art, imbued with strength, honesty and deep feeling as well as by a personal and original conception of tragedy."

Is Fives (1936)

There are two kinds of poets in the world, the "Is Fives" and the "Two Times Two Is Fours." As a matter of fact there is really only one kind, the "Is Fives," since the "Two Times Two" variety are only poets by the grace—or rather disgrace—of those editors that are publishing their works, or by uninformed and undiscriminating public taste. The meaning of these two classifications may still be a little obscure. Perhaps I can clarify it somewhat by quoting directly from the book by E. E. Cummings whose title is the same as that of this paper. "Ineluctable preoccupation with The Verb," says Mr. Cummings, "gives a poet one priceless advantage: whereas nonmakers must content themselves with the merely undeniable fact that two times two is four, he [the "Is Five" poet] rejoices in a purely irresistible truth," namely that five is five or that the quantity of five exists, much in the same way that Miss Gertrude Stein rejoices in the purely irresistible truth of a rose being a rose and continuing to be a rose and purely and simply a rose. This, by the way, is not so ridiculous as it sounds. It has been described by some critics as the repetitious mammerings of insanity. I myself do not think it a particularly felicitous example of Miss Stein's work but it is far from being inexcusable. Miss Stein, an "Is Five" poet, has been so struck, so delighted by the mere fact of the rose's existence, by the truth of the rose being the rose, that she has, quite pardonably, been unable—in her excitement and wonder—to progress beyond that first moment of exquisite divination. A romantic poet or an Elizabethan might and probably would have proceeded to say that the rose was like his mistress's cheek or the color of her lips or the fragrance of her hair. That is typical "two times two" procedure. It does not get at the rose. It may get at the poet's mistress but even that is doubtful. It gets at the printed page and it gets at the popular fancy, both dubious attainments, and that's about all. Miss Stein in her mere statement of the rose in continued existence has gone a great deal further in the right direction despite the fact that she has gone no further than the verb to be.

This paper will no doubt prove to be a series of digressions since it aims to give a definition of pure poetry in necessarily indirect manner. To return briefly to explanations, when we say that a poet is "ineluctably preoccupied with the verb" we mean that he views reality with a direct and penetrating eye. His vision is not refracted, twisted or obstructed by externals or superficialities. The reason that some people love romantic or traditional poetry to the exclusion of all other kinds is that they are incapable of looking directly at things in the modern "Is Five" manner. They can't see the bare trunk of the tree, they can see only the little bright-colored leaves. They cannot and do not wish to see the amazing black root in the soil, they only see and only wish to see the speciously attractive blossom which is its external show. They have not looked, as Euclid has looked, on "Beauty bare." They have not even heard (more faintly and then but far away) her massive sandal set on stone.

I do not mean that no romantic poets are "Is Fives" or that all moderns are. That would be far from true. The "Is Fives" are a human type and not a period or literary type. Possibly there were "Is Fives" among the earliest cavemen. It is rather likely that there were. Possibly there are "Is Fives" among children. I am sure that there are.

But today the "Is Fives" are beginning to have a real audience because of something which we cannot understand at present, some mysterious new yeast that is fermenting the social consciousness, bringing new realities to the surface. You will find me using the word reality perhaps too often throughout this paper, because the word reality contains the whole clue to what I mean by the "Is Five" kind of poetry. In the older periods "Is Fives" could rarely show their true colors. They might have been clapped into lunatic asylums. Only a few giant or exceptional figures like Shakespeare or John Donne or William Blake dared to put their more direct vision before the public eye. And even they did it only in occasional passages. Shakespeare's lyric "The Wind and the Rain" comes to my mind most readily as an example of one of these pioneer "Is Five" or pure poems. Another shining example is, of course, Whitman who in the full bloom of poetry's most innauseatingly over-stuffed and sentimental period dared to lift a totally new and singular voice. It was a shrill voice with rough edges, very much like the screech of an outraged eagle, or an eagle that defies ill-opinion, but nevertheless its sound is extremely grateful upon our ears since it rises above the nauseous cooings of so many sickly grey doves.

Being an "Is Five" then is having a direct view of reality. It is more than that—perhaps much more—but the rest can only be left to individual intuition since it is largely an intuitional thing. Once in reading a passage from H. D.'s verse someone asked me, "What is there good about that?" The obvious answer was complete silence. Nobody can tell anybody else what there is good about pure poetry. No more than he could describe to a lungless person how it feels to inhale pure air.

Arriving at this direct view of reality is like scaling a terrifically high, precipitous range of mountains in order to obtain a clear view of the surrounding country. It is not an easily accessible point of view. That is, in most cases it wasn't. Perhaps some rare individuals are born with it. Children have something approximating it. A wide-eyed innocence of outlook, an unqualifying directness of experience. But theirs is not an intelligent or critical awareness and hence is never perfect. Arriving at this direct view is, then, an apocalyptic experience analogous to that of religious conversion—only it is not in most cases a sudden, inspired, instantaneous thing. It is a thing which may—and usually does—grow very slowly, almost imperceptibly, like a mental disease, only that it grows in the opposite direction, until all at once the individual awakes and looks about him and discovers that he has wandered as if by accident into quite a new and different world. He has left the land of 2 X 2 behind him and entered the high, clear region that is beyond mathematical equations. It is a blinding hour, a holy, terrible day like that of Euclid in Miss Millay's famous sonnet, in which he first beheld "light anatomized."

A great many "In Fives" do not write "Is Five" poetry. It is too difficult. Too abstract. Too private. Being an "Is Five" is not writing poetry any more than it is composing music or drawing pictures or dancing. It is not an art so much as it is an attitude toward life. It is a comprehension of reality. It is a state of wonder. An intensification of emotion. A brilliance and acuteness of perception. A separateness, an individuality. An independence. A standing-aloneness. A purity. An exactness. And also an inexactness. It contains a good many contradictions in terms. Perhaps the closest single word would be the word "intuitiveness."

It is not, I think, an exceedingly rare thing. I doubt if anyone in this room is wholly without it. Artists and people interested in any kind of art—if they have any degree of sincerity—are necessarily "Is Fives" potentially to some degree, for the fact that they are artists or interested in art indicates that they are conscious of something beyond the immediacies of daily living, something beyond inhale and exhale, feel, speak, see, devour. They are conscious of something a little bit out of their reach and they are trying to reach it. They are conscious of certain fundamental rhythms and harmonies. Something is moving them, stirring them up. It is the quality beyond mathematics. Trying to make itself known. Maybe they will get married and have children and build a home in the suburbs and buy a radio and a car and join the Bible Class and the Country Club and the Colonial Dames and take a great interest in the love affairs of Mae West. And in this way their personalities may be gradually diffused, spread out thin over the thousand little facts of possession and belonging, and the fact of simple *being* may lose its original clarity and wonder just as a day fades into twilight and finally into complete dark. Whatever distance they had gotten toward the wonderland beyond mathematical equations will slip from beneath them and they will barely be conscious of the loss, it will come so gradually day by day. They may feel even a little easier on the surface, and say, "When I was young I was an awful fool. I liked poetry and walking alone in the woods and once when I looked out of a high window and saw sunlight cutting in shafts between tall buildings I felt that I was something like God because I felt cold and pure and disassociated from everything that was happening around me and saw it all as a single vast and beautiful pattern as simple and positive and uncompromising as the verb to be!"

Birth of an Art (Anton Chekhov and the New Theater) (1937)

Chekhov and His Critics

Chekhov was one of those rare artists that have the attribute of genius in that they exercise a profound, revolutionary influence on the art of their times. Probably the originator of naturalism in the Russian theater, Chekhov was one of the pioneer naturalists of world literature. He is almost universally recognized as the greatest of all short-story writers, comparable only to Maupassant. His art was peculiarly adopted to this particular form. Chekhov was a lyricist, a creator of moods and atmospheres, a profound analyst of human character. His work has a necessarily limited public. Those who demand exciting narrative, super-ficial cleverness, nerve-shocking drama find little to stimulate their ganglions in his work. They describe him as dull, morbid, colorless. Like most Russians, Chekhov was an intense introvert. He was primarily interested in the life of the soul. Events were secondary to him. Hence he was not strong on plot. Most of his stories strike orthodox critics as being merely anecdotal. They also descry his characters as being unnatural. This is something of a paradox. People will accept the conventional, stock characters of commonplace fiction as thoroughly natural but when they see people on the stage who are transposed directly from life, who are the walking, talking counterparts of their own selves, they imme-diately set up a great cry that these characters are exaggerated, unreal, ridicu-lous—"they behave like lunatics—they are absurdly artificial!" Which proves how little we know ourselves! [. . .]

A Man Without Ideas
In Chekhov's own lifetime, while he enjoyed considerable popularity, he was disparaged by certain readers as a writer who had no ideas to offer. This is in-deed a strange charge to bring against any artist. Art, it has been proven, does not direct itself at the reason or the intellect so much as at that special depart-ment of the mind that is known as the esthetic sense. It is altogether possible for great works of art to be devoid of rational appeal. For substantiation of this we need only point out the charm of imagist poetry, much of which is completely devoid of meaning, but which nevertheless excites a very powerful emotional response in those who like poetry. All abstract beauty is devoid of ideas in the strict sense. In fact I think ideas in that sense may be an encumbrance rather than an asset to certain types of creative art. Ideas in the strict sense are ephem-eral things: truth and beauty are constants. In Ibsen it is not the social themes that have survived: it is the ineluctable artistry with which the plays were writ-ten. It is the Life in them and not the ideas that continue to hold validity—long after the social problems have been resolved. If Shaw's plays survive it will be for the same reason. So the lack of sociological doctrine or new and original "idea" need not be regarded as a fatal defect in Chekhov's work.

However it is only in the narrowest sense that Chekhov can be said to lack ideas. How can any man who gives a true criticism of life be said to lack ideas? His ideas are so large, so comprehensive and so evenly diffused through all his work that they escape the attention of shallow critics. That is the way "Ideas" in literature should be. They should not have the effect of being artificially planted. They should not stick out like a sore thumb. They should be inconspicuously woven through the whole fabric and that is the way they are articulated in Chekhov's works.

I doubt very much if Chekhov can be classified as either right or left, in the popular fashion of these times. Is that a defect or an asset? I think it is distinctly the latter. His was a spirit too large for partisanship. Was he a defeatist? That may be a valid charge. But I don't think it is a damning one. However it must be remembered that he lived in a period and in a society of defeat. The defeatism was not so much his as it was the culture's which he represented. Today we speak of the lost generation as that which immediately followed the war. Chekhov's generation in Russia was even more hopelessly lost. And they knew it. And yet in that unhappy twilight of a social order some of the finest art in the world's history came into being. It was the swan song—which is said to be the loveliest music of all! [. . .]

Chekhov and the New Theater
The problems of playwriting are so peculiar that they usually demand almost a lifetime of application and study. Most major dramatists have lived more or less constantly in some association with the theater. Ibsen was always a dramatist. Shakespeare was an actor and theater-manager. Eugene O'Neill was the son of a veteran Thespian. The list could be extended further. But Chekhov did not even become interested in the theater until near the close of his career. Roughly about the last ten years of his life. And yet in that short time he achieved an absolute mastery. He flew directly in the face of the old theater: defied their conventions: created a new theater for which the general public was quite unprepared: produced four or five plays which stand among the greatest dramatic work of all time.

Chekhov's first dramatic writings were two one-act farce comedies called *The Bear* and *The Proposal*. These were highly popular vaudeville pieces and unlike most of Chekhov's work can be appreciated by English-speaking audiences of mass culture. His first long work was *Ivanov*, a more conventional work than his later plays, which enjoyed a conventional success when presented by the Imperial Theater in St. Petersburg.

Chekhov's first important production was *The Sea Gull*, produced by the same theater, which was a miserable failure. This failure demonstrated the inability of the old theater methods to translate modern art to the stage. The cast was picked from the best stage favorites. Chekhov himself attended rehearsals. But from the beginning failure was apparent. The actors could not understand the pervasive lyricism of the piece. They could not discard their stock mannerisms and voices which were of course totally unsuited to the new art. Chekhov was desperate. "Why don't they stop *acting?*" he exclaimed. No one knew what he meant. They were so used to expressing themselves in these out-worn cliches of speech and gesture that they could use nothing else. The production was elaborate and painstaking. But a complete failure. The audience—in Russian style—was loudly contemptous. They hissed during the intermissions, burst into rude laughter at the climax when the unfortunate young Treplieff shoots himself. Chekhov during this fiasco walked around backstage in a daze. Afterwards he disappeared from the theater: it is said that he walked for hours in the rain, catching a cold which seriously undermined his already failing health. The next morning, without seeing anyone, he departed from St. Petersburg. In a letter he declared that he would never, never write another play if he lived to be seven hundred years old!

The Moscow Art Theater

At about this time one of the most important things in dramatic history was shaping itself. The two great impresarios, Stanislavsky and Dantchenko, were planning to create a new art theater in Moscow. This theater was to have all the virtues that the old theater lacked and was to lack all the old defects. Members were solicited not from the established favorites but from young and ambitious new-comers who were not afraid of revolutionary methods. Hauptmann, Ibsen, Strindberg, Maeterlinck, Tolstoi, Ibsen, Chekhov were the writers whose work they wished to present: in other words, it was a naturalist movement.

Many striking reforms were intended. First of all it was necessary to create a new audience or to re-educate the old. Many horrible practices were tolerated in the old theater. When an audience was pleased it was customary to demand bows in the middle of a dramatic scene. The favorites would advance to the footlights and bow while the other players stood in doll-like attitudes till the ovation ended and the action could resume. Of course this was fatal to that illusion of reality which a good production demands.

The audience usually came late and was seated during the performance. The corridors were noisy. During interludes there was orchestral music. Booing and hissing were unconstrained.

All of these bad practices were taboo at the new Moscow Art Theater.

There were also many technical improvements. Stock scenery was discarded. In the future each play must have its own specially designed set. Stage-craft became a fine art. Performances must not lag through mechanical hitches. Scenes must be shifted promptly without the once-inevitable clamor. Curtains must operate smoothly. And they must be closed, not lowered. Careful attention must be given to lighting. No more sickly green moonlight. The orchestra may be eliminated: usually it interrupts rather than enhances the mood of a play and is, at any rate, an artificial device for stimulating playgoers. There will be no curtain-bows except at the end of the play.

Of course the main reforms were to be in actual play presentation. There is to be a new style of acting: an acting that does not depend upon clichés of speech and gesture. Each speech and movement is to be thought out carefully rather than left to the haphazard virtuosity of stars. Each play will receive individual treatment. The old method of letting the main actors run the show is out. The company must work as an ensemble, a unit. The play will be the thing. The *Régisseur* will be the chief potentate and what he says will go.

There will be acting classes. Each scene of a new play will be rehearsed separately until completely mastered. Rehearsals will be far more painstaking and intensive than was ever the case in the old theater.

Chekhov's Success in the New Theater

Though *The Sea Gull*'s failure in St. Petersburg had a saddening effect on the author, it did not damage his reputation as a writer. It was felt that such a fine story writer could be forgiven a dramatic failure. Chekhov's health was rapidly falling and his works were less frequent and more finely wrought. Each new story was a literary event. Now that every one knew he could not live much longer, he was held in much higher regard.

About two years after the St. Petersburg production Dantchenko began to correspond with Chekhov about presenting *The Sea Gull* at the New Moscow Theater. It took eloquent persuasion. Once badly bitten, Chekhov was more than twice shy of the theatrical world. "Perhaps the play will not provoke storms of applause," wrote Dantchenko, "but that a genuine production with *spontaneous* qualities, *liberated from routine,* will prove a triumph of art—this I can guarantee." Two other letters followed before Chekhov was won over to the new presentation.

At this time Chekhov's health was so delicate he could not risk a Moscow winter. So he was not present at the play's *premiere.* This *premiere,* was a sensational success. It was a complete reversal of what had happened two years before in St. Petersburg. Thus rapidly did naturalism come into its own in Russia!

Writing of this momentous *premiere,* Dantchenko says: "The atmosphere was charged with excitement and perturbation, not only among those participating in *The Sea Gull* but in the entire theater. There was a sense of impending storm. The whole existence of the young theater depended on this performance." Stanislavsky, the other impresario, was so nervous that the day before the performance he begged Dantchenko to remove his name from the bills. He did not wish to be associated with this inevitable failure. Dantchenko, however, was certain of the play's success.

The audience was spell-bound throughout the performance. When the final curtain closed, quoting from Dantchenko's memoirs: "Something occurred which can occur in a theater only once in a decade; the curtain closed and there was silence, a complete silence both in the theater and on the stage; it was as though all held their breath, as though no one quite understood; had it been a vision? a dream? a sad song from some familiar melody? Whence had it come? From what memory of everyone there? This mood lasted quite a long time, so long indeed that those on the stage decided that they had failed, failed so completely that not a single friend in the audience dared applaud. A nervous chill seized the actors, close to hysteria. Then suddenly in the auditorium something happened. It was as if a dam had burst, a bomb had been exploded—all at once there was a deafening crash of applause, from all, from friends and from enemies."

This prodigious oration continued until all the actors embraced each other and wept. Dantchenko appeared on the stage in reply to insistent demands for the author and asked if they authorized him to send Chekhov a telegram. At this the oration was extended for an incredibly long time.

"The New Theater was born!"

A Review of Several Chekhov Plays
I. *The Sea Gull*
This like the other major plays of Chekhov is a tragedy of inaction. I will not attempt to give the Russian names of the characters as they are both difficult to spell and pronounce and I have returned the plays to the library.

The main figure in this play is a young writer whose mother is a famous actress. He is about twenty-five years old. His mother has always left him at her country estate. She is one of those miracles of perpetual youth whose fascination for men never wanes. She is ashamed of having such an old son and his presence always depresses her. There is a suggestion of Oedipus complex in the boy's character, although he has no father to envy. His mother's indifference toward him has probably turned his mind inward. He has become introspective and wretchedly unhappy. [. . .]

The essential idea behind this play is the aimless frustration of certain lives: they are like sea-gulls shot down by chance. What happens to them is mainly outside of their own control. Circumstances make them captives. Nina is captured by her hopeless love for Trigorin, who loves the superficial older actress. Masha is captured by her love for Constantine, Constantine by his love for Nina. It is a tangle in which all are helpless victims: no one is really to blame.

The charm of the play is in its haunting atmosphere and the emotional poignancy built up by each scene. It has an exquisite unity of color: a sort of nostalgic twilight pervades it from beginning. There is always the atmosphere of late summer evening with fire-flies and the droning music of locusts. What happens has a dream-like quality: yet it is as real as though we ourselves were the tragic protagonists.

Uncle Vanya

This is another picture of Russian country life. It is somewhat less sombre than *The Sea Gull* and not quite so lyrical. It is likewise a tragedy of inaction: a static drama. Ivan Voitski (or Uncle Vanya) has spent his whole life managing the estate of his brother-in-law. His sister is dead. The estate was her dowry and Vanya has sacrificed his own inheritance and given up his whole existence to preserving it. He has made an idol of his brother-in-law, who is a famous scholar. [. . .]

The theme of this play is the futile sacrifice of certain lives to others. It is a poignant characterization: all the people of the play are vivid, human types. The realism is superb. A fault lies in the use of soliloquies. This was no doubt an approved device of the Russian theater but for me it always injures the illusion of reality.

The Cherry Orchard

This culminating masterpiece of Chekhov's was the last of his four great plays. It was produced for the first time at the Moscow Art Theater exactly four month's before Chekhov's death in Germany where he had gone to make a last stand against his disease. It is the most finished, the most poignant, the most lyrical of all his plays.

I have read *The Cherry Orchard* twice and seen it produced once by the Little Theater of St. Louis and with each contact my appreciation of this masterpiece has deepened. It is to me the most moving piece of realism ever created for the stage.

There is a great division of opinion even among informed persons upon this drama, one's response to it being, apparently, not so much a matter of intellectual acumen or critical skill as of personal temperament. I have heard many persons far more intelligent than I admit that they could see nothing in it; that the characters are fantastic, the story pointless, the dramaturgy very slow and ineffective. I think these critics are probably persons of the extravert type who cannot understand the intense introspection of Russian realism.

Then, too, the play suffers a distinct disadvantage in most of its English stage interpretations. *The Cherry Orchard* has a very strong element of comedy—in some respects it is almost a Russian comedy of manners—but this element is often completely overlooked in English productions with the result that the play is keyed much too low, the gloom is overemphasized to the point of morbidity, the light, lyrical touch is completely lost.

This was nowhere more apparent than in the production given by the St. Louis Little Theater. The main fault in this production was miscasting. The woman who played Mme. Ranevsky was too firm, assured and vigorous-looking. She looked like the typical American business woman and could not help acting like one. Her characterization, while earnest and painstaking, was never at any point convincing. None of the other characters, with the exception of Director Strickland in the role of Leonidas, seemed to catch the nostalgic atmosphere of the play.

To produce this play one must have a cast especially selected for psychological insight and sensitivity. The mood is the paramount thing. Unless that is captured, the whole thing is bound to collapse. This of course is equally true of Chekhov's other major plays.

The theme of *The Cherry Orchard* is essentially the end of an old order and the beginning of a new. It is an epic theme presented with marvelous delicacy. The cherry orchard is symbolic of the graceful, nostalgic charm of old things. In the end when we hear, in the deserted country house, the muffled, hollow ring of the axes on the trees, we realize it is not just the cherry orchard but a whole civilization that is being ruthlessly chopped down to make room for the new. [. . .]

General Characteristics of the Dialogue

In his dialogue Chekhov departs altogether from the tradition of the "well-made" play. If his speeches were carefully analyzed I suppose about forty or fifty percent of them would be found to have no direct bearing upon the story as such. They are included solely for the purpose of characterization or creating atmosphere. In the well-made play every line was intended to "advance the plot." Even in Ibsen one does not find superfluous speeches. Ibsen was a superior craftsman to Chekhov but never achieved, I think, such complete realism. It is this apparent superfluity of speeches that accounts for the magical effect of verisimilitude we find in Chekhov's plays. It is not an actual superfluity, only apparent. Actually Chekhov was a highly selective artist. Every line belongs in its place. Each contributes toward the total effect of the picture.

Chekhov's poetry is a striking contrast to that of Eugene O'Neill. O'Neill's is obvious and often artificial. When his characters become lyrical one suspects them of having had a few drinks on the sly. Chekhov's lyricism, on the other hand, is intrinsic. It never has the effect of being slapped or poured on. It permeates the whole play. When a lyrical speech occurs, it occurs inevitably, in the heat of an emotional excitement which makes such language altogether fitting and natural.

Bibliography:
Nemirovitch-Dantchenkco—*My Life in the Russian Theater*
Frank W. Chandler—*Aspects of the Modern Drama*
Constance Garnett (translator)—*Letters of Anton Chekhov to his Family and Friends*
Collected Plays of Chekhov

Comments on the Nature of Artists with a few Specific References to the Case of Edgar Allan Poe (1937)

There are certain members of the human family cursed or blessed, as the case may be, with what I have seen defined more sharply in French than in English as "la volonté de puissance." This means a fund of uncontrolled energy that exceeds the demands of ordinary living. Dr. Heller has defined the same thing as "L'élan vital." But I think that leaves too much unsaid. The energy of an artist is something that possesses him rather than something that he possesses. It is a "volonté": an unleashed force. The artist's position strikes me as analogous to that of the prophet Daniel in the den of lions. I do not recall my Biblical folk-lore quite distinctly enough to know what was the exact outcome in Daniel's case. I believe he was saved by an act of God. It takes something nearly as unexpected to preserve the artist from dismemberment in the physical cell which he is forced to occupy with his savage beasts. If he succeeds in domesticating them, at least partially, he may train them to perform circus-acts that will startle and delight the whole world. He may lead his beautiful feline pets through graceful routines that will make the big tent resound with his acclaim. Nevertheless they are a constant peril: no matter how beautifully they are trained to perform they are still potential destroyers—that is, of their master!

The reasons for this vital excess is probably unknown: perhaps it is physiological or hereditary, the result of glandular disturbance or of marriage between hyper-sensitive types. At any rate, the man who possesses it finds himself completely unsatisfied with the usual acts of living. They leave a large portion of him still unused. This portion is his den of lions. Unless he puts them to creative use they will take out their vitality on him: they will make him sickly, neurotic or utterly mad. The red meat which they want is art—art is the "something else" of human life. It has been said by a philosopher (I believe James Branch Cabell) that laughter is the only distinctly human attribute: the only quality which man does not share with any of his animal cousins. But that is mistaken. I have seen dogs laugh: my Boston terrier is highly amused

whenever I look for my socks in the morning and he knows that they are
behind the water-boiler in the basement. Art is really the only thing that man
does which none of the beasts can imitate. Some may mention religion as another: but religion is of course a form of art: it is another "something else":
another exercise for the mysterious new perceptions which are beginning to
slowly evolve from the human consciousness. . . .

The number of artists that survive out of the number of potential artists
is probably comparable to the number of vitalized sperms in an act of sexual
conjugation: millions are ejaculated: one out of that number achieves the fertil-
ization which is its object. The artist is made out of an especially perishable substance: this is a fact which literary biography leaves beyond dispute. This may
suggest that art is a compensatory gesture: something that the owner takes up
to compensate for physiological or nervous weakness just as a blind man may
develop acute auditory and tactile senses. I think it is rather a demonstration of
the tremendous drain that the creative energy makes upon the physical being.
Artists have always been particularly prone to degenerative diseases such as tuberculosis: the greatest of the moderns were afflicted with respiratory disorders:
Chekhov, Mansfield died of tuberculosis: Marcel Proust of a similar disease:
O'Neill has an arrested case of tuberculosis. It is rumored that he is now dying
of it. Sidney Lanier struggled against that disease his whole creative life. John
Keats died of it. Nervous maladies are so general among artists as to be almost
universal. To offer a list of nervously afflicted artists would be an extravagant
use of paper [essay breaks off here].

Van Gogh sent his amputated ear to a prostitute in a fit of madness: later shot
himself through the stomach. Tchaikovsky went mad several times: deliberately
drank cholera-infected water. Nijinsky is drawing weird and meaningless designs in a Swiss sanitarium. Hart Crane needed the tangent release of constant
drink, and finally self-destruction.

Edgar Allan Poe is held up—or down—as a superlative example of the abnormal artist. This is merely because he is one of the few great artists that have
received popular recognition and hence the irregularities of his life are more
widely known than those of artists whose fame was more selective.

Until modern times there has never been an organized school of writing in
America. The few great figures that emerged were isolated figures. They had
no predecessors, no companions, no satellites, no followers. The three major
writers of the pre-modern American era are, to my mind, Whitman, Poe, and
Emily Dickinson. Whitman was the most audacious adventurer of them all.
His poetry sounded like the scream of an eagle above the sickly mammerings

of a flock of grey doves. Nevertheless he was the least in talent of the three poets. Poe was probably the greatest: he was less successful in liberating himself
from the literary conventions of his time than Whitman but his art was a firier
brand. In form he did not differ conspicuously from the borrowed elegance of
his American contemporaries: but his subject matter was more truly original or
individual than the subject matter of any artist before or since. [essay breaks
off here] it was so individual that no one has imitated it. His influence was felt
most strongly in France: Baudelaire came closest to being a follower of Poe:
Maeterlinck reflected the weird radiance that was Poe's particular quality. Yet
Poe really has no true successor.

Clark Mills has remarked that the greatest writers commit more obvious
breaches of taste than do the minor writers. We were once arguing the reasons
for this phenomenon. It was Clark's theory that the great writers take less trouble to revise than do the minor ones: they are led on too swiftly toward fresh
creation to polish up material of the past. This is plausible. But my own theory
is that the fires of their creative ardor—to use a trite phrase—make them blind
at times to the most extreme lapses of taste: lapses which would be immediately
apparent to less bedazzled visions.

   Be that as it may, Poe is undoubtedly guilty of some of the worst trash that
has ever been produced in metre. He shares this distinction with Whitman and
Sidney Lanier, both of whom made incredible mistakes in literary taste. Yet all
three of these men, with Emily Dickinson, produced a handful of verse that tops
our national pyramid of art.

   I doubt if Poe's really good poems exceed the number of eight or ten. The
rest are almost insignificant. Among these chief creations I would list, first, the
brilliant piece, "Israfel": then the short but perfect lyric, "Helen, thy Beauty—":
third on the list I would place "The Raven," which is a magnificent *tour-de-force,*
a little too full of artifice, of mechanical devices, of phrase-mongering—but so
deep and moving in its mood that persons ordinarily [essay breaks off here]
   Crane, Eliot, Spender and Auden.

   The value of Poe's verse has been appraised so thoroughly that any remarks one might now make upon it seem painfully obvious. Poe's great gift,
of course, is that of creating a mood. This is better represented in his short-
stories than in his verse: but there is scarcely a line or phrase of Poe's best
lyrics that do not evoke an emotional response. He was a supreme master of
"stage-effect." Each detail of the raven is a vivid progression of atmospheric
effects.

   Poe's mastery of musical alliteration and of rhyme is also unexcelled. Poe has offered an elaborate analysis of "The Raven" and of his other works. Apparently he would have us regard these as products of studious and precise craftsmanship. Anyone who has written poetry recognizes the fact that no amount of craftsmanship could produce the brilliant musical effects of "The Raven": they are the mysterious fire-works of spontaneous art.

"FORGIVE THE DIGRESSION": AN AFTERWORD

"Forgive the digression: it is characteristic of my awkward adventures in the field of nonfictional prose."
—Tennessee Williams, "Let Me Hang It All Out"

Williams's *Memoirs* (and to some extent his novella *Moise and the World of Reason*, published the same year) reveals more about his life than about his art or his theory of artistic production. In it, we are rarely offered insight into the creation of a character or the genesis of a play, rarely provided a philosophy of his dramaturgy. Instead, we encounter story after story of the playwright's past struggle to become a writer and his present struggle to continue being one. "Truth is the bird we hope to catch in 'this thing,'" he writes midway through the autobiography, and "truth" for him was something "better approached through [his] life story than an account of [his] career." To a great extent, the same could be said about Williams's essays.

Anyone interested in Williams's non-fiction would do well to begin with the *Memoirs*, for it provides a roadmap by which to navigate one's way through the essays. One of the obvious reasons for this is that several of his essays found their way into the *Memoirs*, such as his tributes to Laurette Taylor, Carson McCullers, and William Inge. Even portions of his 1960 essay, "Prelude to a Comedy," on his experiences at the American Hospital in Neuilly, France, and his 1973 essay "Homage to Key West" are there. Recycling essays was certainly a way for Williams to fill the pages of a book he declared at times that he did not want to write. Another reason, though, is that the *Memoirs* reproduces on a larger canvas what the essays frequently accomplish on a smaller scale.

"Why do I resist writing about my plays?" Williams asks himself provocatively in the *Memoirs*. "The truth is," he responds,

[. . .] I feel that the plays speak for themselves. And that my life hasn't and that it has been remarkable enough, in its continual contest with madness, to be worth setting upon paper. And my habits of work are so much more private than my daily and nightly existence.

Williams's "truth" was not always pretty in the *Memoirs*, or flattering, either to himself or to those about whom he candidly wrote. While many of the facts used to construct the memories recounted in the book are not always accurate, the *Memoirs* was, as far as Williams was concerned, truthful, and that counted for everything in his world. Simply put, non-fiction was Williams's public confessional, a place where parable-like recollections of his past could resonate certain truths about his vision of humanity and the directions he thought it was taking.

Like the *Memoirs,* many of the essays gathered in this collection claim "truth" through exaggerated or, at times, questionable facts, and they also frequently end up neglecting to address the plays many were meant to introduce prior to their Broadway opening. And yet, these essays *do* talk about the plays or, at least, they talk *around* the plays, substituting narrative digression for interpretative analysis. In many ways, the essays collected here form individual chapters of Williams's shadow memoirs that when read in parallel with the *Memoirs* demonstrates how his non-fiction prose constituted for him singular pieces of a complex mosaic: by themselves, the essays capture those significant moments in Williams's personal and professional life, to which he referred time and time again; reconstituted as a whole, they display the splendor of Williams's lifelong pursuit of the truth, personal and artistic alike.

What these non-fiction pieces also reveal is Williams's paradoxical nature as an essayist. He never wanted to have to *explain* his work to his audiences and critics, but, when they did not "get" it (or if Williams suspected that they might not), he also never turned down the frequent requests by newspaper and magazine editors to contribute a pre-opening piece ostensibly aimed at providing interpretational direction to, or serving as a "trailer" for, a new play prior to its Broadway premier. In "Questions Without Answers" (1948), Williams articulates his skepticism to write directly about his plays:

> Writing an article about your play prior to its New York opening is not going to improve the quality of the play and, moreover, it may have the disadvantage of suggesting to the suspicious that an effort is being made to load the dice. [. . .] To explain is okay if there is something that needs explaining.

And yet, in an unpublished fragment draft of "Person–To–Person," entitled "A Thing Called Personal Lyricism" (ca. 1955), Williams shows that he recognized the essay's potential to "soften-up the New York critics as just the proper moment," though a history of having received mixed press notices had taught him that "an author's disarmingly modest 'pitch' in front of the tent will have little if any effect upon the show's reception in the press." Consequently, Williams was simultaneously eager and hesitant to write these invited pieces of what he called his "Apologia": eager because he understood the author's role in promoting himself within the economy of Broadway, and hesitant because he knew that perceived personal self-promotions could readily backfire.

Evidence of this paradoxical, self-effacing Williams abounds in both his published and his unpublished non-fiction works. In "T. Williams's View of T. Bankhead" (1963), for example, Williams redirects his reader's attention away from the play under discussion in order to preempt charges of authorial pretension:

> I have been invited to contribute to these pages an explication of the meaning and history of my latest version of my "last long play for Broadway," but I am sure you will forgive me for hoping that the play will speak for itself, and to choose the relevant subject of Miss Tallulah Bankhead.

Redirection of the kind expressed here was Williams's signature line of defense in his essays. "There is nothing more 'loaded' than the self-defense of a writer," Williams expresses in another draft fragment entitled "Past, Present & Perhaps" (ca. 1957), for "[a]ll the honest things that a writer has to say about his work are said in the work itself." In redirecting readers away from the subject at hand, Williams also risked alienating his editors and his readers. Because of this, Williams frequently did not know which of these to two essayists he should be and, moreover, when. As a result, he often adopted a third position, one we encounter repeatedly throughout the essays: that of the raconteur of personal anecdotes.

Numerous critics faulted the *Memoirs* at the time of publication for its lack of discernible structure. They complained that it stumbles illogically from one anecdote to another, some set in the present as with his travails concerning the production of *Small Craft Warnings*, some set in the distant or recent past. Much of the same criticism could be leveled against his essays, however, since they, too, seemingly ramble through remembrances and recollections. Williams predicted this criticism, because it was not the first time he had heard it, and defends his apparent "disregard for chronological order" in a statement in the foreword to the *Memoirs*, which could also serve as the doctrine for nearly all his non-fiction prose:

> This whole book is written by something like the process of "free association," which I learned to practice during my several periods of psychoanalysis. It concerns the reportage of present occurrences, both trivial and important; and of memories, mostly much more important. At least to me.
>
> I will frequently interrupt recollections of the past with an account

of what concerns me in the present because of many of the things which concerned me in the past continue to preoccupy me today.

Scattered throughout the *Memoirs* are Williams's personal anecdotes, stories about his sister Rose's lobotomy or his antics during a preproduction reading of *Sweet Bird of Youth*. What appears as uncontrolled digression, though, is in fact a palimpsest of authorial intrusion where one anecdote directly informs another, and the layers of meaning they both contain separately intertwine to construct a large sense of Williams's artistic "truth." If the essays, like the *Memoirs*, seem preoccupied more with *telling* than with *showing*, it is because Williams treats them as he does his short fiction and drama and places the burden of interpretation on the reader/audience.

Williams had perfected this style of deferral, innuendo, connotation, and parable earlier in the essays themselves. Many of the pieces reprinted in this collection wax philosophical about issues of violence ("The World I Live In") or decadence in modern drama ("Tennessee Williams Presents His POV"). Or they supply endless strings of personal anecdotes about Williams's family ("The Man In the Overstuffed Chair"), success ("The Catastrophe of Success"), injuries ("The Wolf and I"), work ethics ("I Have Rewritten a Play For Artistic Purity"), politics ("We Are Dissenters Now"), or thorny relationships with the glitterati and literati of the theatre world ("'Tennessee, Never Talk to an Actress'"). In short, they seem to talk about anything and everything except the plays themselves. In "Prelude to a Comedy," for example, Williams offers a "Philosophical Shop Talk On the Art of Playwriting" in lieu of commentary on *Period of Adjustment*, and the anecdotes recounted in it were so far-reaching that the papers' editors felt the need to add the following apologetic deck, "Without mentioning his new play [. . .]."

Many of the essays in this book similarly leap from one point to another, from one era to another, only to return again to the original idea at hand:

> "But I am supposed to be writing about my relations with actresses. I'm sorry I got off the track"   —"'Tennessee, Never Talk to an Actress'"

> "With little effort at cohesion, let's turn sharply south"
>   —"A Writer's Quest for a Parnassus"

> "I hope I will not annoy you again in this 'Sunday piece' by another statement as pretentious-sounding as that one, so let us go quickly back to the safer ground of simple recollections"
>   —"The Past, the Present and the Perhaps"

> "To return to the woman in the alcove"
>   —"Questions Without Answers"

"Now let's get on the 'Streetcar'"
                            —"T. Williams's View of T. Bankhead"

"Enough of these philosophical abstractions, for now. To get back to
writing for the theatre [. . .]"   —"Foreword to *Sweet Bird of Youth*"

"Now let me attempt to entertain you once more with an anecdote"
                                            —"Too Personal?"

"Having bored you quite enough with talk about my plays, let me try
to amuse you with an anecdote about Mother at the retirement home"
                                    —"Let Me Hang It All Out"

These digressions appear too frequently to be insignificant. Whether as anecdotes about dog bites that rightly foreshadowed those lacerations he would
soon receive from the critics in their press notices, as recollections of overstuffed
chairs that he would soon sit in himself, or as digressions about retirement
homes to which *he* was not ready to retire from the stage, Williams used the
allusion to negotiate his way through the paradox of explaining his work while
appearing to have said nothing at all.

Williams was a master of digressions in his essays, not with the intention to
obfuscate but precisely to clarify. Each contributed to his overall design of the
work, something he would explain in his 1948 essay "Something Wild . . .": "I
have a way of jumping from the particular to the abstract, for the particular is
sometimes as much as we know of the abstract." Like the abstract painters he
admired—evinced in both his essay "An Appreciation of Hans Hofmann" and
novella *Moise and the World of Reason*—Williams never created linear work,
be it a single play, or an essay, or the total sum of his oeuvre. Personal anecdotes
and parables were simply the oils with which he frequently painted, and Williams spent a lifetime exploring ways in which to combine them on the canvas.

It is fairly certain that Williams rarely wrote non-fiction in the morning, for
that was a creative time devoted to the plays, and prose writing was considered
more or less an exercise or a distraction. When he encountered writer's block,
he would not let it cheat him of a day's work. In his "Preface" to *Slapstick Tragedy*, Williams explains that "since I can't just stop working, I divert myself with
some shorter project, a story, a poem, or a less ponderous play." To that list, we
could add the essay. "These diversions," he continues, "are undertaken simply
as that, as diversions, and they nearly always have a quality in common, which
is experimentation in content and in style, particularly in style. The fatigue I felt
before this escapade is lifted. I find myself enjoying my work again." Creative
writing for Williams was simply more demanding than expository writing. This
does not mean Williams disparaged his non-fiction writing, though he did refer

to himself in *Moise and the World of Reason* as "a distinguished failed prose writer." On the contrary, he wrote in the *Memoirs* that he felt he had "written a goodly quantity of prose works, some of which [he] prefer to [his] plays." With exemplary essays such as "Grand" and "The Man In the Overstuffed Chair," there is little room to disagree with him.

"With little effort at cohesion, let's turn sharply south" to the topic of how this book is constructed.

The first edition of this book, *Where I Live: Selected Essays*, edited in 1978 by Christine R. Day and Bob Woods, reproduced significant essays Williams wrote from 1944 to 1978. Many of his important essays not included in the previous edition are now collected here, along with smaller prose works—some previously unpublished; others published but imprisoned in out-of-print books or microfilm and microfiche on the dusty shelves of august libraries. For the Williams admirer, there are the essays of *Where I Live* plus those left out of the original edition; for the Williams scholar, there are those essays plus the more obscure author's notes, statements, and endorsements that will help expand an understanding of Williams's artistic vision.

This collection is divided into three categories: "Essays," "Miscellany," and "Juvenilia and College Papers." In each rubric, essays are ordered chronologically by date of first publication or, when unpublished, by date of composition. If an essay's date of composition was not available, I surmised it based on internal and external evidence: see my notes at the beginning of the section "A Complete List of Tennessee Williams's Non-fiction Prose Writings." Commentary is provided in the "Notes" section following this afterword to clarify obscure references in the essays or to explain certain points in more detail. When available, I reprinted the original published versions of the essays, and not versions subsequently reprinted as introduction or forewords to his plays. The exceptions to this rule are the essays that appeared in *Where I Live,* which bear the imprint at times of Williams's later editorial hand. I cross-referenced multiple versions for imported errors or variations and listed these in my notes for each essay concerned. When I was able to compare the published essay with its manuscript drafts, I noted any significant changes or deletions. When no published version existed, I reproduced the essay from Williams's original manuscript (or composite manuscripts) and included any holograph changes Williams later emended. These manuscripts were edited only to correct for spelling or for grammar on the assumption that Williams would have done so himself in preparing the essay for publication.

Though the non-fiction pieces are arranged chronologically within their respective rubrics, the categories themselves are not. Since this is not a "collected works" edition, the showcasing of individual essays was privileged over the displaying of Williams's growth as a non-fiction writer. As such, the book concludes with Williams's juvenilia, youthful writings, and a selection of college papers which together show Williams as a non-fiction writer from a very young age. His prize-winning essay for *Smart Set*, "Can a Wife Be a Good Sport?," demonstrates Williams's talent for voice and for creating a persona entirely different from his own. The ten short high school newspaper pieces that recount Williams's 1928 European tour with his grandfather exemplify his skill at noting detail, which he had hoped would serve him the following year when he left St. Louis to attend the celebrated journalism school at the University of Missouri in Columbia. His three years at Mizzou may have helped Williams's writing career in ways he could not have foreseen at the time. Though he left in 1932 without taking a degree, Williams's writing experiences there taught him that his passion and his abilities lay in creative and not in expository writing, academic or otherwise. The six college papers (among the twenty-five or so housed at Texas), all but one published here for the first time, exhibit not only the breadth and depth of Williams's literary and dramatic education, but also his understated exasperation with having had to spend precious energy concentrating on the works of other writers when, as his *Notebooks* inform us, he was in full stride writing and submitting poems, stories, and plays to various magazines and contests.

The "Miscellany" section includes several short introductions, reviews, eulogies, appreciations, prefaces, and forewords to the work of his fellow writers. By the early 1940s, before his "catastrophe of success" with *The Glass Menagerie*, Williams learned that non-fiction prose could serve to advance his career as a creative writer. Essays such as "'Amor Perdido,'" "Te Morituri Salutamus," and "Preface to My Poems" were all carefully crafted pieces intended "to sell" his creative work to his audiences, his critics, and his readers. After the success of *The Glass Menagerie*, Williams was often asked by friends, newspapers, or publishers to produce non-fiction pieces to promote the writing of others. If "The Author Tells Why It is Called *The Glass Menagerie*" helped to draw audiences for the Dowling production of the play, "The History of a Play (With Parentheses)" gave James Laughlin's *Pharos* a boost in publishing a play that many Boston audiences and critics found in 1940 to have been written by the Devil himself. His essay "A Playwright's Statement" similarly bolstered Margo Jones's work in her Theatre '45 in Dallas. This decade, and the one that followed, saw Williams devoting a significant amount of energy to writing long and complex introductions or reviews for his friends: Carson McCullers, Paul Bowles, Marian Gallaway, Donald Windham, Oliver Evans, Gilbert Maxwell, and later, Jane Bowles, Virginia Spenser Carr, and Richard Leavitt. During the 1950s, when Williams was struggling for another Broadway sensation, these introductions became shorter, darker, and less effulgent.

The diminishing length and complexity of these essays evince in part how Williams felt himself being lured away from composing his own art in support of another's. Notable is his curt reply to Audrey Wood when was asked to write the introduction to William Inge's play, *The Dark at the Top of the Stairs*: "it is one thing to type three words—'For Tennessee Williams'—on a dedication page [but] quite another thing to write several pages of introduction." This attitude is best revealed in his brief and unsettling handwritten foreword to Dakin Williams's legal memoirs, *The Bar Bizarre*. In a piece that damns as it praises, Williams demonstrates what little effort he was willing to devote to the promotion of his brother. These "appreciations" are nonetheless significant to a collection of Williams's non-fiction since in each we find him talking as much about himself and his own developing troubles with audiences and critics as he does about the writer whose work he is appraising.

Most significant, though, are the "Essays" themselves, those journalistic pieces that appeared in many of America's important newspapers and magazines. What is perhaps most striking about them is how Williams kept returning over the years, in essay after essay, to the same people, the same places, and the same year: Tallulah Bankhead, Acapulco, 1940. It was as if Williams's essays formed a compass, and *Battle of Angels* was his North. Whenever he felt lost in the theater world, worried that another play of his would not be received favorably by the press or by the public, Williams would repeatedly steer his response in an essay toward the direction of the needle, which would guide him safely back to the security of a past just prior to fortune and fame. Strangely absent from these essays are the names of people like Kip Kiernan and the writing havens like Provincetown. Instead, we repeatedly encounter Andrew Gunn, a name that barely figures in any of Williams's writing, or Jim Parrott or Clark Mills. Perhaps it was because they both influenced Williams's aesthetics at an impressionable time in his life, whereas Kip and Provincetown were matters of the heart. We do find New Orleans and Key West mentioned in the essays, but more in their relation to his break-out year with *Battle of Angels* than with the later theatric successes they are more commonly aligned. Like Bankhead, Laurette Taylor frequently makes an appearance in the essays, perhaps because she is associated with the end to Williams's obscurity, and her performance in *The Glass Menagerie* is inseparably from his being thrust into a life of celebrity and wealth (and all the trapping that go with it) from which he never really recovered.

While his 1940s essays contain the most ebullient of Williams's non-fiction, his classic essays, "The Catastrophe of Success," "Questions Without Answers," and "Something Wild . . ." in 1947 and 1948 mark the beginning of the end of his Broadway honeymoon. By the 1950s, his essays grow gradually more defensive in tone. No Williams production on Broadway after *A Streetcar Named Desire* (1948) would ever be met again with such deference to the playwright, and consequently no later essay would speak with that confident insouciance he displays in "'Amor Perdido'" or "The History of a Play (With Parentheses)." Each essay of the 1950s would to some extent portray a playwright on the attack against philistine critics or prejudiced audiences ("The Timeless World of a Play," "The Meaning of *The Rose Tattoo*," "Foreword to *Camino Real*"), or on the defensive against a growing rumble of dissatisfaction with the one-time darling of the Great White Way ("Afterword to *Camino Real*," "Critic Says 'Evasion,' Writer Says 'Mystery,'" "The Past, the Present, and the Perhaps," "Tennessee Williams Presents His POV," "Prelude to a Comedy"). Perhaps the decade is best captured by his essay "The World I Live In," which projects simultaneously these attacks and these defenses of a writer who found success again in 1955 with *Cat on a Hot Tin Roof*. The essays from this decade, most of which appeared in the *New York Times*, represent the golden age of Williams's non-fiction writing and, perhaps, his most significant contributions to the essay as literary genre.

By the 1960s and 1970s, Williams's essays become so complex that they belie classification. The success of *The Night of the Iguana*, for instance, can be felt in the returned confidence of his essay "A Summer of Discovery." And the autobiographical masterpieces, "The Man In the Overstuffed Chair" and "Grand," capture a Williams still very much at the heights of his non-fiction skills. Most of the later essays, however, bring Williams's defensive stance to their apex (or nadir). Time and time again, we find in them a Williams writing to convince his public and his critics that he was still America's greatest living playwright. The later essays, from his preface to *Slapstick Tragedy* to the program note for the Vancouver production of *The Red Devil Battery Sign*, are both rhetorical attempts to defend his social politics in his plays and pleas for audiences to be indulgent with their experimental natures. Essays such as "Happiness Is Relevant," " 'Tennessee, Never Talk to an Actress,' " "Too Personal?" "Let Me Hang It All Out," "Where My Head Is Now and Other Questions," "I Have Rewritten a Play For Artistic Purity," and "I Am Widely Regarded as the Ghost Of a Writer" provide evidence of an artist on the brink, a writer whose frustration with myopic audiences and belligerent theater critics is echoed in his interviews, his letters, and his bitter, unfinished essay, *Mes Cahiers Noirs*. The fact that Williams's signature plays—*Streetcar* and *Cat*—were enjoying revivals at the time did not bode well for his attempts to convince his public that his dramaturgy had changed. Time and the success of recent revivals of Williams's post-*Iguana* plays have, to a certain extent, justified his venting evident in the essays "Where My Head Is Now and Other Questions" and "The Blessings and Mixed Blessings of Workshop Productions."

His two most political essays of the 1970s, "We Are Dissenters Now" and "The Misunderstanding and Fears of an Artist's Revolt," demonstrate as well how his frustration, compounded by heavy alcohol and drug abuse during his "stoned age" in the 1960s, was so extreme that it affected his ability to write cogently. Many of the fragments and drafts Williams wrote during this decade show (though perhaps no more authentically) Williams teetering on the verge of collapse. In his unpublished essay fragments, such as "These Scattered Idioms

[III]" (ca. 1977), we get a clearer sense of his painful rambling and (it would appear) drug- and/or alcohol and fatigue-enhanced *cri du cœur*:

> About my recent book of <u>Memoirs</u>, there have been some com-
> plaints that they were not well-organized ~~or~~ nor in a very good literary
> style. Now I will let you in on one disgraceful secret about the <u>Memoirs</u>
> which <u>they</u> did <u>not</u> ~~contain confess~~ let you in on.
> I did all my writing on them while I was working on a play, and
> I only worked on the <u>Memoirs</u> when I was too exhausted to continue
> work on the play. No excuses: just an explanation . . .

We must ask ourselves, as we do with all of Williams's confessions, where Wil-liams draws the line between truth and "truth." His anger during the last two decades of his life clouded not only his personal judgments of people but also his perception and assessment of his own work.

Williams was indeed a paradoxical writer in his non-fiction, but that fact no more slights his essays than the paradoxical natures of his many characters damage his plays. Like them, his essays need to be read from multiple, often conflicting angles. Near the end of the foreword to his *Memoirs*, which he dis-ingenuously called "these trivialities," Williams writes:

> Is this book, then, with its rather unusual structure, a professional mat-
> ter? Has any of my writing been "a professional matter"? I have always
> written for deeper necessities than the term "professional" implies, and
> I think that this has sometimes been to the detriment of my career. But
> more of the time to its advantage.

All of the essays in this collection, from the pre-opening pieces to the book re-views, attest to Williams's one consistent effort to find and express in them what he believed to be the truth—the truth about himself and, above all, about his work. To read one essay in isolation, then, is to encounter Williams the rhetori-cian, a prose writer who keenly discerned and attempted to satisfy those needs of his audience, one unlike any of those to whom he wrote his drama, his short fiction, his poetry, his candid letters, or his personal notebooks. To read this collection of essays from cover to cover is to discover Williams the artist, the thinker, the revolutionary, the man who could never let go of the past because he understood the necessities of its ties to his present and his perhaps.

John S. Bak,
Nancy, France
December 2008

ACKNOWLEDGMENTS

Many hands were involved in the production of this book, not the least of which was Williams's.

I would like to thank the ever-reliable staffs of the various Williams archives for helping me track down manuscript drafts and fragments of his published and unpublished non-fiction: Department of Special Collections, UCLA; Rare Book and Manuscript Library, Columbia University; Tennessee Williams Collection, University of Delaware; Williams Research Center of Historic New Orleans Collection, New Orleans; and the Harry Ransom Humanities Research Center, University of Texas (Austin).

Certain individuals at these collections warrant particular praise for their efficiency and friendliness: Siva Blake and Mark Cave of the Historic New Orleans Collection Historical Society, Michael T. Ryan, Director of Columbia University's Rare Book and Manuscript Library, and Richard Workman, Associate Librarian at Harry Ransom Center.

Other individuals, Williams scholars and aficionados alike, deserve recognition here for their help in locating certain materials: Fred Todd, Robert Bray, Allean Hale, George Crandell, Gregg Barrios, and Thomas P. Adler.

I would also like to thank Annette Saddik, W. Kenneth Holditch, R. Barton Palmer, and Colby Kullman for their collegial support, and Rachel Eustache at Northwestern University for her material support in requesting or photocopying many of the sources for me.

Unconditional thanks are extended to my editors at New Directions, in particular Thomas Keith, who had confidence in me from the start to see this collection through to the end and who was always there to steer me back on track when it seemed as if the project was either coming to a standstill or spinning wildly out of control.

Finally, I want to thank my wife Nathalie for her love and support in having held down *le fort flévillois* all while I trekked off to Chicago, New Orleans, London, Manchester, or Paris in the seemingly endless search for more materials.

LIST OF ABBREVIATIONS

Books

Conversations = *Conversations with Tennessee Williams*
Crandell = *Tennessee Williams: A Descriptive Bibliography*
Dakin = *Tennessee Williams: An Intimate Biography*
Edwina = *Remember Me to Tom*
Letters I and *Letters II* = *The Selected Letters of Tennessee Williams* (volumes one and two)
Leverich = *Tom: The Unknown Tennessee Williams*
Notebooks = *Notebooks by Tennessee Williams*
Poems = *Collected Poems*
Spoto = *The Kindness of Strangers*
St. Just = *Five O'Clock Angel: Letters of Tennessee Williams to Maria St. Just*
Where I Live = *Where I Live: Selected Essays*
Windham = *Tennessee Williams' Letters to Donald Windham, 1940-1965*

Archival Holdings

Columbia = Columbia University Rare Book and Manuscript Library
Delaware = Tennessee Williams Collection, University of Delaware
NOLA = The Williams Research Center of Historic New Orleans Collection
Texas = Harry Ransom Humanities Research Center, University of Texas (Austin)
UCLA = Tennessee Williams Papers, 1930-1970, Department of Special Collections, UCLA

NOTES

Essays

"'Amor Perdido,' or, How It Feels to Become a Professional Playwright." First published in *Michigan Quarterly Review*, Summer 2003. Originally from a typescript at Texas, the manuscript carries no date, but the essay was written sometime after October 1940, the month following Williams's departure from Acapulco where he fled to rewrite *Battle of Angels* for the Theatre Guild. Williams's original title, "Amor Perdida" ["Lost Love"], is a misspelling of "Amor Perdido," a bolero written by the Puerto Rican composer Pedro Flores. In a September 3, 1940 letter to Joe Hazan from Mexico City, Williams writes about singing "a beautiful song called 'Amor Perdida'—very haunting" (*Letters I*, p. 274). In the 1930s and 1940s, Lucius Morris Beebe wrote "The New York," a column in the *New York Herald* about New York café life. Joe Jones was an artist and a Communist activist in St. Louis who in 1934 established an arts class in the city's old courtroom (see Williams's essays, "A Summer of Discovery" and "We Are Dissenters Now").

"Te Morituri Salutamus." Previously unpublished (ca. 1941-1942), this essay comes from a typescript at Texas filed with *Battle of Angels*. When *Battle of Angels* closed on January 11, 1941, the Theatre Guild told Williams to rewrite the play for a possible New York premiere the following Broadway season, which it was never given. Addressed to a "First Night Audience" of *Battle of Angel* after its inauspicious opening in Boston, this was written for another production of the play, probably also meant for Broadway. At the top of the manuscript is a note Williams wrote to Audrey Wood, "Keep this on ice for me—I intend to deliver it before the next production. 10." One possible date of the essay is thus between May 1941, when he delivered the revised script to Langner, and August 1941 when Langner rejected it. Another possibility is that the essay was written in early 1942 when Erwin Piscator expressed an interest in producing *Battle of Angels* at his experimental Studio Theatre at the New School for Social Research; however, the play was never produced there either. "Te Morituri Salutamus" ["Those who are about to die salute you"] was the ritual announcement of gladiators to the Roman Emperor just before battle.

"Preface to My Poems" First published in *Five Young American Poets, 1944*. Williams offered James "Jay" Laughlin, publisher of New Directions, a choice of two prefaces to accompany his collection of twenty-nine poems entitled "The

Summer Belvedere." Neither could decide which one to publish. Reviews of the book were vituperative, particularly Williams's contribution. As Williams later wrote to Laughlin in December 1944: "I have seen only one review of my poems, in the *Herald Tribune*. It was pretty condescending but not really evil.—as the *View* would have been" (*Letters I*, p. 540). In early July 1942, Williams and Paul Bigelow were picked up by the police on Cherry Street in Macon, Georgia, and taken to jail because Williams "did not have [his] draft card" (*Notebooks*, p. 299). In January 1941, Williams was classified as IV-F due to his poor eyesight by his draft board. Jesse Stuart was a local color writer and poet of rural Kentucky. Williams first refers to a New Orleans prostitute named Irene "who painted the marvelous pictures and disappeared" in his essay "'Amor Perdido.'" She also becomes the protagonist of his story "In Memory of an Aristocrat" (ca. Winter 1939-1940). In several drafts of a prose piece entitled "A Letter to Irene" (ca. December 1940), Williams recalls having testified on behalf of the Irish prostitute Irene who was arrested for having thrown "green snowballs [made] out of the mint sherbet" (Texas, [p. 1]). Joe Turner was someone Williams could count "on one of those 10 fingers that I reserve for O.K. people" (*Notebooks*, p. 137), while working at "The Quarter Eat Shop" in New Orleans in January 1939.

"The History of a Play (With Parentheses)." First published in *Pharos* Spring 1945 (written in March 1944). James Laughlin, founder of the magazine *Pharos* (1945-1947), wanted to publish *Battle of Angels* in its first volume. It was scheduled for publication in July 1944 but was postponed almost an entire year. The five years between *Battle of Angels*'s premiere and publication gave Williams time to reflect (and dramatize) the events behind its theatrical failure. Laughlin had a hard time getting the first issue of *Pharos* printed. The magazine was printed in Utah, and the Mormon printers found the play objectionable. In a July 1944 letter to Laughlin, Williams asked if *Pharos* was "still at the mercy of the Mormons" (*Letters I*, p. 529). During the late Hellenistic Age, Athenian actors often wore *cothurni*, or buskins, with the heels raised to give them stature. Greek tragedy in general has been called *cothurnus* for this reason. Andrew Gunn, "a spoiled creature [. . .] who has never learned honesty and is now too old to learn it" (*Letters I*, p. 277), was one of Williams's lovers during his summer visit to Acapulco in 1940 (see Williams's essays, "A Summer of Discovery" and "We are Dissenters Now"). Philip Barry, George S. Kaufman, and S. N. Behrman were American dramatists who wrote "art" plays that Williams greatly admired. Shakespeare's lyric verse, "Nothing of him that doth fade [. . .]," comes from the "Full fathom five" song by Ariel in act one, scene two of *The Tempest*. Jack Kirkland dramatized Erskine Caldwell's novel *Tobacco Road* (1932) in 1933, and the play ran on Broadway for 3,182 performances over a span of eight years.

"Notes to the Reader." Previously unpublished (written ca. May-June 1945), this essay comes from a typescript at Texas. The essay may be an early version of what would eventually become the "Production Notes" to the published version of *The Glass Menagerie*. From 1940-1944, Williams met several artists in Provincetown, New York, New Orleans, and Key West. In New York in March 1942, he roomed briefly with New Orleans artist Fritz Bultman, whom he had met in Provincetown the previous summer. Bultman was studying with Hans Hofmann, who had established art schools in New York City and on the Cape, and who would later influence Williams's notion of the plastic theater (see Williams's essay on Hofmann). Williams's reference to Lorca's surrealist play, *If Five Years Pass*, helps to date the essay. An English performance of play was given in April 1945 at the Provincetown Playhouse, New York City, by the Jane Street Cooperative, artists who were all heavily influenced by Hofmann's Abstract Expressionism.

"The Author Tells Why It is Called *The Glass Menagerie*." First published in the *New York Herald Tribune* April 15, 1945. Edwina Williams refuted the tale of the alleycats behind the apartment building and recalled the 4633 Westminster Place apartment as "a gloomy place" (Edwina, p. 28). Lyle Leverich added, "Although [Williams] had a tiny space off a side hall to call his own, he spent more time in his sister's room or sitting on the iron fire escape" (Leverich, p. 51). There is some debate about which of the apartments in St. Louis provided the basis of the setting for *The Glass Menagerie*. Both Williams and Edwina associate the Westminster apartment with the play, while Leverich suggests that their five-room apartment on 6254 Enright Avenue in University City, where they lived "for nearly ten years during the Depression," served as the play's setting (Leverich, p. 601).

"A Playwright's Statement on Dallas' Theater '45 Plans." First published in *The Dallas Morning News* July 22, 1945. Williams wrote this essay in Guadalajara, Mexico, where he had fled (via Dallas) to escape the "catastrophe of success" of *The Glass Menagerie*. He submitted the essay, entitled "A Playwright's Statement," in a letter in early July to Margo Jones. Williams confessed to Guthrie McClintic on May 23, 1945, that he did not like Dallas at all and was "trying to hide" from Margo Jones the fact that he did "not feel the atmosphere here in which anything really progressive is likely to happen" in theater or in anything else (*Letters I*, p. 561). A week later, he had changed his mind, writing to Eddie Dowling that he felt the "outlook" for Margo's Dallas Theater "is really wonderful," a theater in which he could "experiment and clarify," and "remain in touch with [the] stage while at the same time escaping the exhausting responsibilities of Broadway" (*Letters II*, p. 3). The San Francisco Charter refers to the United Nations, which was founded on June 26, 1945, at the Veterans Auditorium in San Francisco. When Williams passed back through Dallas en route to New York later that summer, Jones apparently asked him for a $1,500 contribution to "the Project," which Williams declined.

"The Catastrophe of Success." First published in the *New York Times* November 30, 1947, as "On a Streetcar Named Success," this was the pre-opening piece for *A Streetcar Named Desire*, which premiered on Broadway at the Ethel Barrymore Theater on December 3, 1947. This is a longer version Williams later used as the introduction to *The Glass Menagerie*. Williams's critique of the film industry was likely related to his unhappy stint as a screenwriter for M.G.M. in 1943. Williams stayed in a guesthouse at a resort on Lake Chapala, where he returned to working on *The Moth*, which he was then calling *Blanche's Chair in the Moon* (the title *The Poker Night* was used in later drafts). William Saroyan's *The Time of Your Life* opened October 29, 1939 on Broadway. It was co-produced by the Guild Theater, which would soon take out an option on Williams's *Battle of Angels*, and by Eddie Dowling, who directed and starred opposite Julie Haydon, as they later would in *The Glass Menagerie*.

"Chicago Arrival." Previously unpublished (written ca. August/September 1948), from a typescript housed at NOLA. The essay carries a typed message at the top of the first page that it was "quoted in Chicago Sunday Tribune / September 19, 1948 / by Claudia Cassidy." Though Eddie Dowling announced to the *New York Times* his plans for a London production of *The Glass Menagerie* in August 1945, problems over British rights to the play and contractual disputes between interested American and British parties delayed its West End opening at the Haymarket Theatre until July 28, 1948. Williams attended rehearsals of the London production of *The Glass Menagerie* in mid-June. He arrived in England "late in the week of June 6" (*Letters II*, p. 199) and "escaped from England" on July 25 (Windham, p. 222) to head to Paris, missing opening night.

"Questions Without Answers." First published in the *New York Times* October 3, 1948, as the pre-opening piece for *Summer and Smoke*, which premiered on Broadway at the Music Box Theater on October 6, 1948. From 1948 until the 1970s, Williams would write numerous pre-Broadway-opening essays destined for the *New York Times*, often with a similar self-effacement. On August 13, 1948, Williams wrote to his Grandfather that "Miss Hayes is not as good as Laurette Taylor but she is good as any <u>living</u> actress" (*Letters II*, p. 207).

"Something Wild . . . ." First published in the *New York Star* November 7, 1948, as "On the Art of Being a True Non-conformist" and later published under its current title in *27 Wagons Full of Cotton* in 1953. Williams refers to the Mummers in his journal as a "delightful bunch of young people. Nothing snotty or St. Louis 'Social' about them" (*Notebooks*, p. 65). They produced three of Williams's first plays: *Headlines* (1936), which he wrote as the curtain raiser for Irwin Shaw's antiwar play, *Bury the Dead*, and the full-length *Candles to the Sun* (1937) and *Fugitive Kind* (1937). The Mummers planned to produce *Spring Storm* in 1938, but the company disbanded when director Willard Holland left for Hollywood to be an actor.

"Carson McCullers's *Reflections in a Golden Eye*." First published in 1950 as the introduction to the New Directions reissue of *Reflections in a Golden Eye*. Writing to McCullers from Napoli on March 23 1950, Williams acknowledges receipt of "the copies of 'Reflections' from both you and Laughlin. It seems absurd for me to write a preface to a great work by such a completely established writer and I should feel almost embarrassed to try, but I <u>will</u> try if you really want me to [. . .]" (*Letters II*, p. 240). The first meeting of Williams and McCullers on the island of Nantucket in the summer 1946 in the company of Williams's fiery lover, Amado "Pancho" Rodriquez y Gonzalez, is legendary. The three of them lived in a rented "lopsided frame house" at 31 Pine Street, with Williams working on *Summer and Smoke* and McCullers on the dramatization of her successful novel, *The Member of the Wedding*. Williams is citing the poetic introduction to E. E. Cummings's World War I autobiographical novel, *The Enormous Room* (1922): "Did it ever occur to you that people in this socalled world of ours are not interested in art?"

"A Writer's Quest for a Parnassus." First published in the *New York Times Magazine* August 13, 1950. During the summer of 1950, Williams was working simultaneously on revisions of *The Rose Tattoo* and the screenplay of *A Streetcar Named Desire*. Williams did not find his "magic" writing place this summer in

Rome: "How infinitely <u>wrong</u> this Roman period has turned out!—Key West seems like heaven in retrospect—" (*Notebooks*, p. 515). From a papal bull, Pope Pius XII declared 1950 a Holy Year of pilgrimage to Rome, a tradition dating back 650 years. Ernest Hemingway's *Across the River and Into the Trees* would be published the following month, September 7, 1950. Williams had read the serialized version of novel in *Cosmopolitan* from February to June 1950. Williams's predictions about the novel's poor reviews proved accurate.

"The Timeless World of a Play." First published in the *New York Times* January 14, 1951, as "Concerning The Timeless World of a Play," the pre-opening piece for *The Rose Tattoo*, which premiered on Broadway at the Martin Beck Theater on February 3, 1951. Williams begins the essay with a line from Carson McCullers's poem, "When We are Lost," that captures best the "configured Hell" and "agony immobilized" that he experienced prior to the play's premiere: "While Time / The endless idiot, runs screaming around the world." The Elia Kazan-production of Arthur Miller's *Death of a Salesman* opened in London at the Phoenix Theatre on July 29, 1949. Williams repeatedly tried without success to get Kazan to direct *The Rose Tattoo*. The "skeptical critic" here is most likely British critic Ivor Brown, whose review of *Death of a Salesman* in the *New York Times Magazine* (August 28, 1949) attempted to explain to American audiences why the British could not feel sorry for Willy Loman because "in their offices [they] would brush him aside as just one more shabby and ineffective nuisance [. . .]."

"The Meaning of *The Rose Tattoo*." First published in *Vogue* March 15, 1951, as "Tennessee Williams Explains His Elusive, Brilliant, Allusive Comedy, 'The Rose Tattoo.'" According to Catholic tradition, the Virgin Mary appeared to Sister Pierina Gilli as a vision of the "Mystical Rose" seven times (from November 24, 1946 to December 8, 1947) in a little church in Montichiari, a small town in northern Italy. Williams first arrived in Italy with Frank Merlo in the winter of 1948-1949.

"Facts About Me." First published in 1952 on the back of the record jacket of "Tennessee Williams Reading From His Works" (Caedmon Records). This essay was first written in April 1945, following the success of *The Glass Menagerie*, updated in December 1945, then printed for publicity and promotion in 1947 by Williams's agent, Audrey Wood. The essay later appeared in the theater program for *A Streetcar Named Desire* after the New York Drama Critics' Circle Award (April) and the Pulitzer Prize (May) were announced. It would be repeatedly updated over the years. Caedmon had apparently asked Williams to write a new essay to accompany the recordings. On June 22, 1952, Williams wrote to Audrey Wood: "P.S. I have not had time to write the 'essay' they want for the recordings. Tell Miss Roney that perhaps she could use something from my introduction to the published version of 'Battle of Angels.' States my philosophy of art" (*Letters II*, p. 435). Many of the "facts" about Williams's life are part fiction, part memory. He was not twelve but seven years old when his family moved to St. Louis during the summer of 1917, and over the years he gave numerous accounts as to why he changed his named to Tennessee. Due to a war-related housing shortage, the Williams family first lived in a boarding house on Lindell Boulevard. The "dim" apartment here is either their apartment on 4633 Westminster Place or on 6254 Enright Avenue. Williams studied at the University of Missouri for three years, not two (1929-1932), and his father pulled him out because of his poor grades, including an "F" in ROTC, and not because of a lack of funds, despite the Depression. Williams spent three years (1932-1935) at the Continental branch of the International Shoe Company, where he had worked previously during the summers while attending the University of Missouri. Williams technically spent one year at Washington University College (1935-1936) and one at Washington University (1936-1937) before finally completing his bachelor's degree at the University of Iowa in the summer of 1938. He is exaggerating when he writes that he put himself through school.

"Foreword to *Camino Real.*" First published in the *New York Times* March 15, 1953, as "On the 'Camino Real,'" the pre-opening piece for *Camino Real*, which premiered on Broadway at the National Theater on March 17, 1953. Williams first began work on *Ten Blocks on the Camino Real*, the one-act play from which *Camino Real* evolved, in 1946. American poet Archibald MacLeish wrote "Ars Poetica" (1926), which contains the line, "A poem should not mean / But be."

"Afterword to *Camino Real.*" First published in October 1953 as the afterword to the New Directions edition of *Camino Real*. Parts of this essay, written and signed "Tennessee Williams, June 1, 1953," appear in a letter Williams wrote to Brooks Atkinson in early April 1953 (*Letters II*, pp. 474-76). In both the letter and the afterword, Williams is defending his play as he had in the *New York Times* piece.

"Person–To–Person." First published in the *New York Times* March 20, 1955, as the pre-opening piece for *Cat on a Hot Tin Roof*, which premiered on Broadway at the Morosco Theater on March 24, 1955. Many of the drafts to this essay were revised two years later for the essay "Tennessee Williams on the Past, the Present and the Perhaps." The character referred to is Val Xavier, and the line comes from act two, scene one of *Orpheus Descending*: "Nobody ever gets to know *no body!* We're all of us sentences to solitary confinement inside our own skins, for life!" In *Battle of Angels*, Val says, "We're all of us locked up tight inside our own bodies. Sentenced—you might say—to solitary confinement inside our own skins." The preface Williams cites (almost verbatim) comes from his essay "A History of a Play (With Parentheses)," which he wrote in March 1944.

"Critic Says 'Evasion,' Writer Says 'Mystery.'" First published in the *New York Herald Tribune* April 17, 1955. The essay is a direct response to two of Walter Kerr's reviews for *Cat on a Hot Tin Roof* in the *New York Herald Tribune* (March 25 and April 3). After the second review ("A Secret Is Half-Told In Fountains of Words") appeared, Williams wrote a letter to Kerr (April 9, 1955) and included a rejoinder that he wanted Kerr's paper to publish (*Letters II*, p. 570). Kerr charged Williams in both reviews for having never provided an adequate reason for the "emotionally paralyzed" Brick. In his second review, Kerr boldly asks, "Is he a homosexual? At one moment he is denouncing 'queers,' at another describing the way he clasps his friend's hand going to bed at night [. . .]. Listening, we work at the play in an earnest effort to unlock its ultimate dramatic meaning. But the key has been mislaid, or deliberately hidden." New Directions published the play in July 1955, along with the two versions of act three, plus Williams's "Note of Explanation," and the "long note" about the necessity of Brick's "mystery." Williams is approximating Brick and Maggie's dialogue in act one. The August Strindberg quote is from *The Dance of Death, Part I* (1901).

"The Past, the Present, and the Perhaps." First published in the *New York Times* March 17, 1957, as the pre-opening piece for *Orpheus Descending*, which premiered on Broadway at the Martin Beck Theater on March 21, 1957. The events of the "evening before" are well documented in Williams's essay "Te Morituri Salutamus." Tennessee Williams (along with Lemuel Ayers, who designed the set for *Camino Real*) studied with Professor E. C. Mabie at the University of Iowa in 1937-1938. Williams left New Orleans with friend and clarinet player Jim Parrott on February 20, 1939, and arrived in Los Angeles (via San Antonio, El Paso, Mexico, Phoenix, San Bernardino, and Palm Springs) on March 7. As published in the *New York Times*, paragraph nine began with this sentence: "I hope I will not annoy you again in this 'Sunday piece' by another as pretentious-sounding as that one, so let us go quickly back to the safer ground of simple recollections." When this essay was reprinted as the introduction to *Orpheus Descending*, Williams added the current final sentence after deleting this original ending, which appeared in the *New York Times*: "On my work bench are two unfinished plays, *Kingdom of Earth* and *Sweet Bird of Youth*. I don't know which I'll return to, and like all writers that I have known in a long time of knowing writers, I have the unreasonable but disturbing fear that this one's the last one. Of course, I would not 'make book' on the possibility that I will get up any morning and find it more inviting to live than write about living."

"The World I Live In." First published in the *New York Post* March 17, 1957, as "A Talk with Tennessee." A revival of *The Glass Menagerie*, starring Helen Hayes as Amanda (a role she played in the 1948 London production), opened in November 21, 1956, at the City Center Theater in New York for a limited run. The Gypsy says in block twelve of *Camino Real*, "The Camino Real is a funny paper read backward!"

"Author and Director: A Delicate Situation." First published in *Playbill* September 30, 1957. Williams's "first phase" describes his experiences with Lawrence Langner and the Theatre Guild's production of *Battle of Angels* in December 1940. The "second phase" concerns his success after *The Glass Menagerie* in 1944. The "third phase" describes Williams's experiences throughout most of the 1950s. The "exception" to this cycle probably concerns the recent failure with *Orpheus Descending*, which Williams felt (and voiced frequently in his letters) was his most significant play in terms of revealing all that concerned him as a writer. In the end, Williams is potentially alluding to his on-again, off-again relationship with Elia Kazan.

"If the Writing Is Honest." First published in the *New York Times* March 16, 1958, this essay was originally written as the introduction to William Inge's play *The Dark at the Top of the Stairs* (published later that May). The play's dedication reads, "For Tennessee Williams." Both Inge and Audrey Wood asked Williams to write the introduction, but he at first demured. "[I]t is one thing to type three words—'For Tennessee Williams'—on a dedication page," Williams wrote to Audrey Wood, but it is "quite another thing to write several pages of introduction" (Spoto, p. 249). Williams met Inge for the first time in November of 1944 (and not January 1945), when Williams was preparing for his Broadway debut with *The Glass Menagerie*. Inge's article for the St. Louis *Star-Times*, "Home Town Boy Makes Good," ran November 11, 1958, as "'Tennessee' Williams, Playwright, Author."

"Foreword to *Sweet Bird of Youth.*" First published in the *New York Times* March 8, 1959, as "Williams' Wells of Violence," the pre-opening piece for *Sweet Bird of Youth*, which premiered on Broadway at the Martin Beck Theater on March 10, 1959. Williams's dinner date at the Algonquin Hotel was William Inge, who had asked him prior to Williams's June 1953 departure for Rome if he was "blocked as a writer" (*Memoirs*, p. 146). This is an approximation of the lines in "The Marvelous Children" (revised as "In Jack-O'Lantern's Weather," *Poems*, pp. 3-6), a poem Williams included in *Five Young American Poets, 1944*. Williams's *Period of Adjustment*, which was entering tryouts at the Coconut Grove Theater in Miami before its premiere there in December 1958, did not open on Broadway until November 1960. Though he had spoken about undergoing psychotherapy as early as 1954, Williams only started analysis following the poor reviews of *Orpheus Descending* and the death of his father on March 27, 1957. On and off from June 1957 to March 1958 (sometimes daily, other times three or four times a week), Williams underwent treatment with Dr. Lawrence S. Kubie, a strict Freudian analyst. Kubie told Williams to give up his writing and to fight his homosexual desires, which prompted Williams to flee his therapy for extended periods until finally breaking with Kubie in March 1958 after the success of *Garden District*.

"The Man In the Overstuffed Chair." First published in *Antaeus* Spring/Summer 1982. Though Williams wrote in one draft fragment that he was "never going to get around to writing [his] memoirs" (Columbia, [p. 1]), this essay reflects the manner in which the essays would record his personal, rather than professional, life. Edwina recalled writing Williams while he was still in California, telling him to come home because Grand "was fading fast" (Edwina, p. 143). Williams did not return to St. Louis until late December 1943. "Mr. J.," Cornelius's boss, was Paul Jamison, whose strict morals earned him the role of Edwina's confidant. Williams resigned from his job in April 1935, a week after suffering what he thought was a mild heart attack. He was diagnosed as having suffered from "total exhaustion" (Leverich, p. 148).

"Reflections on a Revival of a Controversial Fantasy." First published in the *New York Times* May 15, 1960. José Quintero directed an Off-Broadway revival of *Camino Real*, which ran at the St. Marks Theater from May 16 to July 31, 1960. During this time, Williams began drafting a response to a review (probably Brooks Atkinson's "'Camino Real,' Williams Play Restaged In Second Avenue" [May 29, 1960]), praising the reviewer's courage in defending the play.

"Tennessee Williams Presents His POV." First published in the *New York Times Magazine* June 12, 1960. This essay was written in response to Marya Mannes's *New York Times Magazine* piece, "Plea for Fairer Ladies" (May 29, 1960). The title of Manne's essay was a reference to Alan J. Lerner and Frederick Lowes's 1956 Broadway musical, *My Fair Lady*, which ran for a then-record 2,717 performances. Mannes complained about recent plays on Broadway as being "snake pits" and how only a "psychiatrist or a nurse in a mental institution would have spent several hours of so many nights in the company of addicts, perverts, sadists, hysterics, bums, delinquents and others afflicted in mind and body." Noted for her outlandish hats, Hedda Hopper was a silent movie star who began writing gossip columns about Hollywood following the demise of her acting career in the mid-1930s. From 1938-1965, Dorothy Kilgallen wrote the syndicated column "The Voice of Broadway" for the *New York Journal-American* (it became a weekly radio talk show in 1941).

"Prelude to a Comedy." First published in the *New York Times* November 6, 1960, as the pre-opening piece for *Period of Adjustment*, which premiered on Broadway at the Helen Hayes Theater on November 10, 1960. Williams paraphrases the start of his own foreword to Oliver Evans's *Young Man with a Screwdriver* (1950): "In this time of false intensities, an art that exists as a natural and joyful accompaniment to living is a thing of exquisite rarity." Williams goes on to say: "He lives *with* his art instead of *by* and *for* it, which is happier for him and even, somehow, more comforting to his listeners." Williams left New York for Cherbourg then Paris at the end of December 1947, following the successful premiere of *A Streetcar Named Desire*. Years later, in the December 30, 1953 entry of his journal, Williams writes, "But then, remember the panicky night at the American hospital in Paris, I said (wrote on a fly leaf of Crane's 'Bridge')—'the jig is up'" (*Notebooks*, pp. 615-17). Williams mentions the "rondini" (not "ronzini") birds in his novella, *The Roman Spring of Mrs. Stone*, which he wrote in Rome in 1949: "[. . .] the rondini don't have any legs [and stay afloat until their deaths]." Williams would repeat this image in act two, scene four of *Orpheus Descending* when Lady asks Val Xavier it is true "[t]hat thing about birds with no feet so they have to sleep on the wind." In his journal for July 14, 1958, Williams calls them "rondinelli" (*Notebooks*, p. 715). Here, Williams fuses two separate lines that Meg Bishop delivers to Karen Stone: "You can retire from a business but you can't retire from an art," and "[. . .] even of you did have more energy than talent, what do you think you are going to do with that energy now? Slip it in your pocket like the key to a house where you don't live anymore?"

"Five Fiery Ladies." First published in *Life* February 3, 1961. Though Williams wanted Magnani to play Serafina Delle Rose in the play version of *The Rose Tattoo*, she starred in the film instead. Vivian Leigh played Blanche DuBois in the London premiere of *A Streetcar Named Desire* and in Elia Kazan's 1951 film version. In addition to playing the Princess Kosmonopolis in *Sweet Bird of Youth* (in both the 1959 play and the 1962 film), Geraldine Page played Alma Winemiller in Peter Glenville's 1961 film and in José Quintero's revival of *Summer and Smoke* at the Circle in the Square Theater in Greenwich Village, which was the surprise hit of the 1952 season. Williams writes in his journal for June 10, 1952, that it was "best thing that I've had this year" (*Notebooks*, p. 551). Page also created the role of Zelda Fitzgerald in Williams's last play for Broadway, *Clothes for a Summer Hotel*. Mauritz Stiller was a Swedish director who discovered Greta Lovisa Gustafsson, taught her cinematic acting techniques, and gave her the stage name "Greta Garbo." Eleonora Duse was a world-renowned Italian actress, who toured the United States at the end of 19th century and throughout the first decade of the 20th century. Katherine Hepburn played Violet Venable in Joseph L. Mankiewicz's film version of *Suddenly Last Summer* (1959). She later played Amanda Wingfield in Anthony Harvey's 1973 made-for-TV film of *The Glass Menagerie*. Elizabeth Taylor starred in several films based on Williams's work, including Richard Brook's *Cat on a Hot Tin Roof* (1958), Mankiewicz's *Suddenly Last Summer*, Joseph Losey's *Boom!* (1968), and Nicolas Roeg's made-for-TV film of *Sweet Bird of Youth* (1989).

"Carson McCullers." First published in the *Saturday Review of Literature* September 23, 1961, as "The Author." This essay was written to promote McCullers's novel *Clock Without Hands*, which was published by Houghton Mifflin on September 18, 1961. Truman Capote was the novelist who told Williams that theater was an "Art Manque." In an early draft of Williams's introduction to *Reflections in a Golden Eye*, he writes, "I cannot offer you a scholarly dissertation upon the novel-form or the history of the novel. I am a lowly playwright, and I have been assured by one Truman Capote that the theater is really a little to the southwest of the literary arts." In August 1947, McCullers suffered a stroke and another in November, which paralyzed the right side of her face but the left side of her body. McCullers's two plays are *The Member of the Wedding*, which ran for over 500 performances at the Empire Theater and won the Donaldson Award and the New York Drama Critics' Circle Award for 1950, and *The Square Root of Wonderful*, which opened on October 30, 1957, at the National Theater, but closed after only forty-five performances.

"A Summer of Discovery." First published in the *New York Herald Tribune* December 24, 1961, as the pre-opening piece for *The Night of the Iguana*, which premiered on Broadway at the Royale Theater on December 28, 1961. Alternative versions of his time in Mexico City are given in Williams's September 3 letter to Joe Hazan (*Letters I*, pp. 273-76), his journal (*Notebooks*, pp. 215-17), and his September 21 letter to his family (*Letters I*, pp. 280-82). In Acapulco, Williams's "fantastic hotel" was Todd's Place, "a resort run by a drunken 'Georgia cracker' and his 'fat Mexican' wife and 'occupied mainly by lizards—and Tennessee Williams'" (*Letters I*, pp. 277, 279). Williams left this hotel after the proprietors "vamoosed" (*Letters I*, p. 278) and moved to the Hotel Costa Verde (*Letters I*, p. 281). The "young writer" friend obsessed with suicide is Andrew Gunn (see Williams's essays, "The History of a Play (With Parentheses)" and "We Are Dissenters Now"). As Devlin and Tischler write, Williams's "monthly option check of $90.00 was 'delayed' because he had not informed the Theatre Guild, or Audrey Wood, of his departure from Mexico City," and they were still sending him mail at the Wells-Fargo office there (*Letters I*, p. 279). Williams describes the tropical downpours, the pro-Nazi Germans, and his "bad humor" in a September 24/25 letter to Hazan (*Letters I*, pp. 284-88).

"The Agent as Catalyst." First published in *Esquire* December 1962. Williams worked with Audrey Wood for thirty-two years, officially ending their professional and personal relationship in July 1971 after a bitter dispute that had been building for over a decade. Molly Day Thatcher first recommended Wood to Williams as an agent in April 1939 after the Group Theater awarded him a special prize of $100 for a group of his one-act plays, *American Blues*. Wood founded the Liebling-Wood Agency in 1937, which the Music Corporation of America (MCA) bought out in 1954. MCA, a giant in the talent industry, represented so many Hollywood stars that Robert Kennedy ordered its break-up in July 1962. As a result, Wood worked for Ashley-Steiner-Famous, which became the International Famous Agency later acquired by the International Creative Management in 1974.

"T. Williams's View of T. Bankhead." First published in the *New York Times* December 29, 1963, as the pre-opening piece for *The Milk Train Doesn't Stop Here*

Anymore, which originally premiered on Broadway at the Morosco Theater on January 16, 1963, and closed sixty-nine performances later, a critical and a commercial failure. Ten months later and after several rewrites, it opened again in New York. Bankhead replaced Hermione Baddeley as Flora Goforth in the second production, which opened at the Brooks Atkinson Theatre on January 1, 1964, and closed three days later. Bankhead was in poor health, exacerbated by her alcohol and drug abuse, and reportedly could not be heard onstage. Bankhead played Blanche DuBois in the 1956 revival of *A Streetcar Named Desire* (see Williams's essays, "A Tribute from Tennessee Williams to 'Heroic Tallulah Bankhead'" and "'Tennessee, Never Talk to an Actress'"). In the winter of 1939, Williams saw Bankhead perform Regina Giddens in Lillian Hellman's *The Little Foxes*, and later the next summer he sent her and Miriam Hopkins a script for *Battle of Angels*. Bankhead was touring in summer stock when Williams went down to Dennis Port to see her performing *The Second Mrs. Tanqueray* "at the Cape Playhouse" in July (Leverich, p. 363). The producer Williams met in Charleston was Irene Mayer Selznick. A newspaper strike in New York City began on December 8, 1962, stopping the publication of nine newspapers for 114 days.

"Grand." First published in a limited edition of 326 copies by House of Books December 15, 1964. In the summer of 1928, Williams's grandfather brought him along on one of his "Episcopalian" tours through Europe (see Williams's high school columns for *U. City Pep*). In an April 1929 letter to his grandfather, Williams curiously refers to Raulston as "John T."—the same first name and middle initial of John T. Scopes—which may have been his way of implicating his kin's infamous ties with the southern "heretic" Scopes (*Letters I*, p. 27). Williams's disdain for Raulston is evidenced in his November 15, 1936 letter to his grandparents, where he expresses his hope that "Grand has not sold her farm" because he thinks "that sly John T. is trying to put something over on her" (*Letters I*, p. 91). Grand died on January 6, 1944, a year before Williams achieved critical and financial success with *The Glass Menagerie*. Williams's six-month contract at M.G.M. studios was from May to October 1943. On May 22, 1943, Williams wrote in his journal that "Grand got better and was around the house" (*Notebooks*, p. 365). By October, he noted: "Grand and Grandfather still alive—the falling monuments on all the sweet things in my childhood and later" (*Notebooks*, p. 397).

"*Slapstick Tragedy*: A Preface." First published in *Esquire* August 1965 as the "Preface" to "*Slapstick Tragedy*: Two Plays by Tennessee Williams." A loyal Williams collaborator, Charles Bowden produced *The Night of the Iguana* and several of Williams's later plays, including *Slapstick Tragedy* (the double-bill of *The Mutilated* and *The Gnädiges Fräulein*). The "Theatre of the Absurd" is a term coined by critic Martin Esslin, whose book on the experimental plays of Samuel Beckett, Arthur Adamov, Eugene Ionesco, and Jean Genet was landmark in the identification of a new trend taking place in the theater.

"The Wolf and I." First published in the *New York Times* February 20, 1966, as "Tennessee Williams: The Wolf and I," the pre-opening piece for the double-bill *Slapstick Tragedy*, which premiered at the Longacre Theater in New York on February 22, 1966, and closed after seven performances. The dog, Satan (Williams calls him Satin in *Memoirs*), was a black Belgian shepherd that Anna Magnani advised him to buy in Rome in the fall of 1960. Williams's parrot's name was Laurita and the bulldog, one of many Williams had throughout his life, was Gigi. The biting incident took place during the two-week tryout of *The Night of the Iguana* at Detroit's Fisher Theater, which was undergoing renovations, in November 1961.

"Happiness Is Relevant." First published in the *New York Times* March 24, 1968, as "'Happiness Is Relevant' to Mr. Williams," the pre-opening piece for *The Seven Descents of Myrtle* (*Kingdom of Earth*), which premiered on Broadway at the Ethel Barrymore Theater on March 27, 1968, and ran for twenty-nine performances. The "period play" Williams quotes from would become *Will Mr. Merriwether Return from Memphis?* Hart Crane's poem "Praise for an Urn" (1922) concludes "Scatter these well-meant idioms / Into the smoky spring that fills / The suburbs, where they will be lost. / They are no trophies of the sun." Edwina Williams's great-great-grandfather, Preserved Fish Dakin, moved to Waynesville, Ohio, "where he acquired a large parcel of land known as Dakin's Corner" (Leverich, p. 18). The "huge dog" was Satan (see Williams's essay, "The Wolf and I").

"'Tennessee, Never Talk to an Actress.'" First published in the *New York Times* May 4, 1969, as the pre-opening piece for *In the Bar of a Tokyo Hotel*, which premiered Off-Broadway at the Eastside Playhouse on May 11, and closed, after twenty-two previews and twenty-five performances, on June 1. Rehearsals for *A Streetcar Named Desire* took place on the roof of the New Amsterdam Theater. The actress who "burst into tears" was presumably Kazan's then-lover, Kim Hunter, who played Stella Kowalkski. Williams told Margo Jones in an October 1947 letter that Hunter was "very bad at first, is now improving but will, I am afraid, always be the lame duck in the line-up" (*Letters II*, p. 128). "[T]hat Italian" is Anna Magnani, for whom Williams wrote *The Rose Tattoo*. Diane Barrymore played Blanche DuBois during a 1959 road-tour rival of the play directed by George Keathley. Estelle Parsons created the title role of *The Seven Descents of Myrtle* (*Kingdom of Earth*). Anne Meacham was currently playing Miriam in *In the Bar of a Tokyo Hotel*. Maureen Stapleton played Serafina Delle Rose and Lady Torrance in the Broadway premieres of *The Rose Tattoo* and *Orpheus Descending* (in the film version of the play, *The Fugitive Kind*, Magnani played Lady and Stapleton played Vee Talbot).

"We Are Dissenters Now." First published in *Harper's Bazaar* January 1972. This essay is related to Williams's speech on December 6, 1971, at a demonstration against the Vietnam War. The Peoples' Coalition for Peace and Justice benefit took place in New York City at the Cathedral of St. John the Divine. Norman Mailer's anti-war play, *D.J. or A Fragment from Vietnam: A One-Act Play* (based on his 1967 novel, *Why Are We In Vietnam?*), was given a staged reading, which Williams did not appreciate (no doubt he was bothered by its homophobic discourse) and left the church. 1972 was a presidential election year fueled by concerns of America's involvement in Southeast Asia and the negotiations for a cease-fire and withdrawal of American troops. Two Valentine Seviers—(1747-1800) and (1780-1840)—were Tennessee ancestors on Williams's father's side. In a 1941 letter to Lawrence Langner, Williams writes, "My people were Tennessee Indian-fighters who never asked for mercy but lost their scalps whenever they lost a battle" (*Let-*

ters I, p. 306). The reference comes from John Keats's poem, "When I have fears that I may cease to be" (1818): "When I behold, upon the night's starr'd face, / Huge cloudy symbols of a high romance, / And think that I may never live to trace / Their shadows, with the magic hand of chance." Williams's mentioning the American comic Lenny Bruce, who was arrested for having spoken obscenities during a performance, is most likely a reference to *Lenny*, Julian Barry's play on Bruce's life and work, which opened at the Brooks Atkinson Theatre on May 26, 1971. The author/guru with whom Williams shared a verandah in Acapulco was Andrew Gunn, the son of a Pullman Company executive. He had fled to Mexico from Tahiti to avoid the war (see Williams's essays, "The History of a Play (With Parentheses)" and "A Summer of Discovery"). Friend and fellow-poet Clark Mills introduced Williams to "The League of Artists and Writers" in St. Louis, where he attended their weekly meetings in 1936. *Candles to the Sun*, Williams's first full-length play, premiered March 20, 1937, at the Wednesday Club in St. Louis. *Fugitive Kind*, Williams's second full-length play, premiered there a few months later on December 4. Williams offers details of his confrontation with Washington University professor William Carson in his journal (*Notebooks*, p. 89), as well as in an interview for the *New York Post* (April 28, 1958). Kate "Ma" Barker was a notorious criminal during the 1930s.

"Too Personal?" First published as the foreword to *Small Craft Warnings* on November 15, 1972. This essay (written March 26, 1972) was meant to be the "pre-opening piece" for *Small Craft Warnings*, which premiered Off-Broadway on Easter Sunday (April 2, 1972) at the Truck and Warehouse Theater. The *New York Times* "chose to interview [him] instead" (Mel Gussow's "Williams Looking to Play's Opening" [March 31]). Williams is referring to his 1970 television interview with David Frost when he publicly alluded to his homosexuality, as well as to Tom Buckley's tell-all piece, "Tennessee Williams Survives," which appeared in the *Atlantic Monthly* later that same year. The second write-up was a 1970 interview with Don Lee Keith.

"Homage to Key West." First published in *Harper's Bazaar* in January 1973. From 1972 till 1979, Robert Carroll was Williams's tempestuous lover, who "alternat[ed] between great sweetness" and "down-right beastliness" (St. Just, p. 292). Williams dedicated *Moise and the World of Reason* (1975) to Carroll.

"Let Me Hang It All Out." First published in the *New York Times* March 4, 1973. This essay was written as a post-production response to the critical attacks against *Out Cry*, which opened at the Lyceum Theater on March 1, 1973, and closed after only twelve performances. *Out Cry* first premiered in the summer of 1971 at the Ivanhoe Theater in Chicago, which was a rewrite of an earlier play, *The Two-Character Play*, which played at the Hampstead Theatre Club in London in 1967. The 1974 revival of *Cat on a Hot Tin Roof* for the American Shakespeare Theater (based on a 1973 version Williams produced at Stage/West, a regional theater in Springfield, Massachusetts, in November 1973) would restore much of the play's original third act, while maintaining the rest of Elia Kazan's suggestions for the Broadway version in 1955. Williams's *Memoirs* was published by Doubleday in November 1975. In it, he writes, "Truth is the bird we hope to catch in 'this thing,' and it can be better approached through my life story than an account of my career" (p. 173). In his 1976 interview with George Whitmore for *Gay Sunshine*, Williams reiterated that he did not want to "write a gay play" simply because he did not "find it necessary." In celebration of *Streetcar*'s silver anniversary, revivals were staged at the Ahmanson Theater in Los Angeles and at the Lincoln Center in New York. Lord Byron delivers the line *"There is a passion for declivity in this world!"* in block eight of *Camino Real*. "Right On!" is the translation of Williams's signature cry, *En avant*. The second outcry is Macbeth's final line to Macduff in Shakespeare's tragedy: "Lay on, Macduff, / And damn'd be him that first cries, 'Hold, enough!'"

"Where My Head Is Now and Other Questions." First published in *Performing Arts* April 1973. This essay resulted from Williams's visit to California where he gave an introduction to a screening of the film *A Streetcar Named Desire* at the Los Angeles County Museum. On March 18, Williams spoke at a luncheon hosted by the University of Southern California. Williams left at the end of March for the Orient on his *Cherry Blossom Cruise*, about which he writes extensively in various manuscript fragments devoted to *Vieux Carré* (ca. 1976-1977), written during the ocean crossing. Williams quotes from his 1939 poem "Cried the Fox" (*Poems*, p. 6).

"The Blessings and Mixed Blessings of Workshop Productions." First published in *Dramatist Guild Quarterly* Autumn 1976. *The Two-Character Play* was restaged in New York at the Quaigh Theater in August 1975. Williams's "great pride" on the Guild Council would not last for long. In the manuscript version, there is a passage that does not make it into the final essay but which is worth mentioning: "I am certain that the time will come when an all-black company, should it choose to present 'Streetcar', will do it brilliantly and the offenses of their race would not be involved" [p. 4]. Peter Shaffer's *Equus* and Edward Albee's *Seascape* were both financially successful. "Oh, Dry Those Tears" was a popular song written by British composer Florence Aylward in 1877.

"I Have Rewritten a Play For Artistic Purity." First published in the *New York Times* November 21, 1976, as the pre-opening piece for *The Eccentricities of a Nightingale*, which premiered on Broadway at the Morosco Theater on November 23, 1976, and closed after twenty-four performances. Armenian-British author Michael Arlen's best-selling novel, *The Green Hat* (1924), was made into a successful play the following year and premiered almost simultaneously in London and New York that September. While Katherine Cornell played Iris (March) Fenwick in the Broadway production at the Broadhurst Theater, Tallulah Bankhead incarnated the role on the West End, so Williams is not entirely mistaken here as he later suggests. Williams reworked a new version of *Summer and Smoke* in Rome but was disappointed with it, writing in his journal on August 9, 1951: "The experience of reading over the 'New S. & S." was a staggering blow. Probably the worst job I've ever done. Quite pitiful" (*Notebooks*, p. 531). Nonetheless he submitted it to John Perry at H. M. Tennent, who was going to put on *Summer and Smoke* that autumn. Nellie Ewell is the "what's-her-name" character who does not appear in the new play.

"I Am Widely Regarded as the Ghost Of a Writer." First published in the *New York Times* May 8, 1977, though written as the pre-opening piece for *Vieux Carré*, which premiered on Broadway at the St. James Theater on January 11, 1977, and closed after five performances. The essay evolved out of numerous essay frag-

ments written between the summer of 1976 and January or February 1977 when
he was preparing to speak at the Sophomore Literary Festival at the University
of Notre Dame. *Vieux Carré* returns to the "poetic naturalism" that character-
ized Williams's earlier dramatic triumphs. Williams began work on *Vieux Carré*
as early as 1938 during his first stay in New Orleans, which may account for its
similarities in style to these earlier plays. The entire poem excerpted here (with
slight variation) was later sent to Maria St. Just in 1982 (St. Just, pp. 387-88).
"The Misunderstanding and Fears of an Artist's Revolt." First published in *Where I
   Live* in November 1978, though actually written earlier that spring in Key West.
   "Begin the Beguine" is a popular ballroom dance song written by Cole Porter for
   the 1935 musical *Jubilee*. Williams may also be punning on Israeli Prime Minister, Menachem Begin, who later that year signed the Camp David Accords with
   Egyptian President Anwar Sadat. Williams began referring to his Key West studio
   as "The Madhouse" in 1976.

Miscellany: Reviews, Introductions, Appreciations, & Program Notes

"A Reply to Mr. Nathan." Previously unpublished (written April 9, 1945), this essay
   comes from a typescript at Texas. This essay was Williams's response to the eminent
   drama critic, George Jean Nathan, his literary "nemesis" (*Memoirs*, p. 114). Nathan's
   review of *The Glass Menagerie* in the *New York Journal-American* (April 4, 1945)
   claimed that the "wooden" role of Tom Wingfield had been "rewritten" by Dowling
   in order to add "some living plausibility" to the play. Whatever praise Nathan attributed to the play was directed toward its production, which he says outright hides the
   faults in the play's structure. Nathan had taken a special interest in the play because
   he was in love with Julie Haydon, who played Laura Wingfield and whom he would
   eventually marry. Williams writes in his *Memoirs* that Dowling and Nathan conspired
   to write the drunk scene for Tom, which Williams detested and rewrote himself (p.
   82).The line "already cited" which Williams admits was Dowling's actually comes
   later in the essay: "'Here's where my memory stops and your imagination begins.'"
   Though the line does not appear in the Random House edition of 1945, it is retained
   in the Drama Play Service's edition of 1948, much to Williams's chagrin.
"An Appreciation: The Creator of *The Glass Menagerie* Pays Tribute to Laurette
   Taylor." First published in the *New York Times* December 15, 1946. Laurette
   Taylor played Amanda Wingfield in the original Broadway production of *The
   Glass Menagerie*. It was her triumphant return to the stage, after a seven-year
   hiatus due to alcoholism. She died of coronary thrombosis on December 7, 1946.
   Taylor's failing health, along with friction between her and Eddie Dowling, were
   two reasons for the play's early closing on Broadway on August 3, 1946, after
   561 performances. Pauline Lord succeeded Taylor in the role of Amanda in the
   touring company of *The Glass Menagerie*, which was set to open in Pittsburgh
   on September 2, 1946.
"An Appreciation of Hans Hofmann." First published in *Women: A Collaboration
   of Artists and Writers* in 1948 as "An Appreciation." This essay reflects the lessons Williams learned in the plastic arts that helped form his idea of the plastic
   theater. Hofmann was one of the most important painters and art teachers in
   postwar America who, along with Jackson Pollock and Willem de Kooning, de-

veloped Abstract Expressionism (see Williams's essay, "Notes to the Reader"). Williams attributes his appreciation of the notion of plastic space to Hofmann in his novella, *Moise and the World of Reason*—though he misspells his name—as well as in act two, scene two of *Will Mr. Merriwether Return from Memphis?*

"An Allegory of Man and His Sahara." A review of Paul Bowles's *The Sheltering Sky*, first published in the *New York Times Book Review* December 4, 1949. This essay actually concludes on "a very lyrical last sentence about 'time'" (*Letters II*, p. 271) that was edited out in the published version: "[. . .] wandering blindly into, conducted only by time, a guide to whom every instrument of reconnaissance seems to be equally and totally dispensable." On November 19, 1949, Williams wrote to Paul Bowles about the manner in which he was asked to write the review and how, after Gore Vidal's interests to do the same, the editor became wary of asking for a book review from a friend (*Letters II*, p. 271). Williams first met Bowles and his wife Jane in Acapulco in 1940, where they became good friends, often traveling together to places like Tangiers. Bowles was principally a composer whom Williams commissioned to compose incidental music for *The Glass Menagerie*, *Summer and Smoke*, and several other plays, as well as for his poems, *Blue Mountain Ballads* (1946). The "frisky [. . .] kids" were Gore Vidal, who was only twenty-four at the time, and Truman Capote, then twenty-five. In a 1972 interview with Jim Gaines, Williams said that writers should never compromise their truth for success: "He's much better off if he compromises not at all, providing he has talent and something to say. People like Genet never compromised. William Burroughs never compromised. Paul Bowles never compromised" (*Conversations*, p. 222).

"A Movie by Cocteau. . . ." First published in the *New York Times* November 5, 1950. In 1946, Cocteau published the discursive diary he kept while making the film *Beauty and the Beast* (*La Belle et la Bête*). It was translated into English by Ronald Duncan in 1950 and published as *The Diary of a Film*, which Williams reviews here. Williams first met Cocteau in Paris in late July 1949. Cocteau was about to direct *Un Tramway nommé Désir* later that October, which starred Jean Marais, Cocteau's lover. Williams, who was already familiar with Cocteau's 1930 film, *The Blood of the Poet* (*Le Sang d'un poète*), saw *Beauty and the Beast* in 1948. Williams often recalled Cocteau's having smoked opium to excite his poetic inspiration (he was addicted to it in the 1920s, finally curing himself in 1929) to justify his own drug use for similar creative stimulation. Christian (Bébé) Bérard, whom Williams incorrectly calls "Bésé" in his *Memoirs* (p. 149), designed the décor for Cocteau's *Beauty and the Beast*. Williams first met him at a theater party in London in June or July 1948 while overseeing the rehearsals of *The Glass Menagerie*.

"The Human Psyche—Alone." A review of Paul Bowles's *The Delicate Prey and Other Stories*, first published in the *Saturday Review of Literature* December 23, 1950. In December 1948, when Williams read the title story about a thief who slices off a boy's penis, he advised Bowles "against its publication in the States" (*Memoirs*, p. 159). On the eve of Thanksgiving, November 22, 1950, a Long Island Railroad train leaving Penn Station for Babylon, New York, rear-ended another passenger train that had stalled on the tracks in Queens, killing seventy-nine people. Williams's comments about an artist retreating into the "cavern of himself" anticipate the "[a]nxiety over all these weeks" (*Notebooks*, p. 519) that he felt prior to the Broadway opening of *The Rose Tattoo*, following its out-of-town preview in Chicago.

"Notes on the Filming of *Rose Tattoo*." Previously unpublished (written April 21, 1952), this essay comes from a typescript at NOLA. *The Rose Tattoo* had caused quite a stir on Broadway in 1950, given its frankness with sexual intercourse outside of marriage. Williams was even criticized by one reviewer for having a condom fall out of Alvaro's pocket in act three, scene one. Williams submitted a revised scene to Audrey Wood to "alleviate some of the 'moral' antipathy" (*Letters II*, p. 374) that the play was causing. Hal B. Wallis was the eminent Hollywood producer to whom Audrey Wood sold the film rights for *The Rose Tattoo*. Williams did not like Antonia Rey in the role of Assunta and wrote to Audrey Wood in July 1951 hoping that "someone" could be found "to replace the present Assunta, if it goes on tour [. . .]" (*Letters II*, p. 391).

"A Tribute from Tennessee Williams to 'Heroic Tallulah Bankhead.'" First published in the *New York Times* March 4, 1956. *Time* magazine ran a brief review of the play in its gossip column on February 13: "As Streetcar's wild run began, Playwright Tennessee Williams had unwarily cozied up to Tallulah in her dressing room [. . .]. After catching her first performances, he began attending a nearby bar. Groaned he into his cups and to all who would listen: 'That woman is ruining my play.'" Williams wrote this letter-to-the-editor to set the record straight. In March 1947, Audrey Wood suggested to Williams that Tallulah Bankhead play Blanche DuBois. "My fear," he replied, "is that Bankhead would not be sympathetic enough in the softer aspects of the character. But she would certainly be thrilling in the big scenes" (*Letters II*, p. 89). Two years later, when Jessica Tandy left the show, Williams wrote to Irene Selznick about the possibility of Bankhead taking over: "Frankly, I am ~~very~~ frightened of her, and I don't think she should be put in the play without very earnest assurance, from her, that should play the play and not just Tallulah as she has been recently doing. In other words, we don't yet want the 'Camp' streetcar!" (*Letters II*, p. 236). Williams was prescient on both accounts, for when Bankhead did perform Blanche in 1956, the revival became notorious. While her opening night performance was typically campy, her next performance was "legitimate and brilliant" (*Letters II*, p. 599). Juan Belmonte García and Manuel Laureano Rodríguez Sánchez ("Manolete") were legendary Spanish bullfighters.

"On Meeting a Young Writer." First published in *Harper's Bazaar* August 1956. Françoise Sagan's 1954 novel, *Hello, Sadness (Bonjour tristesse)*, a bestseller both in France and in the U.S., gave her international celebrity status at age nineteen. In the spring of 1955 during her U.S. book tour, Williams sent Sagan a telegram, inviting her to Key West to meet him and Carson McCullers. She stayed for a "riotous two weeks" (*Letters II*, p. 572). Sagan later translated Williams's *Sweet Bird of Youth* for André Barsacq's Théâtre de L'Atelier in Paris, where it was performed in 1971. Williams said of the translation and of Sagan: "she did a beautiful job on it. She was a close friend of mine; although we didn't see much of each other, whenever we did, the friendship continued as if there had been no interruption" (*Memoirs*, p. 176). Sagan's wealth fueled her passion for sports cars, which culminated in her crashing her Aston-Martin the following year on April 14, 1957, fracturing her skull and putting her into a coma for several weeks. Sagan's second novel, *A Certain Smile* (*Un Certain sourire*), was published in 1956. Ramond Radiguet, whose *The Devil in the Flesh* (*Le Diable au corps*) was an instant success in 1923, died the following year of typhoid fever at the age of twenty.

"Concerning Eugene O'Neill." First published in *Playbill* September 12–October 21, 1967. This tribute was included in the Souvenir Program for the first production of O'Neill's *More Stately Mansions* at the Center Theater Group in Los Angeles in September 1967. Several theater celebrities (playwrights, directors, critics) each wrote a piece on O'Neill's contribution to American theater for the program. In the fall of 1936 while studying at Washington University, he was required to "read all of O'Neill's plays to make a term paper on his work" (*Letters I*, p. 91) (see Williams's college paper, "Some Representative Plays of O'Neill And a Discussion of his Art"). Several of Williams's early one-act plays, such as *Moony's Kid Don't Cry*, were directly influenced by O'Neill's naturalistic plays— *Before Breakfast*, *The Hairy Ape*, and the *S. S. Glencairn* cycle plays.

"Tennessee Williams Talks about His Play *In the Bar of a Tokyo Hotel*." First published in the *New York Times* May 14, 1969. The short essay was a brief statement Williams wrote to the cast during rehearsals of the play. In talking about the artist's commitment to his work over his personal relationships, Williams is perhaps justifying his failed relationship with Frank Merlo, whose death in 1963 haunted Williams throughout the 1960s.

"Notes for *The Two Character Play*." First published in the *Tennessee Williams Review* in 1982 (written in March 1970). These "Notes" were written during the transformation of *The Two-Character Play* into *Out Cry*. Williams gave the notes to Thomas P. Adler when Williams attended the Literary Awards Ceremony at Purdue University on April 27, 1972. There is little doubt that Williams considered this play to be the best he had written in a long time. Its repeated rejection by critics and audiences alike in its various forms and revivals troubled Williams deeply, as his many unpublished essay fragments, such as "Final Material" and "Stylistic Experiments in the Sixties" (Texas, ca. 1973), demonstrate.

"To William Inge: An Homage." First published in the *New York Times* July 1, 1973. This eulogy was written following Inge's suicide by carbon monoxide poisoning on June 10, 1973, and most of it reappears in Williams's *Memoirs* (pp. 87-90). Barbara Baxley played Esmeralda in Williams's *Camino Real* and Isabel Haverstick in *Period of Adjustment*. Maureen Stapleton starred as Serafina Delle Rose in *The Rose Tattoo*, Lady Torrance in *Orpheus Descending*, and played in several other Williams plays. Helene Grace Connell (née Inge) was Inge's older sister by six years; she often looked after him later in his life. Inspired by the Mayo Clinic, the Menninger Clinic in Topeka, Kansas, was founded by Dr. C. F. Menninger and his father in 1919 to treat the mentally ill with respect to the patient's complete environment. Rehearsals of Williams's "most difficult play" was *Out Cry*. See my previous notes on Williams and Inge's first meeting in Williams's essay, "If the Writing Is Honest." Williams learned of the death of Jane Bowles on May 4.

"W. H. Auden: A Few Reminiscences." First published in the *Harvard Advocate* in 1975. Williams first saw W. H. Auden at a poetry reading at the New School for Social Research in February 1940. Auden was teaching poetry there, and Williams was taking John Gassner's drama course. In July 1944, Bill Cannastra, a Harvard student with whom Williams was infatuated, brought Williams to Auden's apartment, where he found the poet to be "polite but conspicuously cool" (Leverich, pp. 541-42). Chester Kallman was "the perennial Auden lover" (Windham, p. 237) whom Williams met in March 1949. Kallman and Auden were living on the island of Ischia, off the Neapolitan coast in Italy, when Williams and Frank Merlo were living in Rome. By this time, however, Williams was already turning sour toward Auden despite the adulatory tone of his essay. Williams was actually in New York at the time of Auden's death, attending a service at the Lady Chapel of St. Patrick's Cathedral for Anna Magnani (who died on September 26). On September 27, 1973, Williams wrote a letter to Maria St. Just using Beverly Hills Hotel letterhead (which may account for his inaccuracy): "Last night—W. H. Auden died in Vienna. I called Isherwood at once, he was very shaken" (St. Just, p. 302). Auden died on September 28 after a poetry reading in Vienna.

"Foreword to Jane Bowles's *Feminine Wiles*." First published in 1976 (written November 11, 1974). Throughout his life, Williams championed Jane Bowles's writing, calling her the greatest prose stylist of the 20th century. When he built a gazebo on his Key West compound in the early 1970s, he baptized it the "Jane Bowles Summer House" after the title of her 1953 play, *In The Summer House*, which Williams saw performed at the University Theater in Ann Arbor, Michigan, starring Miriam Hopkins.

"Program Note for *The Red Devil Battery Sign*." First published in the *Vancouver Playhouse Program Magazine* October 1980. This preface was written to accompany the Vancouver Playhouse's production of *The Red Devil Battery Sign*, which opened on October 18. In the fall of 1980, Williams accepted the offer of a Distinguished Writer in Residence post at the University of British Columbia. Part of the deal was that they produce *Red Devil*. On October 17, Williams wrote to Maria St. Just that he was in Vancouver for "the definitive production of *Red Devil Battery Sign* being staged by a brilliant director" (St. Just, p. 381). In a December 1964 interview for the *New York Times*, entitled "Edward Albee and a Mystery," Albee claimed that his play *Tiny Alice* (1964) was a "mystery play, in two senses of the word," in other words, "it's both a metaphysical mystery and, at the same time, a conventional 'Dial M For Murder'-type mystery."

"Foreword to Dakin Williams's *The Bar Bizarre*." First published in 1980, using a reproduction of Williams's original handwritten note. Williams's younger brother Dakin referred to this piece as "a generous foreword" (Dakin, p. 330), despite its brevity. Implicit here, in the haste that the "foreword" was written, is Williams's continued anger toward his brother for having had him committed to the psychiatric ward of the Barnes Hospital in 1969 (hostilities less transparent than those expressed in his prose poem, "What's Next on the Agenda, Mr. Williams?").

"Homage to J[ames Laughlin]." First published in *Conjunctions* in the winter of 1981-1982. This short statement is similar in sentiment, though vastly different in language, to Williams's short speech in tribute to James Laughlin, which was read at the National Arts Club on February 25, 1983, the evening of the day that Williams died. As founder of New Directions and Williams's principal publisher, Laughlin had an inestimable role in establishing and preserving Williams's name in American letters.

Selected Juvenilia and College Papers

"Can a Good Wife Be a Good Sport?" First published in *Smart Set* May 1927. This essay won the sixteen-year-old Williams a third-prize award of five dollars, as well as an admonishment from his grandfather in a letter of April 12 not to publish in pulp magazines or, if he continued to do so, to use a "non-de-plume instead of your own name" (Leverich, p. 81). It demonstrates Williams's affinity even at a tender age for writing in a persona entirely different from his own.

"A Day at the Olympics" (October 30, 1928), "The Tomb of the Capuchins" (November 12, 1928), "A Flight over London" (November 27, 1928), "A Night in Venice" (December 20, 1928), "A Trip to Monte Carlo" (January 16, 1929), "The Ruins of Pompeii" (February 5, 1929), "A Tour of the Battle-fields of France" (February 19, 1929), "A Festival Night in Paris" (March 5, 1929), "The Almalfi Drive and Sorrento" (March 19, 1929), and "The First Day Out" (April 16, 1929). First published in *U. City Pep* from October 1928 to April 1929. All of these travelogue essays, based on a diary he kept during the trip, were written following Williams's European tour with his grandfather from July 6 to September 1/2, 1928, and published in his high school newspaper, *U. City Pep*, during his senior year. Williams writes that "the high-school paper, at the suggestion of my English teacher, invited me to narrate my European travels, which I did in a series of sketches, none containing a reference to the miracles of Cologne and Amsterdam nor the crisis, but nevertheless giving me a certain position among the student body, not only as the most bashful boy in school but as the only one who had traveled abroad" (*Memoirs*, p. 23). The series of articles do not reflect the order in which Williams visited the cities. Embarking at Southampton on July 12, the group traveled to Paris on July 14, visiting Versailles and the battlefields of the Marne valley. They then left for Marseilles on July 20, moved on to Nice, taking in a day trip to Monte Carlo. Afterwards, they visited "the principal Italian cities, including Rome, [Naples], Venice, and Milan, followed by Montreux, Cologne, Amsterdam, and London" (*Letters I*, p. 12). *Time* magazine on April 29, 1929, contained the following article on "Airports": "Aviation still does not know what it requires in fields. Bad example is England's Croydon field. It was remodeled and enlarged just a year ago. Now it must be altered again at great cost. [. . .] Croydon's chief merit is that planes have a 1,400-yd runway in any direction. Practically all the field is grass-covered. That permits comfortable landings and takeoffs, except in rainy weather. Then the planes tear up the sod." Mary Garden was a Scottish-American opera star from 1900 to the 1930s, whose career brought her acclaim in Paris and in Monaco. Williams wrote his grandfather on January 31, 1929, "The editor of the school-paper, who is in my Latin class, wants me to continue my writing for the paper. I have just completed an article on Pompeii this evening which I will send to you as soon as it is published" (*Letters I*, p. 26). The Battle of Belleau Wood, which took place from June 1 to 26, 1918, was one of the bloodiest battles the American Marines fought in World War I. The Aisne-Marne American Cemetery contains the graves of 2,289 American soldiers killed in the battle. From 1925 to 1934, the Eiffel Tower served as a giant electric billboard for the French automaker Citroën. *Hallelujah*, an all-black musical film that King Vidor directed for M.G.M. in 1929, was based on popular black spirituals. Williams was hardly the "excellent sailor" during the ocean crossing. In a letter dated July 13, 1928, he confessed to his family: "The first day out I was just desperately sea-sick but have become fully adjusted to the ship's motion since then and am now quite well [. . .]" (*Letters I*, p. 14). In a previous letter, he had expressed to his mother that "I will never again see anything humorous in people being sea-sick," adding "I should not have eaten so much in N.Y. before embarking" (Leverich, p. 91).

"Candida." First published in the *Shaw Review* May 1977 (written ca. 1936-1937). Originally from an incomplete, three-page typescript at Texas, this essay was probably written for professor William G. B. ("Pop") Carson's "English 16" course, "Technique of Modern Drama," which Williams enrolled in during the academic year 1936-1937. Williams wrote no less than ten play reports during this time, all based on the same model that he noted in his course spiral notebook for the year: "Report on 'Mérope'—Monday[.] briefest possible outline of plot—background—Voltaire's theatrical value of play—Voltaire's plays did impress audiences" (Texas). There were no corrections or teacher's comments on the typescript. The essay itself ends in mid-sentence (pages were lost).

"Review of Two Plays by John M. Synge." Previously unpublished (written ca. 1936-1937), this five-page typescript at Texas was again written during the academic year 1936-1937 at Washington University. Given the essay's comparison of Synge to Shaw, as well as its few grammatical corrections in a hand other than Professor Otto Heller's, it was probably written for Carson's "English 16" course.

"Some Representative Plays of O'Neill And a Discussion of his Art." Previously unpublished (written ca. Fall 1936), this sixteen-page typescript at Texas was written during the fall of 1936 for Otto Heller's "General Literature III" course, "Principal and Problems of Literature." In a letter to his grandparents (ca. November 15, 1936), Williams writes, "All my mornings, including Saturday are taken up at the University and I have three courses which require a tremendous amount of outside reading. For one course I am having to read all of O'Neill's plays to make a term paper on his work" (*Letters I*, pp. 90-91). In his course spiral notebook for the year 1936-1937 (which contains titles, poetry analysis and play dialogue for "April is the Cruelest Month"), Williams listed "O'Neill plays read": "In The Zone Moon Of The Carribbees (Smitty a love lorn Englishman) The Hairy Ape, Anna Christie, Beyond The Horizon, Electra, Strange Interlude" (Texas, all *sic*). In his journal for September 25, 1936, he writes, "I love school— Especially Heller and [Harcourt] Brown" (*Notebooks*, p. 59). Brown was Williams's professor for "French 16," "Origins of the Philosophic Movement." By October 7, Williams's impressions of Heller had turned sour: "Dr. Heller bores me with all his erudite discussion of literature. Writing is just <u>writing</u>! Why all the fuss about it?" (*Notebooks*, p. 61). There are several corrections and marginal notes in Heller's hand. In one comment, following Williams's analysis of the "ludicrously incongruent" speech of the farm boy in *Beyond the Horizon*, Heller writes, "You are right about the dialogue." At the end of the term paper, however, Heller provides the following commentary: "Not quite in accord with your earlier estimate. Your style is a bit too truculent." He nonetheless gave Williams the grade "AB" for the paper, and an "A" in the course.

"Is Fives." Previously unpublished (written December 1936), this six-page typescript at Texas, signed and dated at the end, was Tom Williams's "poetic manifesto"

(*Poems*, pp. xxv-vi). The title refers to E. E. Cummings's collection of poems entitled *Is 5* (1926). Williams wrote this "paper" under the modernist influences of poet-friend Clark Mills, whom he met in 1933 and with whom he studied at Washington University in 1936-1937. An earlier version of this essay appears handwritten in his college spiral notebook for that year. Gertrude Stein's line "*Rose is a rose is a rose is a rose*" comes from the 1913 poem "Sacred Emily," first published in *Geography and Plays* (1922). Shakespeare's "Sonnet 130" contains the line "I have seen roses damasked, red and white, / But no such roses see I in her cheeks." The line "Ineluctable preoccupation with The Verb" appears in Cumming's foreword to *Is 5*. "Euclid alone has looked on Beauty bare" and "Have heard her massive sandal set on stone" are the first and last lines of a 1923 sonnet by Edna St. Vincent Millay.

"Birth of an Art (Anton Chekhov and the New Theater)." Previously unpublished (written ca. Spring 1937), this twenty-three-page typescript at Texas was written during the spring of 1937 for Otto Heller's "General Literature III" course, "Principal and Problems of Literature." Williams now "despised" Heller for having given him a "D" in his "Principals and Problems of Literature" course, for which this term paper was written (Leverich, p. 217). This affront, compounded by William Carson's not having selected Williams's play *Me, Vashya!* among the three finalists of the "English 16" playwriting contest, may have prompted Williams to write the anonymous essay, "What College Has Not Done For Me," which appeared in the June issue of the *Eliot* (Crandell, pp. 482-83). On the title page of this lightly corrected essay, Heller wrote these two comments: "Page numbers? This paper is no way fulfills the requirements of a term paper as indicated repeatedly. O.H." and "All of this, or nearly all, was written without reference or relation to literary standards and criteria as studied in the course. O.H." [p. 1].

"Comments on the Nature of Artists with a few Specific References to the Case of Edgar Allan Poe." Previously unpublished (written ca. October 18, 1937), this incomplete six-page typescript at Texas was written for Wilbur L. Schramm's "comprehensive survey of English literature" course at the University of Iowa (*Letters I*, p. 105). Williams had been corresponding frequently with Schramm since 1936, when he began submitting poems and stories to the magazine he edited, *American Prefaces*. In his journal for October 18, 1937, Williams writes, "Schramm has almost definitely accepted my ~~poem~~ story—~~(I gave him my silly paper on Poe and artists this morning~~—[. . .]" (*Notebooks*, p. 111). The essay is lightly marked up with Schramm's comments and corrections.

A COMPLETE LIST OF TENNESSEE WILLIAMS'S
NON-FICTION PROSE WRITINGS

The following is a list of all the non-fiction essays, statements, occasional pieces, blurbs, and fragments by Tennessee Williams that I have collected and examined over the course of editing this book. All major Williams archives are represented here except Harvard, whose collection remains uncatalogued. Though extensive, I am sure this list remains incomplete, in particular in the manuscript section.

The titles used here represent those that Williams chose himself for his individual essays, either in manuscript draft or at the time of its reprinting as the foreword to a given play or in the collection *Where I Live*. Since many of the essays first appeared in newspapers or magazines, their titles were supplied by editors or modified by editorial standards. I have placed these more familiar titles in square brackets following Williams's specific title or the title he most likely attributed to the essay.

Dating Williams's unpublished non-fiction is daunting. One reason is that at all the main repositories of his manuscripts there are files which combine drafts of different essays or which contain numerous untitled fragments with obscure or no internal or external evidence in which to date them precisely (in these cases, I have written "n.d." for "no date" and "ca." for "circa" and have offered an approximate date in parentheses). To complicate matters, Williams often took up previous manuscripts five, ten, sometimes thirty years later and began writing them, frequently using the same opening phrase. Where these fragments should fall in terms of a chronology remains a difficult issue to resolve. Williams did, however, frequently use signature phrases and metaphors that link certain essays or made references to specific current events—like a recent hurricane that swept through the Keys, a snow storm or train wreck in New York, a newspaper strike, or a recent film released—that help situate the manuscripts within a particular time frame. Examining external evidence in the manuscripts, though, remains problematic. While certain essays share identifiable keystrokes or hotel letterhead, Williams's habits of rarely staying in one place beyond a few months frequently translated into his using whatever typewriter that was on hand and filling it with blank or recycled typing paper (with previous work of his already on it) that was stuffed into his suitcase or steamer trunk. The result is that two manuscripts separated by as little as a month could be typed on different typewriters, whereas two fragments that were obviously typed on the same typewriter might have been written years or decades apart.

Moreover, in the files at Texas, Columbia, and New Orleans, disparate fragments have been placed in one folder, with no consistent order and often without logical sequencing. It becomes apparent that the ten or fifteen sheets of paper included in one folder either make up Williams's different attempts to restart the same essay or reflect the uncertainty of a given sheet's origins. Since many of the manuscripts are typed with different typewriters (Williams preferred typing to handwriting during composition) and deal with entirely different subjects, it would be prudent to separate them all into individual files; doing so, however, would easily quadruple the length of the list presented below.

I am certain that some dates I have listed here are wrong—some by as little as a month; others by perhaps as much as a year. My goal was not to establish a definitive chronology of Williams non-fiction prose manuscripts, but rather to offer a starting point for future scholars. There remains a considerable amount of research to be done to piece together Williams's unpublished non-fiction prose, and I would recommend that the person who undertakes the task follow Blanche's advice to Stanley *viz.* the Ambler & Ambler papers of the lost Belle Reve: study them "with a bottle of aspirin tablets."

Essays

"'Amor Perdido,' or, How It Feels to Become a Professional Playwright," *Michigan Quarterly Review* n.d. (ca. 1940)

"Te Morituri Salutamus" n.d. (ca. 1941-1942) (Texas)

"Preface to My Poems," *Five Young American Poets,* 1944

"The History of a Play (With Parentheses)," *Pharos* Spring 1945

"Notes to the Reader" n.d. (ca. 1945) (Texas)

"The Author Tells Why It is Called *The Glass Menagerie,*" *New York Herald Tribune* April 15, 1945

"A Playwright's Statement on Dallas' Theatre '45 Plans," *The Dallas Morning News* July 22, 1945

"Tennessee Williams" December 1945 (Texas)

"The Catastrophe of Success" ["On a Streetcar Named Success"], *New York Times* November 30, 1947

"Chicago Arrival" August/September 1948 (NOLA)

"Questions Without Answers," *New York Times* October 3, 1948

"Something Wild . . ." ["On the Art of Being a True Non-conformist"], *New York Star* November 7, 1948

Carson McCullers's *Reflections in a Golden Eye* ["Introduction"], January or March 1950

"A Writer's Quest for a Parnassus," *New York Times* August 13, 1950

"The Timeless World of a Play" ["Concerning the Timeless World of a Play"], *New York Times* January 14, 1951

"The Meaning of *The Rose Tattoo*" ["Tennessee Williams Explains His Elusive, Brilliant, Allusive Comedy, 'The Rose Tattoo'"], *Vogue* March 15, 1951

"Facts About Me," Caedmon Records 1952 (Texas, NOLA)

"Foreword to *Camino Real*" ["On the 'Camino Real'"], *New York Times* March 15, 1953

"Afterword to *Camino Real*" June 1, 1953

"Person–To–Person" ["Williams: Person–To–Person"], *New York Times* March 20, 1955

"Critic Says 'Evasion,' Writer Says 'Mystery,'" *New York Herald Tribune* April 17, 1955

"The Past, the Present, and the Perhaps" ["Tennessee Williams on the Past, the Present and the Perhaps"], *New York Times* March 17, 1957

"The World I Live In" ["A Talk with Tennessee"], *New York Post* March 17, 1957

"Author and Director: A Delicate Situation," *Playbill* September 30, 1957

"The Writing Is Honest," *New York Times* March 16, 1958
"Foreword to *Sweet Bird of Youth*" ["Williams' Wells of Violence"], *New York Times* March 8, 1959
"The Man In the Overstuffed Chair," *Antaeus* (ca. 1960) 1982
"Reflections on a Revival of a Controversial Fantasy," *New York Times* May 15, 1960
"Tennessee Williams Presents His POV," *New York Times Magazine* June 12, 1960
"Prelude to a Comedy," *New York Times* November 6, 1960
"Five Fiery Ladies," *Life* February 3, 1961
"Carson McCullers" ["The Author"], *Saturday Review of Literature* September 23, 1961
"A Summer of Discovery," *New York Herald Tribune* December 24, 1961
"The Agent as Catalyst," *Esquire* December 1962
"T. Williams's View of T. Bankhead," *New York Times* December 29, 1963
"Grand" December 15, 1964
"*Slapstick Tragedy*: Preface" ["Preface," "*Slapstick Tragedy*: Two Plays by Tennessee Williams"], *Esquire* August 1965
"The Wolf and I" ["Tennessee Williams: The Wolf And I"], *New York Times* February 20, 1966
"Happiness Is Relevant" ["'Happiness Is Relevant' to Mr. Williams"], *New York Times* March 24, 1968
"'Tennessee, Never Talk to an Actress,'" *New York Times* May 1969
"Some Memoirs of a Con-Man" July 1971 (St. Just)
"We Are Dissenters Now," *Harper's Bazaar* January 1972
"Too Personal?" (ca. 26 March 1972), *Small Craft Warnings* November 15, 1972
"Survival Notes: A Journal," *Esquire* September 1972
"Homage to Key West," *Harper's Bazaar* January 1973
"Let Me Hang It All Out," *New York Times* March 4, 1973
"Where My Head Is Now and Other Questions," *Performing Arts* April 1973
"Le cinéma et moi," *Le Figaro* May 14, 1976
"The Blessings and Mixed Blessings of Workshop Productions" (ca. September 18, 1975), *Dramatist Guild Quarterly* Autumn 1976
"I Have Rewritten a Play For Artistic Purity," *New York Times* November 21, 1976
"I Am Widely Regarded as the Ghost Of a Writer," *New York Times* May 8, 1977
"The Misunderstanding and Fears of an Artist's Revolt" (ca. Spring 1978), *Where I Live: Selected Essays* November 15, 1978
"The Pleasures of the Table" (ca. May 1987), *Where I Live: Selected Essays* 1978

Author's Notes and Statements

"Program Note," Sinclair Lewis, *It Can't Happen Here* 1938 (Leverich)
"Random Observations," *Stairs to the Roof* 1941
"Author's Note," *I Rise in Flames, Cried the Phoenix* September 1941
[Letter to the Editor], *Herald American* February 25, 1945
"A Reply to Mr. Nathan," April 9, 1945 (Texas)
"Production Notes," *The Glass Menagerie* July 31, 1945
"Foreword," *Stairs to the Roof* February 26, 1947
[Letter to the Editor] "Tennessee Williams Explains," *St. Louis Post-Dispatch* January 2, 1948

"Author's Production Notes," *Summer and Smoke* March 1948
"My Current Reading," *Saturday Review of Literature* March 6, 1948
[A reply to] "A Streetcar Named Desire," *Esquire* May 1948
"History of *Summer and Smoke*" November 7, 1949 (Texas)
"To Mr. Ustinov, a gentle objection" n.d. (ca. November 1949–July 1950) (Texas)
"Loading the Dice," *Saturday Review of Literature* August 19, 1950
[Letter to the Editor] "Letter from a Playwright," *New York Post* May 16, 1951
[Letter to Walter Winchell] in "Behind the Scenes" January 31, 1952
"Notes on the Filming of *Rose Tattoo*" April 21, 1952 (NOLA)
Statement, Helen Chinoy, *Directing the Play* 1953
"The Dylan Thomas Fund," *Partisan Review* January–February 1954
"Notes for the Designer," *Cat on a Hot Tin Roof* 1955
"*The Rose Tattoo* in Key West," *Harper's Bazaar* February 1955
"Note of Explanation," *Cat on a Hot Tin Roof* July 20, 1955
"American Playwrights Self-Appraised," *Saturday Review of Literature* September 3, 1955
[Letter to the Editor] *Theatre Arts* October 1955
"I have three homes," *Perfect Home* November 1956
Statement, *Film en Roman* 1956
"Author's Note," *Sweet Bird of Youth* [playbill] April 1956
[Letter to the Editor] "Mal de Merde," *Time* October 22, 1956
"Reply to Charles Samuels," *Syracuse Review* January 1957
"What They Are Saying," *Look* July 9, 1957
[Letter to Robert Rice] "A Note from Tennessee Williams," *New York Post Daily Magazine* May 4, 1958
Statement, *Grand Kabuki* [playbill] May 1960
[Letter to the Editor], *Time* March 16, 1962
"Letter to Stubs Preview Club" June 12, 1962
Statement, *The Milk Train Doesn't Stop Here Anymore* [playbill] July 1962
[Letter to the Editor] "Quote, Unquote," *Newsweek* February 18, 1963
"Author's Notes," *The Milk Train Doesn't Stop Here Anymore* February 24, 1964
"These Ladies" *Sunday Herald Tribune Magazine* February 20, 1966
Statement, *Eccentricities of a Nightingale* [playbill] January 1967
"Production Note," *The Mutilated* March 7, 1967
"Production Notes," *The Gnädiges Fraülein* March 7, 1967
"Tennessee Williams Talks about His Play *In the Bar of a Tokyo Hotel*," *New York Times* May 14, 1969
"Notes for *The Two Character Play*," *Tennessee Williams Review* March 1970
"Acceptance by Mr. Williams," *Proceedings of the American Academy of Arts and Letters and the National Institute of Arts and Letters* 1970
[Letter to the Editor] "An Open Response to Tom Buckley," *Atlantic Monthly* January 1971
"Notes after the Second Invited Audience," *Small Craft Warnings* March 29, 1972
[Letter to the Editor] [on Max Jacobson], *New York Times* December 12, 1972
Statement, Evelyn Byrne, *Attacks of Taste* December 25, 1972
"Author's Note," *One Arm* [screenplay] n.d. (ca. 1972)
"A Dispensable Foreword," *Out Cry* October 24, 1973
"Quarterly's 1974 Questionnaire," *Dramatists Guild Quarterly* Winter 1974
"Author's Note," *A Cavalier for Milady* n.d. (ca. mid-1970s)

"Tennessee Williams Writes," *Gay Sunshine* Winter 1977
"Author's Note," *Stopped Rocking* 1977
[Letter to the Editor] "Tennessee Williams–Donald Windham," *New York Times* January 15, 1978
"Broadway Stars Talk About Critics," *New York Theatre Review* June/July 1978
"Author's Note," *All Gaul is Divided* July 1979
"Author's Production Note," *Will Mr. Merriwether Return from Memphis?* January 1980
[Statement on the Greene St. Theatre], *Tennessee Williams Newsletter* Spring 1980
"Author's Note," *The Loss of a Teardrop Diamond* May 1980
[Letter to the Editor] "Tennessee Williams Replies," *New York Times* August 3, 1980
[Letter to the Editor] "A Rave for a Critic," *Time* September 8, 1980
"Playwright's Preface" ["Program Note for *The Red Devil Battery Sign*"], *Vancouver Playhouse Program Magazine* October 18–November 15, 1980
"Grits," Dean Faulkner Wells, *Great American Cookbooks* 1981
"Something Tennessee," *Other Stages* July 30, 1981
"Author's Note," *Clothes for a Summer Hotel* n.d. (ca. pre-March 1983)

Miscellany: Reviews, Introductions, Appreciations
"The Darkling Plain (For Bruno Hauptmann who Dies Tonight)" March 31, 1936 (Texas)
"Return to Dust" September 1938 (Texas)
"An Appreciation: The Creator of *The Glass Menagerie* Pays Tribute to Laurette Taylor," *New York Times* December 15, 1946
"An Appreciation [of Hans Hofmann]," *Women: A Collaboration of Artists and Writers* January 2, 1948
"A Movie Named *La Terra Trema*," *'48* June 1948
"Thomas Benton Paints the Rough Side of *Streetcar* . . . and Playwright Tennessee Williams Likes It," *Look* February 1, 1949
"An Allegory of Man and His Sahara," [Review] Paul Bowles, *The Sheltering Sky*, *New York Times* December 4, 1949
"Foreword," Marian Gallaway, *Constructing a Play* **June 14, 1950**
"A Movie by Cocteau . . . ," *New York Times* November 5, 1950
"Foreword," Oliver Evans, *Young Man with a Screwdriver* May 5, 1950
"The Human Psyche—Alone," [Review] Paul Bowles, *The Delicate Prey and Other Stories, Saturday Review of Literature* December 23, 1950
Blurb, Donald Windham, *The Dog Star* 1950
Statement on Licia Albanese, RCA Victor Records 1950
"The Theatre," Donald Windham, *The Starless Air* [playbill] May 13, 1953
"Some Words Before," Gilbert Maxwell, *Go Looking* November 17, 1954
"Anna Magnani, Tigress of the Tiber. She Retains 'Uncanny Sense of Truth' in an English Speaking Movie Role," *New York Herald Tribune* December 11, 1955
"A Tribute from Tennessee Williams to 'Heroic Tallulah Bankhead,'" *New York Times* March 4, 1956
"On Meeting a Young Writer," *Harper's Bazaar* August 1956
Blurb, Gore Vidal, *Visit to a Small Planet* 1957
Blurb, James Purdy, *Malcolm* 1959
Blurb, James Leo Herlihy, *All Fall Down* 1960

"Authors and Critics Appraise Works" [on Ernest Hemingway], *New York Times*
  July 3, 1961
Blurb, James Purdy, *Color of Darkness* Summer/Fall 1961
Blurb, Richard Yates, *Revolutionary Road* 1961
Blurb, Donald Windham, *Emblems of Conduct* 1963
Blurb, Jane Bowles, *Two Serious Ladies* 1965
Blurb, Donald Windham, *Two People* 1965
Blurb, James Leo Herlihy, *Midnight Cowboy* 1965
"Tennessee Williams Reads Hart Crane," Caedmon Records 1965
"Gore Vidal," *McCall's* October 1966
"Concerning Eugene O'Neill," *Playbill* September 12–October 21, 1967
Blurb, Walter Starcke, *This Double Thread* 1967
Blurb, Lucy Freeman, *Celebrities on the Couch* 1967
Blurb, James Kirkwood, *Good Times / Bad Times* 1968
Blurb, Frederick Nicklaus, *Cut of Noon* 1971
"To William Inge: An Homage," *New York Times* July 1, 1973
Statement, Jeanine Basinger, *Working with Kazan* September 1973
Blurb, Mohamed Choukri, *For Bread Alone* 1973
"Some Words Before," Virginia Carr, *The Lonely Hunter: A Biography of Carson
  McCullers* July 3, 1975
"W. H. Auden: A Few Reminiscences," *Harvard Advocate* 1975
Blurb, Coleman Dowell, *Island People* 1976
Blurb, Darwin Porter, *Butterflies in Heat* 1976
"Foreword," Jane Bowles, *Feminine Wiles* (ca. November 11, 1974) May 24, 1976
Blurb, Joan Didion, *A Book of Common Prayer* 1978
"At the Expense of the Future," Richard Leavitt, *The World of Tennessee Williams*
  September 18, 1978
Statement, Mohamed Choukri, *Tennessee Williams in Tangiers* June 1, 1979
"Williams Recalls John Cromwell's Death," *New York Times* September 30, 1979
"Foreword," Dakin Williams, *The Bar Bizarre* November 15, 1980
"Homage to J[ames Laughlin].," *Conjunctions* Winter 1981-1982
"National Art Club Speech [on James Laughlin], *The Way It Wasn't* January 1983
Blurb, Charlotte Chandler, *The Ultimate Seduction* 1984
Blurb, Elia Kazan, *The Assassins* 1985

Juvenilia and College Papers
"Isolated," *The Junior Life* November 7, 1924
"Can a Good Wife Be a Good Sport?" *Smart Set* May 1927
"A Day at the Olympics," *The U. City Pep* October 30, 1928
"The Tomb of the Capuchins," *The U. City Pep* November 12, 1928
"A Flight over London," *The U. City Pep* November 27, 1928
"A Night in Venice," *The U. City Pep* December 20, 1928
"A Trip to Monte Carlo," *The U. City Pep* January 16, 1929
"The Ruins of Pompeii," *The U. City Pep* February 5, 1929
"A Tour of the Battle-fields of France," *The U. City Pep* February 19, 1929
"A Festival Night in Paris," *The U. City Pep* March 5, 1929
"The Almalfi Drive and Sorrento," *The U. City Pep* March 19, 1929
"The First Day Out," *The U. City Pep* April 16, 1929
"The Wounds of Vanity" December 2, 1930 (Texas)

"Tristam by Edward Arlington Robinson" n.d. (ca. 1936-1937) (Texas)
"Daisy Miller by Henry James" n.d. (ca. 1936-1937) (Texas)
"The 'Nigger' of the Narcissus by Joseph Conrad" n.d. (ca. 1936-1937) (Texas)
"A Report On Four Writers Of The Modern Psychological School" n.d. (ca. Fall 1936) (Texas)
"Some Representative Plays of O'Neill And a Discussion of his Art" n.d. (ca. Fall 1936) (Texas)
"[Exam] I. "Mr. Krutch is probably correct [. . .]" n.d. (ca. Fall 1936) (Texas)
"Art, Clive Bell" n.d. (ca. 1936-1937) (Texas)
"The Literary Mind by Max Eastman" n.d. (ca. 1936-1937) (Texas)
"Is Fives" December 1936 (Texas)
"As A Man Thinketh" n.d. (ca. 1936-1937) (Texas)
"Antigone" n.d. (ca. 1936-1937) (Texas)
"An Ancient Greek Poet's Address to a Convention of Modern Artist" n.d. (ca. 1936-1937) (Texas)
"Thinking Our Own Thoughts" n.d. (ca. 1936-1937) (Texas)
"Rain from Heaven" n.d. (ca. 1936-1937) (Texas)
"You Never Can Tell The Depth Of A Well" n.d. (ca. 1936-1937) (Texas)
"'Holiday' by Philip Barry" n.d. (ca. 1936-1937) (Texas)
"The Wind and the Rain (Merton Hodge)" n.d. (ca. 1936-1937) (Texas)
"'The Late Christopher Bean' by Sidney Howard" n.d. (ca. 1936-1937) (Texas)
"Candida" n.d. (ca. 1936-1937) (Texas)
"Review of Two Plays by John M. Synge" n.d. (ca. 1936-1937) (Texas)
"Candide ou L'Optimisme" n.d. (ca. 1936-1937) (Texas)
"Tucaret" n.d. (ca. 1936-1937) (Texas)
"Merope" n.d. (ca. 1936-1937) (Texas)
"Birth of an Art (Anton Chekhov and the New Theatre)" n.d. (ca. Spring 1937) (Texas)
"What College Has Not Done For Me," *Eliot* June 1937
"Comments on the Nature of Artists with a few Specific References to the Case of Edgar Allan Poe" n.d. (ca. October, 18 1937) (Texas)
"Scenario" ["Prof. Baker..."] n.d. (ca. 1938) (Texas)

Essay Drafts and Manuscript Fragments
"The 'Boss' Complex" n.d. (ca. 1930) (Texas)
"Yesterday morning the city of Midland [. . .]" ["corr. in class"] n.d. (ca. 1931-1932) (Texas)
"Imagism Old and New" [fragment] n.d. (ca. 1936-1937) (Texas)
"Chekhov and the New Theatre" n.d. (ca. Spring 1937) (Texas)
"A Letter to Irene" (ca. December 1940) (Texas)
"Hedda Gabler by Henrik Ibsen" [holograph fragment] n.d. (ca. May 1941) (Texas)
"Technical Foreword and Notes on the 'Plastic Theatre'" [fragment] n.d. (ca. 1945) (Texas)
"I think it was about ten 37 years ago [. . .]" [fragment] n.d. (ca. 1945) (NOLA)
"Eulogy of Laurette Taylor" n.d. (ca. 7–15 December 1946) (Texas)
"The Sculptured Play" n.d. (ca. 1945-1950) (Texas)
"Facts About Me" n.d. (ca. 1947) (Texas)
"Some Informedal Thoughts on Success" n.d. (ca. 1947) (Texas)

"An Old Lady Falls with Two Books" [fragments, review of Windham] n.d. (ca. Winter 1947-1948) (Texas)

"A Film in Sicily" February 14/15, 1948 (NOLA)

"Writing an article about [. . .]" [Draft of "Questions Without Answers] Detroit, September 1948 (Texas)

"A true piece of creative writing" [fragment] n.d. (ca. September 1948) (Texas)

"I realize now that I have taken probably inexcusable liberties [. . .]" [McCullers's *Reflections in the Golden Eye*] n.d. (ca. March–April 1949) (Texas)

"Some Words of Introduction" [McCullers's *Reflections in the Golden Eye*] n.d. (ca. April 1949) (Texas)

"This Book" [McCullers's *Reflections in the Golden Eye*] n.d. (ca. April 1949) (Texas)

"Praise to Assenting Angels" [McCullers's *Reflections in the Golden Eye*] n.d. (Delaware, ca. May 1949; NOLA, ca. May–July 1949)

"The Idea of Theatre by Francis Fergusson" [fragment] n.d. (ca. 1949-1950) (Texas)

The Dog Star [fragment blurb/review] n.d. (ca. December 16, 1949) (Texas)

"Writers Abroad: 1950" Rome, June 1950 (Texas)

"The Delicate Prey by Paul Bowles" n.d. (ca. 1950) (Texas)

"Timeless World of a Play" n.d. (ca. 1951) (Texas)

"Almost more important than being [. . .]" [fragment] n.d. (ca. 1952) (Texas)

"Some Notes on 'Camino Real'" n.d. (ca. 1953) (NOLA)

"The Art of Acting and Anna" n.d. (ca. 1955) (Texas)

"A Thing Called 'Personal Lyricism" [fragment for "Person–To–Person"] n.d. (ca. 1955) (Texas)

"Some Qualifications" [fragment for "Person–To–Person"] n.d. (ca. 1955) (Texas)

"Personal Lyricism (?)" [fragment for "Person–To–Person"] n.d. (ca. 1955) (Texas)

"Lyric Theatre: a faith" [fragment for "Person–To–Person" and "Past, Present & Perhaps"] (n.d. (ca. Fall 1955/1956) (Texas)

"Tennessee Williams (The Author)" n.d. (ca. 1956) (Texas)

"Preface" to *Playbook* [fragment] n.d. (ca. February/March 1956) (Texas)

"The Problem of a Long Run" n.d (ca. July 1956) (Texas)

"After Ten Years" [fragment originally for "Person–To–Person" used later for "Past, Present & Perhaps"] n.d. (ca. 1957) (Texas)

[Untitled holograph fragment of "Past, Present & Perhaps"] n.d. (ca. 1957) (Texas)

"Having been asked once again to compose a Sunday piece [. . .]" [fragment for "Past, Present & Perhaps"] n.d. (ca. 1957) (Texas)

"There is nothing more 'loaded' [. . .]" [fragment for "Past, Present & Perhaps"] n.d. (ca. 1957) (Texas)

"These invitations to write Sunday pieces [. . .]" [fragment for "Past, Present & Perhaps"] n.d. (ca. 1957) (Texas)

"One early Spring day long ago [. . .]" [fragment for "Past, Present & Perhaps"] n.d. (ca. 1957) (Texas)

"When people ask me if 'Something Wild in the Country' [. . .]" [fragment for "Past, Present & Perhaps"] n.d. (ca. 1957) (Columbia)

"A Do-It-Yourself Interview" [fragments for "Past, Present & Perhaps"] n.d. (ca. January 1957) (UCLA)

"Playwright Williams Interviews Himself" [draft of "World I Live In"] n.d. (ca. February 1957) (Texas)

"Time and Life and Drama" n.d. (ca. 1957-1960) (Texas)

"~~12~~ 13 Golden (?) Rules for New Playwrights" n.d. (ca. August 1959) (UCLA)

"Deepest Instinct, or Fate. . . ." n.d. (ca. 1960) (Texas)

"The drama critic of this newspaper" [fragment for "The Play of Character"] n.d. (ca. June/July1960) (Texas)

"The Play of Character" n.d. (ca. June/July1960) (Texas)

"Elizabeth Taylor," "Katherine Hepburn," "Anna Magnani" [drafts for and proofs of "Five Fiery Ladies"] July 12–13, 1960 (NOLA)

"[. . .] in a legal separation arranged by my little brother [. . .]" [fragments of "The Man in the Overstuffed Chair" as "Prelude to a Comedy"] n.d. (ca. 1960) (Columbia)

"The Man In The Overstuffed Chair" n.d. (ca. 1960) (Columbia)

"The Man in the Overstuffed Chair" [fragments] n.d. (ca. 1960) (Columbia)

"The last time I did a piece [. . .]" [fragment for "Prelude to a Comedy"] n.d. (ca. 1960) (Texas)

"The last time I wrote a piece [. . .]" [fragment for "Prelude to a Comedy"] n.d. (ca. 1960) (Columbia)

"[. . .] some intensely personal ~~personal~~ experience [. . .]" [fragment for "Prelude to a Comedy"] n.d. (ca. 1960) (Columbia)

"Since I am never going to get around to writing my memoirs [. . .]" [fragment for "Prelude to a Comedy"] n.d. (ca. 1960) (Columbia)

"The 'correction' of a playwright is rarely [. . .]" [fragments for "Prelude to a Comedy" and other essays] n.d. (ca. 1960) (Columbia)

"These Scattered Idioms [I]" [fragment for "Prelude to a Comedy"] n.d. (ca. 1960) (NOLA)

"These Scattered Idioms [II]" [fragment for "Prelude to a Comedy"] n.d. (ca. 1960) (Columbia)

"First Draft: Some Philosophical Shop Talk, or, An Inventory of a Remarkable Market" (numerous fragments of Williams randomly collected together in lieu of his memoirs that he felt he would never write; some would find their way into "Prelude to a Comedy," some into "Man in the Overstuffed Chair" and some into his *Memoirs* n.d. (ca. post–September 10, 1960-1972) (Columbia)

"Some Philosophical Shop-Talk" n.d. (ca. October 1960) (Columbia)

"Shop Talk" n.d. (ca. October 1960) (Columbia)

"Sam, You Made the Interview Too Long" n.d. (ca. October 1960) (Columbia)

"Personal as Ever" and "Sequiturs & non-sequiturs" n.d. (ca. October 1960) (Columbia)

"What the American novel needs [. . .]" [draft of blurb for Richard Yates, *Towers*] n.d. (ca. 1961) (NOLA)

"That Greek Island in times so ancient [. . .]" [fragment] n.d. (ca. post–April 1961/1963) (Columbia)

[Fragment statement on the "new wave" theatre] n.d. (ca. 1961/1963) (NOLA)

"Of My Father (A Belated Appreciation)" [fragments] n.d. (ca. 1964) (Columbia)

"A. Take any child who is terribly introverted [. . .]" (fragment) n.d. (ca. 1966-1967) (Columbia)

"[. . .] are its social aims [. . .]" [fragment of speech at The Peoples' Coalition for Peace and Justice?] n.d. (ca. December 1971) (NOLA)

"We Are Dissenters Now" [draft] n.d. (ca. December 1971) (NOLA)

"We are now into the seventies [. . .]" [fragment on *Confessional/Small Craft Warnings*] n.d. (ca. December 20,1971-January 1972) (NOLA)

"Who would have thought that [. . .]" [fragment on *Confessional/Small Craft Warnings*] n.d. (ca. January-March 1972) (NOLA)

"Certainly in one important respect I feel I have been lucky as a writer [. . .]" n.d. (ca. February/March 1972) (NOLA)

"The best thing that has happened [. . .]" [fragment statement on other playwrights] n.d. (ca. 1972) (NOLA)

"Unbreakable Habit of Work" [draft of University of Hartford honorary doctorate speech?] n.d. (ca. 1972) (Texas)

"Final Material" n.d. (ca. September 1972) (NOLA)

"I had met Bill Inge" n.d. (July 1973) (NOLA)

"Stylistic Experiments in the Sixties [. . .]" n.d. (ca. 1973) (Texas)

"Experiments of the Sixties" n.d. (ca. 1973) (Texas)

"It is the accidents [. . .]" [holograph statement on the back of a prescription] n.d. (ca. 1974) (NOLA)

"In my present and future plans [. . .]" [fragments for *The Red Devil Battery Sign*] June 1975 (NOLA)

"Afterword" [to *Memoirs*] n.d. (ca. June 1975) (NOLA)

"I have never believed in villains [. . .]" [fragment for *The Red Devil Battery Sign*] n.d. (ca. 1975) (NOLA)

"The Blessings and Mixed Blessings of 'Show-Case' Productions" n.d. (ca. September 18, 1975) (Columbia)

"My last two full-length works . . ." [statement on *This is . . .* and the Vienna production of *The Red Devil Battery Sign*] n.d. (ca. mid–December 1975) (NOLA)

"The Romantic Last Stand" n.d. (ca. September 1975) (NOLA)

"A play may find itself a failure . . ." [fragment for *The Red Devil Battery Sign*] n.d. (ca. 1976/1977) (NOLA)

"The Curious History of This Play and Plans for its Future" n.d. (ca. April 1976) (NOLA)

"A Playwright's Prayer," *Tennessee Williams Annual Review* n.d. (ca. November 1976)

"Mes Cahiers Noirs" n.d. (ca. 1976-1979) (Columbia)

"Finally Something New" n.d. (ca. August/September 1976) (Texas)

"[. . .] infinitely overshadowing question mark [. . .]" [fragment for *Vieux Carré*] n.d. (ca. January/February 1977) (Texas)

"These Scattered Idioms [III]" [fragment for *Vieux Carré*] n.d. (ca. January 1977) (Texas)

"What is 'Success' in the Theatre?" [fragment for *Vieux Carré*] n.d. (ca. February 1977) (Texas)

"Vieux Carre was start<ed> [. . .]" [fragments for *Vieux Carré*] n.d. (ca. February 1977) (Texas)

"Keith Baxter has been [. . .]" [fragments for *Vieux Carré*] n.d. (ca. September 1978) (NOLA)

"Valediction" December 24, 1982 (Columbia)

"The old way of life" (fragment) n.d. (ca. mid to late-1970s or early 1980s) (Texas)

"You suffer too much [. . .]" [holograph fragment] n.d. (NOLA)

INDEX

Whitehead, Robert, 180
Whitman, Walt, 14, 245, 255, 256
Whitmore, George, 283n
Wilde, Oscar, 237
Williams, Cornelius Coffin (father),
     x, 65, 93, 97–98, 99–100,
     101–2, 103–6, 278n
Williams, Dakin (brother), 97, 99,
     105, 106, 173–74, 219, 266,
     289n
Williams, Edwina (mother), ix–x,
     65, 98–100, 101, 105, 109,
     145, 173–74, 219, 273n, 278n,
     282n
Williams, Ella (aunt), 105–6
Williams, Rose (sister), 27, 65, 100,
     140, 164, 262
"Wind and the Rain, The" (Shake-
     speare), 245
Windham, Donald, 57, 121, 265

Wolf (dog), 149–52, 281n, 282n
"Wolf and I, The" (Williams),
     149–52, 262, 281n–82n
Wood, Audrey, 12, 14, 17, 79, 82,
     124, 130–33, 136, 194, 206,
     215, 265–66, 271n, 275n,
     277n, 280n, 287n
Wood, Grant, 168
Woods, Bob, 264
"World I Live In, The" (Williams),
     83–85, 262, 267, 277n
"Writer's Quest for a Parnassus,
     A" (Williams), 54–58, 262,
     274n–75n

Yeats, William Butler, 137
Young, Laura, 17
You Touched Me! (Williams), 94

Zoo Story, The (Albee), 172

ONE-ACT PLAY COLLECTIONS
BY TENNESSEE WILLIAMS

27 WAGONS FULL OF COTTON
Thirteen one-act plays

27 Wagons Full of Cotton ✦ The Purification ✦ The Lady of Larkspur Lotion
The Last of My Solid Gold Watches ✦ Portrait of a Madonna ✦ Auto-Da-Fé
Lord Byron's Love Letter ✦ The Strangest Kind of Romance
The Long Goodbye ✦ Hello From Bertha ✦ This Property is Condemned
Something Unspoken ✦ The Unsatisfactory Supper
Talk to Me Like the Rain and Let Me Listen

MISTER PARADISE
AND OTHER ONE-ACT PLAYS

Edited, with an introduction, by Nicholas Moschovakis and David Roessel
Foreword by Eli Wallach and Anne Jackson

These Are the Stairs You Got to Watch ✦ Mister Paradise
The Palooka ✦ Escape ✦ Why Do You Smoke So Much, Lily?
Summer At The Lake ✦ The Big Game ✦ The Pink Bedroom
The Fat Man's Wife ✦ Thank You, Kind Spirit
The Municipal Abattoir ✦ Adam and Eve on a Ferry
And Tell Sad Stories of The Deaths of Queens...

THE TRAVELING COMPANION
AND OTHER PLAYS

Edited, with an introduction, by Annette Saddik

The Chalky White Substance ✦ The Day on Which a Man Dies
A Cavalier for Milady ✦ The Pronoun 'I'
The Remarkable Rooming-House of Madame LeMonde
Kirche, Küche, Kinder ✦ Green Eyes ✦ The Parade
The One Exception ✦ Sunburst
Will Mr. Merriwether Return from Memphis? (full-length)
The Traveling Companion

DRAGON COUNTRY
A book of nine short plays

In the Bar of a Tokyo Hotel ✦ I Rise in Flames, Cried the Phoenix
The Mutilated ✦ I Can't Imagine Tomorrow ✦ Confessional
The Frosted Glass Coffin ✦ The Gnädiges Fräulein
A Perfect Analysis Given by a Parrot